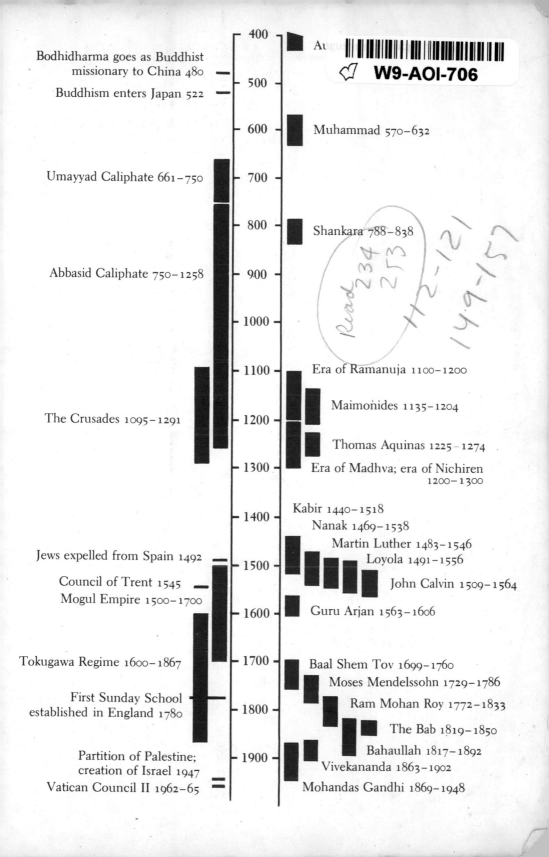

Bodhidharma goes as Buddhist
missionary to China 480

Buddhism enters Japan 522

Umayyad Caliphate 661–750

Abbasid Caliphate 750–1258

The Crusades 1095–1291

Jews expelled from Spain 1492

Council of Trent 1545

Mogul Empire 1500–1700

Tokugawa Regime 1600–1867

First Sunday School
established in England 1780

Partition of Palestine;
creation of Israel 1947

Vatican Council II 1962–65

400
500
600
700
800
900
1000
1100
1200
1300
1400
1500
1600
1700
1800
1900

Augu...

Muhammad 570–632

Shankara 788–838

Era of Ramanuja 1100–1200

Maimonides 1135–1204

Thomas Aquinas 1225–1274

Era of Madhva; era of Nichiren
1200–1300

Kabir 1440–1518
Nanak 1469–1538
Martin Luther 1483–1546
Loyola 1491–1556
John Calvin 1509–1564

Guru Arjan 1563–1606

Baal Shem Tov 1699–1760
Moses Mendelssohn 1729–1786
Ram Mohan Roy 1772–1833
The Bab 1819–1850
Bahaullah 1817–1892
Vivekananda 1863–1902
Mohandas Gandhi 1869–1948

RELIGIONS OF THE WORLD

SECOND EDITION

LEWIS M. HOPFE

GLENCOE PUBLISHING CO., INC.
Encino, California
Collier Macmillan Publishers
London

To Elizabeth, Lewis, and Cathleen,
in whom there is hope.

Cover painting: Water color *Touch* by Beverly Judd

Copyright © 1979, 1976 by Lewis M. Hopfe

Printed in the United States of America

Glencoe Publishing Co., Inc.
17337 Ventura Boulevard
Encino, California 91316
Collier Macmillan Canada, Ltd.

Library of Congress Catalog Card Number: 77-094769

2 3 4 5 6 7 8 9 RRD 80 79

ISBN 0-02-474820-X

CONTENTS

RELIGIONS ORIGINATING IN
CHINA AND JAPAN

RELIGIONS ORIGINATING IN THE
MIDDLE EAST

PREFACE

RELIGIONS OF THE WORLD is written for the student who wants a concise introduction to the historical and philosophical foundations of the major religions of the world. This new edition follows the same narrative style and approach that met with such a positive response in the first edition. Readers first are introduced to the basic vocabulary of the field and to some of the theories of the origins of religion. The text then goes on to explore the major religions: the historical and cultural factors that produced them, the lives of their founders, their basic teachings, and their historical development and current status in the world.

New Features

The second edition of RELIGIONS OF THE WORLD offers some important new features. It provides a broader coverage of the philosophical statements of the leading thinkers of each religion and includes more primary source material from the scriptures and writings of each religion. Primary materials have been chosen very carefully from the enormous body of philosophical and scriptural material available to most effectively highlight the narrative discussion.

An entirely new chapter on the religions of Africa has been added to the book. The rising importance of the African continent in world affairs makes it essential that all who would study human culture become familiar with at least the broad outlines of both the native and imported religions of the African people. This chapter should whet the intellectual appetite of its readers for this fascinating subject. In addition, the coverage of Baha'i has been expanded to give the reader a fuller picture of this relatively modern religion.

Student Aids

To make the second edition more helpful to the student, a map locating the major religions in the world today has been added to the text. With the same goal in mind, a selected bibliography has been added at the end of each chapter; the major concern in the choice of these readings was the accessibility and readability of the books. The visual impact of this new edition has been heightened by a completely new selection of photographs. The time line comparing the major events of each religion has been retained from the first edition.

Organization

The organization of the second edition is substantially the same as that of the first. The text begins with an exploration of the definitions of religion and the various theories of the origins of religion. This overview is followed by a section on basic religions, which opens with a chapter on the religions of prehistoric peoples and of the so-called primitive peoples of the contemporary world. In this context, Native American religions and African religions are outlined in two broad chapters. The four great religions that arose in India— Hinduism, Jainism, Buddhism, and Sikhism—are explored next. This section is followed by one presenting the religions of China and Japan, including Taoism, Confucianism, and Shinto. The text concludes with a section covering those religions that arose in the Middle East and with which the student is possibly most familiar: Zoroastrianism, Judaism, Christianity, Islam, and Baha'i.

Acknowledgments

In the preparation of this text I am indebted to my students at Kendall College and the University of Houston who studied the religions of the world with me for the past twelve years and whose interests were foremost in the selection of the materials which make up this book. I am also indebted to my patient editors at Glencoe Publishing Co., Judy Ziajka and Marie Enders, and to the reviewers who have guided and encouraged the development of this text.

LEWIS MOORE HOPFE
Pentacost 1978

Critical Reviewers

Professor Larry Axel, Purdue University

Professor Surrendra Gangadean, Phoenix College

Professor Thomas Nuelle, Chaffey Community College

Professor Alfred Painter, Orange Coast Community College

Professor Judith Saltzman, California Polytechnic State University, San Luis Obispo

Professor Robert Shuler, El Camino College

Professor Clara Wood, Diablo Valley College

RELIGIONS OF THE WORLD

Religions of the World

RELIGION OF THE MAJORITY
OF THE POPULATION

- Christianity
- Islam
- Buddhism
  - Buddhist, Confucianist,
    Taoist, and other elements
    mingled (China, Korea, Vietnam)
  - Buddhism and Shinto
    intermixed (Japan)
- Hinduism
- "Animism"
  (includes Shaminism)
- Judaism

Where followers of a religion
form a substantial minority of
the population, the following
symbols are used:
A "Animism"
B Buddhism
C Christianity
H Hinduism
J Judaism
M Islam
O Chinese religious blend
  (see above)

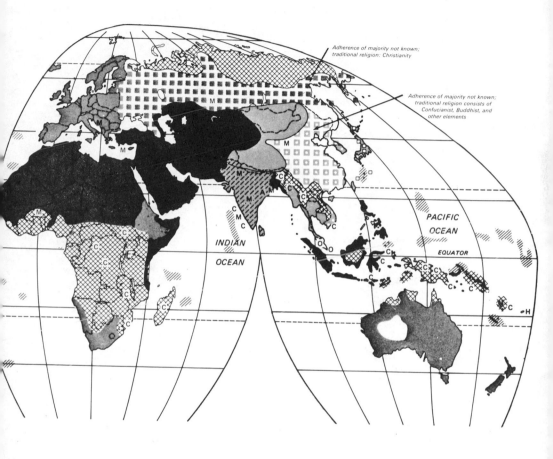

Adherence of majority not known;
traditional religion: Christianity

Adherence of majority not known;
traditional religion consists of
Confucianist, Buddhist, and
other elements

PACIFIC
OCEAN

INDIAN

OCEAN

EQUATOR

INTRODUCTION
OVERVIEW

Religion: The service and adoration of God or a god as ex-
pressed in forms of worship, in obedience to divine com-
mands . . . and in the pursuit of a way of life regarded as
incumbent on true believers.

WEBSTER'S NEW INTERNATIONAL DICTIONARY
OF THE ENGLISH LANGUAGE, SECOND EDITION

Why study religion?

Any student embarking upon a study of the religions of the world, whether it be for a semester, a year, or a lifetime, must question his or her reasons. After all, we have been told that religion is a personal matter and that while we should be informed about the nature of our own religion, the religion of others need scarcely concern us. We have heard that religions are of little real consequence; that we might more profitably spend our time studying subjects of immediate practical value in the pursuit of a career; that religions are becoming passé in a scientifically progressive world. Why, then, should any student take time from his or her academic career to study the religions of the world?

We might justify the study of religions in the same manner that we justify the study of Shakespeare or art history: the subject can be worth studying simply because the student is interested in it. Certainly anyone who is interested in the history of the world and in the antecedents of his or her own culture will find the study of world religions imperative. An art historian lecturing to a class on the art of sixteenth- and seventeenth-century Europe presented picture after picture of the art of that period, which was filled with religious themes. To his class he said, "Because you may have no religious interest yourself, please do not assume that the people of the past had none." Indeed, we could not understand the art of 90 percent of the world's cultures without knowing the religious themes of those cultures. Likewise the student of

1

world literature must know religions. We cannot understand the Bhagavad-Gita without understanding Hinduism; we cannot truly understand Hermann Hesse's *Siddhartha* without a knowledge of Buddhism; we cannot understand the literature of Herman Melville without a knowledge of Christian themes; even the contemporary literature of a writer such as Philip Roth is misunderstood without a knowledge of Judaism.

Perhaps the greatest contribution that a knowledge of world religions can make to a citizen of the fourth quarter of the twentieth century is in the area of world politics. At the time of this writing, as at almost any time in history, major political conflicts have at their roots religious differences. Catholic Christians war against Protestant Christians; Muslims war against Eastern Orthodox Christians; Hindus war against Muslims; Buddhists war with Christians; and Jews struggle with Muslims. Certainly these conflicts have other dimensions, but the religious differences are imposing. If we are to understand these conflicts fully, we must know that Christians, Jews, Muslims, Hindus, and Buddhists have basic philosophical differences. This is not to say that people of different religions and cultures cannot live in peace together; it is to say that if there is to be peace, these differences must be known and respected. In the early 1960s a young professor and his wife gave a dinner party on a Friday evening. The guest list included Jews, Catholics, and Muslims. The dinner entrée was ham! Needless to say, it was not a happy party. Whether the choice of food was made in ignorance or arrogance does not matter. The guests, because of their religions, were offended. The dinner party is all too frequently a microcosm of what happens in the larger world because of ignorance of the religions of the world.

A DEFINITION OF RELIGION

Assuming an interest in religions and a willingness to study them, what constitutes the subject matter of a course in world religions? Humankind has been on earth for a long, long time. Our cultures, historic and prehistoric, are too numerous to even begin to detail. Which cultures and religions shall we study? Whole texts have been written solely on prehistoric religions, not to mention the great families of religion such as those found within Hinduism. Therefore, any one text or course on religions must of necessity be selective about its subject, and a definition of the subject is necessary.

The English word *religion* is derived from the Latin *religio*, which refers to the fear or awe one feels in the presence of a spirit or a god. The average person seeks to define religion in terms of a set of beliefs, having to do with the gods, through which one is taught a moral system. While elements of this definition may be found within many of the religions of the world, it cannot do justice to them all. For example, some religions may recognize the existence of gods but actually have very little to do with them. Jainism and to some extent early Buddhism may be called atheistic religions because their emphasis was on people's delivering themselves from their plights without the help of gods. There are also religions that are not naturally tied to moral systems. A majority of the religions that have existed upon earth have probably been far more concerned with humanity's proper relationship to gods, demons, and spirits than with ethical relationships between people. One distinctive characteristic of the religion of the early Hebrews was the ethical dimension that Yahweh required of them. This was also found in Zoroastrianism and was in turn passed on to Christianity and Islam. Modern adherents to those religions associate the word *religious* with the word *moral*. But among the majority of religions it is not necessarily so.

A definition of religion that is widely accepted today was offered by the late Paul Tillich, who identified religion as that which is of "ultimate concern."[1] Taking Tillich's definition one step further, some might say that in its basic form a person's religion is that which is so vital to that person that he or she would die for it. In this sense, then, the intense patriotism one finds in many nations could be called *religion*. Men and women have been known to die for their families. In terms of this definition their intense love for their family thus may be seen as their religion. However satisfying Tillich's definition may be, it is probably too broad for most of us. People have been known to have ultimate concern for their automobiles, their professions, their homes, food, and golf. Only in the broadest sense of the word can these things be considered *religions* or even *religious*. For the purposes of this book a more restrictive definition must be used.

The contents of this text have been chosen from the hundreds of religions that have existed in the world on the following five bases: (1) They are religions that usually deal in some way with people's relationship to the unseen world of spirits, gods, demons. (2) They are religions

---

[1]See Paul Tillich, *The Protestant Era*, trans. James Luther Adams (Chicago: The University of Chicago Press, 1948), pp. xv, 59, and 273.

that usually have developed a system of myths about the unseen world and rituals designed for communing with or propitiating the spirits. (3) They are religions that usually have developed a cult of organized rituals, temples, priests, and scriptures at some point in their history. (4) They are religions that usually have some statement about life beyond death, either as survival in some shadowy hades, in some version of heaven and hell, or through reincarnation. (5) Finally, the religions discussed in this text generally have attracted large followings, either currently or at some time in the past.

As there are many religions from which we must choose, so there are many methods by which we might deal with these religions. We might present the religions of the world in terms of their effects upon the societies that support them; in terms of their forms or style of worship; in a comparative manner in which each religion is compared with the others in terms of its outlook toward God, the nature of humankind, sin, and so on; or we might present the religions of the world in terms of their histories and their effects upon the histories of the nations where they were found. It is the intent of this text to combine some of these methods and to present the major religions of the world as simply and yet as thoroughly as possible. For each religion, four major points will be considered: (1) The world that produced this religion: What was the culture that hosted this religion? (2) The life of the founder(s): Where there is a founder and where anything can be known of this person's life, what factors caused this person to found this religion? (3) The sacred texts: Where there are scriptures or sacred books, what does the literature tell us about this religion? (4) The major historical developments of this religion.

THE UNIVERSALITY OF RELIGION

Wherever people are found, there too religion resides. Occasionally religion is hard to find or pin down, but in the great metropolitan capitals and in the most primitive areas of the world, there are physical and cultural temples, pyramids, megaliths, and monuments that societies have raised at tremendous expense as an expression of their religion. Even when we explore the backwaters of time in prehistoric civilizations, we find altars, cave paintings, and special burials that point toward our religious nature. Indeed, there is no other phenomenon so pervasive, so consistent from society to society, as the search for gods.

THEORIES OF THE ORIGIN OF RELIGIONS

Where does religion come from? This is a very basic question, as our answer tends to reflect our view of the very nature of religion. Some would say that human beings developed religion because they were weak and ignorant of the forces of nature that surrounded them. They were at the mercy of these forces and therefore devised a scheme of gods and spirits that tended to explain the mysteries of the universe and to whom they could pray for support. According to this view, religion was needed as a crutch to lean upon. The implication is that when human beings come to fully know and understand their universe, they will no longer need the crutch of religion to support them. Others would say that religion was developed by a few as a means of suppressing the masses. The traditional view held by those who are themselves religious is that God revealed religion and religious truths to human beings at some point in their development.

In the nineteenth century, when the social sciences were being developed and anthropologists were first beginning to investigate the remaining primitive cultures, certain theories of the origin of religion were proposed by pioneers in this field. No longer satisfied with mere guessing about the origin of religion or with the orthodox religious views on the subject, early anthropologists based their theories on their observations. These nineteenth- and early twentieth-century scholars, enamored of the belief that the biological theories of evolution taught by Darwin could be applied to the social sciences, investigated contemporary "primitive" religions, reread ancient reporters such as Herodotus, and hypothesized ad infinitum about the origin and development of the phenomenon of religion. A few of the more outstanding and enduring of their theories follow.

The Animistic Theories

The most outstanding exponent of one animistic theory of the origin of religion was the English scholar Sir Edward Burnett Tylor. In his book *Primitive Culture*, which was published in 1871, Tylor maintained that primitive people had difficulty in distinguishing dreams from reality. Therefore, when they dreamed of the recent dead, particularly outstanding members of their society, they believed that the dead were not really dead, or at least they continued to exist in some other form. On the basis of their visions of the ghosts of the dead in their dreams, primitive people came to believe in the existence of souls or spirits that continued to exist after physical death. According to Tylor, primitive peoples also believed that these souls (Latin, *anima*) were to be found not only in people but in all of nature. There were souls in stones, trees, animals, rivers, springs, volcanoes, and mountains. The entire world, the very air itself was seen to be alive with spirits of all kinds. These spirits could be helpful or harmful to human beings, and they had personalities that could be offended or flattered. Therefore, it became a part of the life of primitive societies to pray to these spirits, to offer sacrifices to them, to seek to appease them, and to avoid offending them. From this animistic understanding of the world there arose the multiple deities that became the basis for the more developed religions of the world.

Another theory of the origin of religion that can be loosely defined as animistic was developed and propounded in 1891 by a Christian missionary to the Melanesian people, Bishop Codrington. In the course of his work Codrington discovered that the Melanesians believed in a mysterious and awesome force that inhabited all of nature and caused nature to act as it did toward humankind. The Melanesians called this force *mana*, and Bishop Codrington theorized that all primitive people had begun their religions with an awareness of such a force. Investigators studying other primitive cultures found a similar phenomenon, although it was called by other names. The theory that a force like *mana* existed in nature and was acknowledged by primitive societies differed from Tylor's animistic theory. The animists tended to recognize the unseen forces in nature as personal. One could communicate with these forces as well as flatter or offend them. Those who recognized a force like *mana* thought of it as an impersonal force. One did not offer sacrifices to it; one only sought to avoid its evil consequences. The Melanesians avoided the destructiveness of *mana* by establishing what they called *taboos*. For example, if a man married his sister and the marriage produced an evil effect or resulted in no children, then it might be construed that somehow marriage between brother and sister was responsible for the evil effect. Therefore, in later generations such a marriage would become a tribal taboo and be forbidden.

The Nature-Worship Theory

Another theory regarding the origin of religion was developed by the German scholar Max Müller. Müller taught at Oxford University in the last quarter of the nineteenth century and was primarily concerned with mythology and Indian religions. From his studies he became convinced that human beings first developed their religions from their observations of the forces of nature. According to this theory, primitive people became aware of the regularity of the seasons, the tides, and the phases of the moon. Their response to these forces in nature was to personalize them. Thus they gave a name to the sun, the moon, and so on, and began to describe the activities of these forces with tales that eventually became mythology. An example of this process is found in the Greek myth of Apollo and Daphne. Apollo was in love with Daphne, but she fled from him and was changed into a laurel tree. By searching out the etymology of these names, Müller found that Apollo was the name given to the sun and that Daphne was the name for the dawn. Thus the original myth is simply a primitive story describing the manner in which the sun chases away the dawn. In applying similar etymological studies to the mythologies of the world Müller became convinced he had found the key to the origin of all religions: Primitive people identified the forces in nature, personified them, created myths to describe their activities, and eventually developed pantheons and religions around them.

The Theory of Original Monotheism

A completely different approach to the origin of religion was presented early in the twentieth century by a Jesuit, Father Wilhelm Schmidt, in his book *Der Ursprung der Gottesidee*. Schmidt had examined the religions of many contemporary basic cultures in Australia and Africa and found that they all held a common belief in a distant high god. While the predominant form of religion for these primitives was animism or polytheism, there was always the belief that originally there had been one great god above all others. He may have been the creator of the world or the father of the many lesser deities. After initially establishing the world, this high god went away and now has little contact with the world. Some of the mythologies go on to say that one day he will return and reestablish himself. In these societies the local deities receive the majority of attention and worship, although the distant high god has a small part in mythology. Father Schmidt inferred from this phenomenon that primitive societies were originally monotheistic, but because the worship of one god was difficult, religion was corrupted into polytheism. Later, more advanced religions recovered the true monotheistic religion. Naturally, Schmidt was accused of allowing his Christian prejudices to be active in the formulation of this theory.

The Magic Theory

Between 1890 and 1915 Sir James George Frazer produced his encyclopedic work on religion, *The Golden Bough*. Unlike Codrington and Schmidt, Frazer did not personally study contemporary basic religions but rather constructed his theories from reading the reports of anthropologists, missionaries, and ancient writers such as Herodotus. On the basis of his studies Frazer came to believe that humankind had gone through three phases of development regarding the spirit world. First, people had attempted to control the world of nature through magic. The magician is one who believes that through certain processes such as dances, rituals, formulae, incantations, and so on, nature can be forced to act in one's favor. For example, if people need rain they employ the services of a magician who leads the tribe in the proper rain magic (dances and incantations, for example). The premise behind magic is that if the ritual is done properly nature will have no choice but to cooperate. Finally, people came to realize that nature could not be coerced by magic. Therefore, in a second phase, people turned to religion whose premise seems to be that nature can be implored to cooperate. Whereas the witch doctor might perform a rain dance, a priest would pray and offer sacrifice to the powers of nature hoping to please them and thus bring rain. In a third phase, people turned from religion to science, in which a more rational understanding of nature is operative. Therefore the modern farmer who needs rain will turn neither to the magician nor to the priest but to the scientist, who will seed the clouds and cause it to rain. A skeptic might note that there is little proof that seeding the clouds produces rain any more frequently than did rain dances or prayers.

The Wish-Fulfillment Theory

One of the most influential thinkers of the nineteenth century was the German philosopher Ludwig Feuerbach. Feuerbach, who had originally been a theological student, taught that there were no gods and that belief in gods was merely wish fulfillment. People who were troubled and could not cope with the problems and challenges of life simply projected their wishes and developed gods and religions.

Two of the leading disciples of Feuerbach's thinking in the nineteenth and twentieth centuries were Karl Marx and Sigmund Freud. Each of these men took Feuerbach's position on the origin of religion and added his own distinctive touches. Marx saw the origin and development of religion in terms of his personal view of history and the economic and social struggle between classes. Marx's opinion of religion is summed up in his most widely remembered statement, "Religion is the opiate of the people." According to Marx, religions were developed by the few as a means of controlling the masses and preventing revolution. The few, the rulers and their allies the priests, wished to possess and control the wealth. Therefore they created a scheme of gods, heavens, and hells. With this scheme they persuaded the masses of people that if they would accept poverty in this life and be obedient to the rulers and priests, they would then inherit bliss in another life. Thus the people, believing these lies, are opiated against the misery that they suffer in the present evil social structure.

Sigmund Freud, the founder of psychoanalysis, gave Feuerbach's ideas a psychological dimension. He saw religion originating from the guilt that individuals supposedly feel in hating their fathers. Freud saw in the ancient Greek myth of Oedipus a pattern of human experience. Oedipus was a man who, through a long and tragic series of events, killed his father and married his mother. Freud said that in all of us there was a similar tendency to desire our mothers and therefore to hate our fathers. Because of this subconscious hatred and ensuing guilt, Freud believed that we project a great father image in the sky and call him God. The truly healthy mature person, according to Freud, is content to stand alone and face the problems of life without gods or religions.

TYPES OF RELIGIONS

In the long period of human life on earth there have been hundreds of religions and religious systems. Since recorded history covers only the last five thousand years of our million-year existence, there are undoubtedly more unknown than known religions. In addition, many religious systems have lived and died within the relatively short span of recorded history. This text does not pretend to deal with all religions, historical or prehistorical. It deals only with religious systems that are active and viable today. These religions are grouped into four categories.

Basic or Primitive Religions

The term "basic religion" is generally applied to the religions of people in undeveloped areas of the world and to the religions of prehistoric peoples, about which we know very little. This category embraces a great variety of beliefs and practices, including animism, totemism, and demonism. In the following chapters we will examine American Indian religions and African religions as examples of the basic religions. Probably the most common characteristic of this group is an animistic view of nature. No one knows the numbers of persons whose religions may be categorized as basic.

Religion's Originating in India

Four of the great religions of the world originated in India: Hinduism, Jainism, Buddhism, and Sikhism. India remains the home of Hinduism, Jainism, and Sikhism; while Buddhism is now found in other Asian nations such as China, Japan, Korea, Vietnam, Cambodia, and Thailand. The basic beliefs of these religions are that there are many gods (Sikhism is the exception, taking its belief in one god from Islam) and that one person may lead many lives through a system of reincarnation. The goal of these religions is release from the cycle of life, death, and rebirth and the achievement of nonlife, which is called *moksha* or *Nirvana*. Sometimes this goal is achieved through the aid of the gods, but often believers are expected by their actions or lack thereof to work out their own release.

Religions Originating in China and Japan

Religions that originated in China and Japan include Taoism, Confucianism, and Shinto. There is some question as to whether Taoism and Confucianism are truly religions, but since they have at times developed religious cults they are usually considered world religions. They have in common the belief in many gods and include the worship of nature, the worship or veneration of ancestors, and, in the case of Shinto, a reverence of the nation itself. Like most of the religions of India, they are relatively tolerant, allowing their adherents the freedom to accept and even adopt the religious positions of others.

Religions Originating in the Middle East

Religions originating in the Middle East include Zoroastrianism, Judaism, Christianity, and Islam. All four hold to the common belief in one supreme creator god. In contrast to the Indian religions, they believe that each person lives only one life and will spend an eternal destiny in either reward or punishment based upon the deeds and actions of this one life. Christianity and Islam have been two of the great missionary religions of the world. Today their adherents are found all over the globe and number in the billions.

At one time in history human religions may have shared certain characteristics no longer visible in the contemporary religions that dominate the world. Through an examination of archaeological evidence and of certain cultures that are judged to be "primitive" by modern standards, the student of religions may be able to gain an insight into what the earliest religions may have been. At the same time, by studying the characteristics of these so-called basic religions of the past and present, the student will also learn more about the bases upon which such major contemporary religions as Hinduism, Christianity, and Islam rest. The key to an appropriate and valuable study of these religions is an openness and a willingness to appreciate their strengths and beauty.

BASIC
RELIGIONS

CHAPTER ONE

CHARACTERISTICS OF BASIC RELIGIONS

MUSÉE D'AQUITAINE

The Venus of Lausanne. The exaggerated breasts, hips, and abdomen indicate that this was an image connected with fertility worship.

*It has its wild and demonic forms and can sink into an
almost grisly horror and shuddering. It has its crude, barbaric
antecedents and early manifestations, and again it may be
developed into something beautiful and pure and glorious.
It may become the hushed, trembling, and speechless humility of the creature in the presence of—whom or what? In the
presence of that which is a* mystery *inexpressible and above
all creatures.*

RUDOLF OTTO, THE IDEA OF THE HOLY

Typically the religions and total culture of prehistoric peoples and the
current practices in geographical areas not technically classified as
civilized are referred to as *primitive.* Unfortunately the word *primitive*
carries with it the connotations of backward, simple, even childlike.
Thus the Christian or Muslim or Jew may tend to look down upon
these religions as superstitious or uncivilized. However, the religion of
the bushman of Australia or the Indian of the Americas may be fully as
intricate in its rituals and mythology and as satisfying to its adherents
as is the worship of the high-church Episcopalian. In studying the
religions of the world we can assume no evolutionary scale that moves
from basic religions to Zen Buddhism or any other highly developed
religion of the so-called civilized world. There is satisfaction and
beauty in all religions, and there is ugliness and baseness in all, too.
Nevertheless, because basic religious elements are found in the religions of prehistoric people and people of the less-developed areas of
the world, the term *basic religions* is not inappropriate.

It follows, of course, that of all the world's religions, we know least
about these basic religions simply because they spring from prehistory
or out-of-the-way places that have not been penetrated by civilization.
However, the study of these religions is extremely important because
from them have sprung all of the other religions of the world. Elements of the basic religions are found to a greater or lesser degree in all
religions. It is therefore important that we have an understanding of

these elements and the manner in which they operate. Second, it is important that we study basic religions because they represent approximately 75 percent of the total religious experience of humankind since the dawn of human history.

SOURCES OF INFORMATION CONCERNING BASIC RELIGIONS

Humans have been active on planet Earth for a million or more years, depending upon which anthropologist one chooses to believe. However, we know but a tiny fraction of human history. Only within the last five or six thousand years has *Homo sapiens* utilized writing. While nonwritten sources such as cave paintings, burial sites, religious statuary, and archaeological remains indicate human culture and religious experiences, our strongest source of knowledge is the written record. Of the total period of time in which people have been upon Earth, we have written records of perhaps less than one-half of 1 percent. From these records we know a great deal about peoples' culture and religious experience, but there is an enormous amount we do not know.

There are two primary sources of information about basic religions. The first is contemporary basic religions. The anthropologist visits a contemporary basic culture and studies its religious beliefs and practices. From this study the anthropologist then infers that many or all basic and prehistoric religions may have had similar attitudes and religious practices. Thus Bishop Codrington studied the Melanesian people in the nineteenth century and reported their awareness of the unseen force in nature called *mana*. He and others were led to believe that a similar awareness of a force like *mana* might have been humankind's original religious impetus.

However interesting the study of contemporary basic religions may be, it obviously leaves much to be desired as a source for knowledge of prehistoric basic religion. It is possible that the Melanesians of the nineteenth century were very different from civilized people or even from pre-nineteenth century Melanesians. Their religious awareness and practices might have changed within the nineteenth century itself. They might only recently have adopted the belief in *mana*, or they could have been affected by the visits of former missionaries or traders or even by the visit of the anthropologist. There is also the possibility

Corroborree dancers enacting a myth sacred to the
Australian Aborigines.

that even if the anthropologist arrived and found a virgin primitive
society in the exact state of prehistoric time, the anthropologist's observations and reporting might not be accurate. The anthropologist
must learn the language of the group that is being studied and live with
that group long enough to be thoroughly conversant with its customs
and religions. The reliability of the chieftains and the priests with
whom there is contact must also be taken into account. If any of these
factors is missing, then the data that the anthropologist gathers can be
questioned. Therefore, while the study of contemporary basic religions
may be helpful, it cannot be relied upon to give a total picture of basic
religions as they have always been.

A second source of information comes from the science of archaeology. Although human beings have always been interested in
their past and have doubtless always attempted to investigate the physical remains of that past, the scientific examination of those remains is
less than two hundred years old. In fact most of the serious archaeological work that has been done has been achieved in the twentieth century.

17

Archaeologists, working very carefully, attempt to uncover the physical remains of past civilizations and reconstruct the life and history of their cultures. In their examinations of relatively recent cultures, such as the Roman or the Mayan, the task is simplified because of the wealth of buildings, burials, coinage, and other elaborate artifacts that these civilizations left. The task is further simplified when the cultures that are examined have been literate, and scrolls, clay tablets, and inscriptional material are found.

In dealing with distant prehistoric cultures, the task is more difficult. Here the main sources of information are likely to be burials, weapons, and tools, and the archaeologist must reconstruct very carefully. However, even in dealing with either distant or recent cultures, archaeological results depend upon the interpretations of the investigator. What one archaeologist calls a temple another may call a stable; controversy and mistakes within this field are too numerous to list. Therefore we must be very careful to give archaeological investigation its due value and no more. Some archaeologists may assure us that Neanderthal people worshiped bears because bear skulls have been found in their burial sites. This may or may not be the case. Bear skulls may have been buried with these primitive people because they worshiped the bear, or bears may have been buried there as trophies of the hunt. Until the day when the Neanderthals speak for themselves in one form or another, we cannot be certain about their religion.

PREHISTORIC BEGINNINGS OF BASIC RELIGIONS

Neanderthal Religion

One of the earliest human species was the so-called Neanderthal, who lived from approximately 100,000 to 25,000 B.C. Little is known about Neanderthals except that physically they were smaller than present *Homo sapiens* and probably survived in a hostile environment by means of hunting and food gathering. Of course Neanderthals did not leave written records of their society or of their religion. Our only evidence that they were religious at all comes from archaeology, and this is slender evidence indeed. In the Neanderthal burials of several regions archaeologists have found the remains of animal bones and stone tools. Some suggest that these remains indicate that the dead were buried with food and with their tools and weapons, perhaps as offerings to the gods or as necessary accompaniment into the world of the dead. In addition archaeologists have found bear skulls, apparently carefully arranged, in Neanderthal burials; and this suggests a worshipful attitude toward the bear. None of this proves that Neanderthal was religious or had any concept of life beyond the grave, however.

Cro-Magnon Religion

A later species of *Homo sapiens* to appear and displace Neanderthal was Cro-Magnon, who appeared some 25,000 years ago. Cro-Magnon was physically larger and had a larger brain capacity than Neanderthal. Often living in caves, Cro-Magnon seems to have survived primarily as a hunter. When we picture "the caveman" we probably are thinking of Cro-Magnon. Like Neanderthal, Cro-Magnon did not leave any written records of culture or its religion. Again our only information comes from the work of archaeologists. Like the Neanderthals, the Cro-Magnons apparently buried their dead with tools and weapons. Graves have also yielded ornaments with which the dead were buried. In addition some Cro-Magnon graves have yielded bones that were painted red. Archaeologists have interpreted these factors as indicating a concern for life beyond the grave.

The most outstanding artifacts associated with Cro-Magnon are the famous cave paintings on the walls of caves. These paintings, located in dark recesses far from the entrances, were identified as Cro-Magnon and apparently had been placed in such difficult places to keep out the uninitiated. Their location had inadvertently protected them from damage for thousands of years. Most of these paintings depict animals being killed during a hunt. The animals, bison, horses, wild boar, and bears, are shown with arrows and spears entering their bodies at critical points. While the animals are painted in a very lifelike fashion, the humans hunting them are depicted by mere stick figures. The most commonly held interpretation of these paintings is that they were placed on the hidden walls of the caves by priests or magicians of the Cro-Magnon people before the hunt. It is believed that by painting the animals being killed or by retracing the paintings, the priests were hoping to predict the events of a successful hunt. Similar practices are followed by the witch doctors of contemporary basic religions either in the form of graphic art or a drama in which members of the tribe play the part of animals being killed during a hunt.

In addition to the cave paintings, which may have had religious significance, the Cro-Magnons also left figurines carved from stone. One of the best known of these is the so-called Venus of Willendorf, a

*Cave art from Dordogne Valley, Lascaux. Typical of
primitive religious art, this painting depicts animals
being pierced by spears and arrows. It may be an example
of imitative magic through which a hunter sought to
insure success in a hunt.*

small figurine depicting a female form. While the figure has no face,
her breasts, hips, and abdomen are greatly exaggerated. It is suggested
that this figure was part of a fertility cult that may have been associated
with Cro-Magnon religion.

Neolithic Religion

Since Neanderthal and Cro-Magnon societies primarily utilized
stone tools and weapons, their cultures are identified archaeologically
as Stone Age cultures. The eras that followed the Cro-Magnon period

also utilized stone weapons and implements, but they were much advanced in other ways. The Neolithic or late Stone Age ran from approximately 7000 to 3000 B.C. and was characterized by many new developments in civilization.

One of the most significant advances that greatly influenced the development of religion was the development of agriculture as a way of life. When primitive people found that they could live by planting seeds, harvesting their crops, and storing the crops against their future hunger, their lives changed enormously. For the first time people did not have to move constantly from place to place in search of wild game; they could settle and live in one place as long as the soil was fertile. This meant that they now needed more permanent dwellings and that they could live in larger groups. This in turn led to the development of cities that were located close to farming areas.

In Egypt the advancement to agriculture led to the development of the ownership of land. The sciences of surveying and mathematics were developed to establish ownership of the fields after the annual flood of the delta by the river Nile. Above all else the development of agriculture gave people more leisure time than they had ever known. They could, in effect, afford to sit back and allow the soil to provide them with their nourishment. For the first time certain people in the community could afford to be free to devote their total time to the mysteries of religion. A true priesthood prior to an agricultural society is really unthinkable. In addition agricultural society for the first time became dependent upon the fertility of nature. People became aware that one year would be a year of great harvest, while the next might be a year of drought. They became aware of the regularity of the seasons, the tides, the phases of the moon, and the movements of the stars. Each of these factors caused Neolithic people to develop religions based upon the fertility of the soil as well as the fertility of humans and animals. These factors also caused them to develop mythologies in which deities became personifications of the sun, the moon, the stars, and the seasons.

Archaeological remains from the Neolithic period give some indication of the religious attitudes of the time. Large burials from this era contain the bones of men, women, and animals along with tools, weapons, and ornaments. This suggests to some that Neolithic people may have buried the chieftain with his wives, servants, and favorite animals so that they might serve him in the next life. This practice has been followed in many cultures, and as late as the nineteenth century the *suttee* was practiced in India; this involved a wife throwing herself upon her husband's funeral pyre or allowing herself to be buried alive in his grave.

It also appears that Neolithic societies erected megaliths in several parts of the world. The two best examples of this practice are the great stone monuments erected at Stonehenge in England and the hundreds of megaliths set up in the fields of Brittany in France. Apparently these massive stones were quarried at a distance and transported with great effort to the place where they were erected. Since Neolithic societies left no written records about these stones it is assumed by many that their purpose was at least in part religious, but this cannot be proved.

COMMON FEATURES OF BASIC RELIGIONS

The following features appear to be common to many of those basic religions that still exist or at least existed in some form in the nineteenth and twentieth centuries when anthropologists began to study them. These features have also appeared in the historical religions of which we are aware. Many of these features are evident in one form or another in the so-called advanced or developed religions. Sacrifice, for example, appears in the earliest form of nearly every extant religion. Finally, some of the features not currently a part of religions are to be found subliminally in modern cultures. For instance, while few of the developed religions would admit that magic is part of their theology, belief in the lucky coin, the unlucky day, the avoidance of the number *thirteen*, and so on, is widely found, even in the most advanced societies of the twentieth century.

Animism

Tylor suggested that primitive people originally envisioned the world as alive with souls or spirits and on the basis of this understanding of nature developed religions. Indeed, the belief that nature is alive with spirits that have feelings and can be communicated with is one of the most common to human religious experience. In many of the basic religions people seem to believe that they are not the only spirit, that animals, trees, stones, rivers, mountains, the heavenly bodies, the seas, and the earth itself have *anima* (spirit), and that these spirits can communicate with people, can be flattered or offended by them, and can either help or hurt them. Basic religions tend to see these forces as either personal, as in the case of the typical animist, or as impersonal vague forces, which are identified as mana by Bishop Codrington and others.

On the basis of an awareness of life in nature the basic religions tend to revere nature in a way in which modern religions do not. Before building a house upon a hill, primitive peoples might ask the permission of the hill; before cutting a tree, they might ask the tree's permission, offer a sacrifice to it, and promise to use every bit of the tree to good purpose; upon hunting an animal they might apologize to the animal for killing it and treat the corpse with great respect.

On the basis of an animistic understanding of life, basic religions and many advanced religions have revered or openly worshiped nearly everything in nature. Almost any animal one can think of has at some time or another been worshiped; stones have been worshiped or have been the sites where the gods have spoken to people or received the blood of their sacrifices; mountains have frequently been the objects of worship or the places of revelation; the seas and the creatures in them have been objects of veneration; trees have frequently been the objects of religious cults; the heavenly bodies, the sun, moon, and stars, play a part in nearly every religion; and fire, water, and the earth itself have become objects of worship or important elements in worship. The list of animistic expression is almost endless.

Modern people place historic stones at the corners of their new buildings; they build expensive, elaborate, and useless fireplaces. Christians bring evergreen trees into their homes to celebrate Christmas, knowing full well that there is no basic connection between an evergreen tree and the birth of Jesus; Muslims march around the sacred black stone and kiss it during their pilgrimage to Mecca; Hindus seek to bathe in the sacred river Ganges; the Parsee bring gifts of sandalwood to be burned in the sacred fire temple; and on and on. The animistic understanding of life is one of the most pervasive and influential of all the religious and nonreligious impulses of mankind.

Magic

When modern people speak of magic, they often think in terms of sleight-of-hand tricks or illusions performed by a professional whose job is to deceive and amuse them. In basic religions the term *magic* takes on far more serious meaning.

Magicians in basic societies attempt to control nature for either the benefit of their people or the detriment of their enemies. These magicians believe that if they perform their rituals, their formulae, their dances, or their incantations properly, they will in fact be able to control nature: they can make rain, cause the crops to be bountiful, create conditions for a successful hunt, or kill their enemies.

Technically the line between religion and magic is drawn by the intent of the practitioner. Magicians believe that by performing rituals they can force nature to act, as they desire, whereas the practitioners of religion only seek to implore the gods on their behalf. The magician knows his will shall be done, but the priest hopes that the gods will act favorably toward him. Actually the distinction between religion and magic is never that clear, and elements of magic appear in religion, elements of religion appear in magic. Sir James Frazer, a Scottish anthropologist, believed that magic was a phase through which humankind passed on its way to religion and ultimately to science.

The most common form of magic at work among basic societies is sympathetic or imitative magic. In this form of magic one attempts to coerce nature into some act by performing that act oneself on a smaller scale. The most common example of this involves the so-called voodoo doll with which the magician seeks to do evil to enemies. The doll is created in the rough image of the enemy and may contain such personal elements of the enemy as bits of hair or nail parings. Since the doll looks like the victim, whatever is done to the doll will happen to the victim. If the doll is pierced with a needle through the leg, then the victim will be injured in the leg; if the doll is pierced through the heart, then the victim will be killed or at least have severe chest pains. In primitive societies many of the rain ceremonies are based upon imitative magic. Many believe that the Cro-Magnon cave paintings that showed animals being pierced by weapons during a hunt were made by priests seeking to work imitative magic.

Another aspect of magic frequently found in basic religions is the fetish. A fetish is any object that is used to control nature in a magical fashion. In modern society such objects are called good-luck charms. The fetish is used to bring good fortune to the one who possesses it and to ward off evil. In basic societies the fetish may be almost anything: a wooden stick, a stone or collection of stones, a bone, a feather, even a special weapon. Fetishes may be held singly or in a collection or they may be used as ornamentation of some kind. Fetishism is never very far from even the most advanced human society. In any group of people one is likely to encounter a large collection of lucky coins, rabbits' feet, religious medallions, and so on. The value which most twentieth century people place on their fetishes probably varies considerably from that which primitive people placed on theirs. Nevertheless, the existence of fetishes and other elements of basic religion in advanced and scientific societies speaks of their inherent value to the human race.

Divination

The prediction of the future through divination is a very important function in basic societies. Usually this is the work of priests or someone who is especially prepared for the task, and it is accomplished by various means. Frequently divination is done through the examination of the entrails of a sacrificed animal. Sometimes it is accomplished by observation of the flights of birds or the casting of sacred dice. In ancient China a tortoiseshell was heated until it cracked, and the pattern of the cracks was interpreted as a prediction of the future. This was later refined into the practice of casting yarrow stalks, and these patterns were interpreted in a book called the *I Ching*. Among the ancient Greeks the future was predicted when a priestess sat on a tripod and breathed fumes that escaped from the ground at Delphi. What she said after breathing the fumes was interpreted by a priest as the message from the gods regarding the future.

Frequently primitive societies sought knowledge of the future from a member of the group who was believed to have been possessed by the gods. Among the peoples of Siberia this person was called a *shaman*. While the word *shaman* often bears the connotation *"priest"* or *"magician,"* the original meaning related to one who was possessed by the gods and spoke their messages to the group.

Taboo

In the primitive scheme of life there are certain actions that must be avoided lest the spirit world release harmful effects upon the person or group. These acts to be avoided are known by the Polynesian word *tabu*. Generally in basic societies holy persons, places, and objects are considered taboo to the ordinary person. Chieftains, priests, sacred places, fetishes, and so on, are to be avoided by the unordained person except on very special occasions or when there is special preparation. In basic societies one does not touch the person of the chief nor does one enter the sacred areas without great fear. Great harm can come to someone who violates these tribal taboos. In the Jewish Bible we find occasions when people either knowingly or accidentally violate taboos. II Kings 2:23–25 speaks of an occasion when boys mocked and taunted the prophet Elisha. As a result the children were mauled by two bears. II Samuel 6:1–7 tells of a man who merely touched the ark of the covenant in order to prevent its falling off a cart and as a result was struck dead by God. Isaiah, chapter 7, relates the calling of the young man, Isaiah, and his great fear and awe as he entered the holy Temple of Yahweh, which was taboo. In many other cultures the person of the king is so sacred that it is considered taboo to come into his presence without special invitation. Until fairly recent times the Japanese people considered it taboo to look upon the face of the emperor, even when he toured the streets of a city.

Other examples are numerous. In basic societies the birth of twins is so rare as to be considered taboo. Thus when twins are born they are either killed or exiled or they are treated as special sacred persons. The dead are often the object of taboos. Among many cultures those who handle the dead for burial are considered ritually unclean, at least for a certain period of time. Women during their menstrual period are frequently considered taboo and are often required to live in houses separate from the rest of the group. Many cultures have developed taboos regarding certain foods. Usually the food set aside for the chieftain is forbidden to the rest of the community. Certain kinds of food such as pork, beef, and shellfish are considered by particular groups to be ritually unclean and thus taboo. In the caste system of India certain foods are perfectly acceptable to members of some castes and totally forbidden to other castes.

Totems

Another practice found in some basic religions, but by no means all, is that of totemism. Totemism was first identified by white settlers in the eighteenth century when they found the practice among American Indians. Totemism was later identified within other basic societies in other parts of the world. The word *totem* is a corruption of the Ojibwa word *ototeman*.

Totemism is apparently based upon the feeling of kinship that exists between humans and other creatures or objects in nature. As such it is an extension and expression of animism. Generally it involves some form of identification between a tribe or a clan and an animal, although totems in some parts of the world have been identified as plants or even as the sun, moon, or stars. For example, a clan may understand that it is basically related to the bear. The bear may be the ancestor of the clan, the clan may possess the characteristics of the

Totem Poles located in the Kitikshan Village, Kitwan-coal, B.C. These massive wooden poles are carved with various totem animals and figures placed in a sacred relationship by the artist.

bear (strength, ferocity, or size), or clan members may believe that when they die they will take the form of the bear. If the bear is the totem of the clan, members may not eat or kill this animal except in cases of self-defense or on very sacred occasions when they may eat its flesh in a ceremonial meal that has the effect of binding the clan closer together. Members of another, neighboring, clan whose totem may be the deer may hunt and eat the bear while members of the first clan may hunt and eat the deer.

27

Highly developed societies, although they do not clearly and religiously adhere to totemism, still hold to the vestiges of this practice. Nations are symbolized by animals such as the eagle, the bear, or the lion, and schools choose mascots to symbolize the spirit of their athletic teams. Some highly developed religions still utilize animal sacrifices on sacred occasions: To bind their communities together and to renew ancient covenants, they eat the flesh of a sacred animal.

Sacrifice

One of the most common practices in all of the religions of the world, both basic and advanced, is sacrifice. Throughout history one finds people offering sacrifices of nearly every imaginable material to the gods, the spirits, the demons, and the ancestors. Most often the sacrifices are animals, which are slaughtered and then burned or cooked and eaten before the gods. However, the sacrifice of nearly every other item of value can be found. People have sacrificed grain, wine, milk, water, wood, tools, weapons, and jewelry to the gods. Occasionally religions will call for the sacrifice of a human, but this is a relatively rare practice. Usually the human who is sacrificed is an enemy who has been taken prisoner in a battle, but on infrequent occasions it is a beloved child or a young person who has been chosen especially for the altar. Human sacrifice is rarely mentioned in religious literature and is usually considered an extreme but effective method of persuading the gods.[1]

The act of sacrifice has a variety of meanings. Originally it was probably considered a means of feeding the residents of the spirit world, the idea being that the deities need to be fed just as humans do. How does one feed the spirits? One may pour water, wine, and milk on the ground and believe that as the fluid is soaked up the spirits are drinking it. One may leave food in a sacred place and assume that when the food has disappeared the gods have been fed. Or one may burn meat or grain, and the gods may inhale the smoke of the offerings. Thus the spirit world is sustained by the human world and acts favorably toward it.

At other times the sacrifice is understood simply as a gift of some sort to the spirit world. Gifts of tools, weapons, ornaments, money,

---

[1]Human sacrifice is mentioned only occasionally in the Jewish Bible, for example. When it is mentioned it is regarded as the supreme and outstanding sacrifice which is usually prompted by extremely rare circumstances. See Genesis 22, Judges 11, II Kings 3:27, and Micah 6:7.

incense, or even tobacco may be left in sacred places for the spirits by a person who wishes the favor of the spirits or who simply wishes to avoid offending them.

Sacrifice in some basic religions also implies the establishment of a communal bond between spirits and human beings. The worshiper brings food to the sacred place, burns a portion of it for the gods, and then eats a portion of it or shares it with the clan. Thus the spirits and the living share a meal together, and their bond is renewed and strengthened.

Rites of Passage

Another almost universal practice among basic societies is the establishment of certain rituals at key points in the life of the individual. These are called rites of passage. The usually recognized key points in life are birth, puberty, marriage, and death. In developed societies the ceremonies at birth are most important. Frequently this is the occasion for circumcision, baptism, and so on. The infant is officially recognized as a member of the community, given a name, and at least symbolically initiated into the religion of the group.

Among the basic societies a great many babies die before puberty, and therefore it is at puberty that the society places its heaviest interest. The rites of passage at puberty are preceded by a period of instruction in the basic knowledge of the society, as well as in the arts of survival, hunting, agriculture, fire making, and so on. At puberty the child may have to undergo an ordeal of some kind. Among some American Indians, children are expected to live apart from their families for a while, fast, and seek a vision from the spirits. Among other basic societies children may be painted white or given some other highly visible mark and be sent away to live alone until the paint or the mark disappears. During this time they are expected to fend entirely for themselves. Of course many children are not lucky or skillful enough to survive this period. Those who do survive and return are then initiated into full adulthood in the society. The individual may also be circumcised or given some other mark of identity such as facial scars. During these ceremonies the young person will be more fully instructed in the religious traditions, secrets, and lore of the society and thereafter may take his or her place as a fully matured member of the group.[2] The counterpart to the puberty rites of passage in more

---

[2]For examples of these rites see the chapters on American Indian and African religions.

modern societies is confirmation for Christian youths and Bar Mitzvah or Bat Mitzvah for Jewish young people.[3]

Other key points at which religious rituals and symbols are important are marriage and death. Marriage within almost all religions is frequently celebrated with fertility rituals of one kind or another and with the full attention of religious functionaries. The passage at death is likewise given the attention of religious rituals, both at the time of death and at the burial.

Ancestor Worship

One final characteristic of basic religions is the veneration or worship of deceased members of the family. Tylor theorized that primitive people dreamed of their departed family and friends and therefore assumed that they were not truly dead or gone but simply living in another realm. Whether this was the occasion of the beginning of religion or not is a matter of speculation. However, from what is known of basic religions, it is apparent that these people recognized that the dead lived on in some form, at least for a time, and that the dead could either help or hurt the living.

These people greatly feared the evil that the dead might do and frequently took great pains to prevent the dead from returning from their graves to harm the living. Bodies were buried with large stones on them or with stakes implanted in their chests, apparently to prevent them from roaming. Among some basic societies the names of the dead were dropped from common usage for a time, and the houses in which they died were burned to discourage their return.

At the same time, people also seemed to feel that the dead could benefit the living. Therefore steps were taken to please the dead. Their possessions, tools, weapons, favorite foods, ornaments and sometimes even their wives and servants were sent into the grave with them. Graves and tombs were decorated and elaborately cared for in order that the dead might be comfortable. Among the ancient Chinese, grave mounds were rebuilt each year, and offerings of food, drink, flowers, and even blankets were left for the comfort of the deceased. Perhaps no people made such a great effort to placate the deceased as the ancient Chinese. Their special concern was to keep alive the memory of their ancestors by memorizing their names and biographies and passing this information on to future generations.

---

[3]Some have suggested that the twentieth-century secular version of the puberty rite of passage is the acquisition of a driver's license with its intensive preparation, its ordeal, and the admission to adulthood of those who "pass."

SUGGESTED READING

Eliade, Mircea. *The Sacred and the Profane*. Translated by Willard Trask. New York: Harper Torchbooks, 1961.

Frazer, Sir James. *The New Golden Bough*. Abridgment by Theodore H. Gaster. New York: Criterion Books, 1959.

Freud, Sigmund. *The Future of an Illusion*. Translated by W. D. Robinson-Scott. Garden City, N. Y.: Doubleday, 1964.

Malinowski, Bronislaw. *Magic, Science and Religion, and Other Essays*. Boston: Beacon Press, 1948.

Otto, Rudolf. *The Idea of the Holy*. Translated by John W. Harvey. London: Oxford University Press, 1948.

CHAPTER TWO

AMERICAN INDIAN RELIGIONS

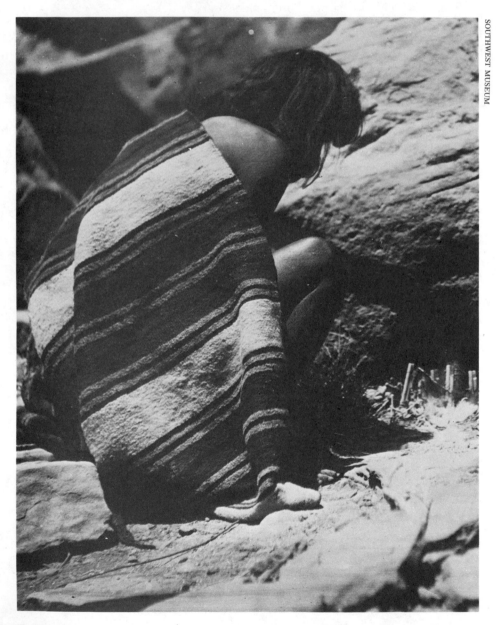

Tu-Bang-Vin-Tiwa, chief priest of antelope fraternity, makes an offering at the shrine of the spider woman and prays.

Holy Mother Earth, the trees and all nature, are witnesses of your thoughts and deeds.

A WINNEBAGO WISE SAYING

The recent American Indian Movement has raised interest in the plight of contemporary Native Americans as well as in their culture, religions, and contributions to American history. Along with almost every other aspect of their heritage, the religion of the Native Americans is widely misunderstood and misrepresented.

Hollywood would have us believe that the religion of these people has to do with the "Great Spirit" and the eventual trip to some "happy hunting ground." While a concern for the unseen spirit world is very important to American Indians, the terms *Great Spirit* and *happy hunting ground* are almost total fabrications. Many American Indian tribes were primarily agricultural in their life-styles, and an eternity in a hunting ground would be meaningless to them.

Another popular misconception regarding American Indian religions has to do with the use of hallucinogenic drugs. Carlos Casteñeda's recent books emphasize the use of peyote and mescaline as a means to understanding the spirit world. One might conclude from reading these books that the use of such drugs was of primary importance in American Indian religions. However, the use of hallucinogenics was extremely limited; the use of the sacred pipe and tobacco was far more widespread, as we shall see.

When speaking of the religion of Native Americans, we must be aware that we are not speaking of a monolithic structure. These people, whom we identify as American Indians, arrived on this continent some 15,000 to 20,000 years ago. Since then they have lived in

33

nearly every section of the Americas. They have lived in many different climates with many different life-styles. They have lived in very primitive conditions in simple hunting and gathering societies and in relatively advanced agricultural societies. After 1800 A.D., when the horse became available to the Indian, many tribes that had been primarily agricultural societies moved to the American plains and developed new ways of living based on the pursuit of the American bison. Considering such a long time span and in the midst of so many various life-styles and societies, it is impossible to talk about one "American Indian religion."

In studying these religions we must also be aware of the poverty of our sources. With American Indian life covering perhaps 20,000 years, we have literary sources from only the last four hundred years. Frequently these writings come to us from Christian missionaries who were scarcely sympathetic to Indian religions. Those sources not produced by missionaries tend to come from the last one hundred years or so, after the Indian had had some contact with the Western civilization, its religion, and its technology. Beyond our literary sources, all that we know of Indian religions prior to contact with the white settlers derives from archaeological research; since the majority of Indian tribes were preliterate, these sources are also limited. Therefore, it behooves us to speak very carefully about our "knowledge" of the subject.

In describing American Indian religion we have two major options: we can either describe the specific religion of one tribe at one point in history, or we can make statements about the religious outlook of Native Americans in general according to the information available. In this text we will take the second path. Following are some characteristics found in almost all American Indian religions of which we are aware.

ANIMISM

Much is made of the contrast between the Indian attitude toward nature and that of the whites. Generally the argument is stated that the Indian had a reverential attitude toward the land, its trees, its rivers, and its streams, whereas the white people looked upon nature as something to be exploited on their behalf. Thus the whites were willing to sacrifice the beauty and even the life of the land to build a technology that would temporarily make life more comfortable and pleasant for them. Whether or not this is an accurate statement and whether or not the whites inherited this attitude from their Judaeo-Christian religion is a matter of some speculation, but it does seem to be true that the American Indian had a more reverent attitude toward nature.

The term *animism* when applied to the American Indian simply means that to him there was not the clear-cut distinction between the animate and the inanimate world that other cultures seem to see. To the Indian all of nature was alive and animate. Thus the trees, the rivers, the soil, and even the stones of the land were believed to contain a form of life that could be either helpful or harmful to human beings. Among the natives of the Pacific Islands, who viewed nature in a manner similar to that of the American Indian, this force was called *mana*. *Mana* was never seen as either good or evil but affected humans according to the way it was used. The attitude of the American Indian toward the forces in nature seems to have been similar to that of modern people toward electricity. That is, the forces are unseen and may be helpful if handled properly; if they are not handled properly these forces can be extremely dangerous.

Thus the Native American did not view nature as the creation of a supreme deity for the subjugation of humankind. Rather, nature was seen as a collection of multiple spirits with which people must live in harmony. And so all of life had a religious nature. Hunting was a religious occupation in which the animal was not just an object to be killed and devoured; rather, the animal was a fellow creature with a spirit similar to that of the hunter. Therefore, before a hunt Indians prepared themselves religiously. Hunters prayed to the spirit of the animal they were hunting. They observed certain taboos to protect themselves from disaster. One of the most common taboos connected with the hunt was that against women, particularly menstruating women. Among some tribes it was believed that if a menstruating woman even accidentally touched a hunting weapon or crossed the path of a hunting party, the hunt would be ruined. During the hunt only those animals which were needed would be killed. After the hunt all of the animal's body was used in some way; nothing was wasted. Among some tribes special care was taken of the bones to insure success in the next hunt.

Not only was hunting a holy occupation shrouded with religious rituals and preparations, but nearly every other relationship between the Native American and nature was similarly religious. Planting and harvesting were surrounded with rituals and taboos. Even the gathering of clay for the production of pottery revealed an animistic understanding of nature. The Papago women of southern Arizona spoke to the clay that they dug for pots: "I take only what I need. It is to cook for my children."[1] If possible the woman digging the clay from the earth left a small gift. A similar attitude toward nature is revealed among American Indians when they cut trees. A Fox Indian said:

> We do not like to harm the trees. Whenever we can, we always make an offering of tobacco to the trees before we cut them down. We never waste the wood, but use all that we cut down. If we did not think of their feelings, all the other trees in the forest would weep, and that would make our hearts sad, too.[2]

The reverent attitude of the American Indian toward nature and its contrast to that of the white person is best summarized in the words of an Indian:

> The work of the white man hardens soul and body. Nor is it right to tear up and mutilate the earth as white men do. . . . We simply take the gifts that are freely offered. We no more harm the earth than would an infant's fingers harm its mother's breast.[3]

CONTROLS OVER THE SPIRIT WORLD

Animists do not see the universe under the control of one supreme god in the pattern of Western religions such as Judaism or Islam. Neither do they see the world under the direction of many gods in a pantheon as in many Eastern religions or in the Graeco-Roman world view. Animists may recognize many gods and may in fact acknowledge one of them as a high god above all the rest, but this god is not their major concern. The major concern of the animist is day-to-day life among the multiple spirits which make up the world. Native Americans may have recognized a kind of "Great Spirit," or "Great Mystery," but the

---

[1] Ruth M. Underhill, *Red Man's Religion* (Chicago: The University of Chicago Press, 1965), p. 116.

[2] William Jones, *Ethnography of the Fox Indians* (Washington, D.C.: Government Printing Office, Bureau of American Ethnology Bulletin, 1939), p. 21.

[3] James Mooney, "The Ghost-Dance Religion and the Sioux Outbreak of 1890," *14th Annual Report of the Bureau of Ethnology, Part II* (Washington, D.C.: Government Printing Office, 1896), p. 724.

Sacred bags of the Horn Society of the Blood Indian tribe. These bags would likely contain various religious items believed by these Plains Indians to have great medicinal or religious power.

bulk of their religious attention was directed toward good relationships between themselves and the multiple spirits of the forests, streams, mountains, and plains.

Absent for the most part from the religions of the American Indians was the nearly universal practice of animal and human sacrifice to placate the gods. "North America had almost no sacrifice, even of animals. Mother Earth did not demand it."[4] Perhaps the animistic spirit of the American Indian felt that human or animal blood spilt out to the spirits would be wasteful. For whatever reason, the great blood sacrifices of many religions of the Eastern and Western worlds were usually missing from most American Indian religions.

Taboos

One of the ways Native Americans protected themselves from evil that might come from the spirit world was through the use of taboos. As we have already mentioned, one of the most widely held taboos was that regarding menstruating women. In many cultures women are held to have special powers for either good or evil, but the menstruating woman is particularly powerful. It is during this time that she is

---

[4]Underhill, *Red Man's Religion*, p. 48.

obviously set apart by the spirits as one who can participate in the miracle of birth, a power than no man can have. Thus during this period the menstruating woman was kept away from the tribe. In some communities she was required to leave her family and live in a special hut. At this time she could be especially damaging to the magic necessary for the hunt, and hunters therefore avoided her. Native Americans believed that even a glance from a menstruating woman could destroy the hunting ability of a man for the rest of his life, that she could also destroy the magic of hunting weapons, and that her presence in the forests might drive away the game forever.

Another taboo widely observed among American Indians was avoidance of the dead, whom they feared and respected. No matter how beloved the dead may have been in life, after death it was feared that the spirit would continue to stay around its former home and perhaps attempt to take the friends and family of the dead with it. At best, the spirits of the dead might haunt their families, causing them bad dreams. Therefore, the dead had to be buried or burned and every step taken to prevent them from returning. Measures were taken to confuse the dead so that they might not recognize their former homes, and sometimes even their names were forbidden to be spoken for years after their deaths. They were buried by special members of the tribe apart from the immediate family, and these corpse handlers were considered to be ritually unclean for a period of time after they had touched the corpse. They were separated from the tribe for a period of perhaps ten days and forbidden to eat the regular food of the tribe. Thus the dead and those who handled them were widely considered to be taboo.

Ceremonies and Ritual

Along with the observance of taboos, American Indians sought to control the capricious forces of the spirit world with ceremonies. As is the case with many other religions, ceremonies were extremely important to Native American religions. The purpose of their ceremonies, rituals, and dances was not necessarily for worship but as a means of renewing the partnership between humans and the spirit world. Frequently they involved dances, fasting, ordeals, bathing, and the observation of taboos.

One of the most common elements in American Indian religions was the use of the dance as a means of contacting the spirit world in preparation for some special event in life. The dance was an event in which the entire community participated. It was used to prepare the tribe for the hunt or for the agricultural season or for war. It was also frequently used in the rites of passage and when a member of the tribe died. Whatever the occasion, the dance was usually accompanied by song, the beating of drums, and the shaking of rattles. The song might be made up of only a few lines, but these lines would be repeated over and over again. The drum beat might be nothing more than several people beating on a log with sticks, but the effect of hours of song and steady rhythm was hypnotic and prepared the participants for contact with the spirit world.

Among the American Indian Tribes whose livelihood depended upon hunting, rituals prepared the hunters for their work. Hunting, like agriculture, tends to develop highly religious societies because of its capricious nature. During one season the hunters may go forth and find an abundance of game. They may find their weapons extremely accurate and effective. In the next season the same hunters may find game scarce or their weapons virtually useless. Therefore the spirits of the animals and the hunters themselves, along with their weapons, must be properly prepared for the hunt in order to ensure success. It is believed that the cave paintings of France from the era of Cro-Magnon are attempts by primitive hunters to depict the game being killed in an effort to ensure success in the hunt. In addition to preparing their weapons with special rituals, Native Americans, as we have already mentioned, did not allow women, particularly menstruating women, to touch their weapons, and employed special dances to ensure a successful hunt. Ruth Underhill describes a Pueblo ritual preparing the hunters and their game for a good hunt:

> One of my most dramatic memories is that of standing in the plaza of a Pueblo, in the dark of a January morning, to watch the Mother of Game bring in the deer. It was almost dawn when we heard the hunter's call from the hillside. Then shadowy forms came bounding down through the piñon trees. At first we could barely see the shaking horns and dappled hides. Then the sun's rays picked out men on all fours, with deerskins over their backs and painted staves in their hands to simulate forelegs. They leaped and gamboled before the people while around them pranced little boys who seemed actually to have the spirit of fawns.
>
> In their midst was a beautiful Pueblo woman with long black hair, in all the regalia of white boots and embroidered *manta*.

> She was their Owner, the Mother of Game. But she was also
> Earth Mother, the source of all live things including men. She
> led the animals where they would be good targets for the hunters,
> and, one by one, they were symbolically killed.[5]

As discussed in the previous chapter, such a ritual is called sympathetic or imitative magic. Those persons who are imitating the game animals in the ceremony are symbolically called forth and killed in the belief that during the actual hunt the real animals will similarly be killed.

Because of the animistic identification of a kindred spirit between the American Indian and the game, the ritual of the hunt also included a merciful killing of the animal and a festive treatment of its body. For example, we have reports in which hunting Indians apologized to the animal before they killed it. After it was killed and brought back to the tribe the animal was treated as an honored guest. Following the hunt every item of the animal's body was used; nothing was wasted. If bones or hide or flesh were wasted in any way, then the animal might have died in vain and there would be retribution against the hunters.

Visions and Fasting

In order to gain special power at some point in life, Native Americans often sought visions that would put them in contact with the spirit world. Visions were especially sought by boys at puberty. Early in life the Indian boy was taught that one day he must go alone into the wilderness and seek a vision from the spirits. At some point in his youth, usually at the age of nine or ten, the child was sent away from his family and tribe into the forest, where he was required to live alone and apart for some time until he received a vision. The quest for the vision was nearly always accompanied by several days of fasting. Usually the child lived without food, perhaps without water, and with only the barest of possessions and clothing in order that he might appear quite poor and humble before the spirits. Sometimes he painted his face or his body in such a way as to identify himself as a special member of his tribe. Under such conditions he awaited the vision. The spirits frequently appeared in visions as animals, but they might also appear as men or women. If the vision did not appear after two or three days of fasting and prayer, the person seeking it might feel compelled

---

[5]Underhill, *Red Man's Religion*, pp. 117, 118.

to take more extreme measures, such as cutting his flesh or perhaps even hacking off a finger and offering it to the spirits as a sign of sincerity. When the vision finally came, the child returned to the tribe as a fuller member of the group, having passed through this rite of passage.

Visions were also sought by men at other times in life. Visions were particularly important on the eve of a great battle when extraordinary strength was needed to achieve honors. Visions were also connected with the buffalo hunt among members of the Plains Indian tribes. The most widely known example of this was the sun dance. During the summer months, if a member of the tribe felt the need for special power or needed to overcome some problem in his life, he would pledge to do the sun dance. During a tribal gathering the participant then fasted, danced, and looked constantly at the sun in order to force the sun to bless him. On some occasions and among some tribes the sun dance also involved self-torture. Among the Oglala Sioux the dancers put thongs through the flesh of their pectoral muscles and hung from the center pole of their lodge as they gazed at the sun. As gruesome as this sounds, it apparently inflicted no permanent injury.

Religious Leadership

Native American religions were remarkably free of a priesthood. While there were those in every tribe who had a special connection with the spirit world, basic religious functions were performed by every member of the group. In a sense the religion of the American Indians was a very personal religion that encouraged the individual to get in contact with the spirit world alone. Prayers, dances, songs, and visions were all to be done, not by the specialist in religion, but by every member of the tribe according to each person's need. Since there was a very limited use of sacrifice, there was little need for the trained professional to perform the ritual on behalf of the untrained layperson—the procedure so common to so many religions of the world. Nevertheless, among Native Americans there were several categories of religious specialists who were used occasionally in encounters with the spirit world.

The specialist most often connected with American Indian religions is the so-called medicine man. The designation *medicine man* was given to this functionary by early white settlers because they recognized him as one who specialized in healing. To the Indian, sickness was caused by the invasion of the body by a foreign object, and healing

Navajo medicine man.

came about when the foreign body was removed. It was the work of the medicine man to remove such objects. The person designated as the medicine man for his tribe received his power over the powers that caused sickness through visions from the spirit world. The spirits might appear to the medicine man after a period of fasting and prayer, or they might appear without any preparation. They usually took the form of some special animal such as the bear or the badger since these two animals were connected with healing in Indian mythology. The spirits did not take possession of the medicine man; they only appeared to and instructed him on a frequent basis, perhaps giving him a song or instructing him in taboos.

Because of his special contacts with the spirit world the medicine man was empowered to heal, but he could also curse and bring sickness and even death to those who incurred his wrath. This brought a great responsibility to those recognized as medicine men. If the medicine man encountered a sickness too serious for him to heal, he could claim that it was the work of a more powerful medicine man. At the same time, if a number of the medicine man's patients were dying, he might have been held responsible for the deaths and even have been put to death himself.

The healing process the medicine man conducted usually consisted of a sucking ritual in which the healer literally attempted to suck the offensive object or spirit from the body of the sick person. This was often accompanied with songs and dancing or incantations.

Another specialist found in American Indian religions is that person designated by anthropologists with the Siberian name *shaman*. The shaman was found mainly among the Eskimos and the tribes of the Pacific Northwest. Unlike the medicine man, who simply dreamed about the spirits, the shaman was actually possessed by them. The spirits chose a future shaman and caused him to have a serious illness. He could not be cured unless he allowed the spirits to take possession of him and he became a shaman. After he entered a trance the spirits took possession of him and spoke through his voice. Shamans were also distinctive in that they could work wonders similar to those of the Yogins. Shamans have been known to walk on hot coals, swallow hot coals, and stab themselves without leaving a wound. They were also known to speak an ecstatic tongue when under the control of the spirits and to foretell the future—probably their most useful function.

Among American Indian tribes whose lives revolved directly around a settled life and an agricultural community, ceremonies were maintained from one generation to the next and a form of priesthood was needed to maintain and pass on the rituals. These priests did not claim a vision from the spirits, nor were they possessed by the spirits; they were individuals who memorized and carried on prayers and ceremonies for the fertility of the soil and for the general welfare of the tribe.

Other Means of Contact with the Spirit World

One of the most common elements of all American Indian religions was the use of tobacco and the sacred pipe in religious ceremonies. Tobacco was the incense of Native American religions; it was a part of nearly every ceremony. It was smoked when people gathered to talk of peace, or war, or the hunt. It was smoked by the medicine man as he performed healing ceremonies. The pipes themselves were carried as the talismans of the tribes when they went to hunt or into battle.

Tobacco was apparently grown and used only for religious purposes. There is no indication that American Indians used it as a daily narcotic in the fashion of twentieth-century civilization. One of the reasons tobacco was reserved for special religious occasions was that it was far too strong to be used more frequently. American Indians did not have the tobacco that is commercially available today, *Nicotiana attenuata*, but used a far stronger variety, *Nicotiana rustica*. The fumes of this tobacco were so strong as to be intoxicating. Present-day smokers who have tried this variety marvel that Indians were ever able to smoke the six puffs usually required in their ceremonies.

The pipes in which this tobacco was smoked were called calumets after the French word *chalumeau*, which means "reed." The bowls of these pipes were made from either clay or stone and the stems were made from reeds. Sometimes the most ceremonial of the pipes were known to have stems up to four feet in length. They were frequently decorated with paints and feathers, indicating their importance as tribal talismans.

It is popularly believed that peyote and other hallucinogenic drugs were a regular part of American Indian worship, but this was not the case. With the extremely intoxicating tobacco that was used in the ceremonial pipes, no other hallucinogenics were necessary for most American Indian tribes. Peyote was used as early as four hundred years ago by the Aztecs and other Indian groups in Mexico, and it may have been introduced to the North American Indians as late as the nineteenth century.

The peyote plant (*Lophophora williamsii*) is a small cactus with

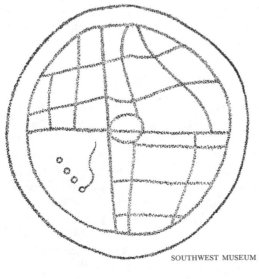

Sand-altar painting used in initiation ceremony by the Luiseño Chinigchinix cult of Southern California. (After DuBois.)

SOUTHWEST MUSEUM

bulbous or button growths on it. These buttons contain eight alkaloid substances. Some of these substances are stimulating and some are depressing. The alkaloid that produces hallucinations is mescaline. The peyote buttons may be eaten fresh from the plant or they may be dried and later brewed in a tea. It is estimated that a person would have to ingest forty peyote buttons to hallucinate.

With the defeats that the Native Americans suffered at the hands of the United States government at the end of the nineteenth century, many turned to the use of peyote as a means of achieving a vision from the spirits. Previously the vision was sought only occasionally in Indian religions, at the rite of passage at the time of puberty, prior to a great hunt or battle, or by the medicine man at crucial points in his life. However, when so little was left to the American Indian, many tribes felt the need of a vision on a more regular basis without the preparatory fasting and ordeals. Small amounts of the peyote button could help in achieving this vision.

In 1941 the peyote cult was introduced into the Native American Church of Oklahoma. This church combined many of the elements of Christianity that were appealing to the American Indian people[6] and the use of peyote to stimulate the vision. In 1945 the group became known as the Native American Church of the United States and spread via Indian missionaries from the tribes of Oklahoma to those of Arizona. Today the use of peyote is banned by some Indian tribes, and nine western states have laws against its importation. However, its moderate use is still maintained by some groups within the Native American Church.

DEATH AND LIFE AFTER DEATH

In discussing the beliefs of the American Indian about death and life after death we must be reminded again that we are discussing a great variety of people who lived in various climates and had a variety of

---

[6]From the sixteenth century onward American Indians have been exposed to various forms of Christianity. Sometimes the exposure has been forced upon them. Apparently there were many elements within Christianity that appealed to them and that could be adopted into their religious system with little difficulty. One element that never seemed to fit, however, was the Christian concept of original sin. To the Indian mind when there was real evil in the world it was the result of witchcraft rather than personal evil.

cultural systems. Therefore attitudes toward death and practices regarding death varied widely. We can no more talk about *the* American Indian concept of life after death than we can talk about *the* American Indian religion. Here again we can only generalize.

As we noted earlier, Native Americans tended to fear the dead and to handle them with great care and concern lest they return and somehow trouble the lives of the living. Many of the most serious taboos of American Indian life were built around the treatment of the dead. It should also be noted that in spite of the awe and dread that American Indians expressed regarding the dead, there was little fear of death itself. Missionaries, anthropologists, and other white observers have noted again and again the remarkable lack of fear demonstrated by them when they faced death.

Picture writing on a buffalo skin, depicting the principal events in the life of a Pawnee chief.

Generally American Indians seem to have believed in the existence of two souls, neither of which could be considered immortal in any sense. One soul was the life or breath that accompanies the body. When the body died, or at least when it decaycd, this soul also died. The second soul was what might be called a free soul. This soul wandered about during dreams or left the body during sickness. After death this free soul went to the land of the dead. Little is said about this land of the dead among Indians. Sometimes it is considered a happy place and sometimes a place of sadness. Some tribes attempted to aid the deceased in the journey to the land of the dead by also burying food and drink in the grave. Occasionally this was carried further when an important person died, and an attempt was made to send along a guide to aid the deceased in finding the land of the dead. Sometimes an animal was killed to act as a guide, and on other occasions an enemy was killed for the same purpose. Among the Natchez Indians of Mississippi, when a great chieftain died, large numbers of wives, children, friends, and animals were sacrificed to accompany the dead man.

When the free soul reached the land of the dead it did not live forever there. Perhaps like the Hebrews' concept of *Sheol* or the Greeks' idea of *Hades*, the American Indian believed that the soul existed in the land of the dead only as long as the person was remembered by the living. When the person began to be forgotten, the free soul began to fade and eventually disappeared.

The closest thing to immortality that can be found among American Indian religions was the belief among some tribes in reincarnation. Apparently some believed that a dead relative might reappear as a newborn infant. Sometimes there was an attempt to recognize the deceased in the baby by virtue of facial similarity or the child's recognition of its former name. When the child was identified as a deceased relative, the youth might be given the name of the relative or he might be treated with the respect that the aged person received while still alive. Although this concept of reincarnation was found among some American Indians, it was by no means universal.

With the coming of the white settlers and their religions, Native American cultures and religions have undergone severe stress. Native Americans have been pressured to convert to Christianity in one of its many forms and to accept the educational and cultural values of the Europeans. Many Native Americans have yielded to this pressure and have entered the mainstream of twentieth-century American society.

Others have accepted only parts of the European culture and religious schemes, while maintaining a part of their native culture. An example of this attempted amalgamation is the Native American Church. Still other Native Americans have clung to their culture and have maintained the religions of their forebears. The modern revival of interest in Native American life has strengthened this third alternative.

SUGGESTED READING

Benedict, Ruth Fulton. *The Concept of the Guardian Spirit in North America*. Menasha, Wis.: The Collegiate Press, 1923.

Brown, Dee. *Bury My Heart at Wounded Knee*. New York: Holt, Rinehart & Winston, 1970.

Deloria, Vine. *God Is Red*. New York: Grosset & Dunlap, 1973.

Underhill, Ruth M. *Red Man's Religion*. Chicago: The University of Chicago Press, 1956.

CHAPTER THREE

AFRICAN RELIGIONS

*Mask worn in a ritual dance by the women's society of the
Mende tribe of Sierre Leone.*

We worship the *Orisha*.
If we worship the *Orisha*
We will always have money,
We will always have children.

YORUBA SONG

During the past thirty years Europe's control over its former empires has declined, and many of the countries that were once members of these empires have begun to form independent empires of their own. Much of this activity has taken place on the vast continent of Africa. Today these new African nations have become a vocal and active segment of the so-called Third World. Many of them control raw materials that are essential to the industrialized nations of the world. The leaders of today and of the future must learn to deal with Africans on both political and business levels if there is to be peace and prosperity in the world.

Essential to understanding the leaders of black Africa is a knowledge of their culture. A major step in understanding customs and values is a basic knowledge of religion. As it is in the case of nearly every other people in the world, religion is one of the keystones of African culture. A basic understanding of African religions will provide an awareness of African customs, the African approach to the family, the African appreciation of land, and, of course, the African view of death and life beyond death.

Perhaps no religions have been so confused in the minds of Western audiences as the religions of Africa. The images of these religions as presented in films and popular literature depict the black African as a hopeless savage and African religion as ugly superstition. Most people

associate African religions with the image of a missionary in the canni-
bal's pot about to be boiled and eaten. Or people remember the many,
many motion pictures in which the evil witch doctor in a horrible mask
tries to put a voodoo curse upon a victim. Even supposedly factual
sources are likely to contain images of blood sacrifice, fetishes, shrunk-
en heads, and babies sacrificed to crocodile gods. All these are dis-
torted images drawn from half truths and fertile imaginations.
Nevertheless, they have left their impression on most Westerners. As
with American Indian religions, the full truth about African religions
cannot be told in such a brief and general text as this because the topic
is simply too broad. There is no "African religion" as such, and beliefs
and practices vary widely throughout the African continent. However,
general truths, concepts, and trends about certain areas of African
religions can be highlighted and some of the popular misconceptions
dispelled.

NON-NATIVE AFRICAN RELIGIONS

The emphasis of this chapter will be on the basic concepts of native
African religions. However, we cannot overlook several non-native
religions that have had enormous influence upon the continent in the
past, and which may influence it even more in the future. Today
approximately one-half of the African population is estimated to
adhere to non-native religions.

Christianity

Christianity has had a long and illustrious history in Africa. Indeed
Africa may have been one of the first locations for Christianity outside
of Palestine. The earliest known fragment of the New Testament is a
section from the Gospel of John which was found in Egypt. This
fragment is dated approximately 125 A.D. It is reasonable to assume
that Christian missionaries took the east trade routes by land and sea to
North Africa early in the first Christian centuries.

Regardless of the date that Christianity entered Africa, it found
fertile ground there. Some of the finest minds and leaders of early
Christianity were from this region. Leaders such as Augustine, Origen,
Arius, Athanasius, Tertullian and Cyprian came from North Africa.
The libraries, universities, and fine scholarly traditions found in such

communities as Alexandria contributed much to early Christian thought.

In the seventh and eighth centuries the new religion of Islam swept across northern Africa and eventually became the religion of most of the African people. The only African nations that remained Christian after the Muslim conquest were Ethiopia and Nubia. In Egypt a minority sect of Christians called *Copts* remains to this day.

It was not until the fifteenth century that any part of Africa south of the Sahara was exposed to Christianity. Portugese traders of that era were the first Europeans to venture along the west and east coasts of Africa, bringing their religion and its missionaries with them. They succeeded in converting many Africans all over the continent to Christianity. The period from the seventeenth through the nineteenth centuries was the era of the slave trade, so the encounter between Christian Europeans and black Africans was not pleasant. With the end of the slave trade in the nineteenth century and the eventual rise of the colonial empires, Christian missionaries made a serious effort to convert black Africans. Because these missionaries were representatives of the dominant European and American cultures and because they brought with them modernity, medicine, and education, in many cases they were successful. It is estimated that of a total population of approximately 413 million, today there are 101 million Christians in Africa.[1]

In addition to the traditional Catholic and Protestant groups in Africa, many independent Christian sects developed there. In many cases these sects are amalgamations of Christian doctrines and native African religious concepts. In other cases these sects are Christian groups that have developed around the charismatic leadership of a prophet or a faith healer. It is estimated that there may be as many as six thousand independent Christian churches in Africa.[2]

Islam

As it moved out of the Arabian desert, Islam conquered nearly all of northern Africa within a century of the death of the prophet Muhammad. However, like Christianity before it, Islam seemed restricted or

---

[1]*The World Almanac of* 1977 (New York: Newspaper Enterprise Association, 1977), p. 349.
[2]Benjamin C. Ray, *African Religions* (Englewood Cliffs, N. J.: Prentice-Hall, 1976), p. 194.

bounded by the Sahara desert and with rare exception did not move southward for many centuries.

In the eleventh and twelfth centuries Muslim traders began to spread Islam southward. Several of the large African empires of that era such as Ghana, Mali, and Songhai were converted to Islam. During the centuries that followed, Islam continued to grow in black Africa. However, it too was impeded by the slave trade, because many of the agents of the slave trade were Arab. Because Islam is a religion that stresses the brotherhood and equality of all Muslims before Allah, it was difficult for Muslims to convert those whom they might later enslave. With the end of the slave trade in the nineteenth century and with the travel advantages of the colonial period, Muslim missionary activity enjoyed a tremendous upsurge.

In the twentieth century Islam has had a great entree into black Africa for several reasons. First, Islam is widely identified as the religion of Third World nations, and many Africans find this appealing. Second, Islam can be more easily adapted to native African customs and beliefs than other world religions. Islam speaks of the one true High God, Allah, and this is a concept shared with many native African religions. Finally, Islam allows polygamy under certain conditions, and this too has been a regular feature of African life. Today it is estimated that there are approximately 99 million Muslims in Africa.[3]

Other Religions

Christianity and Islam are the two largest non-native religions in Africa, but there are elements of several other religions of the world to be found on the continent. A distinct branch of Judaism is found in Ethiopia among a group of people called the Falashas. The Falashas trace their ancestry back to the Queen of Sheba in the tenth century B.C. They practice a form of Judaism that is influenced by the Pentateuch but which does not seem to be aware of the Talmud.

On the east coast of Africa there are settlements of people from India. Here live one-half million Hindus and small groups of Buddhists and Confucianists. Although there is speculation that some of these Indian religions may have influenced certain aspects of African Islam, they seem to offer little attraction for the native African. The major choice seems to be among native African religions, Christianity, and Islam.

---

[3]*World Almanac*, p. 349.

NATIVE RELIGIONS

When we speak of native African religions, we cannot speak with authority about a single religion, theology, world view, or cult. Africa is a huge continent that has supported millions of people for many centuries. Undoubtedly almost every imaginable form of human religion has been expressed by people on this continent. Unfortunately most of the religions of Africa have existed in preliterate times, so the modern student of religion must realize that only the tip of the iceberg can be known. What *is* known about African religions has been gathered by modern anthropologists or has been remembered from the past by Africans. Furthermore, religious beliefs and practices of any one group of Africans are not necessarily shared by other groups. Therefore, when we speak of basic concepts within these religions we must keep in mind that these ideas do not always apply universally; there is a great variety of beliefs.

The High God

A belief that above all local deities there is one supreme High God who created the world and then withdrew from active participation is frequently found among many of the polytheistic religions of the world. This belief is also found among some African peoples. Although most of the native religions of Africa are basically polytheistic in their day-to-day practices, there is an overriding belief that beyond all the minor gods, spirits, and ancestors, one High God exists. When this became known among early anthropologists some of them concluded that Africans had originally been monotheistic but had lapsed into polytheism.[4] There are few, if any, authorities on African religions who advocate this position today, however.

In many African religions the High God seems to have been a creator god who did his work and then retired to some distant place. It is currently believed that this god has little contact with the world and its daily operations. Typical of the African understanding of the High God is the Yoruba story of Olorun. The Yoruba are native to the central west Africa territory now governed by Nigeria. In their mythology the High God, Olorun, gave the job of creating the world to his eldest son, Obatala. This son failed to complete the task, so it was

---

[4]The best known advocate of this position was Father Wilhelm Schmidt in his book *Der Ursprung der Gottesidee*.

passed on the the younger son, Odudua, but he too failed. Therefore Olorun had to complete the work of creation himself. He assigned the other tasks of creation to various *orisha*, who are regarded as lesser deities. After the work of creation was done, Olorun seems to have retired to the heavens with little interest or control over his universe. While various Yoruba villages have special *orisha* who have saved them or helped them in times of trouble, there is no record that the Olorun ever has been of direct assistance. He remains detached from the problems of the world and allows the *orisha* to intervene when necessary.

A legend from the people of Upper Zambezi reveals the retiring nature of the High God even more clearly.

In the beginning Nyambi made all things. He made animals, fishes, birds. At that time he lived on earth with his wife, Nasilele. One of Nyambi's creatures was different from all the others. His name was Kamonu. Kamonu imitated Nyambi in everything Nyambi did. When Nyambi worked in wood, Kamonu worked in wood; when Nyambi forged iron Kamonu forged iron.

After awhile Nyambi began to fear Kamonu.

Then one day Kamonu forged a spear and killed a male antelope, and he went on killing. Nyambi grew very angry at this.

"Man, you are acting badly," he said to Kamonu. "These are your brothers. Do not kill them."

Nyambi drove Kamonu out into another land. But after awhile Kamonu returned. Nyambi allowed him to stay and gave him a garden to cultivate.

It happened that at night buffaloes wandered into Kamonu's garden and he speared them; after that some elands, and he killed one. After some time Kamonu's dog died; then his pot broke; then his child died. When Kamonu went to Nyambi to tell him what had happened he found his dog and his pot and his child at Nyambi's.

Then Kamonu said to Nyambi, "Give me medicine so that I may keep my things." But Nyambi refused to give him medicine. After this, Nyambi met with his two counselors and said, "How shall we live since Kamonu knows too well the road hither?"

Nyambi tried various means to flee Kamonu. He removed

himself and his court to an island across the river. But
Kamonu made a raft of reeds and crossed over to Nyambi's
island. Then Nyambi piled up a huge mountain and went to
live on its peak. Still Nyambi could not get away from man.
Kamonu found his way to him. In the meantime men were
multiplying and spreading all over the earth.

Finally Nyambi sent birds to go look for a place for Litoma,
god's town. But the birds failed to find a place. Nyambi sought
council from a diviner. The diviner said, "Your life depends on
Spider." And Spider went and found an abode for Nyambi and
his court in the sky. Then Spider spun a thread from earth to
the sky and Nyambi climbed up on the thread. Then the diviner advised Nyambi to put out Spider's eyes so that he could
never see the way to heaven again and Nyambi did so.

After Nyambi disappeared into the sky Kamonu gathered
some men around him and said, "Let us build a high tower and
climb up to Nyambi." They cut down trees and put log on log,
higher and higher toward the sky. But the weight was too great
and the tower collapsed. So that Kamonu never found his way
to Nyambi's home.

But every morning when the sun appeared, Kamonu
greeted it saying, "Here is our king. He has come." And all the
other people greeted him shouting and clapping. At the time
of the new moon men call on Nasilele, Nyambi's wife.[5]

Occasionally the High God is an object of worship, and some communities have temples and priests dedicated to him. Apparently, however, most Africans regard the High God as too high, too distant, and
too great to pay much attention to his worship. It is the lesser spirits
and the ancestors that receive the greatest attention in African religions.

The Lesser Spirits

When we get beyond the stories of the High God which are found in
many African religions, we encounter true animism. Like many other
people of the world, the Africans tend to people the universe with
spirits. All the earth, the seas, and the skies are believed to contain a
spiritual or life force similar to that in humankind. These forces can be

[5]Susan Feldmann, ed., *African Myths and Tales* (New York: Dell, 1963), pp.
36–37.

Serpent temple, Dahomey.

beneficial or harmful, they are subject to flattery and sacrifice. Therefore it behooves humans to be aware of these spirits and to seek their
favor.

Africans recognize the life force in mountains, forests, pools,
streams, trees, and animals. They are aware of it in the sun and the
moon. Not only is it found in these objects, but Africans also see it in
storms, thunder, and lightning. In fact, in some west African villages
there are temples, priests, and cults established to worship the storm
gods. The earth, too, is worshiped. As in ancient Europe and nearly
every other ancient culture, the earth is often pictured as a goddess
and receives worship by some Africans. Among the Ashanti people
there are regular ceremonies to the Earth Mother in which the following lines are recited:

> Earth, while I am yet alive,
> It is upon you that I put my trust,
> Earth who receives my body . . .
> We are addressing you,
> And you will understand.[6]

Among native Africans water is frequently recognized as a sacred
element. Water is used in religious rituals the world over and is particularly important and sacred in many of the basic religions. When the life

---

[6]Geoffrey Parrinder, *African Traditional Religion* (London: Hutchinson
House, 1954), p. 48.

57

of a people is dependent upon rainfall, rivers, and streams, or when water appears to have a life of its own, its religious significance is accentuated. When Africans use water for an essentially religious ritual such as bathing a new-born baby, the water must come from a source of *living water* (for instance, a spring or a river), and must not be boiled because that would kill the spirit or power in it. Throughout Africa, rivers, streams, lakes, springs, and the seas are venerated for the spiritual powers which abide in them. Because serpents are often connected with bodies of water, they too are often regarded with awe, and cults are sometimes developed for their worship.

Although the nature gods and lesser spirits of the universe are seldom a major aspect of African worship, they are recognized and do receive veneration. Worship may vary from fully established cults, complete with temples, priests, and rituals, to less formal types of worship. Perhaps the most common form of worship of these lesser spirits is the simple libation or offering. The African wishing to acknowledge the spirits may pour out a bit of water, wine, beer, or milk upon the ground or may offer a bit of foodstuff to these gods at each meal.

Ancestors

The most commonly recognized spiritual forces in African religions are departed ancestors. In perhaps no other part of the world except China and Japan is such high regard and concern for the dead apparent. Africans believe that departed members of the family exist in a spirit world and yet maintain an interest in the lives of those who continue to live. They are regarded as a great *cloud of witnesses* who watch the spectacle of life. More important, the dead are believed to be able to interfere in the affairs of the living. They can help a person, a family, or an entire nation if they wish. Therefore ancestors are often consulted before a battle, before an agricultural season, or before the birth of a child. In some areas no one may eat the first fruits of a harvest until proper sacrifice has been made to the ancestors.

It is the ancestor's ability to do harm that makes ancestor veneration such a potent force in Africa. Africans' fear of any god is of no consequence when compared to the dread which Africans feel toward their ancestors. While the Chinese attitude toward their ancestors may be described as one of respect and reverence, the attitude of Africans toward their ancestors can only be described as awe and dread. Ancestors are believed to be capricious and unpredictable. In spite of all offerings and reverence, ancestors may turn on one person or an entire group and cause great damage. Ancestors are believed to be the cause of droughts, famines, and earthquakes. They are held responsible for many forms of sickness and even death. One of the most terrible misfortunes that can befall any African couple is childlessness, and this curse is often attributed to the wrath of offended ancestors.

Because of the tremendous fear of ancestors that is a part of the African consciousness, it is the spirits of the ancestors rather than of the recognized deities who enforce the social and moral codes of the people. Apparently people would rather incur the wrath of a god than the wrath of the ancestors.

Because of this great concern for the ancestors, Africans frequently offer sacrifices and libations to them. It is believed that the ancestors are in control of the land and its produce. Therefore, before anyone enjoys this produce a bit of it must be offered to the ancestors. At harvest time there are larger offerings to them. When new animals are born to the flocks, some must be slaughtered and their blood spilled to the ancestors in order to insure continued blessings in the future.

Ancestors are believed to communicate with the living from time to time. One of the most common forms of this communication is the dream. Sometimes the message in the dream is direct and needs no interpretation, but at other times the message is not clear, and the dreamer must seek the help of a diviner to understand it.

Sometimes the ancestors use a more direct means to communicate with the living. Among the Tallensi there is a story of a young man named Pu-eng-yii who left his family and settled with a rival family because he felt he could earn greater wealth with them. In this manner he effectively cut himself off from his family and offended his ancestors. In his pursuit of wealth Pu-eng-yii suffered a serious leg injury in an auto accident. He consulted a diviner as to the cause of the accident. The diviner told him that his ancestors were angry with him and had caused his injury. Actually they had intended to kill him but had failed to carry through their plans. The diviner told Pu-eng-yii that he must make restitution to his family and his ancestors and give up his association with the other family. The hapless man gave in to the demands of his ancestors and returned to his family, offering the proper sacrifices, and making full restitution because he feared death.[7]

Diviners who can contact the departed ones are also in demand to gain knowledge about the future. Not only do the dead know what is happening among the living at the present, but they also know what the future will bring. Therefore, before special events such as battles,

---

[7]Ray, *African Religions*, p. 149.

Africans often will consult the ancestors through a medium to predict the outcome. Parallels to this practice in many other religions are too numerous to mention.

Sacrifice

African religions have developed a series of rituals that seek to appease the gods and the ancestors and provide proper transition through the various stages of life. At many points of contact between Africans and the spirit world, various forms of sacrifice are used to smooth the way and provide a point of communion between humankind and the spirit world.

Perhaps the most common forms of sacrifice in African religions are the daily libations offered to the gods and the ancestors. As a display of recognition to the deities and the ancestors, those who are living in this world pour out a bit of their drink or toss away bits of their food.

On more serious occasions, there is animal sacrifice. The blood of such animals as dogs, birds, sheep, goats, and cattle is ritually poured out upon the ground to placate the gods or to assure their support in some trying and difficult period. Blood sacrifice may be offered when a group is preparing for battle or when there has been a long drought or in times of illness. A person who is engaged in the dangerous business of hunting may wish to offer a sacrifice to one of the deities before the hunt begins. In modern times the Yoruba god, Ogun, for centuries considered the god of iron, has become known as the god of automobiles and trucks. Therefore drivers engaged in the deadly business of operating automobiles will offer a dog to him and will decorate their cars with his symbols. His protection is sought for other objects of iron as well, as is illustrated in this sacrifice song:

> Ogun, here are Ebun's kola nuts:
> He rides a bicycle,
> He cultivates with a matchet,
> He fells trees with the axe.
>
> Do not let Ebun meet your anger this year;
> Take care of him.
> He comes this year,
> Enable him to come next season.[8]

---

[8]Ray, *African Religions*, p. 80.

On many occasions of African animal sacrifice the worshiper partakes of the sacrificed flesh with the deity or ancestor. After the blood has been poured out of the animal onto the altar or the ground, the flesh is roasted or boiled. A portion of it is given to the deity upon the altar, and a portion is eaten by the person who brought the sacrifice and that person's family. In this way a communion is established between the living and the spirits; it is almost universally believed that eating together forms a bond.

On rare occasions in the past human sacrifice has been a part of native African religions. This aspect has been grossly exaggerated by the movies and by nineteenth century tales of cannibalism and great stacks of human skulls. While it is true that in the past Africans did sacrifice humans to their gods, such sacrifices were rare and occurred only on the most serious occasions. An Akikuyu legend tells of a time when there was a great drought in the land. A diviner determined that only when a certain maiden was sacrificed would it rain. The girl was placed in the center of the village where she gradually sank into the ground. When she had sunk to the depth of her nose, rain began to fall. Her family allowed her to sink completely out of sight as the rain continued. It was only the action of a lover who followed her into the earth that spared her life. Eventually he was able to find her and bring her back to the surface again.[9]

The most common form of human sacrifice occurred when a great king died and it was believed that he needed servants in the next life. At such times certain persons were sacrificed to accompany their leader into the world of the dead. Apparently human sacrifice was practiced only under the most severe circumstances and was never intended to establish a communion with the spirit world. The flesh of the victim was almost never eaten after the sacrifice. Cannibalism in any form seems to have been restricted to only a few tribes.

Rites of Passage

As in every other society, certain points along the pathway of life are marked by the African community and religion with rituals. These passage points are usually birth, puberty, marriage, and death. In societies where there is no clear distinction between the secular and the religious, these rites of passage are often regulated by religious practices and functionaries.

---

[9]Feldmann, *African Myths and Tales*, pp. 278–280.

The birth of children is an event of great rejoicing among African people. Children are regarded as great blessings from the world of the spirits, and conversely childlessness is considered to be a curse. A childless woman will go to great lengths to determine the reason for her plight and to alleviate it. Not all childbirths are welcomed however. For example, African people tend to regard the birth of twins as something unusual and evil. Sometimes twins are regarded as a sign that the woman has been unfaithful to her husband and that each of the babies has a different father. Occasionally one or both of the twins is killed. Sometimes the twins and their mother are forced to live apart from the rest of the community. Among other African people the taboo against twins is reversed, and they are considered to be extremely lucky to the community into which they were born.

In many African societies, such as the Ashanti, children are not named or given much consideration for the first week of life. Because of the high infant mortality rate, it is considered unwise for a family to become attached to what may be a ghost child who has come to deceive them into loving it. If the child lives through the first week of life then it is considered a true human baby and attention and joy may be lavished upon it. At this point the baby is named. In some cases a lengthy process of divination may be invoked in order to choose the proper name for the child. Other peoples recite the names of ancestors until the child makes some motion or gesture of recognition. In this manner the names of the ancestors are kept alive.

The ceremony of naming is often followed by the practice of showing the child to the moon. The Gu people of Dahomey throw their children gently up into the air several times, instructing them to look at the moon. The Basuto people of South Africa lift their children toward the moon and say, "There is your father's sister."[10] Some African people practice circumcision at the time of birth, but the majority wait until puberty.

During childhood young Africans receive instruction in their roles in society. As they approach puberty, instruction becomes more intensive. Special classes are established separately for the boys and girls. In these groups they are instructed in the adult roles expected of them and prepared for initiatory rites. For the boys these rites may involve whippings and harsh trials designed to test their courage and resourcefulness. During these rituals they learn tribal religion, myths, and

---

[10]Parringer, *African Traditional Religion*, p. 94.

morality. Among some tribes the girls may be shut away in a fattening house where they will be encouraged to eat a great deal and grow plump in order to make them more attractive brides. Both boys and girls receive special training in sexual behavior and conduct. These puberty rites and instructions may take anywhere from a few days to several years, depending upon the tribe. However, their length and severity has declined in recent years because of the opposition of certain governments and the decline in power of village life.

Puberty rites for boys often culminate in the ritual of circumcision. No one seems to know where or how circumcision began among African people, but it is widely practiced. It may be, as Freud suggested, the final domination by the older males of the community over the young. Because circumcision is performed at puberty without any form of anesthetic, it is often regarded as a test of courage. The initiate is expected to accept the operation without flinching or crying out. Among some African people the operation is performed by a man wearing a mask who represents the ancestors of the tribe.

Female circumcision is still practiced among some African peoples, but there is a growing sentiment against it. Sometimes this circumcision is a clitoridectomy, while at other times the labia is mutilated. Like male circumcision, there seems to be no clear reason for the practice.

After puberty rituals and instruction, the young person is considered to be an adult and is expected to partake in the privileges and responsibilities of adult life. One of the first of these adult roles is marriage. There is little of a religious nature about African tribal marriage. It is often more of a secular contract between the families involved. Virginity is highly prized at the time of marriage, particularly among the young women. Chastity after marriage is also strongly encouraged by tribal customs and mores. Often one finds polygamy in African societies, especially polygyny. Frequently a husband is forbidden sexual contact with his wife during her pregnancy and as long as she is nursing her infants. Since this can often be two years or more, it is considered wise for a husband to have several wives living in separate houses. There also have been rare instances of polyandry, where one woman is the wife of several brothers.

As in many societies, African religion tends to surround death with a great deal of ritual. The purpose of death rituals in these religions is to make the spirits of the newly dead as comfortable as possible with their new existence so they will not return to the living and haunt them. Many steps are taken during and after the burial of the dead to prevent them from returning to their villages, homes, and families. Women fear that their husband's ghosts will return and cause their wombs to die and become unproductive.

Because of the warm climate of much of Africa, the dead are buried as quickly as possible. On rare occasions there are attempts to embalm or mummify the corpses of outstanding people such as kings. There are also a few examples of corpses regularly being turned over to the hyenas for disposal, but burial seems to be the most common practice. Buried with the dead are money, trinkets, tools, and weapons to make life in the next world as pleasant as possible. As has been mentioned before, a notable king might be buried with some servants to aid him in the life beyond.

Some African societies believe that no illness, no misfortune, and no death "just happens." These things must have been caused by witchcraft or foul play of some kind. In the past the dead sometimes were allowed to identify the individuals who caused their deaths. Often the corpse would be seen to point out the house or the person that was responsible. Sometimes the corpse would fall from the backs of the bearers as it passed the guilty party. A person accused this way had to find some way to prove his or her innocence.

African religions generally have no system of eschatology with a scheme of judgment and retribution after death. The dead simply move into the world of the spirits but continue to be interested in and effective among the living. An exception to this is the belief of the LoDagaa people of Ghana. According to their religion the departed person takes a long journey toward the land of the ancestors. Just before this land is reached, there is a river. There waits a ferryman who must be paid to take the deceased across the river. If the deceased has had a good life, the crossing will be easy. If the person has been wicked, he or she must swim across the river, and this will take three years. Individuals who owe anything to people who are still living must wait at the edge of the river until these creditors arrive so they can be paid. Once the deceased is in the land of the dead there are further tests and ordeals in which the person's lifetime deeds play a great part. Those who are judged to have been evil and suffer for it question the great God:

> "Why do you make us suffer?" . . . God replies, "Because you sinned on earth." And they ask, "Who created us?" To which God replies, "I did." And they ask, "If you created us,

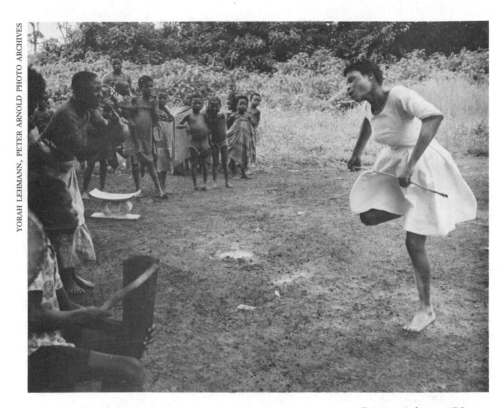

YORAH LEHMANN, PETER ARNOLD PHOTO ARCHIVES

Priestess' dance, Ghana.

did we know evil when we came or did you give it to us?" God replies, "I gave it to you." Then the people ask God, "Why was it that you knew it was evil and gave it to us?" God replies, "Stop, let me think and find the answer."[11]

Religious Leaders

Since a great deal of native African religion is based upon rituals which are performed regularly by individuals without the aid of priests, such as the pouring out of libations to the ancestors, the need for religious functionaries is not as great as it is in religions that rely on

---

[11]Ray, *African Religions*, p. 146.

complex theology and rituals. Nevertheless African religions do have leaders who are essential at special times or places.

African religions generally do not require a priesthood. In western Africa, however, some communities maintain temples and altars to their deities. The existence of a temple virtually requires a priesthood to maintain and control it, and so in these areas priests, and occasionally priestesses, exist. Priests are required to go through a lengthy training period before they are allowed to serve. They must be trained in rituals, mythology, dances, and taboos connected to their religion.

One of the more common religious functionaries in Africa is the so-called witch doctor. Since the term *witch doctor* has a negative connotation, a better choice of names might be "doctor to the bewitched." As has been previously mentioned, the African world view does not include the idea of "natural" causes of death and disease. There is always a spiritual cause for these misfortunes. Someone has cast a spell or placed a curse on the one who is stricken, or the stricken person may have in some way offended the ancestors or one of the deities. Therefore it is the task of the witch doctor to ascertain the cause of the illness and prescribe a cure. The doctor will use the magic of divination to determine the nature of the curse and who is responsible for it. Once that has been done it is the doctor's duty to use magic and herbs to drive away the witchcraft and dispel the curse. Often the doctor is called upon to clear a house of witches and curses before an owner will live in it.

Among the Acholi people of Uganda the evil spirits that cause a person to become ill are called *jok*. The healer is called *ajwaka*. When the *ajwaka* enters the presence of the sick person he will attempt to draw the *jok* up into the head of the patient by the use of music and song. When this is accomplished the *ajwaka* enters into conversation with the *jok*. "Why have you come? What do you want? What is your name?" Finally the evil spirit is driven out of the sick person by the *ajwaka*, captured in a gourd, and buried in the ground.[12]

Obviously the doctor to the bewitched is part religious functionary, part herbalist, and part psychologist. The skills this doctor has are highly valued and are sometimes imported into modern hospitals by Africans who don't want to leave anything to chance. When a young person decides on a life as a healer the youth must be apprenticed to an established doctor for several years in order to learn the many skills and secrets involved.

---

[12]Noel Q. King. *Religions of Africa* (New York: Harper & Row, 1970), p. 30.

Closely allied to the healer in many African communities is the diviner. It is the diviner's task to utilize magic and divine the causes of present misfortune, past secrets, and things to come. This individual can also ferret out witches and sorcerers. In some African communities the diviner is primarily one who investigates the causes of trouble, while in other communities the function of prediction is more important.

Among the Ndembu people of northwestern Zambia individuals are chosen as diviners by being inhabited by a spirit. The spirit Kayong'u seeks out those whom he will have become diviners, and it is believed that he first makes them ill. The deity thus shows people what he wants. A person so selected then goes through an elaborate initiation ritual and a long period of training.

The tools that African diviners use are widely different. Most commonly they cast the shells of nuts to form a pattern and then read the pattern to find the answer they seek. Among the Yoruba people, a diviner shakes sixteen palm nuts out into a pattern. This allows for as many as 256 different patterns. Each pattern is associated with several poems, each of which contains a message. Even the beginning diviner is supposed to know from memory a minimum of four poems for each pattern. This means that a person must memorize at least 1,024 poems to be a diviner; an experienced diviner will know many more. When the pattern has been cast and the poems recited, the person who has sought divination will select the poem that he or she believes to be the most meaningful.[13] Other methods of divination include casting dice and gazing into a bowl of water. At one time among many African people trials by ordeal were used to determine the guilt or innocence of a person accused of some crime. The person being tried was given a poisonous substance to drink. If the person did not die, innocence was proven. In more recent times a fowl has been substituted. When the fowl dies from the poison, guilt or innocence is determined by the way in which it falls.

Another religious functionary found from time to time in many parts of Africa is the prophet. Like the biblical prophet, this person is seen as one who speaks the words of the gods. When there is a political upheaval or an impending religious revival, charismatic leaders may arise and proclaim the words of the gods to their people. In the late nineteenth century there were several prophets who led African people in resistance to the Arab slave trade and to the European colonial

---

[13]Ray. *African Religions*, pp. 106–108.

efforts. One of these was a man named Ngundeng who arose among the Nuer people of the southern Sudan and who spoke in the name of the sky god, Dengkur. Usually the prophetic figures in Africa gain their authority by the power of their personalities and their message. Therefore, they seldom leave successors.

One of the most enduring of the religious figures in Africa is the chief-king. While there are some societies in Africa without monarchs, those which have kings and queens look upon them with great awe and reverence. These rulers are regarded as the tribal connection to the world of the ancestors and are revered as the living symbol of the tribe. Because of this, they are the objects of many taboos. In some societies they are considered to be so sacred that commoners may not look upon their faces. In other societies it is regarded as certain death to eat food that has been prepared for the monarch. Some peoples, such as the Bantus, actually look upon their rulers as gods incarnate.

Since the rulers represent the community, their health must be good at all times. A sick monarch means a sick land. Therefore, any infirmity of the ruler must be dealt with quickly. In some societies, rulers are required to take their own lives when ill health or old age begins to weaken them. The queen of the Lovedu people of South Africa carries poison with her at all times and is expected to use it to prevent her death by other means. In other areas and at other times there have been stories indicating that the people feel it is necessary to kill an aged or infirm king themselves. In some cases a substitute king is chosen to rule for a few days and ritually killed in order to spare the true king.

Once the monarch is dead, the death often is kept secret until a successor can be chosen and enthroned. It is believed that the former king or queen fully becomes a god as he or she enters the land of the ancestors.

THE FUTURE OF AFRICAN RELIGIONS

Today native African religions are under enormous pressure, not only from the missionary efforts of Islam and Christianity, but from the urbanization and industrialization of Africa which weakens village life and customs. Nevertheless there are still signs of vitality among these religions, and there are Africans who seem to prefer the ways of their ancestors to the ways of the modern world.

SUGGESTED READING

Courlander, Harold, *Tales of Yoruba Gods and Heroes*. Greenwich, Conn.: Fawcett Publications, 1973.

Idowu, E. Bolaji. *African Traditional Religion*. Maryknoll, N. Y.: Orbis Books, 1973.

King, Noel Q. *Christian and Muslim in Africa*. New York: Harper & Row, 1971.

King, Noel Q. *Religions of Africa*. New York: Harper & Row, 1970.

Parrinder, Geoffrey. *African Traditional Religion*. London: Hutchinson House, 1954.

Ray, Benjamin C. *African Religions: Symbol, Ritual and Community*. Englewood Cliffs, N. J.: Prentice-Hall, 1976.

To the modern student of religions no series of religions is so fascinating as those that began in India. The great depth and variety of religious teaching and experience one finds in Hinduism, Jainism, Buddhism, and Sikhism are indeed awesome. Today the beauty of the Bhagavada Gita, the complexity of Vedanta, the simple mysteries of Zen Buddhism, and the concept of *ahimsa* taught by the Jains are appreciated by students in Western nations as never before. An understanding of the basic literature, history, and doctrines of these religions is essential for the person who would understand modern Asia.

RELIGIONS ORIGINATING IN
INDIA

HINDUISM

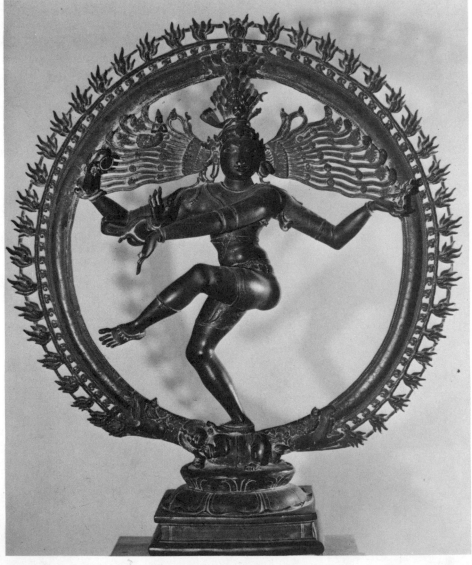

One of the more popular gods of Hinduism is Shiva, the god of death and reproduction. He is shown here in a dancing pose.

As a man casts off his worn-out clothes and takes on other
  new ones,
So does the embodied soul cast off his wornout bodies and
  enters others new.
He cannot be cut by sword,
Nor burnt by fire;
The waters cannot wet him,
Nor the wind dry him up.

BHAGAVAD GITA, II, 22, 23

Perhaps the oldest and most complex of all the religions of the world is Hinduism. Whereas most of today's active religions seem to have begun sometime around the sixth century B.C. or later, Hinduism traces the beginnings of some of its religious themes and forms to the third millennium B.C. One can find within Hinduism almost any form or style of religion that has been conceived or practiced. It is probably the most tolerant of all religions, and its scope ranges from simple animism to some of the most exalted and elaborate philosophical systems ever devised. In this vast tolerance, Hinduism allows for literally millions of major and minor gods, their temples, and their priests. Therefore, for the Hindu, the possible religious views are virtually infinite.

Hinduism has also been the source for three other religions. In the sixth century B.C. two reform movements, Jainism and Buddhism, arose from within Hinduism and challenged traditional Indian religious concepts. For a time it appeared that both movements might even replace Hinduism. Within a few centuries, however, their distinctive features were absorbed by Hinduism, which reemerged as the major religion of India. Today Jainism is a minority religion in India and Buddhism, while having great influence in other Asian nations, has almost no following in India. In the fifteenth century A.D., after Muslim invasions of India, Sikhism arose as a combination of the features of Islam and Hinduism. However, it has never become more than a minority religion. Hinduism overwhelmed these challengers by absorbing them and adopting their distinctive features into the mainstream of Hindu thought.

Unlike most of the other major religions of the world, Hinduism had no one identifiable founder. While there have been many great teachers and leaders in its history, there has never been one whose teachings became the wellspring of all later Hindu thought.

The word *Hindu* comes from the Sanskrit name for the river Indus, *Sindhu*. While the designation *Hindu* may refer to a great variety of religious beliefs and practices, it generally applies to the religion of the people of India. To be Indian is, in a sense, to be Hindu and vice versa. While there have been many converts to Hinduism throughout its history, it has never been an active missionary religion like Buddhism, Christianity, or Islam.

THE ORIGINS OF HINDUISM

Pre-Aryan India

The history of Hinduism begins with the migratory waves of Aryan conquerors of the people of India during the second millennium B.C. The religion that these conquerors brought with them mingled with the religion of the native people, and the culture that developed between them became classical Hinduism.

However, before we can speak of the Aryan religion we must first take notice of the pre-Aryan natives of India. Actually very little is known about these people. Prior to the 1920s the only source that spoke of the pre-Aryan people was the Vedic literature of early Hinduism. Since this was the religious literature of the Aryans, references to the natives of India and their religions were mainly negative, and the people were presented as uncivilized and barbarian. However, in the 1920s archaeological excavations were carried out in the Indus valley and at least two pre-Aryan cities were uncovered. Contrary to the image presented in the Vedas, these excavations revealed that as early as 2500 B.C. there was a fairly highly advanced civilization in the Indus valley. The cities had well-planned streets with drainage systems; they were supported by rather advanced agricultural communities which surrounded them; and these pre-Aryan people had a written language. Unfortunately this language has not yet been translated, and the great amount of information that it could supply regarding the life and religion of these people remains hidden.

What we do know of the religion of the pre-Aryan people is revealed by numerous statues and amulets that have been found by archaeologists. Many of these bear the image of what have been interpreted as fertility gods and goddesses. Some of the figures sit in the lotus position that was later adopted by Yoga Hinduism and other meditative sects. It is therefore assumed that far from being barbarian, the pre-Aryan people were highly civilized city dwellers and that later Hinduism took some of its gods and practices from this early period.

The Coming of the Aryans

To the modern student the word *Aryan* usually connotes the various meanings that the twentieth-century Nazi movement gave it. Hitler, in his attempt to depict his own people as the master race, called the large, blond, blue-eyed people of the world "the Aryan race." To the Nazis these people were the superior race who had historically given the world its strength and civilization. Other "races," such as the Semitic Jews and the blacks, were decidedly inferior to these "Aryans." This of course has no anthropological or historical foundation. The true Aryans were not a race and probably possessed none of the physical characteristics that the Nazis ascribed to them.

The term *Aryan* is a Sanskrit word which means "the noble ones"; this word was applied to a group of migrants who moved into the Indus valley in the second millennium B.C. from the regions of Persia. (The kinsmen of the Aryans who did not migrate into India became the founders of the Persian Empire, which ruled the Middle East from the sixth to the fourth centuries B.C. When the modern Persian peoples were seeking a name for their nation they chose to call it Iran, that is, the land of the Aryans.)

During the period between 1750 and 1200 B.C. the Aryans came in migratory waves into the Indus valley. Presumably the highly civilized city cultures of this region had declined because they were easily conquered by the Aryans and assimilated into their culture. Of the early Aryans little is known. Scattered references in the Vedic literature indicate that they were basically wandering nomads following their flocks from place to place. They apparently had no permanent bases or cities. The Aryans of this period were organized along tribal lines, being led by chieftains who were called *rajahs*. The Aryans spoke an Indo-European language which became the basis for Sanskrit and which has many cognates with European languages. It was not until about the sixth century B.C. that these people began to settle into cities in the Indus valley and that some of the rajahs began to collect and build minor kingdoms for themselves.

According to early sources Aryan society began to develop into three basic categories. The highly regarded priests who served the cults of the various Aryan deities were called Brahmins. The chieftains and their warriors, also considered to be near the apex of society, were called Kshatriyas. The commoners and merchants, regarded as subservient to the two upper classes, were called Vaishyas. A fourth group was made up of those conquered pre-Aryan people who were called Shudras. Shudras were not considered full members of the society and generally held the position of slaves or servants to the Aryans. These divisions were maintained in Indian society for centuries and were subdivided into the multiple classes that became the basis of the so-called caste system.

Aryan Religion

The best source of knowledge about the religion of the Aryan invaders is the Vedic literature, but this literature was mainly composed after the Aryans had been settled in India for a time and had intermingled with the native people and with their religions. What is truly Aryan and what is truly pre-Aryan in the Vedas is therefore difficult to delineate. Nevertheless, certain basic assumptions about Aryan religion can be made.

It seems clear that the Aryan invaders of India brought with them a polytheistic religion similar to that of other Indo-European peoples. There have been considerable attempts to identify Aryan deities with those of the Graeco-Roman pantheon.[1] The collection of gods which the Aryans worshiped seem to have been personifications of various natural forces such as the storm, the sun, the moon, and the fertility of the soil.

The chief manner of worship of the Aryan gods was apparently sacrifice. Since the Aryans were primarily nomadic people in the early days of their occupation of India, they built no temples to their gods, but rather offered sacrifices to them on altars built in open places. These offerings were frequently animal sacrifices, but they also included offerings of dairy products such as butter and libations of milk poured out to the gods. Another liquid which apparently was used as a libation was the juice of the sacred soma plant. The exact identifica-

---

[1] The most common identifications are of the Indian god Varuna with Uranus and Dyaus Pitar with the Greek Zeus and the Roman Jupiter.

Entrance to Temple of Sangsit, Bali. The elaborate carvings at this entrance depict many scenes from the lives of the gods.

tion of the soma plant is lost to the modern world.[2] The ancient texts describe it as a sacred plant that was sent to earth by the god Indra. Its juice was described as delicious and invigorating to the worshiper who drank it and shared it with the gods. The plant that modern Indians identify as soma is not delicious and invigorating but produces nausea in those who drink it. Naturally there are those who suggest that the original soma may have been some form of mushroom or other plant that produced hallucinations.[3]

Perhaps the most expensive and elaborate sacrifice ever used in any religion is said to have originated among the Aryans. This was the so-called horse sacrifice. Because of the expense and incredible detail involved, the horse sacrifice was limited to the Aryan rulers. This was a sacrifice that supposedly had extraordinary effects in atoning for a

[2]*Soma* is frequently identified with the haoma plant, which is used in the ancient Persian religions, but that too is not easily identified by modern students of religion.

[3]It is noteworthy that Aldous Huxley named the happiness-producing drug of the future *soma* in his book *Brave New World*.

great sin or in giving great religious power to those who participated in it. The horse sacrifice was also helpful to rulers who wished to expand their territory, and this, of course, was its major attraction to Indian rulers. A young male horse chosen for this sacrifice was set loose to roam the countryside for one year. The attendants of the ruler who supported the sacrifice followed the horse wherever he went. If the horse covered any territory that was not in the domain of the ruler, that rajah had the right to claim that land as his own. After one year the horse was returned. At that time a great many other animals were sacrificed to the gods. This great holocaust included animals of all types, ranging from the bee to the elephant and sometimes involved more than six hundred animals. Next the sacred horse was strangled, and the wives of the rajah participated in fertility rites with the body of the horse. Finally the carcass was ritually butchered and eaten by the ruler and his family. According to legend, if one man could perform one hundred horse sacrifices he would become master over all the gods and the universe. Unfortunately for those who aspired to this, such an act would have required over one hundred years and incredible wealth. Consequently there is no record of a ruler who could or would perform it one hundred times. The horse sacrifice was last performed by an Indian ruler in the eighteenth century A.D.

THE VEDIC ERA

The Vedas

The basic sacred scripture of Hinduism is the Vedic literature. These books are the source of the Hindu understanding of the universe, and all later material refers back to them and is seen as mere commentary upon them. The Vedas were developed as the Aryans came into India, settled there, and mingled their religion with that of the native peoples. There is dispute over the exact period in which the Vedas were written. Some scholars believe that the earliest of the Vedic hymns may have developed prior to the coming of the Aryans, before 2000 B.C., and that they were still developing as late as the sixth century A.D. Others contend that the bulk of the Vedic material came into being between 1500 and 400 B.C. Like much other ancient religious literature, there is no sure way of knowing the exact time of the origin and development of these books. Undoubtedly they were first composed and transmitted orally for many generations before they were committed to writing; thus centuries may have passed between their origin and completion.

There are four basic Vedic books. The first and most important is the Rig-Veda. (The word Veda basically means "knowledge of figures.") This is a collection of over one thousand hymns to the gods of the Aryan pantheon as well as various other materials. It contains the basic mythology of these gods. The other Vedic books are made up of much of the material that was orginally contained in the Rig-Veda.

The second book is the Yajur-Veda ("knowledge of rites"). This is a collection of materials to be recited during sacrifice to the gods. The third book, the Sama-Veda ("knowlege of chants"), is a collection of verses from the basic hymns recited at sacrifices by the priests. The fourth book, second in importance only to the Rig-Veda, is the Atharva-Veda ("knowledge given by the sage Atharva"). It contains rituals to be used in the home and popular prayers to the gods, along with spells and incantations to ward off evil.

Each of the Vedic[4] books is made up of four parts. Each contains a section of hymns to the gods (mantras). As is the case in many ancient religions, hymns and religious poetry are to be regarded as the most ancient of all religious literature since they reflect the period when statements about and to the gods were memorized, chanted, and passed from one generation to the next without benefit of the written word. Each Vedic book also contains a section of ritual materials (Brahmanas) in which the worshiper is given instruction in the proper way to perform his sacrifices, etc. The Brahmanas are considered to be later than the mantra sections. A third section in each of the Vedas is the so-called Forest Treatises (Aranyakas), which are materials for hermits in their religious pursuits. The fourth sections are called Upanishads and are made up of philosophical materials. The mantra and Brahmana sections are considered to be the oldest material in the Vedas, with the Aranyakas and the Upanishads having been added later. The Vedas in their final form are written in a language called Vedic, which is a predecessor of early Sanskrit.

Within the Vedas are basic descriptions and mythology of the various Aryan and pre-Aryan gods. The god who receives the most attention in terms of numbers of hymns is Indra, the god of the thunderbolt, of clouds and rain, and the ruler of heaven. Indra is especially important because he is remembered as the conqueror of Vitra, the

---

[4]The word Veda is used in two ways. Generally, the word refers to only the ancient collection of hymns to the Aryan gods. However, in another sense the word refers to an entire collection of sacred literature which includes the hymns and the later additions: the Brahmanas, the Aranyakas, and the Upanishads. In this text we shall use the word in the latter sense.

personification of evil. Within the Rig-Veda alone there are over 250 hymns specifically addressed to him. Following is one of these.

> O Indra, in the past the sages of old bore your Indra power. This one is on the earth and is of the form of fire; the other in the form of the sun dwells in the heavens. Both are one like two banners.
>
> Indra held the earth menaced by the demons. He fixed it and then expanded it. He killed the demons with the bolt, smote the clouds with it, and made the waters come out of them from the sky. He struck down Ahi, the serpent demon; he rent Rauhina to death and slaughtered Vyamsa in flight.
>
> With trust in his prowess, he roams shattering the cities of the Dasas with his bolt. O wielder of the bolt, O wise one, throw your weapons at the Dasyus, our enemies, and increase the might and glory of the Aryans.
>
> We prepare *soma* to offer him, the author of many great deeds, the Bull, worthy of the *soma* drink. He, the hero, takes the wealth of those who do not perform the sacrifice to give it to those who perform it.
>
> After Indra destroyed the four demons Susna, Pipru, Kuyava, and Vitra, he razed Sambara's fort to the ground. May Mitra, Varuna, Aditi, Prthivi, and Dau grant this prayer of ours.[5]

Many other Aryan gods are also mentioned in the Vedic literature. Agni, the god of fire, is mentioned in over two hundred hymns. He is basically regarded as the god of the priests and the priests of the gods. He leads the gods in proper sacrifice, and as the god of fire it is he who brings the burnt sacrifices to the other gods. The god Varuna receives his share of hymns in the Vedic material also. He is seen as the god over the order of the universe and the one who gives forgiveness to those who have sinned.

> O leader of the whole world, Varuna, lord of many heroes, may we be in your happy abode. May the sons of Aditi, never harmed by enemies, pardon our sins and make us your friends.[6]

---

[5]Rig-Veda, 1:103.
[6]Ibid., 2:28.

Vishnu is mentioned briefly in the Vedas, but at the time they were composed he was not the important deity he was to become in later Hinduism. Another of the gods whose function and name was to change in later Hinduism was Rudra, later known as Shiva, the god of death and destruction. In later times Shiva, Vishnu, and Brahma became the three most popular gods in Hinduism. The god of the dead who receives the greater attention in the Vedas is Yama, who was supposed to have been the first man to die and consequently became the god of the dead.

> O sacrificer, honor the king of our ancestors with oblations.
> He, the son of Vivasvan, Yama, whom all men reach, has led
> all men of good deeds along the path to their respective places
> without trouble.
> Yama, the first, knows our merits and demerits. None can
> mislead him. By whichever path our ancestors went, by that
> path all those born will go.[7]

In addition to hymns to the many gods of the Aryan pantheon, the Vedas also contain legendary and mythological material from early Indian life. One of the most interesting of these is the story of Manu.

> They brought water to Manu for washing, as it is now usual to
> bring it for washing hands. When he was washing, a fish came
> into his hands.
> It said to him in words, "Bring me up, I shall save you."
> "From what will you save me?" "A flood will carry away all the
> creatures. I shall save you from that flood." "How can I bring
> you up?"
> "Fish swallow fish. So long as we remain small, destruction
> awaits us. Keep me first in a jar. When I outgrow it, dig a pond
> and keep me in it. When I outgrow that also, take me to the
> sea. Then I shall be beyond danger."
> It quickly became a Jhasa, which become the largest. Then
> it said, "The flood will come in such and such a year. Take my
> advice then, and build a ship. Enter it when the flood rises,
> and I shall save you from the flood."
> After rearing the fish thus, Manu took it to the sea. In the
> year indicated to him by the fish, he acted according to the

---

[7]Ibid., 10:14.

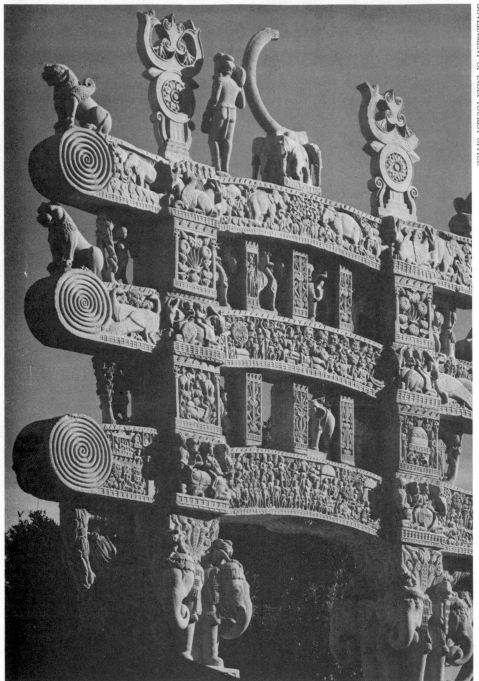

North gateway, Sanchi Stupa, India.

advice of the fish and built a ship. When the flood rose, he entered it. The fish then swam to him. He tied the rope of the ship to the horn of the fish and thus reached swiftly the Northern Mountain there.

The fish then said, "I have saved you. Tie the ship to a tree and do not let the water leave you stranded when you are on the mountain. Descend as the water subsides." Thus gradually he descended, hence that slope of the Northern Mountain is called "Manu's Descent." The flood carried off all the creatures, Manu alone survived.

Wishing for a progeny, he began to worship and do penance. Then he performed a sacrifice of cooked meal. In the waters he offered melted butter, buttermilk, whey, and curd as oblations. In a year, a woman was created out of them. She rose dripping, melted butter collected at her footprints.

Wishing for progeny, he continued to worship and perform penance along with her. Through her this race was generated by him. This is the race of Manu. Whatever blessings he desired through her were all conferred on him.[8]

The Upanishads

As noted earlier, the fourth section of each of the Vedas is called the Upanishads.[9] Within these materials one finds the early philosophical statements that became the basis for all later Hindu philosophy. Although there originally may have been more of these treatises, there are currently about two hundred Upanishads. They vary in length from one page to over fifty pages. Of these, fourteen are called the principal Upanishads. Scholarly research indicates that the earliest of the Upanishads probably originated in the ninth century B.C. and the most recent in the sixth century A.D.

Some scholars contend that the Upanishads are an integral part of the Vedas and that they are a natural commentary upon the early hymns and ritual texts. These persons tend to see the Upanishads as the philosophical expression of what one finds in the rest of the Vedas.

[8] Satopoda Brahmana, 1:8.
[9] The basic meaning of the word *Upanishad* seems to be "near sitting," indicating that these are materials that were developed in the discussions between teachers (*gurus*) and their students as they sat together and spoke of the philosophical implications of the Vedas.

Others disagree and point out the basic disharmony between the two. Whereas the hymns, chants, legends, and rituals in the rest of the Vedic material are clearly polytheistic, giving instruction on the proper worship of myriad gods, the Upanishads operate from a monistic pre-supposition. They assume that there is only one reality, the impersonal god-being called Brahman. All other beings are but an expression of Brahman. All that is not Brahman is an illusion (maya). Not only is there this basic distinction between the Upanishads and the rest of the Vedic material, but the Upanishads also seem to have been written as a reaction to the priestly form of worship that was prescribed by the other Vedic books. Whereas most of the Vedas seem to teach that the proper way to worship is by sacrifice to the various Aryan gods, the Upanishads emphasize meditation as a means of worship. They teach that people's real problem is ignorance (avidya) of their plight and that only when people realize this ignorance and come to true knowledge will they find salvation. Those scholars who point to these essential differences between the Upanishads and other portions of the Vedas believe that the Upanishads may have had a different point of origin and may have become attached to the Vedic literature at a later time. It is probably fair to say that while the Upanishads have been tremendously influential as the basis for later Hindu philosophy, they have never been extremely popular with the common people. They are complicated and difficult discussions, and they require the acceptance of a world view that is not easily understood. While the remainder of the Vedas may have been for the masses to use in their worship of the gods, the Upanishads have been popular with a relative handful of Indian intellectuals.

As we have indicated, the fundamental assumption of the Upanishads is that there is but one true reality in the universe; that reality is known as Brahman. Brahman is eternal, infinite, unknowable, sex-less,[10] without a past, present, or a future, and totally impersonal.

> Verily, in the beginning this world was Brahman, the limitless One—limitless to the east, limitless to the north, . . . limitless in every direction. . . . Incomprehensible is that supreme Soul, unlimited, unborn, not to be reasoned about, unthinkable—He whose soul is space![11]

---

[10]The word, Brahman is neuter. Basically it means "ever growing."
[11]Maitri Upanishad, vi. 17.

The living beings that inhabit our world are really only expressions of the Brahman. They are souls which are a part of the great ocean of souls which make up the Brahman. Therefore all phenomenal existence is illusion arising from ignorance of the true nature of reality. A person's individuality apart from the Brahman—the world in which one lives, that which one sees, hears, touches, and feels—is all an illusion, a dream.

> This whole world the illusion-maker projects out of this [Brahman].
> And in it by illusion the other is confined.
> Now, one should know that Nature is illusion,
> And that the Mighty Lord is the illusion-maker.[12]

The plight of human beings is that they are bound up in this world of illusion and ignorance, thinking that it is real, unaware of their true identification with Brahman. "Those who worship ignorance (avidya) enter blinding darkness."[13] Those who continue in this ignorance are bound to life by karma which keeps them endlessly in the cycle of birth, life, death, rebirth (samsara). Salvation from this cycle and release from life comes when there is true knowledge of the illusion of life. "By knowing God man is freed from all bonds."[14] When true knowledge of the illusion of life is realized, one can be freed from the bondage of life and achieve unity with the Brahman. This is difficult. It comes only after much study. "Arise, awake, go to the sages and learn. The wise say that the path is sharp like the edge of a razor, hard to walk on, and difficult to obtain."[15]

Within the Upanishads one finds a collection of materials similar to that found in the Jewish Talmud. Various legends and tales are used to illustrate the philosophical material of these books. They are frequently cast in the form of a student's discussion with a guru and apparently have been collected over centuries of use. The Chandoya Upanishad records a conversation between a son and his father. The father instructs his son in the following manner:

> "Put this piece of salt in the water and come to me tomorrow morning."

[12]Svetashvatara Upanishad, 4, 9–10.
[13]Isavasya Upanishad, 9.
[14]Svetashvatara Upanishad, 4:6.
[15]Katha Upanishad, 1, 14.

[Svetaketu] did as he was told. [Then his father] said to him: "[Do you remember] that piece of salt you put in the water yesterday evening? Would you be good enough to bring it here?"

He groped for it but could not find it. It had completely dissolved.

"Would you please sip it at this end? What is it like?" he said.

"Salt."

"Sip it in the middle. What is it like?"

"Salt."

"Sip it at the far end. What is it like?"

"Salt."

"Throw it away, and then come to me."

He did as he was told but [that did not stop the salt from] remaining ever the same.

[His father] said to him: "My dear child, it is true that you cannot perceive Being here, but it is equally true that it *is* here.

"This finest essence, the whole universe has as its Self: That is the Real: That is the Self: That *you* are, Svetaketu!"

"Good sir, will you kindly instruct me further?"

"I will, my dear child," said he.[16]

The Code of Manu

Another piece of traditional Indian literature produced during the classical era is the ethical Code of Manu. This code, which was probably written sometime between 300 B.C. and 300 A.D., is of value not because of its great religious or philosophical teachings but because of what it reveals about Indian life during the period. Within this book the student finds the ethical and social standards that were held up as ideals during the classical era of Indian history and the effects that the religious and philosophical teachings of the Vedas had upon Indian society. Furthermore, one finds here the roots of many of the social and religious traditions that were to characterize Hinduism into modern times.

One of the basic assumptions of the Code of Manu is the caste system which had apparently developed from the early Aryan divisions

---

[16]Chandoya Upanishad, VI, 13.

Pilgrims travel from all over India to bathe in the sacred Ganges River at Benares.

of society. In the Code of Manu the caste divisions are seen as divinely ordained.

> For the growth of the worlds, (Brahman) created Brahmanas (Brahmins), Kshatriyas (warriors), Vaishyas (traders) and Shudras (manual workers) from his face, arms, thighs and feet respectively.[17]

The first three castes are called "twice born" while the fourth caste, the shudras, are "once born," indicating that the members of the higher castes had already experienced at least one life and that the lowest caste members were only beginning their cycle of birth and rebirth. Members of each caste have certain specified duties (*dharma*) and opportunities and must obey them only.

---

[17]The Code of Manu, 1:31

For the Brahmanas (Brahmins), he created teaching, studying, sacrifice, officiating at sacrifice, giving gifts, and accepting
gifts.

For the Kshatriya, he created in short the protection of
people, giving gifts, performing sacrifices, studying, and non-
attachment to sense pleasures.

For the Vaishya, he created the protection of cattle, charity,
performance of sacrifices, studying, trading, lending on interest, and agriculture.

The Lord created only one profession for the Shudra: service without envy of the above three castes.[18]

Apparently people were expected to begin life as Shudras, serve
willingly and obediently and gradually move from life to life through
the caste system until they came to the exalted rank of Brahmin. Thus
even at this early stage the Indian society was stratified into fixed
classes, and the only mobility through these classes was by the means
of reincarnation.

The Code of Manu also demonstrates the state of the understanding
of reincarnation at this period.

Man obtains the life of motionlessness (of plants, and so on) as
a result of the evil committed by the body, the life of birds and
beasts because of the evil committed by speech, and the life of
the lowest born because of the evil committed by mind.

If a man performs only good actions, he will be born a god; if
he performs mixed actions, he will be born a man; and if he
performs only evil actions, he will be born a bird or an animal.
The result of evil speech is the destruction of knowledge; that
of evil mind is the loss of the supreme destiny; and that of the
evil body is the loss of the worlds. So let one protect the three
in every way. The punishment prescribed for evil speech is
silence; that for evil mind is fasting; and that for evil action is
breath control.[19]

Another of the central teachings of the Code of Manu is the various
stages through which a man was expected to pass in a successful life. In
the first stage of life the typical Indian gentleman is supposed to be a

---

[18]Ibid., 1:88–91
[19]Ibid., 12:9

student, studying the Vedas and giving careful attention to his teacher. In the second stage of life one is to become a householder and marry a proper girl from his own caste. In the ideal marriage described in the Code of Manu the man is to be considerably older than his wife. "A man, when he enters the stage of the householder, if he is thirty years of age, should marry a girl of twelve whom he likes. A man of twenty-four may marry a girl of eight."[20] The role of householder and provider is one of the most important, for it is the householder who is seen as one of the cornerstones of society. When a man's duties as a householder are completed and when he is aged, he is to retreat to the forest and live there for some years as a hermit, meditating and offering sacrifices. Finally when his days as a hermit are completed, the Indian gentleman should become a wandering beggar (sannyasin). These four stages are only the ideals of the twice born (the three higher castes); the complete role of the shudra is to serve the higher castes all his life.

The four stages of life are also only for the men of the society. The women are supposed to stay in the home under the control and protection of the chief male of the household.

> Even at home nothing should be done independently by a woman, whether she is a young girl, a youthful maiden, or an old lady.
>
> When young, she should be in the control of her father and in her youth of her husband. When the husband dies, she should be in the protection of her sons. She should not love independence.
>
> She should never desire separation from her father, husband, or children. Separated from them, she brings bad name to both the families.[21]
>
> Women are meant for children. They are for the good and light of home. They are to be worshiped. In a home there is no difference between a woman on the one side and wealth, beauty, and splendor on the other.[22]

The Code of Manu is mainly a statement of the moral and ethical ideals of the period. It contains the prohibitions that one would expect against murder, theft, and sexual immorality. The moral aims of the

---

[20]Ibid., 9:94
[21]Ibid., 5:147–149
[22]Ibid., 9:26.

era are summed up in the following ten characteristics: pleasantness, patience, control of mind, nonstealing, purity, control of the senses, intelligence, knowledge, truthfulness, and nonirritability.[23]

It is notable that even at this early date, Indian society placed a premium upon the life of cattle and imposed penalties upon those who slaughtered them. "The Vaishya, having gone through the sacraments, and having accepted a wife, should engage himself in trade and in the protection of cattle."[24] Among the greatest of sins is listed "the killing of cows."[25] For those who have committed great sins the remedy is to: "Live with cows for a year controlling his mind, studying sacred texts. . . . "[26]

The Code of Manu is also helpful in giving an understanding of the Indian conception of divine time, which is virtually endless.

> Eighteen movements of the eyelid are called Kashta, Kala is thirty Kashtas, thirty Kalas constitute a Muhurta, and thirty Muhurtas make a day and night.
>
> The night and day are divided by the sun for men and gods. The night is meant for the sleep of beings and the day for their work.
>
> The night and day of ancestors is one month of men. Its black fortnight is meant for their action and the white for their sleep.
>
> The night and day of gods is the year of men. Its division again is into the summer solstice as the day and the winter solstice as the night.
>
> Now, understand the night and day of Brahman and their duration, and also of each of the aeons in succession.
>
> The Krita aeon consists of 4,000 years. Four hundred years before and four hundred after are the intervening times for this aeon.
>
> In the case of the other three aeons with their prior and posterior twilights, the number of thousands and hundreds is to be less and less by one.
>
> The aeon of the gods is said to be 12,000 times the four aeons counted previously.

---

[23]Ibid., 6:92.
[24]Ibid., 9:326.
[25]Ibid., 11:59.
[26]Ibid., 11:257.

One thousand times the aeon of the gods is the day Brahman. His night also is as long.

The knowers of day and night call the day of Brahman, which is 1,000 aeons long, the auspicious day. His night also is such.[27]

In general, Indian philosophy saw time as moving endlessly through various cycles. When one cycle of time is completed the world dissolves and all souls depart into suspended being. After a period of repose the world begins again and the souls take up new bodies.

Jainism and Buddhism

In the sixth century B.C. there arose in India two new religions that offered alternative salvation schemes within the Indian world view. They will be discussed in detail in later chapters, but it is worth noting at this point in our discussion of classical Hinduism that they did arise as serious challenges to the mother religion.

Both Jainism and Buddhism rejected the sacrificial system as a means of salvation from life as taught in the Vedas. They both taught that one achieved release from life not by offering sacrifices to the gods or by any form of worship but through accomplishments in one's own life. They both rejected the Vedas as sacred scripture, and they both taught that anyone of any caste who lived properly might find salvation.

Jainism taught that one found release from life through asceticism. The more one denied pleasures and satisfactions to the body, the more likely that person was to achieve freedom from the endless cycle of birth and rebirth. In addition the founders of Jainism enlarged upon the traditional Indian concern for cattle and taught that all forms of life were sacred and were to be loved and preserved whenever possible (ahimsa). While Jainism had its moments of popularity, it tended to demand too much of the average person for it to have ever become a mass movement. In the centuries following Jainism's origin, Hinduism absorbed its concern for asceticism and ahimsa, and today Jainism has only a small minority of Indian adherents.

Buddhism grew out of many of the same longings and beliefs that formed the basis for Jainism. However, it taught that while one could

---

[27]Ibid., 1:64–73.

find release from life without priests and a sacrificial system, the extremes of asceticism were not necessary. For a time Buddhism, with its more moderate ways, appeared to have become the religion of India; it even became a missionary religion, sending its preachers to other Asian nations. However, Hinduism eventually reasserted itself and absorbed the distinctive features of Buddhism. Gautama Buddha, founder of Buddhism, was made a member of the Hindu pantheon, and many of his teachings became a part of Hinduism. By the fifteenth century A.D. there were few Buddhists left in India. (Buddhism did, however, become the dominant religion of many other Asian nations and survives in them today.) The rise and popularity of Jainism and Buddhism in the sixth century B.C. in India nevertheless demonstrates that not all Indians found satisfaction in the teachings of classical Hinduism.

Bhagavad-Gita

Perhaps the concluding statement on classical Hinduism is the great epic poem of Indian culture and religion, the Bhagavad-Gita. This poem is to Hinduism what the Homeric epic poems are to Greek and Hellenistic culture. Like the Homeric poems, the Bhagavad-Gita is cast about a great battle; it relates the stories of the struggles of great heroes and gods and contains much of the basic philosophy of the culture.

The Bhagavad-Gita is found within the text of an even longer poem called the Mahabharata.[28] The Mahabharata is the story of the struggles between the two leading families from the beginning of Indian history. Finally these two families come together in the battle of Kurukshetra, which historians roughly place between 850 and 650 B.C. Just before this battle one of the warriors, Arjuna, contemplates his fate and the struggle before him. His charioteer, Krishna, enters into the dialogue with him. Their conversation, found between chapters 25 and 42 of the Mahabharata, makes up the Bhagavad-Gita.

While the Mahabharata is believed to have been composed over a very long period of time, beginning perhaps as early as the ninth or eighth century B.C., the Bhagavad-Gita itself is believed to have been composed sometime between the second century B.C. and the third century A.D. The eighteen chapters that make up the Bhagavad-Gita

---

[28]While the Bhagavad-Gita is a massive epic in itself, it pales to insignificance beside the Mahabharata, which contains 110,000 couplets or 220,000 lines.

are divided into three sections of six chapters each. In the first section Arjuna, the young warrior, looks out upon the battlefield and contemplates the coming war and his part in it.

> Standing there, Partha (Arjuna) saw his fathers, grandfathers, teachers, maternal uncles, brothers, sons, grandsons, friends, paternal uncles, well-wishers in both armies. He, a son of Kunti, saw closely all of them, his relations.[29]
>
> He was overcome by sorrow, felt dejected, and said, "Seeing my own men gathered and ready for battle, my limbs give way and mouth dries up, my body trembles and hairs stand on end. My Gandiva [bow] slips from my hand, and my skin burns. I am unable to stand and my mind whirls."
>
> "Even if they whose minds are struck by greed, do not see the sin in destroying the family and in being unfaithful to friends, why should it be not known by us that we should avoid this sin?"[30]
>
> If the sons of Dhritarashtra, with weapons in their hands, kill me who am without weapons in hand and who do not retaliate in this battle, it will be better for me."[31]

Thus like other warriors in all ages, Arjuna ponders the folly of war, particularly interfamily war, and contemplates going into battle unarmed and thus committing suicide. Arjuna's contemplation is answered by his charioteer, Krishna. The remainder of the poem is the conversation between Arjuna and Krishna about the nature of life and one's duties in life. In the second section of the poem Krishna reveals that he is the incarnation of the god Vishnu. As such he has come to earth to help mortals who are struggling with their problems. In the third section Krishna and Arjuna continue to discuss the problems of life that confront mortals.

Much of the advice and teaching that Krishna gives Arjuna is a reflection of the philosophy of the Upanishads, which says that most of what mortals see as life and its problems is merely illusion. The most direct teaching that Krishna gives to Arjuna is that he should not dread going into battle because he is a member of the Kshatriya class and as such it is his duty (dharma) to be a warrior and to kill. If Arjuna were a

[29]Bhagavad-Gita, II. 26–30.
[30]Ibid., II. 35–39.
[31]Ibid., I. 46.

Vishnu, the preserver, one of the three most popular gods of Hinduism, is depicted with his consort, Lakshmi, on a panel from the temple at Khajuraho, ca. 1000 A.D.

member of another class, such as the Brahmin, he might have reason to reject the battlefield. However, battle is the *dharma* of the Kshatriya, and Arjuna has an obligation to obey that duty.

> Not by leaving works undone
> Does a man win freedom from the [bond of] work,
> Nor by renunciation alone
> Can he win perfection['s prize].
>
> Not for a moment can a man
> Stand still and do no work;
> For every man is powerless and forced to work
> By the "constituents" born of Nature.[32]

The basic teachings and religious implications of the Bhagavad-Gita are many. The obvious teaching is that individuals should perform the duty of their caste and thus avoid *karma*, the force that binds people to

---

[32]*Ibid.*, III, 4–5.

the endless cycle of birth, death, and rebirth.[33] The obligations that are placed upon each caste are raised to the level of religious duties.

A second feature of Indian religion apparent in the Gita is its openness to a variety of means of personal salvation. People can achieve release from life (Nirvana), through asceticism, through meditation, through devotion to and worship of the gods, or through obedience to the rules of his caste. Thus Hinduism is regarded as the most tolerant of all the world religions, and the Bhagavad-Gita makes this clear.

Perhaps the most lasting teaching of the Gita is its revelation of Vishnu as a god who loves and is concerned about human beings. His concern is such that he takes various forms and comes to earth at certain times to aid mortals in their struggles. As Krishna says, "Whenever there is a decline of faith and an upsurge of irreligion," Vishnu makes his appearance in the world.[34]

In postclassical Hinduism, Vishnu became one of the most popular gods. The Bhagavad-Gita makes clear that one of the legitimate means of salvation is through devotion (bhakti) to gods like Vishnu.

> Arjuna, of this be sure:
> None who pays me worship of loyalty and love is ever lost.
> For whosoever makes Me his haven,
> Base-born though he may be,
> Yes, women too, and artisians, even serfs,—
> Theirs it is to tread the highest Way. . . .
>
> On Me thy mind, for Me thy loving service,
> For Me thy sacrifice, and to Me be thy prostrations:
> Let self be integrated, and then
> Shalt thou come to Me, thy striving bent on Me.[35]

POSTCLASSICAL HINDUISM

With the completion of the Bhagavad-Gita the classical era in Indian religion came to a close. This period began with the coming of the Aryans to India. It included the development of the Vedas and other

---

[33]The word karma literally means "deed" or "act." In Indian religions it usually refers to those deeds or actions that have effects upon future lives.
[34]Bhagavad-Gita, III, 12:6.
[35]Ibid., IX, 31, 32, 34.

religious literature such as the Code of Manu and the Bhagavad-Gita. This material, its philosophy, and the pantheon of gods that it presented became the basis for later Hinduism.

Some scholars distinguish between the religion of the classical era and that of the postclassical period by referring to the earlier religion as Brahminism and the later as Hinduism. Within Brahminism the religion of the Indian people was much like that of the Graeco-Roman world. Gods were worshiped with sacrifices offered on altars built in the open. Priests, who were expert in rituals and methods of sacrifice, were very important.

After the close of the classical period subtle changes gradually were introduced into the religion of India. While the existence of many gods was still acknowledged, interest tended to center around the worship of a few major deities. Worship came to be love and devotion to these gods. Temples were built to them, and hymns were composed about their outstanding qualities. Whereas the literature of the classical period tended to deal with the great epics of Indian history, the literature of the postclassical era tended to center about these gods. The major gods were seen as taking various forms and becoming involved in the affairs of men. Of special interest in the postclassical literature were the various wives and consorts of the gods. A number of these goddesses became as popular as their mates, and many of the people of India became devotees of these goddesses, developed cults about them, and built temples for their worship of them.

Some scholars also point to the change that occurred in the basic attitude toward life in India between the classical and the postclassical eras. When the Aryans came to India they were an aggressive and optimistic people. Pessimistic and passive peoples do not migrate thousands of miles from their homes, conquer a land, and establish themselves as its rulers. However, by the beginning of modern Hinduism one sees certain negative and life-denying forces emerging. If the basic world view of Hinduism is that life is an endless cycle of birth, life, death, and rebirth, and that the goal of religion is to cease living, then this is essentially a negative and world-denying religion. The ascetic who refuses the pleasures and comforts of this life becomes the religious and cultural hero rather than the warrior.

None of these changes occurred overnight or even over one century. Their roots appear even in the Vedas. However, by the beginning of the Christian era certain changes in the basic religious structure did appear.

Devotion to Three Major Gods

As we have observed repeatedly, Hinduism offers its devotees many paths to salvation. Individuals may find release from life by devotion to one or more of the Indian gods. They may give full religious attention to each of these gods or goddesses by worshiping at their temples, offering sacrifices, praying, supporting the priests of the temple, and so on. In this manner the gods or goddesses may look with favor upon the devotee, support the believer in life, and help in the struggle for salvation. This path to salvation is called *Bhakti Marga* ("the way of devotion").

Brahman, who is ultimate reality, is at the core of Hindu thought. He is one and undivided. Yet postclassical Hinduism sees him in terms of three forms or functions. These three, called the Trimurti, are creation, preservation, and destruction. Each of these three functions of Brahman is expressed by a god from the classical literature: Brahma, the creator; Vishnu, the preserver; and Shiva, the destroyer. Devotees of any of these three gods tend to see all of the functions of Brahman in their chosen deity.

Brahma. Of the three leading deities of the Hindu pantheon, Brahma[36] receives the least attention. Although Brahma is widely respected and recognized as the creator of the world, there are only two temples specifically dedicated to him in all of India, and he has no cult of devotees. When Brahma is depicted in Indian art he is shown as red in color with four bearded faces and four arms. His chief wife, Sarasvati, is the goddess of science and wisdom. Although Brahma is not mentioned in the Vedas, considerable mythology has grown up about him and his work of creation in the post-Vedic era.

Shiva. By far the most popular god in postclassical Hinduism is Shiva, who is known as "the destroyer." Shiva is the god of death, destruction, and disease. Like Brahma, Shiva does not appear in the Vedic literature, but he is believed to have been developed from the Aryan god Rhudra.

The functions of Shiva are many. Not only is he the god of death, disease, and destruction, but he is also the god of the dance. In the

---

[36]The god Brahma is to be distinguished from the all-pervading god-force of the Upanishads, Brahman. The word *Brahman* is neuter. The word *Brahma* is masculine and refers to a distinct entity.

mythology connected with Shiva there is frequently some statement about his dancing, usually in some terrible fashion over poor mortals who unwittingly offended him. He is a special god to Hindu ascetics, probably because in the process of tormenting and destroying their flesh this terrible deity is the one who is closest to reality for them. One of the most common symbols of Shiva is the trident. Frequently ascetics will be seen carrying a trident or will have the form of a trident painted upon their faces.

Perhaps the most important reason for Shiva's popularity is the fact that he is also the god of vegetable, animal, and human reproduction. In Indian thought death is but the prelude to rebirth. Therefore it follows that the god of death will also be a god of reproduction and sexuality. In the mythology of Shiva he is described as having a constantly erect penis and being sexually alert at all times. Other symbols that depict Shiva are the *lingam* and the *yoni*, the male and female sexual organs. Thus Shiva becomes the special deity of those who seek fertility or utilize sex as a basis for religion.

Devotees of Shiva are known as Shaivites. There are several sects of Shaivism in Hinduism today. All regard the Vedas and special Shavite texts as scriptures. Their philosophical stance is that Shiva is ultimate reality; he is creator, preserver, and destroyer. Humans are thought to be separated from Shiva because of ignorance, karma, and illusion. In order to achieve union with Shiva, people must follow a prescribed path, worship Shiva, and attend him in his temples. They must also meditate and study under the direction of a guru. Some Shaivites require the repetition of a special *mantra*. All of these acts culminate in a union between Shiva and the worshiper and ultimately result in *moksha* (release from the death-rebirth cycle).

Fully as popular as Shiva are his various consorts. Numerous goddesses are associated with him, but the most important and most popular is Kali or, as she is cometimes called, Durga. Kali is, if anything, more terrible than Shiva. She is frequently depicted as wearing a necklace of human skulls, of tearing away the flesh of sacrificed victims, and drinking blood. Mythology connects her with the founding of the modern city of Calcutta.

> When Kali died, Shiva was both grief-stricken and angry. He placed her corpse on his shoulders and went stamping round the world in a dervish dance of mourning which became more furious the longer it lasted. The other gods realized that unless Shiva was stopped the whole world would be destroyed by his

rage, which was unlikely to end as long as he had his wife's body on his shoulders. So Vishnu took up a knife and flung it at the corpse, dismembering it into fifty-two pieces which were scattered across the face of the earth. By the side of a great river in Bengal the little toe of the right foot landed, and a temple was built there, with an attendant village, and the people called this place Kalikata.[37]

Among the many sects dedicated to Kali was a group known as Thugs. The chief function of this group of devotees was to offer freshly strangled victims to their goddess. Thus they would waylay and slowly strangle some lonely victim while calling for Kali to come and be present in the death struggle. Strangely enough the cult of the Thugs attracted Indian Muslims as well as Hindus after the eleventh and twelfth centuries. The organization was outlawed by the British in the nineteenth century.

Vishnu. The third god of the postclassical Hindu triad is Vishnu, the preserver. In contrast to Shiva, Vishnu is known as a god of love, benevolence, and forgiveness. The chief feature of Vishnu is his concern for humanity, which he expresses by appearing on earth a number of times in various forms. According to mythology, Vishnu has appeared on earth in nine forms and will come a tenth time to close this era *(kalpa)* and bring the world to an end. In some incarnations he has come as a man. According to the Bhagavad-Gita he has appeared as Krishna. As Hinduism absorbed the distinctive features of Buddhism it was taught that Vishnu had appeared as Gautama, the Buddha. He has purportedly also come to earth as various animals and creatures involved in helping people. For example, it is believed that Vishnu appeared as Matsya, the fish who acted to save Manu from the great flood. In every case he has come to aid humankind because he is the preserver and the restorer.

Devotees of Vishnu are known as Vaishnavites. In India they are noted for their deep love of God and the poems and songs that they write in his praise. Kabir and Nanak, the founders of Sikhism, were poets in this tradition. Like the Shaivites, the worshipers of Vishnu regard their god as ultimate reality. Generally they see salvation coming not from the actions of the devotees but through the love and grace of Vishnu.

[37]Geoffrey Moorhouse, *Calcutta* (New York: Harcourt Brace Jovanovich, 1971), p. 6.

An extreme example of devotion to one god that has become familiar in many major American cities in the past few years is the so-called
Hare Krishna movement. This group of devotees of the god Krishna
traces its origin back to the appearance of Krishna in human form as
recorded in the Bhagavad Gita. From that time onward there has been
a group of people in India who have devoted themselves totally to the
worship and adoration of Krishna. The movement in its present form
actually began in the fifteenth century. At that time a man named
Chaitanya Mahprabhu became converted to the sole worship of
Krishna, the incarnation of Vishnu. In his ecstasy he began to dance
and sing in the streets of his home city. He chanted a special *mantra* to
Krishna, which he felt would help him find identity with the god.
Others were attracted to Chaitanya and his message, and a small band
of Krishna worshipers was formed. Chaitanya strangely· disappeared
without a trace in 1534.

In 1922 a man named Abhay Charan De from Calcutta became a
devotee of Krishna after the manner of Chaitanya. He was unable to
do missionary work until 1954, when he retired from his position as a
manager of a chemical firm. At that time he changed his name to A. C.
Bhaktivedanta Swami Prabhupada and began to spread the word of
Krishna. In 1965 he traveled to the United States and began chanting
each day in the parks of New York City. Soon he attracted a following,
and in 1966 Swami Prabhupada opened the first temple for the International Society of Krishna Consciousness (ISKCON) in New York.
The following year another center was opened in the Haight-Ashbury
district of San Francisco. By 1974 there were sixty-eight centers in the
world, with twenty-eight listed in the United States.

The philosophy of the ISKCON movement is expressed in the title
of its major publication, *Back to Godhead*. It is believed that humanity in its current state is separated from the godhead. Humankind is
wrapped up in a trap of illusions and is concentrating its energies on
gaining false possessions. Only when people realize the trap they are in
and begin to seek the godhead can they achieve the true intended
state. According to the teachings of ISKCON, humankind finds its
liberation through what is called Krishna-Consciousness. People
should seek unity with Krishna, who is symbolically the representation
of all the divine forces. Krishna-Consciousness is attained through
chanting the Krishna mantras, through study, and through meditation. Though it is possible to find Krishna-Consciousness in the daily
life of a layperson, the surest path lies in renouncing life and possessions and in joining an ISKCON temple.

Life for the devotees in an ISKCON temple is highly disciplined and regulated. Those who join give up all possessions and exist only on what is provided for them by the society. They dress in distinctive saffron-colored robes, and the male devotees shave their heads, leaving only a topknot. They arise daily at 3 A.M. to begin a day that consists of meditation, study, chores in the temple, and public chanting, selling, and begging. They are forbidden meat, coffee, tea, alcohol, nicotine, and other drugs. Sexual relations are limited to those members who are married, and they may indulge only at certain specified times for the sole purpose of procreation.

Even with these stringent regulations the ISKCON movement in the United States and Western Europe has been modestly successful in attracting converts. It has even sent missionaries to open a center in India.

Devotion to Knowledge

In postclassical Hinduism people could choose one or more of the gods and find salvation through devotion to those gods and their temples. This was probably the most acceptable and convenient way to salvation for the majority of the people. However, an equally acceptable way to salvation for those who could follow it was the so-called way of knowledge *(Jnana Marga)*. For the wealthy or the intellectual who had the time to spend studying the various philosophical implications of sacred writings, the way of knowledge had merit.

Generally when people speak of the way of knowledge as a means to salvation in Hinduism, they refer to the various systems of philosophy which offer paths to salvation. These systems are Sankhya, Yoga, Mimansa, Vaisheshika, Nyana, and Vedanta. All claim to be based upon the Vedas, all aim at salvation, and all believe in rebirth and preexistence. While the number of philosophical systems is usually limited to these six, there are many other lesser systems and variations within the six.

The Samkhya System. The Samkhya system of philosophy is said to have been founded by the sage Kapila, who lived during the sixth century B.C. The Samkhya system arose during the era of the founding of Jainism and Buddhism and apparently influenced both these religions and was in turn influenced by them. Like Jainism and early Buddhism, the Samkhya system recognizes no personal gods and may be viewed as an atheistic approach to life. Like Jainism it sees the

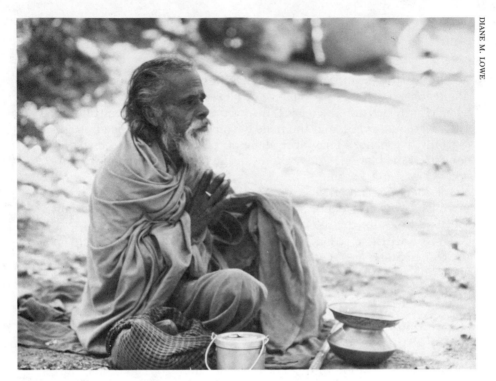

Sadhu holy man. This Hindu has entered the final stage of life and has given himself totally to meditation and acts of devotion.

universe as a dualism with the forces of spirit *(purusha)* and matter *(prakriti)*. All that exists is these two forces and from them springs all that we know in the world.

The Yoga System. Of all the Hindu philosophies Yoga is the best known to Westerners, although they tend to think only of physical, or Hatha, Yoga or of the various extremes of asceticism that the Yogin may achieve. The word *Yoga* is derived from the root *yuj*, which means "to yoke" or "to join." Yoga basically follows the philosophical views of the Samkhya system, viewing the world as a dualism and teaching that one should attempt to yoke or join his individual spirit to God.

Statues depicting persons in various yogic positions have been found in the remains of the pre-Aryan cities dating back to the third millennium B.C. However, the philosophy of Yoga as it is known today was developed by the sage Yajnavalkya. It is believed that he lived sometime between 200 B.C. and 500 A.D. and codified the teachings of Yoga in his *Yoga Sutra*.

The main feature of all Yoga is meditation. Meditation is necessary even for the gods if they are to find release from the cycle of birth, death, and rebirth.

There are several forms of Yoga, each having several features and each emphasizing a different one. Rajah Yoga stresses mental and spiritual development. In this form of yogic discipline one works through various stages in order to free the mind from anger, lust, hatred, greed, and so on.

Another widely known and practiced form of Yoga is Hatha, which stresses physical culture. In Hatha one seeks to move through eight stages.

1. Before one can progress in Hatha one must take certain vows of restraint *(yama)*. These are vows against harming living creatures and unchastity.

2. At this stage one attempts to achieve internal control, calmness, and equanimity *(niyama)*.

3. In the third stage one learns and practices certain bodily postures *(asana)* which are designed to help one achieve the aims of Yoga.[38]

4. Once the postures have been mastered one works on breath control *(pranayama)*.

5. The fifth stage is control of the senses *(pratyahara)* in which one seeks to shut out the outside world.

6. The sixth stage is extreme concentration on a single object *(dharana)*.

7. Then one seeks to achieve meditation *(dhyana)*.

8. Finally the Yogin seeks a trance *(samadhi)* in which the Yogin becomes one with the Brahman.

Those who work through these steps achieve great physical powers and remarkable abilities of concentration. The ascetics who master Yoga are those who perform the outstanding feats of asceticism that have come to be identified with Yoga in the Western mind.

The Mimansa System. Purva Mimansa, the full name of the Mimansa system of philosophy, means "early examination" of the Vedas. The primary scriptures for the advocates of this system are the

---

[38]The most common posture used in meditation is the so-called lotus position in which one sits with his right foot upon his left thigh, his left foot upon his right thigh, and his back erect. In this extremely balanced position concentration is easier than it is in most other seated positions.

Vedas and the Mimansa Sutra, which was written about 200 B.C. The leading advocates of the Mimansa philosophy were Kumarila and Prabhakara who lived in the eighth century A.D.

The primary concern of Mimansa is the avoidance of rebirth. This is accomplished by obeying the laws laid down in the Vedas and by performing the rites established in them. Early advocates rejected the existence of gods, but by the eighth century A.D. some philosophers of this system were known to offer prayers to Shiva.

The Vaisheshika System. The root meaning of *Vaisheshika* is "particularity." The Vaisheshika system of philosophy probably arose in the sixth century B.C. at the time of the founding of Buddhism and Jainism. The founder of Vaisheshika was Kanada, who wrote the primary document, the Vaisheshika Sutra. In contrast to the philosophies that teach that there is no reality except Brahman, the Vaisheshika teaches that the universe is made up of nine distinct elements: earth, water, air, fire, soul, mind, ether, time, and space. Since these elements are eternal and uncreated, no gods are needed in the universe. Later philosophers in this system adopted the idea of a supreme being who guides the universe.

The Nyana System. The Nyana philosophical system has adopted the metaphysical scheme of the Vaisheshika system and is often paired with it by those who classify Indian philosophies. Nyana was founded by a man named Gautama who lived in the third century B.C. and who wrote the Nyana Sutra. This Gautama has been called "the Aristotle of India" by some students of philosophy. Like the advocates of Vaisheshika, he was essentially atheistic and believed in the reality of the world. He therefore reasoned that individuals can have a real knowledge of the world. Thus the Nyana system is primarily concerned with logical analysis as a means of arriving at truth about the world.

The Vedanta System. Another system or set of systems of Hindu philosophy is the Vedanta. The term *Vedanta* is usually translated as "the end of the Vedas," indicating that the major materials in these systems are taken from the Upanishads, which are placed at the end of the Vedic literature. (Contrast this with "Mimansa.") The term is also translated as "the acme of the Vedas," indicating that the Vedanta philosophy is the very peak of the religious teaching found in the Vedas. Regardless of the interpretation, the Vedanta philosophy is based upon the Upanishadic writings and their outlook on life. It is believed that the Vedanta philosophy was first formulated by a sage named Badarayana, who lived sometime between 250 B.C. and 450 A.D. and wrote the *Vedanta Sutra*.

In contrast to the Samkhya system, the Vedanta is monistic and assumes only one true essence in the universe. This essence may be called God, or Brahman. Nothing else exists but Brahman. The world of humankind, its bodies, souls, and material substances, do not really exist. Therefore, humankind's basic problem is not its wickedness but its ignorance. People are ignorant of the true nature of reality and believe that they are separated from Brahman. This ignorance thus binds them endlessly to the cycle of birth and rebirth until they can achieve liberation through knowledge.

One branch of Vedanta which developed in the ninth century A.D. is called "Advaita." The word means "non-dual" and indicates its monistic viewpoint. Its founder was Shankara (788–838 A.D.), who was perhaps the most outstanding scholar of medieval Hinduism. Although this man was a very famous ascetic and teacher in his time, he is best known for the philosophical approach he took in interpreting the Vedas. His abilities and reputation as a philosopher have prompted some Western readers to refer to Shankara as the Aquinas of Hinduism. His most outstanding literary contribution is a commentary which he wrote on the *Vedanta Sutra*. This commentary has become such a classic in Hindu literature that it has been the object of several commentaries itself. In his commentary Shankara asserted the absolute oneness of Brahman in the classic manner of the Upanishads. Brahman is all there is. All else in the universe is an illusion, and people are bound up in endless reincarnations until they rip aside the veil of this illusion. Strangely enough, Shankara himself was a devotee of Shiva because he believed that Shiva was the best representation of the true nature of Brahman.

Shankara is also remembered for his fierce opposition to Buddhism. It is believed that his leadership against Buddhism was a major factor in destroying this religion in India and restoring Hinduism to the dominant position.

According to one story, Shankara did not die; he simply disappeared. This has caused some Shaivites to believe that the great scholar was actually an avatar of Shiva.

A second philosopher of the medieval period in Hinduism who represents a side in the debate over the true meaning of the Vedas was Ramanuja. Ramanuja lived in the twelfth century A.D. and was a teacher who believed that devotion to the gods was extremely important. He was himself devoted to the worship of Vishnu. He reasoned that if Shankara were correct and if each person were merely a part of the God Brahman, then devotion to God would not be possible, for how can one be devoted to oneself? While he could not move away from the traditional Vedanta position of the oneness of God, Ramanuja taught a qualified dualism in which he asserted that the human soul and the divine soul were united and yet somehow separate. The analogy that he used to explain this was the human body and spirit. One cannot exist without the other, but they are separate entities.

The third point of view in this debate was presented by the philosopher Madhva, who lived in the thirteenth century. Madhva was also devoted to the god Vishnu and believed strongly in devotion to the gods as the only proper religious expression. He was willing to go farther than Ramanuja, however. He took the side of dualism even though he remained in the general school of Vedanta. However, he abandoned completely the notion that God was all and that all else was illusion. To him the world and individual souls were completely separate from Brahman and separate from one another. Thus each individual and separate soul is able to worship properly the separate nature of God.

Muslim Influences in India

In the seventh century A.D. a new and vital religion sprang from the deserts of Arabia. Within a few decades the religion of Islam had spread, through conquest and conversion, across the entire Middle Eastern world. By the eighth century it was on the verge of moving into Europe. Islam also moved eastward and by the eighth century had conquered Persia and Afghanistan and made occasional raids into India.

Portions of northwest India were conquered by Muslim leaders as early as 712 A.D. In the eleventh century the Turkish general Mahmud of Ghazni invaded India seventeen times and brought back vast treasure to his headquarters in Afghanistan. By the thirteenth century Islam was so well entrenched in India that there was a Sultanate of Delhi. In the sixteenth century a dynasty of Turkish rulers known as the Moghuls established an empire and ruled most of the subcontinent of India. However, by the eighteenth century this empire had run its course and had decayed into many small warring states which became easy prey for the invading British armies. Today, though Hinduism is the majority religion of India, there are more Muslims on the subcontinent than there are in any other nation in the world.

Relations between Hindus and Muslims have always been touchy. Indeed it would be difficult to find two religions more different than Hinduism and Islam. Whereas Muslims are staunchly monotheistic, Hindus tend to be limitlessly polytheistic; whereas Muslims disdain the representation of Allah in any form, Hindus have richly decorated temples with statuary portraying their many gods; whereas Muslims have been known to occasionally offer a cow as a blood sacrifice to Allah, Hindus tend to regard the cow as a sacred animal and seek to protect it from any harm; and whereas Muslims regard every man as equal before Allah, Hindus have traditionally followed a caste system that divides society into classes with the upper classes having more religious privileges than the lower.

In spite of these vast differences Hindus and Muslims have managed to live side by side for more than one thousand years. Hinduism has not altered its basic theology in light of its contacts with Islam, but Indian society has adopted many of the elements of the Muslim world. Particularly during the years of the Moghul empire Indian society was influenced by the art, architecture, sciences, and even the dress styles of the Muslim world.

In the fifteenth century there arose the most notable attempt at reconciliation between Islam and Hinduism: the religion of Sikhism. Sikhism will be discussed in detail in a later chapter. However, it must be said at this point that Sikhism managed to attain a harmony between the uncompromising monotheism of Islam and the doctrines of illusion and reincarnation of Hinduism. It must also be said that, whereas Hindus and Muslims have somehow managed to live together in India, the religious and political differences between the two peoples remain today as one of the major problems facing India.

MODERN HINDUISM

Hinduism, like all major religions, has had to face the rigors of the modern age with its nationalistic movements, its social reforms, its encounters between religions, and its scientific revolutions. The last four hundred years have been difficult for a religion that is as tied to tradition as is Hinduism.

Of all the factors of the modern era that have affected Hinduism, one of the most important has been Hinduism's encounter with Christianity and its European and American representatives. According to tradition Christianity was brought to India by the disciple Thomas and has been an active religion there since the first century A.D.[39] However, Christianity probably had little effect upon the Indian people until more recent times.

The first serious encounter between India and the modern European nations came in 1510, when the Portuguese conquered Goa. In the seventeenth century the British invaded India and established the British East India Company. This began three centuries of British rule in India. Though the British were present in India as merchants and soldiers, it was not until the nineteenth century that they allowed Protestant missionaries to enter the country to try to convert the Indians. One of the reasons for this late entry was that many Protestant denominations did not actively seek to send missionaries earlier.

One of the first British missionaries to enter India was the Baptist William Carey (1761–1834). Like many other missionaries of the nineteenth century Carey was concerned not only with preaching the gospel of his faith but also with raising the living and educational standards of the people he ministered to. He was the first to begin modern printing in India, and he also initiated many new educational programs for the Indian people. Carey, along with other missionaries, was alarmed at several practices—which he felt were inhuman and harmful—within Indian social life. One of these was the *suttee*, in which an Indian widow was expected to throw herself upon the funeral pyre or into the grave of her dead husband and be destroyed with him. Another practice that was abhorrent to the European missionary was that of child marriages. Because of the rigid caste structure it had become common in India for parents to betroth their young children in order to insure a suitable marriage. Frequently this meant the betrothal of very young children, and the marriage of nine- and ten-year-olds. This was particularly harsh in the case of girls who might have been promised by their parents to men twenty or thirty years their senior. This practice tended to ensure that when a husband died he left behind a fairly young widow who was expected to destroy herself. The missionaries put pressure upon the British rulers, and eventually both the practices of child marriage and the *suttee* were officially outlawed in India.

---

[39]Some scholars believe that Christianity was a factor in the development of devotion to one god (*bhakti marga*) as a means of salvation in the postclassical period and that it was also a factor in the development of the Bhagavad-Gita.

Meenakshi Temple, Madurai, India.

The encounter with Europeans, their missionaries, and with Christianity caused many Indians to carefully reconsider their religion. Thus the late nineteenth and twentieth centuries saw several reform movements in Hinduism. One of the earliest reformers was Ram Mohan Roy (1774–1833), who was called "the Father of Modern India." Roy tended to agree with the missionaries and supported them in their attempts to suppress the *suttee* and child marriages. He also saw in Christianity many elements that he appreciated although he did not accept the divinity of Jesus. Ram Mohan Roy tended to be a monotheist and sought to suppress the polytheism and idolatry of Hinduism. In order to continue his work after his death, Roy organized the *Brahma Samaj* (The Society of God), which became a major force in the renewal of India in the nineteenth and twentieth centuries.

Perhaps the greatest religious reformer of the nineteenth century was Sri Ramakrishna (1834–1886). Once a priest of Kali in Calcutta, Ramakrishna was philosophically a follower of nondualistic Vedanta. He later became convinced that behind all religions there was a single reality which might be called God. Although Ramakrishna was illiterate, his contacts with Christians and Muslims as well as Hindus convinced him that truth was essentially one.

The teachings of Ramakrishna might have died with him in India had it not been for one of his disciples, Narendranath Dutt (1863–1902), who was later known as Vivekananda. Vivekananda became a member of the *Brahman Samaj* early in his life. Later he met Ramakrishna and became his apostle. After a period of several years of retreat in the Himalayas he set forth to be the first Hindu missionary to the modern world. Vivekananda traveled widely, lecturing on the virtues of Vedanta Hinduism, which he described as "the mother of all other religions." He made his greatest impression at the Parliament of Religions in Chicago in 1893 as the spokesman for Hinduism. Wherever he went, this spokesman for the oneness of God captivated audiences and made converts.

The best-known Indian reformer of the twentieth century was Mohandas K. Gandhi (1869–1948). Gandhi is chiefly remembered for his work in bringing political and social benefits to the Indian people near the end of the British rule through a combination of religious idealism and civil disobedience. Gandhi was originally trained as a lawyer in England, where he came into contact with many of the social and political ideas of the nineteenth century. He was also introduced to Christianity, especially to Jesus' Sermon on the Mount. These factors, along with the ideals of his Hindu heritage, molded Gandhi into the figure that he became. As the leader of the Indian people in their struggle for freedom from British rule, he personally led many fasts and strikes against various British policies and was usually victorious. In addition to espousing civil disobedience and nonviolence, Gandhi was also influenced by the Jain teaching of noninjury of life. Thus he was a vegetarian and stoutly defended the Indian practice of cow protection. Gandhi also read and remembered the works of the American Thoreau, works that advocated passive resistance to civil authority. In turn Gandhi became one of the models for the political thinking of Martin Luther King, Jr., who led American blacks in their struggles for civil rights in the 1960s. Gandhi, who advocated nonviolence, died by an assassin's bullet in 1948, just a few months after his people had won their independence.

India of the late twentieth century is a country beset by some of the world's most serious problems. Conflicts between its Hindu and Muslim inhabitants often result in bloodshed; its population has grown and continues to grow seemingly beyond the abilities of the nation to feed its millions; and it desperately fears an invasion from its giant neighbor to the north, China.

As always, Hinduism quietly plays its role in the lives of the Indian people. Some Indians have come to feel that Hinduism has no answers to the problems of their nation and have turned to the secular world for solutions. However, the majority still prefer to seek solace in the many gods, the rich literature, the elaborate mythology, and the extensive philosophies of Hinduism.

SUGGESTED READING

Edgerton, Franklin, trans. *Bhagavad Gita*. New York: Harper & Row, 1965.

Hinnells, John R. and Sharpe, Eric J., *Hinduism*. Newcastle: Oriel Press, 1972.

Hopkins, Thomas J. *The Hindu Religious Tradition*. Encino, Calif.: Dickenson, 1971.

Judah, J. Stillson. *Hare Krishna and the Counterculture*. New York: John Wiley & Sons, 1974. *

Nikhilanada, Swami, trans. *The Upanishads*. 4 vols. New York: Harper & Bros., 1949–1959.

Renou, Louis, ed. *Hinduism*. New York: George Braziller, 1961.

JAINISM

Ceiling of the Jain temple on Mount Abu.

The essence of right conduct is not to injure anyone; one
should know only this, that non-injury is religion.

NALADIYAR, 14, 15

In the sixth century B.C. two protests arose in India against Hinduism. These two heresies were Jainism and Buddhism, and they each offered alternate means of salvation to that presented in the Vedic literature and taught by the Brahmin gurus. Both Jainism and Buddhism denied the validity of the Vedas as inspired scripture, and both rejected the religious implications of the Indian caste system. Of these two new religions (or new forms of Hindusim) Jainism was probably the first.

THE LIFE OF MAHAVIRA

It is difficult to determine precisely the origin of Jainism, although Nataputta Vardhamana, who became known to his followers as Mahavira ("great hero"), has traditionally been identified as its founder. The story of Mahavira's life, however, obviously has been covered with legend. Actually, in orthodox Jainism, Mahavira was only the last in a long line of founders. There are twenty-three figures who preceded Mahavira in the establishment of Jainism. These people, together with Mahavira, are called Tirthankaras, which means "crossing builders." They are believed to be those ideal persons who forged a bridge between this life and Nirvana. A total of twenty-four Tirthankaras receive the veneration of Jains in their temples.

Most sources suggest that Mahavira lived between 599 and 527 B.C., although some authorities place his death as late as 467 B.C. At any rate, he seems to fit best into the sixth century B.C., that century in which the world heard the teachings of Siddhartha Gautama, the Buddha; Zoroaster; the Hebrew prophets Jeremiah, Second Isaiah, and Ezekiel; Confucius; and Lao-tzu.

The reported details of the life of Mahavira are similar in many respects to those of the life of the Buddha, and some suggest that these details are taken from Buddhism. Like the Buddha, Mahavira was born in the sixth century B.C. to parents of the Kshatriya caste and his father was a minor ruler. Mahavira was the second of two sons. According to legend the family possessed great wealth and lived in luxury. They lived in Vesali, the capital city of the region of Mogadah in north India. At the proper age Mahavira married and had a daughter. Despite his position and wealth, he was not happy and sought a religious answer to this unhappiness. When a group of wandering ascetics came to dwell in his village Mahavira became interested in them and longed to join their order. However, being a dutiful son, he waited until his parents died[1] and the business affairs of the family had been taken over successfully by his older brother. Then he bade farewell to his family and his wife and child, turned his back upon his wealth and luxury, tore out his hair and beard by the handfuls, and went off to join the ascetics in their pursuit of salvation.

Mahavira did not find his salvation among this group of ascetics as he had hoped. He came to believe instead that one must practice a more severe asceticism than they practiced in order to find release of the soul from this life. In addition to his concern for extreme asceticism, Mahavira eventually felt that one must also practice *ahimsa* (noninjury to life) in order to find release. Therefore he went forth on his own path.

The legends concerning this period of Mahavira's life emphasize the extreme measures of asceticism that he imposed upon himself. Since he did not wish to become attached to people or things he never stayed more than one night in any one place when he traveled. During the rainy season he stayed off the roads to avoid walking where he might inadvertently step upon an insect. During the dry season he swept the road before him as he walked to avoid crushing insects. He strained all the water that he drank in order to prevent swallowing any creature that might be in it. Like any true ascetic he begged for his food. But he

---

[1]According to some Jain legends, the parents of Mahavira died of self-imposed starvation. Since Jainism places such high value on asceticism, this form of death becomes ideal.

Jain temple, Khajuraho, India.

refused to eat raw food and preferred to eat only food that had been left over from the meal of some other person in order that he might not be the cause of the death of the food. In order to better torment his body he sought out the coldest spots in the winter months and the hottest climates in the summer and went about naked always. Whenever angry or vile persons sent their dogs after Mahavira he allowed himself to be bitten by them rather than resist. Legend also tells of a time when Mahavira was meditating and some people built a fire beneath him to see if he would resist; he did not. After twelve years of the harshest forms of asceticism he achieved release (*moksha*) from the bounds that tie one's soul to the endless cycle of birth, death, and rebirth. Thus he became known to his followers as a Jain ("conqueror") because he had heroically conquered the forces of life. Though he had achieved *moksha*, Mahavira lived for another thirty years and died at the age of seventy-two.

THE TEACHINGS OF JAINISM

Like the other Indian religions, Jainism views life in terms of endless reincarnation. People are born, live out their lives, die, and are born again. This is the religious problem around which Indian religions revolve. How does a person get off the wheel of lives and cease to live? Hinduism offers a variety of answers as do Buddhism and Sikhism. Jainism views people as bound to life because of the karma that they acquire.

> All living beings owe their present form of existence to their own Karman; timid, wicked, suffering latent misery, they err about (in the Circle of Births), subject to birth, old age and death.[2]

Apparently Mahavira taught that karma was built up on an individual as the result of activity of any sort. Thus the ideal life for a Jain might be to simply do as little as possible and thereby escape karma and be freed from life.

> Liberation is absolute freedom from the totality of actions through the absence of the causes of bondage and exhaustion (of past karmas).[3]

The philosophical world view of Jainism is dualistic. According to Jainism the world is essentially made up of two substances, soul *(jiva)* and matter *(ajiva)*. Soul is life; it is eternal and valuable. Matter is lifeless, material, and evil. The entire universe can be identified as either soul or matter. All persons are seen as soul encased in matter. As long as soul is enmeshed in matter it can never be free and is bound to remain in the endless cycle of lives. Thus it is the goal of Jainism to liberate the soul from matter. This philosophical basis that sees the flesh as an evil which thwarts the pure and perfect development of the soul is a universal ascetic belief. If the flesh is evil, then the ascetic answer is to release the soul by tormenting the flesh in some manner. This answer to human sinfulness is found in some form in Hinduism, Buddhism, Christianity, Islam, and nearly every other major religion in the world. Whereas these religions also have other solutions to the

[2]Sutrakritanga, 1, 2, 3, 18.
[3]Tattvartha Sutra, 10, 2.

problem of human being's plight, Jainism is consistent. It views the world as a dualism. Its answer to the dualistic nature of the world is severe asceticism. Whereas not all Jains can be free from the responsibilities of life and dedicate themselves to the ascetic life, it is believed that the Jains who do are closest to salvation. Mahavira set the pattern by turning his back upon the wealth and pleasures of his home and submitting his body to the rigors of asceticism. Thus he found release.

Jainism maintains that the salvation of the soul must be accomplished by the individual. Soul can only be freed from matter by the action of the person involved, and that person cannot and does not receive help from outside. Therefore, the gods are of little consequence in Jainism. Jains have no need for a creator god since they believe that matter is eternal. Thus there never was a creation of the world. It has been here forever and will continue to exist forever. If Jainism has any awareness of gods it is that they are simply creatures living on a different plane from humankind and are trying to work out their own salvation. These gods cannot help humans in their search for salvation. Therefore prayer and worship are worthless. While Jainism may acknowledge the existence of gods it does not rely upon them, and for that reason it may be called an essentially atheistic religion.

In regard to the practice of their religion Jains tend to divide themselves into two distinct groups: the majority who cannot afford to leave their homes and accept the rigors of the ascetic life, and the minority who can and do become monks. The latter represent the ideal life for a Jain. Jain monks take five vows which are to guide their lives:

1. They vow noninjury of life (*ahimsa*). According to Jain tradition Mahavira taught:

> He who injures these (animals) does not comprehend and renounce the sinful acts; he who does not injure these, comprehends and renounces the sinful acts. Knowing them, a wise man should not act sinfully toward animals, nor cause others to act so, nor allow others to act so. He who knows these causes of sin relating to animals, is called a reward-knowing sage. Thus I say.[4]

This vow has become the most dominant characteristic of all Jains and the mark by which they are known to the world. A Jain will go to

---

[4]Ayaranya Sutra, 1, 1, 6, 6

All life, but especially animal life, is sacred to Jains.

DIANE M. LOWE

great lengths to avoid harming any living creature. They are of course vegeterian and avoid the use of products such as leather, which require the death or suffering of life. Jain monks, following Mahavira's example, sweep the path before them when they walk to avoid treading on insects, and they strain the water they drink in order to protect whatever life may have been in it. In certain extreme cases Jains have been known to establish hospitals for sick rats. Thus some have noted jokingly that Jains are those "who deny God, worship man, and nourish vermin." The Jain principle of not injuring life has had widespread influence among non-Jains such as Mohandas Gandhi and Albert Schweitzer.

2. Jain monks vow always to speak the truth, and because of this vow they are widely respected for their truthfulness. However, in its search for truth, Jainism has tended to view truth as relative rather than absolute.[5]

3. Jain monks vow to refrain from taking anything that is not given to them. This too has added to the Jain's reputation for honesty.

4. The monks' fourth vow is to renounce sexual pleasures. This is in keeping with traditional asceticism, which views the pleasures of the flesh as evil; since sex is one of the greatest pleasures of the flesh it must be forsaken. (Mahavira went even further by not only renouncing sexual pleasures but by also renouncing women in general. He is said to have declared that "women are the greatest temptation in the world." Thus the very conservative Jain sects today will not allow a woman even to seek salvation in a monastery.)

5. The final vow is to renounce all attachments. Attachments to and love for other persons or things is one of the elements that keep humans bound to life. (It was for this reason that Mahavira renounced his family and possessions and refused to stay in any place longer than one day lest he build new attachments.)

Generally all Jains seek to follow the first three vows as much as possible, while those who enter the monastic life will keep all five. Thus a Jain layperson may marry and have a family and possessions with the understanding that he is not leading the ideal life and may not expect salvation in this life.

The scriptures of the Jains are called Agamas, which means "precepts," or Siddhantas, which means "treatises." Orthodox Jains believe that these Agamas are the actual sermons or teachings that Mahavira gave to his disciples. The various Jain sects differ as to the number of Agamas that are genuine and authoritative. Many of the lesser known Agamas have not yet been translated into English.

---

[5]The well-known story of the blind men and the elephant is said to have been of Jain origin and illustrates the relativity of truth. In this tale several blind men are asked to describe an elephant. Each touches a different part of the elephant's body and thus each describes the animal in a different way. To one man the elephant is like a stone wall since he has touched the side; to another the elephant is like a rope since he touched the tail; and to another the elephant is like a fan since he touched the ear. Each man truthfully described the animal, but since each had contacted it from a different perspective, their descriptions varied tremendously.

JAIN SECTS

By 80 A.D. the Jains were severely divided over what was to be the true meaning of Jainism, and they split into two sects that still exist today. The sect that takes the more liberal view in the interpretation of Jain teachings is the Svetambara (literally, "the white clad"). Today this group is located mainly in the northern part of India. They are liberal in their interpretation of Mahavira's teachings regarding the wearing of clothing and are called "white clad" because they reject the necessity of nudity and allow their monks to wear a white garment. They are also liberal in that they allow the admission of women to the religion and to their monasteries and even accept the possibility that a woman may find salvation. Of the two sects, the Svetambara is the more popular.

The second sect, the Digambara (literally, "the sky clad"), is the more conservative of the two, and its members live mainly in the southern portion of India. The Digambaras adhere to the old ideals and require their monks to go about nearly nude; total nudity is reserved only for those of greatest holiness. In addition, they believe that women have no chance of achieving salvation and are to be regarded as the greatest of all temptations to a man. Therefore women are prohibited from entering the monasteries and the temples. The Digambaras even refuse to believe that Mahavira was ever married.

In 1473 a third sect arose as a splinter group from Svetambara. This group is known as the Sthanakavasi and is distinguished by its opposition to temples and idols. It also differs from other Jain sects in that it accepts only thirty-three Agamas as authoritative, while others accept as many as eighty-four.

JAINISM TODAY

Hinduism was affected by Jain teaching and was moved to accept its emphasis upon asceticism and *ahimsa* as regular parts of Indian religion. However, while Jainism and its ascetic movement may have been very popular in India at one time, today it is considered a minority sect of Hinduism. In its purest form it appeals to less than two million people, mainly in the Bombay region of India.

Because of their overwhelming concern for the sacredness of life the Jains are forbidden from entering certain occupations. No Jain can belong to any profession that takes life or profits from slaughter. For example, they cannot be soldiers, butchers, leather workers, exterminators, or even farmers, since farmers regularly plow the soil and might be a party to the death of worms and insects that live in the soil. These prohibitions have forced the Jains to enter the commercial professions. This fact, along with their reputation for honesty and morality, have made the Jains excellent businessmen. It is paradoxical that a sect that began with the intention of asceticism and poverty has become, by virtue of its respect for life, one of the wealthiest classes of India.

Though Jains have no need for gods they do venerate the twenty-four Tirthankaras. Jains have erected over forty thousand temples in India for the worship of these figures. Many of these temples are renowned for their beauty, and the one on Mount Abu is considered to be one of the seven wonders of India.

Apart from adoring the Tirthankaras in temples, Jain worship includes many rituals in the home. This worship may include reciting the names of the Jinas (bathing idols) and offering flowers and perfumes to them. Worship may also contain the chanting of Jain hymns, prayers, and formulas. Many Jains also include meditation and the observance of vows in their worship.

SUGGESTED READING

Frost, S. E., ed. *The Sacred Writings of the World's Great Religions.* New York: McGraw-Hill, 1972.

Jaini, Jagmanderlal. *Outlines of Jainism.* Cambridge: Cambridge University Press, 1916.

Stevenson, Margaret. *The Heart of Jainism.* London: Oxford University Press, 1915.

CHAPTER SIX

BUDDHISM

This unusual statue from the marble temple in Uruvela, Thailand, shows an emaciated Buddha during his ascetic period.

Let, therefore, no man love anything; loss of the beloved is evil. Those who love nothing and hate nothing, have no fetters.

DHAMMAPADA, 211

Buddhism began in India in the sixth century B.C. as another interpretation of the Hindu religious system. As such it had great appeal in India for several centuries. However, by the third century B.C. it developed something unusual for any version of Hinduism: a missionary imperative. The rulers of India, who were enamored of this new religion, sent Buddhist missionaries into neighboring Asian countries. At the same time, Buddhism was developing new theologies that became more and more attractive to the Asian people. This combination of missionary thrust and new theologies made it a sweeping success in countries such as China, Japan, Korea, and Indochina. Yet while Buddhism was becoming a success in foreign missions it was slowly being pushed aside in India by a resurging Hinduism. The Muslim conquest of India crushed the final remains of Buddhism there, and today one must look to other Asian nations to find its adherents.

THE LIFE OF GAUTAMA

The founder of Buddhism was a man named Siddhartha, who was a member of the Gautama clan. The dates usually given for his life are 560–480 B.C. However, the life of Gautama, as he has come to be known, is surrounded by legend and his exact dates are subject to question. Nevertheless he probably lived during the sixth century B.C. and was a contemporary of Mahavira.

Gautama was the son of a Kshatriya rajah called Suddhodana and his wife, Maya. The legends say that the birth of the child was surrounded by extraordinary events and portents. According to one story, a soothsayer predicted that the child would either become a great king who would rule India or a great Buddha ("Enlightened One"). Gautama's mother died soon after his birth, and he was reared by his maternal aunt, who became his father's second wife.

Because Gautama's father did not wish him to grow up to become a religious leader, his father sought to protect him and keep him from seeing the ugliness and distress of humanity. The rajah specifically sought to keep the young prince from seeing four sights: a dead body, an aged person, a diseased person, and an ascetic monk. Thus Gautama grew up surrounded by youth, beauty, and health. He received a normal education for a prince of that era. He studied the arts of warfare and received some education in philosophy. When he was nineteen he married his cousin and they shared a happy home together. They had one child, a son.

As Gautama neared his thirtieth birthday he gradually became aware of the ugliness of the real world. According to some of the legends, the gods, wishing to awaken the future Buddha from the wasteful life he was leading, conspired to break through the walls of youth and beauty that had been erected about him. One by one he began to see the things his father had forbidden him to see. He saw a rotting corpse, a wrinkled and bent elderly person, a man with a loathsome disease, and a peaceful monk who had renounced the world for asceticism. Whether these sights were the work of the gods or not, Gautama, reaching his mature years, became aware that the life most people led was one of suffering and pain. It is said that he once entered his father's harem room where there were some of the most beautiful young women in the kingdom. There he received a vision of what these women would soon become, wrinkled, bent, gray, and stooped. These revelations made it impossible for the sensitive young prince to continue to live in his palace surrounded by ease and plenty, and one night he decided to leave his home. He crept into his wife's bedroom and said farewell to her and their infant son.[1] Then he took his best horse and rode off into the night. After going a certain distance he

[1]According to one story the son was named Rahula, which means "fetter," indicating that at the time of the child's birth, Gautama was at the point of considering that all things, even a beautiful child, could bind one to life like a fetter.

clipped off his hair and beard and sent it back with the horse by his charioteer. He changed clothes with a beggar and began a period of searching for answers to life's misery.

At first Gautama thought the answers to the questions that troubled him were to be found in the various schools of philosophy. Therefore he attached himself to a guru and studied with him for some time, but he received no satisfaction in his studies. A second avenue Gautama sought was that of asceticism. As a solution to the problems of life, asceticism was an acceptable pursuit in the sixth century B.C., as can be seen from the life of Mahavira and his followers. Gautama joined five other monks and with them began a life of severe asceticism that lasted for five years. The ascetic measures Gautama took were as severe as any recorded in the history of religion. According to legend he became something of a champion ascetic. Gautama sought out anything that was unpleasant, painful, or disagreeable as a means by which he might find release. He is supposed to have practiced fasting until he reached the point of living on a single grain of rice per day. When most Westerners think of Buddha they tend to think of a fat, jolly person because they have been influenced by the Japanese statuary that depicts plump figures as "Buddhas." However, these are not an attempt to depict the historical Buddha. At this time in his life Gautama reportedly became so thin that when he grasped his stomach he touched his backbone. In addition to eating very little food he ate nauseating food and at one point is even supposed to have eaten his feces. He wore irritating garments and sat in awkward and painful positions for hours. He sat on thorns and for a time slept in a graveyard among the rotting flesh of corpses. In the tradition of many ascetics, Gautama allowed filth and vermin to accumulate on his body. However, in spite of these heroic efforts at asceticism, he did not find the salvation he was seeking.

Apparently the turning point in Gautama's quest came one day when he was walking near a stream. Because he had been terribly weakened by his ordeals, he fainted and fell into the stream. The cold water revived him and when he was able to contemplate his situation he realized that, while he had done everything that could be expected of an ascetic, he still had not found satisfaction. He therefore arose, went to a nearby tavern, and had a meal. His five friends happened to pass by and when they saw him eating and drinking and enjoying himself, they spurned him as a traitor. When Gautama had finished his meal he went to the banks of a river and sat down under the shade

GURU — teacher of spiritual life

Buddha's first sermon at Deer Park, Nagarjunakonda, India.

of a fig tree and began to meditate.[2] He decided to sit and meditate until he received enlightenment. At last, after seven weeks of meditation, Gautama was enlightened, and from then on he was known as the Buddha ("Enlightened One"). In his meditation the Buddha had a vision of the endless cycle of birth and death that is the lot of mankind. It was revealed to him that people were bound to this cycle because of *tanha* (desire, thirst, craving). It is desire that causes karma and thus fetters people. The Buddha had desired salvation and had sought it through asceticism and knowledge, but it had eluded him. When he had ceased to desire he found enlightenment and thus salvation.

The first step the Buddha took after his enlightenment was to go to the holy city of Benares and locate the five ascetic friends who had spurned him. He found them in the Deer Park and, though at first they had contempt for him, they listened as he preached. In this first sermon the Buddha taught that neither the extreme of indulgence nor the extreme of asceticism was acceptable as a way of life and that one

[2]Because he found enlightenment under this tree it has become known as the bo or bodhi tree.

should avoid extremes and seek to live in the middle way. The five ascetics noted the change that had come over the Buddha, and they accepted his teachings. These five formed the first *Sangha* (Buddhist monastic order).

The Buddha was enlightened when he was about thirty-five years of age. During the remaining years of his life he wandered about with his growing band of disciples. Unlike orthodox Hindus, he taught that any person of any caste or sex could find salvation. Therefore his followers included a wide variety of persons. When women asked to join his group, the Buddha was at first reluctant, but he eventually relented and allowed them to form an order of nuns. According to legend, the Buddha's former wife was among the first women to seek admission to this group. Those persons who seriously joined the Buddha as monks shaved their heads and wore coarse yellow robes. Their only possession was a bowl that they carried when they begged for food. Their creed is said to have been, "I take refuge in the Buddha; I take refuge in the *Dharma* ("law"); and I take refuge in the Sangha."

In addition the monks sought to observe the following rules of conduct as described in the Pali Sermons.

And How, O king, is a monk accomplished in morality?

Herein a monk abandons the killing of living things and refrains from killing; laying aside the use of a stick or a knife he dwells modest, full of kindliness, and compassionate for the welfare of all living things. This is his behavior in morality.

Abandoning the taking of what is not given he refrains from taking what is not given; he takes and expects only what is given, he dwells purely and without stealing.

Abandoning incontinence he practises continence and lives apart, avoiding the village practice of sex intercourse.

Abandoning falsehood he refrains from falsehood; he speaks truth, he is truthful, trustworthy, and reliable, not deceiving people.

Abandoning slanderous speech he refrains from slanderous speech; what he has heard from one place he does not tell in another to cause dissension. He is even a healer of dissensions and a producer of union, delighting and rejoicing in concord, eager for concord, and an utterer of speech that produces concord.

Abandoning harsh speech he refrains from harsh speech; the speech that is harmless, pleasant to the ear, kind, reaching the heart, urbane, amiable, and attractive to the multitude, that kind of speech does he utter.

Abandoning frivolous speech he refrains from frivolous speech; he speaks of the good, the real, the profitable, of the doctrine and the discipline; he is an utterer of speech worth hoarding, with timely reasons and purpose and meaning.

He refrains from injuring seeds and plants.

He eats only within one meal time, abstaining from food at night and avoiding untimely food.

He refrains from seeing dancing, singing, music, and shows.

He refrains from the use of garlands, scents, unguents, and objects of adornment; from a high or large bed; from accepting gold and silver; from accepting raw grain and raw meat.

He refrains from accepting women, girls, male and female slaves, goats and rams, fowls and pigs, elephants, oxen, horses, mares, and farm-lands.

He refrains from going on messages and errands; from buying and selling; from cheating in weighing, false metal, and measuring; from practices of cheating, trickery, deception, and fraud; from cutting, killing, binding, robbery, pillage, and violence. . . .[3]

The Buddha reportedly died at the age of eighty after eating some bad mushrooms. According to tradition his final words were, "Subject to decay are all component things. Strive earnestly to work out your own salvation."

THE TEACHINGS OF THE BUDDHA

There is nothing in the life and teachings of the Buddha to indicate that he intended to found a new religion or even to reform Hinduism. His teachings are more concerned with ethics and self-understanding than with anything that might be called religion. Apparently he was opposed to the various existing forms of religious worship, and he was certainly opposed to the Brahmin system of animal sacrifice. In addition he rejected the authority of the Vedas. The Buddha tended to be agnostic and sometimes atheistic in his teachings regarding the gods. He was much more concerned that people work out their own salvation than that they appeal to the gods for help and support. Yet the

---

[3]Pali Sermons, *Morality* (1).

teachings of the Buddha came to be regarded by Hindus as a reformation of their religion and also as the basis for a vast family of religions in
Asia outside of India.

Among the most unique teachings of the Buddha was that the soul
did not exist. According to Buddha, people live in a state of *anatman*
(nonsoulness). What is called a soul is actually a combination of five
mental or physical aggregates: the physical body, feelings, understanding, will, and consciousness. This combination which makes up the
human personality is bound up in the endless cycle of birth, death, and
rebirth that is typical in Indian religions. The Buddha's understanding
of humankind's plight is presented in the classic Buddhist statement of
the Four Noble Truths:

> And what, monks, is the Middle Path, of which the Tathagata
> has gained enlightenment, which produces insight and knowl-
> edge, and tends to calm, to higher knowledge, enlightenment,
> Nirvana? This is the noble Eightfold Way, namely right view,
> right intention, right speech, right action, right livelihood,
> right effort, right mindfulness, right concentration. This,
> monks, is the Middle Path, of which the Tathagata has gained
> enlightenment, which produces insight and knowledge, and
> tends to calm, to higher knowledge, enlightenment, Nirvana.
>
> Now this, monks, is the noble truth of pain: birth is painful,
> old age is painful, sickness is painful, death is painful, sorrow,
> lamentation, dejection, and despair are painful. Contact with
> unpleasant things is painful, not getting what one wishes is
> painful. In short the five groups of grasping are painful.
>
> Now this, monks, is the noble truth of the cause of pain: the
> craving, which tends to rebirth, combined with pleasure and
> lust, finding pleasure here and there, namely the craving for
> passion, the craving for existence, the craving for non-
> existence.
>
> Now this, monks, is the noble truth of the cessation of pain,
> the cessation without a remainder of craving, the abandon-
> ment, forsaking, release, non-attachment.
>
> Now this, monks, is the noble truth of the way that leads to
> the cessation of pain: this is the noble Eightfold Way, namely,
> right views, right intention, right speech, right action, right
> livelihood, right effort, right mindfulness, right concentra-
> tion.[4]

---

[4]Pali Sermon, the first sermon.

The person who follows the Eightfold Path will break the bonds that tie him to life and achieve release from the cycle. The word used to describe this release is Nirvana, which basically means "extinguished" or "put out like a candle." Thus the goal of basic Buddhist thought is not the achievement of some state of bliss in some heaven but the extinguishing of the self and its desire and the cessation of life. Those who have followed the Eightfold Path and arrived at the point of achieving Nirvana are called *arhat*, or "saint."

The teachings of the Buddha became the basis for an organization that took on many of the components of a religion. His followers organized themselves into a monastic order, or Sangha, that was made up of both purely dedicated monks and laypeople. His teachings became codified in the laws of that order and in various forms of scripture. The Buddha himself came to be regarded as the chief of beings. The rules under which early Buddhist monks were expected to live are noteworthy since they demonstrate the practical outworkings of the Buddha's teachings.

THE DEVELOPMENT OF BUDDHISM

When the Buddha died in the fifth century B.C. his teachings could scarcely be called a religion. They denied the existence or the importance of the gods, they denied the necessity of worship or sacrifice, and salvation was seen as totally dependent upon the works of the individual. Those persons attracted to the teachings of the Buddha during his life must have been a special group of very intelligent people who were dissatisfied with life and had the capacity to discipline themselves. Had Buddhism remained as it was in the beginning, it is doubtful whether more than a mere handful of people in the history of the world would have been interested in it. However, in the twentieth century Buddhism is one of the major religions of the world. Its devotees are to be found in nearly every Asian nation. The path by which Buddhism was transformed from a world-denying, god-denying sect into one of the largest of the world's religions is a fascinating one indeed.

As in the case of almost every other founder of a religion, before the Buddha had been dead very long his followers were fighting over the real meaning of his teachings. According to one tradition a schism occurred between the disciples the day after his death. Within the year of his death his followers were forced to call together a council to try to determine the true meaning of his teachings. This council failed to

Great Buddha at Kamakura.

bring unity, and within a very short period of time there were four major Buddhist factions. During the next ten years the number increased to over seventy.

In 390 B.C. a second council was called, and an orthodox minority declared the majority of Buddhists to be heretics. From this point onward Buddhism has been divided into these two major camps, which have in turn been subdivided into numerous sects. The smaller and more orthodox wing of Buddhism is known by its adherents as *Theravada* ("the tradition of the elders") and by its enemies as *Hinayana* ("the smaller vehicle"). The larger and more liberal segment is known primarily as *Mahayana* ("the larger vehicle"). The basic theological differences between these two sects will be discussed in a later section of this chapter.

Buddhism received its greatest impetus when a man who was to become the emperor of India, Asoka, was converted to the new religion. It is said that Asoka was to Buddhism what Constantine was to Christianity. In both cases these rulers of large empires were converted to what had previously been small struggling religions. Both emperors then threw the power of their thrones behind their new faiths, and from that point onward these religions grew rapidly. Asoka was converted in 297 B.C., and he became convinced that unlike other religions of India Buddhism was potentially the religion for all the peoples of the world. Thus he was the first Buddhist to send out missionaries, carrying the teachings of Gautama and urging non-Indians to accept them.

131

According to some, Asoka's missionaries went as far west as Syria and Greece. While this may be an exaggeration, we are reasonably certain that he sent representatives to Ceylon (present-day Sri Lanka), where the king and his court were converted. Today Ceylon boasts the longest history of Buddhism of any Asian nation. Whatever Asoka's motives may have been in sending out these missionaries, the decision proved to be the salvation of Buddhism, since this religion ceased to exist in India as it was there absorbed by Hinduism. Asoka also called the third council of Buddhism in 247 B.C. The purpose of this council was to determine the true canon of Buddhist scriptures.

In spite of the enormous unifying work of Asoka and others, by the first century A.D. there were many major and minor sects within Buddhism. Some estimate that by this time there may have been as many as five hundred. However, the most distinct split was along the lines of the differences between Theravada and Mahayana.

THERAVADA BUDDHISM

As mentioned earlier, Hinayana or Theravada Buddhism is the more conservative of the two major divisions within this religion. As such it is believed to be closer to the original teachings of the Buddha. The major locations of Theravada Buddhism today are Ceylon, Burma, and the nations of Southeast Asia. Ceylon seems to be the model for early Buddhism since it was the object of Asoka's missionary efforts in the third century B.C. and has had a relatively peaceful and untroubled history, escaping the conquests and turmoil that have been the lot of India. Because of this rather peaceful history, the Buddhism of Ceylon has remained relatively unchanged.

According to Theravada Buddhism, people must work out their own salvation without reliance upon the gods or any force beyond themselves. For this reason the monk is the ideal figure. It is he who shaves his head, puts on the coarse yellow robe, takes up a begging bowl, and goes forth to seek release from life. His home is the Sangha just as it was in the days of the Buddha. When a monk achieves the goal he is seeking he becomes a saint, and it only remains for him to die before he attains Nirvana and release from the cycle of birth, death, and rebirth, which is the common lot of humankind.

> There is no suffering for him who has finished his journey, and abandoned grief, who has freed himself on all sides, and thrown off all fetters.

They exert themselves with their thoughts well-collected, they do not tarry in their abode; like swans who have left their lake, they leave their house and home.

Men who have no riches, who live on recognized food, who have perceived void and unconditioned freedom [Nirvana], their path is difficult to understand, like that of the birds of the air.

He whose appetites are stilled, who is not absorbed in enjoyment. . . .

The gods even envy him whose senses, like horses well broken in by the driver, have been subdued, who is free from pride, and free from appetites;

In a hamlet or in a forest, on sea or on dry land, wherever venerable persons [Arahanta] dwell, that place is delightful.[5]

If a Theravada Buddhist cannot or will not join the Sangha and become a monk, then he must content himself with living the life of a layperson now, supporting the needs of the monks, and hoping that in another life he will be in a better position to seek to become a saint. The scriptures of Theravada Buddhism are relatively few in number because scripture is not very important in conservative Buddhism.

Thus Theravada Buddhism, like the Buddhism that Gautama himself taught, contains little that might be called a religion. The gods, sacrifice, and prayer are of minor consequence. However, certain religious elements have evolved. For example, relics of the life of the Buddha have become important to Theravadins. His bones and possessions have become objects of veneration at many of the important sites of Therevadin life. One of the early missionaries reportedly took a branch from the sacred bo tree under which the Buddha found enlightenment and planted it in Ceylon. The resultant tree is supposed to be the world's oldest living tree. Some Theravadins even teach that the Buddha was actually a divine, omniscient, and sinless being who lived many lives before he became Gautama and that another Buddha is waiting now to be born and to give further light to the world through another incarnation.

The characteristic physical structure of Theravada Buddhism is a complex of buildings called a *wat*.[6] The most important building in the wat is the *bot*, a hall used for teaching, preaching, and meditation.

---

[5]Dhammapada, 90–94, 98.
[6]The word *wat* is a Thai word. In Burma similar clusters are called *phongyi chaung*.

Usually this hall contains a statue of the Buddha, with attending altars, candles, and incense. In another portion of the hall there may be a raised seat for lecturing teachers and preachers. Other buildings within the wat include the living quarters for the monks and a number of graceful towers known as stupas or pagodas. Some speculate that the pagodas may have begun as relic mounds, but today they serve as worship or festival centers for the Buddhist community.

Although Theravada Buddhism has had appeal for the peoples of Southeast Asia, its nonreligious attitude of expecting each individual to work out his own salvation as a monk never had the wide appeal that would have made it an international religion. It was necessary for Buddhism to change and develop. If it had not developed a greater religious appeal, as it did in Mahayana, it might have died in India or remained a minor religion of the Southeast Asian nations.

MAHAYANA BUDDHISM

The Principles of Mahayana

In the third century B.C., while King Asoka was spreading the gospel of Buddhism by means of his missionary efforts, certain subtle changes began to occur in the religion itself. When these new principles solidified they produced a Buddhism so different from that which Gautama taught and which was accepted by the Theravada Buddhists that it was virtually a new religion.

One of the basic assumptions underlying these new developments was that, in addition to what the Buddha had taught his disciples openly, there were many other principles that he had taught in secret and which were only for the elect who could properly interpret them. A favorite story of the Mahayanists is that as the Buddha was teaching he took a handful of leaves from the floor of the forest and explained to his disciples that as the leaves in his hand were less than the total leaves of the forest, so were the teachings he had given them openly less than the total amount of truth that could be given in secret. Mahayana Buddhism simply picked up a few more leaves. Once this assumption was accepted, then all manner of new teachings could be added to Buddhism.

A second principle that began to develop in Mahayana Buddhism between the third century B.C. and the first century A.D. was that Gautama was really more than a man. In contrast to the original teachings of the Buddha and those of the Theravada school, the

Buddhist Temple, Tokyo. People burning prayer sticks in fire rite.

Mahayanists began to teach that the Buddha was really a compassionate divine being who came to earth in the form of a man because he loved humankind and wished to be of assistance.

The third principle the Mahayanists put forth was that Gautama was not the only Buddha. If Gautama were a divine being who had come to earth to help people, the Mahayanists maintained that there must have been other such beings. Some of these beings had come before Gautama, some had come after him, and some were yet to come. This new idea did more than anything else to broaden the appeal of Buddhism. If there are many divine beings who are compassionate and have come to earth to help suffering people, then these beings are worthy of worship. Whereas Gautama had been unconcerned about the gods, and worship had meant nothing in his scheme of things, the Mahayana Buddhists could now develop worship around these many divine beings. They could study the lives of these new gods and build temples to them. Priests could be trained in worshiping these gods, and cultic systems of ritual, sacrifice, hymns, and so on, could be raised in their behalf. The discovery of many compassionate Buddhas was the most religious step ever taken in Buddhism. What had essentially been a philosophy based upon self-help now was free to become a religion in every sense of the word.

135

This development was also essential to the Buddhist missionary movement. Now when Buddhist missionaries entered a new country they did not have to ask the natives to give up their old gods; these gods were seen as various incarnations of the Buddha, and their cults could continue. In the same way that Hinduism absorbed Buddhism by saying that Guatama was really an avatar of Vishnu, Buddhism absorbed many other religions by saying that their gods were really incarnations of the Buddha.

In addition to these new principles, Mahayana Buddhists developed a path of salvation for the common person. It was taught that mortals could take vows to become *bodhisattvas* ("enlightened beings") at some point during their lifetimes. Then, by living exemplary lives they could acquire merit. Following death, these bodhisattvas postponed their achievement of Nirvana and shared their merit with humankind. The bodhisattvas are pictured as sitting in heaven answering the prayers of those who need their help. Thus the Mahayanists developed a system whereby mortals could achieve divine status and become lesser deities. In this manner the polytheism that Mahayana developed continued to grow.

The Spread of Mahayana Buddhism

Whereas the original teachings of the Buddha and the more orthodox interpretations of Hinayana Buddhism had limited appeal to a rather select group, Mahayana, with its openness to more traditional religious concepts, developed wide appeal. The attractiveness of Mahayana Buddhism was so great that it eventually became one of the world's most successful missionary religions.

The teachings of the Buddha probably were carried into China as soon as they became popular in India. Surely Asoka must have sent his missionaries into that great land to the north and east of India in the third century B.C. There is some evidence that Hinayana Buddhism had been introduced and had achieved a minor foothold in China by the first century A.D. However, it was not until the third century, when Mahayana was introduced, that Buddhism really began to take hold there. From that era onward Buddhism became the major religion of China, with the native Confucianism and Taoism offering cultural values but taking a secondary position as religions.

From China Mahayana Buddhism spread to other east Asian nations. Because of its close ties to China, Korea was brought under the influence of Buddhism as early as the fourth century A.D. The spread to the East continued in the sixth century, when Buddhism entered Japan. The Japanese at first refused to accept this new religion, but after a short period of time they embraced it to the point that it came to share religious leadership with the native Shinto. In the ensuing centuries other Asian nations such as Mongolia and Tibet also accepted versions of Buddhism. Because of the remote nature of these countries, the religion developed along slightly different lines than it had in other places and remains today an unusual variation.

While Buddhism was becoming a great success as a missionary religion in the East Asian nations it was gradually dying in the land of its birth, India. Waves of invasions by various peoples caused the destruction of many Indian centers of Buddhist strength. This was particularly true of the Islamic invasions in which Buddhists were forced to convert to Islam and Buddhist temples and images were destroyed by the iconoclastic Muslims. Whereas Hinduism, which also suffered at the hands of the Muslims, somehow had the resiliency to recover, Buddhism—in India—did not. In addition to the destruction encountered from the invaders of India, Buddhism suffered from absorption by Hinduism. Since Hinduism has the capacity for openness and toleration of other religions, it was able to absorb the distinctive qualities of the major challenging religions, Jainism and Buddhism. By the seventh century it absorbed many Buddhist features simply by stating that Gautama was an avatar of Vishnu. Therefore anything new, important, or distinctive about Buddhism came to be understood as an expression of Vishnu within the Hindu scheme of things. In this way Buddhism eventually ceased to be a distinctive religion in India, and today only a tiny minority of Indians are truly Buddhists.

Mahayanist Sects

Mahayana Buddhism began as a religion open to innovation and change. It would not be bound to the original teachings of the Buddha. As it moved and grew in the various Asian nations it acquired many new concepts from these peoples. Therefore when we speak of Buddhism today, we are not speaking of a single religion but of a whole family of religions; and within this family nearly every form of religious expression may be found.

The Pure Land Sect (Ching-t'u, Jodo). One of the most popular and widespread branches of Mahayana Buddhism is the so-called Pure Land sect. The goal of its adherents is to achieve salvation when they

die and live in a paradise called "the pure land of the west." As we
mentioned earlier the Mahayanists believe that there have been many
Buddhas and other forms of divine beings, one of which is the
Bodhisattvas. Another form of deity is a group called *Dhyani Buddhas*,
who, unlike the Bodhisattvas, were never humans but are deities who
dwell in heaven and can help humans. One of the most popular of
these is known as *Amitabha*.[7] Amitabha is viewed as the god who
presides over a western paradise called "the pure land."

> This world Sukhavati, Ananda, which is the world system of
> the Lord Amitabha, is rich and prosperous, comfortable, fer-
> tile, delightful and crowded with many Gods and men. And in
> this world system, Ananda, there are no hells, no animals, no
> ghosts, no Asuras and none of the inauspicious places of re-
> birth. And in this our world no jewels make their appearance
> like those which exist in the world system Sukhavati.
>
> And that world system Sukhavati, Ananda, emits many fra-
> grant odours, it is rich in a great variety of flowers and fruits,
> adorned with jewel trees, which are frequented by flocks of
> various birds with sweet voices, which the Tathagata's miracu-
> lous power has conjured up. And these jewel trees, Ananda,
> have various colors, many colors, many hundreds of
> thousands of colors. They are variously composed of the seven
> precious things, in varying combinations, i.e., of gold, silver,
> beryl, crystal, coral, red pearls or emerald. Such jewel trees,
> and clusters of banana trees and rows of palm trees, all made
> of precious things, grow everywhere in the Buddha-field.[8]

To the Pure Land Buddhist, salvation comes through faith in
Amitabha. Some members of this sect believe that simply uttering the
name of Amitabha many times during the day is an aid to salvation.

With faith in Amitabha as its central premise, and eternity in the
Pure Land as its goal, this version of Buddhism is something quite
different from that originally taught by the Buddha. It is possible for
the Pure Land priesthood to marry, have children, eat meat, and live
in the world in a manner very similar to that of the layperson. Worship
for the Pure Land devotee oftens occurs in what may be best described
as "churches"; in fact some Pure Land congregations in Western na-

---

[7]In China this Buddha is known as O-mi-to, and in Japan he is called Amida.
[8]The Pure Land, 15, 16.

tions use that title. Pure Land Buddhists may have "Sunday Schools" for the religious instruction of their children, meet for worship in congregations, hear sermons from their clergymen, and offer prayers to Amitabha.

The Intuitive Sects (Ch'an, Zen). There always seems to have been a group within Buddhism that has emphasized that the truths of religion do not come through rational thought processes, study of scripture, or faith in a deity but rather through a sudden flash of insight. These groups usually trace their origin to the experience of the Buddha under the bodhi tree. As you will recall, here the Buddha realized that he had not found the truth he sought through study with the Brahmin gurus or after five years of extreme asceticism. He therefore resolved simply to sit and meditate. He sat under the bodhi tree for several weeks, and the truth came to him in a flash of inspiration. Advocates of this position maintain that intitution or inspiration which comes after a period of meditation is the key to Buddhist truth. These groups have been known throughout the Buddhist world as meditative or intuitive Buddhists. In India the word for meditation is *dhyana*, in China it is *ch'an*, and in Japan it is *zen*.

Although these Buddhists believe that the Buddha himself received his knowledge intuitively and taught his disciples in this manner, the actual founding of the intuitive sects did not take place until some time in the sixth century A.D. with the work of a monk named Bodhidharma. A great deal about the life of Bodhidharma is legendary, but it seems clear that in the late fifth or early sixth century the concepts of intuitive Buddhism entered China from India. From China they were carried to Korea and Japan, where this version of Buddhism reached its peak in the form of Zen. According to legend, at the invitation of the Chinese emperor, Bodhidharma went as a missionary from South India to Canton in 480 A.D. There he taught the emperor that his scripture, monasteries, philanthropy, and so on, availed him nothing; the truth of Buddhism is only found through meditation and sudden insight. Again according to legend, when he had finished teaching the emperor, Bodhidharma retired to a cave in the mountains where he spent ten years meditating while facing a wall, and during this time his lower limbs withered and he was no longer able to walk.

A purely apocryphal story says that Bodhidharma wished to stay awake for many hours and meditate but he kept falling asleep. In a fit of anger at his own inability to stay awake, the monk took a knife and cut off his eyelids. The eyelids fell to the ground and sprang up as the

*Stone Garden of Tofukuji Temple, Kyoto. The beauty and
simplicity of this garden reflects the teachings of Zen.*

tea plant. Therefore whenever Bodhidharma is depicted he is shown
with harsh staring eyes, and no eyelids. Legend also has it that
Bodhidharma brought tea from India to China. It is true that about
this time in history tea was introduced from India to China and later to
Japan and that the intuitive monks began to use heavily caffeinated tea
as a means of staying awake in order to meditate longer.

The basic principle behind all of the intuitive sects of Buddhism is
that salvation is an individual matter and therefore one cannot receive
much help from other persons or institutions. Individuals find salvation when through an accident or through meditation they are "enlightened." Therefore, the externals of religion are unnecessary. Scripture is not necessary because all people must learn the real truth of
religion and life for themselves. Temples are not important because

individuals can become enlightened while sitting under a tree or sweeping a floor. Statues of the Buddha and other saints are nice to look at but are not essential for enlightenment.[9] The same disregard is shown toward prayer, asceticism, and rituals.

According to the intuitive sects, reason is to be distrusted more than anything else because it cannot possibly lead people to real truth. In fact, people must deliberately confuse reason before they can find the truth. Therefore Zen Buddhism utilizes riddles that are carefully constructed to go beyond or confuse reason in order to lead the initiates into enlightenment. Such riddles of Zen are called *koans* (case studies). Entire books have been filled with these riddles, tales, and short statements which have been used by the Zen masters to aid their pupils. Perhaps the best known of all to Westerners is the simple statement "You have heard the sound of the clapping of two hands, but what is the sound of one hand clapping?" This question makes no sense, but it is designed to induce the initiate to go beyond sense or reason and to ponder. The pupil of Zen first meditates. When the pupil's mind is cleared of day-to-day matters and is ready to be released from reason, the master gives the student a riddle. It is hoped that while the novitiate meditates upon one of these nonsense statements a flash of enlightenment will come and will lead the initiate to the truth beyond reason.

In addition to the riddles, Zen masters utilize other devices to bring a student to insight. Generally any device that confuses the reasoning processes of the pupil will be used. A Zen master might suddenly shout at the pupil or even slap or kick the student in order to do this. Tales from Zen monasteries tell of masters striking their pupils with sticks or even cutting off one of their fingers in an attempt to cause the intuitive flash. The occasions of brutality are the exception rather than the rule, however.

It is in Japan that intuitive Buddhism has had its most profound effect upon the society. The Zen principles of beauty, simplicity, and profundity have deeply touched many areas of Japanese life. Because tea was introduced along with intuitive Buddhism, tea drinking and the rituals that surround it have been affected by Zen principles. The architecture of the teahouse, the pottery used in the tea ceremony, the

---

[9]The best illustration of the attitude of intuitive sects toward the externals of religion is found in a Zen cartoon that shows a monk seeking to warm himself on a cold morning. He has chopped up a statue of the Buddha, set fire to it, and is depicted raising his robe and warming his buttocks by the fire.

music that is played during the tea ceremony, the poetry that is recited, and the floral arrangements that decorate the teahouse, all reflect the principles of Zen. In Japanese art that which is valued most highly is called "the controlled accident." That is, art that is not purely planned or contrived is valued above that which is planned. A teapot that is accidentally broken and glued back together with gold-colored cement is more valued because of the beautiful "accidental" lines of the breakage than a teapot with a contrived design painted upon it. A drawing that is done upon very porous paper with pen and ink and cannot be erased and corrected is considered more beautiful than one that has been planned, worked out very carefully, and corrected by an artist. Thus the concepts of beauty in Japanese life are heavily influenced by the nonrational approach of Zen.

The Rationalist Sect (T'ien-t'ai, Tendai). Whereas the intuitive groups, Ch'an and Zen, tended to distrust the rational process and felt that they had little need for scripture in their search for enlightenment, another group arose in China in the sixth century and taught that in addition to meditation one should utilize reason and a study of the scriptures in order to find the truth of Buddhism. This sect, which was called T'ien-t'ai, was founded by a monk named Chih-i. According to Chih-i, the Buddha had used a variety of teaching methods during his lifetime in order to get across his truths. At one point he taught the Theravada doctrines; at another time he felt that he could communicate better by teaching the Mahayana doctrines; and at still another point he taught in a manner similar to that used by the intuitive sects. In reality there is only one true Buddhist teaching, and individuals must study the scriptures of Buddhism in order to know this truth. Therefore, whereas meditation may be helpful at certain times, it is not the only path, and rational thought and study should not be disregarded. In the ninth century the teachings of Chih-i were introduced into Japan, where this sect became known as Tendai.

The Sociopolitical Sect (Nichiren). From time to time the various sects of Buddhism have come to have great effect upon the social and political dimensions of various nations. One such sect is the so-called Nichiren ("sun lotus") Buddhist group that is a purely Japanese phenomenon. The founder of Nichiren lived in Japan in the thirteenth century. He was the son of humble parents, and at the age of fifteen he entered a Tendai Buddhist monastery. During his ten years there he came to believe that all the current sects of Buddhism were a perversion of the true teachings of the Buddha. He also came to believe that the Lotus Sutra was the only scripture a person needed to study to be a correct Buddhist. While meditating upon this sutra this man underwent a conversion experience. He changed his name to Nichiren, took a vow to faithfully follow and teach the Lotus Sutra, and set forth on a career of preaching and polemics with a fervor that is reminiscent of many of the Jewish prophets. He preached that he alone understood the truth of pure Buddhism and that the other Japanese sects, Zen, Pure Land, and so on, were preaching falsehoods and leading people to hell. Because the majority of the Japanese people followed these false sects, the· nation was suffering from internal and external woes. Naturally this kind of preaching aroused powerful enemies; Nichiren was twice deported and twice condemned to death.

Throughout its history Nichiren Buddhism has expressed hostility toward the rituals and teachings of other Buddhist sects. Consequently it has always been a small and persecuted minority.

The Nichiren sect has also stressed a simpler form of Buddhism and uncompromising patriotism and loyalty to Japan. It teaches that when Buddhism becomes purified in Japan it will reach out to the rest of the world. Although Nichiren itself has only slightly over two million followers today, it has been the source of another Buddhist sect, Soka Gakkai, which is much larger.

Tibetan Buddhism

Another aspect of Mahayana Buddhism is represented by sects that emphasize the use of magical words or formulae as means of achieving various goals. In Buddhism as in nearly every other religion there are those who believe that the recitation of certain phrases, names, or "magical" words has the effect of achieving certain ends. The largest and best known of these is the religion that was once a dominant force in Tibet.

The native religion of Tibet was known as *Bon*. The original meaning of this word has been lost, but it is suggested that it referred to priests who performed acts of magic and taught the Tibetan people various incantations and spells to protect themselves from the demons which lurked in the shadows and dark places of that harsh land. When Buddhism entered Tibet it apparently took this concern for magic and protection from demons as its major emphasis.

Buddhism was officially introduced into Tibet in the seventh century, when King Songtsan-Gampo came to the throne. He was interested in bringing the benefits of Indian and Chinese culture to his
people. One of his wives was Chinese and another was Indian. Both
were Buddhist. Therefore he sent them back to their respective home-
lands and asked them to return with Buddhist books and teachers. In
the eighth century the spread of Buddhism was interrupted when the
Bonists persuaded the Tibetans that a certain epidemic was the result
of the native deities' anger. This interruption did not last long, however, and soon the Buddhists were allowed to return and continue
their missionary activities.

The theology of Tibetan Buddhism is much like that found
throughout the Mahayana world, but because of the isolation of this
nation many unique features have developed and been maintained.
The most important practical feature of Tibetan Buddhism is its concern for magic as a means of coping with the problems of life. Tibetan
Buddhism is frequently referred to as *Tantric* Buddhism. This is because of its heavy use of manuals *(tantras)* that teach the various
magical words and spells that help one to deal with the unknown.
Tantric religion is found in several of the sects of both Hinduism and
Buddhism. In original Indian thought it was believed that within each
deity there were two elements: the male and the female. Sometimes
these elements were separated in the minds of the devotee into a god
and his consort, or wife, as in the case of Shiva and Kali. The awareness of these two divine elements led certain Hindus and later Buddhists to seek a mystical union with them through sexual excesses. It
was also believed that people could conquer passion with an excess of
that passion. Therefore in addition to bringing about a union between
the devotee and the god/goddess, *tantric* religion sought enlightenment
and conquest over the flesh by carrying passion to excessive lengths. It
was also believed that people could conquer the desire for meat, wine,
or other forbidden items by overindulging in them under the guidance
of a guru and the direction of certain rituals. This form of religion
became popular in early medieval Tibet. Eventually it led to uncon-
trolled license within the monasteries. Reform came under the direction of a monk named Marpa (1020–1097) and Tibetan tantric Buddhism was purged of much of its eroticism and given more spiritual
meaning.

Another feature of Tibetan Buddhism is its use of the phrase *Om
mani padmi hum*, which means, "Om, the jewel of the lotus, hum."
While the phrase has no special meaning literally, it is used as an

Man of Nepal with prayer wheel. Prayers written on bits of paper are attached to the spinning cylinder.

all-purpose formula for warding off evil and bringing good fortune. Some Tibetans believe that if this phrase is repeated often enough, magical effects will occur.

Another feature of Tibetan Buddhism that seems to be unique is the use of the prayer wheel. No one knows the origin of this, but its major use has been among the Tibetans. Basically the prayer wheel is a cylinder that contains various prayers and ritual incantations. Within this cylinder is an agitator of some kind. It is believed that by turning the agitator and stirring the prayers, the prayers are somehow prayed. The most common form of the prayer wheel is a small model that can be carried on one's person and activated regularly. Other larger models are found in monasteries. Inventive Tibetan Buddhists have even been known to set up prayer wheels near streams and have them turned by water power.

Still another distinctive feature of Tibetan Buddhism is its clergy, the *lamas*. The word *lama* basically means "the superior one." From earliest days these men who have turned aside from the normal pursuits of life to enter monasteries have been unusually powerful. As early as the ninth century the kings of Tibet gave the lamas certain lands for their monasteries and with these lands the power to gather funds from the people. By the fourteenth century the leaders of the monasteries had become more powerful than the kings. The kings disappeared and for all practical purposes the country was ruled by the Buddhist priests. Although the lamas had originally taken the vows of celibacy, by the fourteenth century they had rejected it and lived in lordly splendor with their wives and children. However, in that same century reform measures were introduced and celibacy again became their lot.

The lamas of Tibetan Buddhism have been divided basically into two orders: One is identified by Western scholars as the so-called Yellow Hat school and is the larger of the two; the other is identified as the Red Hat school. One of the most interesting contributions of the Red Hat school is their scriptural book, *Bardo Thodol (The Book of the Dead)*. It is believed that this book came to written form sometime in the eighth century A.D., although it may contain materials that are centuries older. Of course it contains teachings that are pre-Buddhist in nature. It essentially teaches that after death the human soul abides for forty-nine days in a dream-like state called the *Bardo*. During this period the ultimate destiny of the soul is determined. Individuals who have lived virtuous lives will achieve nirvana from the Bardo; if, on the other hand, a karmic pull has been built up during an individual's life, then that person will be drawn again to rebirth.[10] It is also believed that the immediate pre-death hours can influence the soul in its stay in the Bardo. Therefore Tibetan Buddhist monks are trained to help the dying through this experience. Western witnesses have sometimes observed the elaborate rituals and efforts of monks as they seek to help the dying.

The leader of the Yellow Hat group has been known for centuries as the Dalai Lama[11] and by virtue of his position essentially has been the ruler of Tibet. When one Dalai Lama dies an extensive search is made

---

[10] In a strange manner the *Bardo Thodol* seems to have anticipated Freud when it declares that people to be reborn as males will feel hostility toward their fathers and attraction to their mothers, and people to be females will feel hostility toward their mothers and attraction to their fathers.

[11] The word *dalai* literally means "the sea" and is used to indicate the vastness and depth of the person.

for his replacement. A group of monks scours Tibet for a child who seems to have the qualities and characteristics of the dead Dalai since it is believed that following his death he will reincarnate himself in the body of his successor. When the group has found such a child and agrees that this is the new Dalai Lama, the boy begins a long period of training that prepares him for leadership of the nation.

By the twentieth century Tibet had become a nation in which the clergy once again literally ruled the land. The Dalai Lama served as both spiritual and temporal leader, and the position of lama became so popular and so important that it was estimated in 1950 that almost 20 percent of the entire male population lived behind the walls of the monasteries.

This all came to an end in 1950, when Tibet was invaded by China. For centuries Tibet has been claimed by both China and India, but since neither nation pressed the claim, Tibet enjoyed a virtually independent existence. In 1950 China pressed its claim and set up a puppet government. In 1959, under the leadership of the young Dalai Lama, the Tibetans attempted to overthrow Chinese rule, but their revolution was crushed. The Dalai Lama and a few of his followers escaped to India, where they live today, and so the future of Tibetan Buddhism is very bleak.

MODERN BUDDHISM

After the great missionary movements in the first millennium of its existence, and after Asian nations such as China and Japan had been converted, Buddhism slipped into a state of quiescence. For centuries there were no great movements or changes. However, within the twentieth century Buddhism has begun to revive and grow. One of the factors that led to this revival has been the work of Christian missionaries in Asian nations. In an attempt to know Buddhism and Asian people better, Christian missionaries translated the ancient Buddhist texts and brought them out into the open for all to study. This has aroused many Buddhists to study, reevaluate, and reassert their own religion.

A second factor that has contributed to the revival of Buddhism is the rise of Asian nationalism. With the end of the colonial era the various Asian nations have made a great effort to reassert their national independence. Part of this has involved a restudy of and a new pride in their religions, including Buddhism. In some areas Buddhism has once more become a missionary religion and has even sent missionaries back to the home of the movement, India. However, at the same time that there is a new stirring of Buddhism in the world, Buddhism and all religions also are being repressed by governments in such countries as China and Tibet.

SUGGESTED READING

Conze, Edward, ed. *Buddhist Texts Through the Ages*. Oxford: Bruno Cassirer, 1953.

Gard, Richard A., ed. *Buddhism*. New York: George Braziller, 1961.

Humphreys, Christmas. *Buddhism*. New York: Penguin Books, 1951.

Snellgrove, D. L. *Buddhist Himalaya*. New York: Philosophical Library, 1957.

Suzuke, Daisetz T. *Zen and Japanese Buddhism*. Tokyo: Charles E. Tuttle, 1958.

Watts, Alan. *The Way of Zen*. New York: Pantheon Books, 1957.

CHAPTER SEVEN

SIKHISM

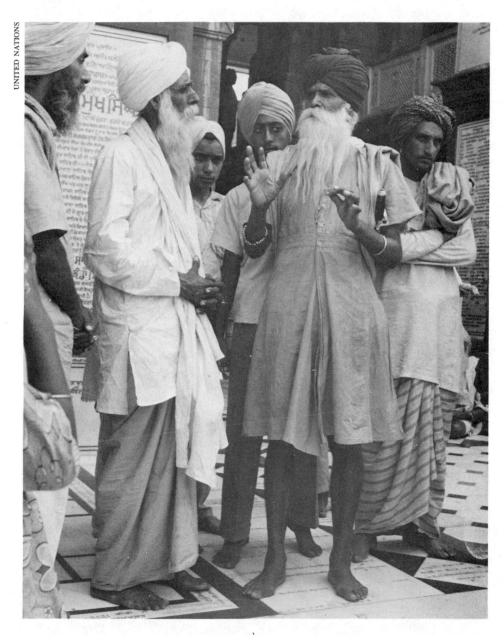

A Sikh preacher addresses an audience in the Golden Temple in Amritsar, India. The Golden Temple houses the holy Granth and is the most sacred of all Sikh shrines.

There is no Muslim and there is no Hindu.

NANAK

One of the world's newest religions, Sikhism, originated in the six-teenth century A.D. Although some call it a new and independent religion, there are those who think of Sikhism primarily as just one more reform movement in Hinduism. Indeed, like Buddhism and Jainism, Sikhism does take its basic theology and world view from Hinduism and does seek to reform certain elements in Hinduism. However, unlike other reform movements in Hinduism, Sikhism en-deavors to incorporate elements from another major world religion, Islam. Interestingly, Islam has an entirely different world view than Hinduism. This attempt to blend elements from two religions that are so diverse is a fascinating story.

The Sikhs have always been a minority among the other religions of India, and today they number only about six million. These people are found mainly in the Punjab region of northwest India, which has traditionally been their home.

THE LIFE OF NANAK

From the tenth century onward various Muslim groups invaded India from their bases to the west. These invasions eventually resulted in the domination of India by the Moghul rulers. While all of India faced Muslim conquest at one time or another, the northwest section was invaded most frequently. It was here that Islam made its greatest number of converts and established its strongest bases. Because Islam and Hinduism were basically so different in so many areas, the encounters between Muslims and Hindus were often hostile and frequently violent.

From the earliest days, however, there were teachers who did not believe that the two religions had to be hostile and thought that a synthesis could be reached. The reformer who is best remembered for attempting to bring Hinduism and Islam together was a man named Kabir (1440–1518). Kabir was born a Muslim but found it possible to worship with his Hindu neighbors. While worshiping the Hindu deities, he was also teaching that the true god was one. It is not clear how he was able to work this out, but he left a profound impression upon the Sikhs and their literature.

The actual founder of Sikhism was a man named Nanak (1469–1538), who was a later contemporary of Kabir and was undoubtedly influenced by him. Nanak was born into a Hindu home in the Punjab region about forty miles from the city of Lahore. Because of the mixed nature of the region, Nanak's schoolmaster was a Muslim and surely had an influence on him.

Nanak is pictured as a dreamer who seems to have had little grasp of the day-to-day world of business or practicality. His interests and talents were more toward poetry and religion than the business of earning a living. His father tried to place him in a variety of occupations, but Nanak apparently was a failure at all of them. He was betrothed to a young woman when he was twelve, and their marriage was consummated when he was nineteen. Two sons were born of this marriage. Nanak eventually left his wife and sons and went to the city of Sultanpur to earn his living. Here he was a bit more successful in business pursuits.

During his stay in Sultanpur, when he was about thirty years of age, Nanak received a vision from God which was to change his life. According to some stories God spoke to him while he was meditating in the forest. The message of the vision was that Nanak had been singled out as a prophet of a true religion. His message was to be, "There is no Muslim and there is no Hindu." Thus he was to become an evangelist, preaching gospel of unity between these two religions. Along with his constant companion, Mardana, Nanak became a wandering preacher of this new message. The two traveled widely in India over the next decades, preaching the essential unity of Islam and Hinduism. To emphasize his message Nanak wore a mixed costume made up of the clothing of both Hindus and Muslims. Wherever he went he sought to organize communities of people who accepted his teachings, and his followers became known as Sikhs, a Punjabi word for "disciple." In his travels Nanak even made the pilgrimage to Mecca, although he aroused antagonism there because of his unwillingness to display proper respect for Muslim shrines.

After many years of wandering Nanak returned home to northwest India, where he continued to teach and form communities of Sikhs. According to a charming Sikh legend, as Nanak was about to die, his followers were still divided over their basic religious loyalties. Those who originally had been Hindus planned to cremate his remains, while those who originally had been Muslim wished to bury him. Nanak, aware of this dispute over his body, requested that each group place flowers beside him, and the group whose flowers were still fresh on the following day could have his body. When the two factions agreed and placed their flowers beside him, Nanak covered himself with a sheet and died. The next morning when the sheet was removed, the Sikhs found that both sets of flowers were still fresh, but that the body of Nanak was gone. Thus, according to this legend, the peaceful and loving Nanak, even in death, sought to bring harmony between Muslims and Hindus.[1]

THE TEACHINGS OF NANAK

Nanak, like Kabir and others, sought to synthesize the best elements of Islam and Hinduism. He took from each religion what he believed to be of most importance. From Islam he took the teaching that there is but one God. While Hindus may see this God at work in many ways and in various disguises, still God is basically one. Sikhs refer to this God as "The True Name."

> There is but one God whose name is true, the Creator, devoid of fear and enmity, immortal, unborn, self-existent; by the favor of the Guru.
>
> The True One was in the beginning; the True One was in the primal age.
>
> The True One is now also, O Nanak; the True One also shall be.[2]

---

[1] The same story is told about the death of Kabir.
[2] The Japji, Preamble.

Nanak also taught that "The True Name" is the creator of the entire universe and that human beings are God's supreme creation. Thus Nanak rejected the teaching of *ahimsa*, which is so important to many Indian religions. Since people are the primary creation they are free to kill and eat animals. Sikhs are among the few Indians who may legitimately eat meat.

Nanak adopted several other elements of Hinduism. He accepted the principle of reincarnation, which is basic to many Indian religions. Sikhs came to believe that the spirit of Nanak was reincarnated in the bodies of those gurus who succeeded him as the leaders of Sikhism. Nanak also taught the Indian principle of karma and believed that people continue to acquire karma and live again and again until they are freed from this cycle by "The True Name."

Nanak rejected the ceremonialism and rituals of both Hinduism and Islam. He taught a very plain and simple form of religion which distrusted and rejected ritual.

> The Musalmans praise the Sharia, read it, and reflect on it:
> But God's servants are they who employ themselves in His service in order to behold Him.
> The Hindus praise the Praised One whose appearance and form are incomparable;
> They bathe in holy streams, perform idol-worship and adoration, use copious incense of sandal.
> The Jogis meditate on God the Creator, whom they call the Unseen,
> Whose form is minute, whose name is the Bright One, and who is the image of their bodies.[3]

According to one story, Nanak was ejected from Muslim worship once because he laughed aloud during the sermon of the *imam*. When he was asked why he was so disrespectful to Muslim worship, he replied that he had perceived that the *imam* was not really thinking about God while he was preaching but was in fact thinking about his horse and worrying lest the horse fall into a well. This perception struck Nanak as being so ludicrous that he burst into laughter.

Another element in the religion of Nanak was his pacifism. This man, in all his travels and with all the rejection that he received, maintained the stance of a pacifist. He never struck out at his enemies,

---

[3]Asa Ki War, Slok VI.

and apparently he taught his disciples to follow this pattern. In contrast to the teachings of Nanak, Sikhs, in their later history, became known as the most militant of warriors.

THE HISTORICAL DEVELOPMENT OF SIKHISM

Upon the death of Nanak the leadership of the new movement was taken over by a man named Angad, who ruled until 1552. Nanak and Angad were the first two in a series of ten gurus who led Sikhism until the mid-eighteenth century. Usually the word *guru* in Indian religions has the connotation of "teacher," but to the Sikhs the word means "leader." The first four of the ten gurus of Sikhism tended to follow the teachings of Nanak and to be rather pacific toward their enemies. Angad is remembered because he devised a new script and began to compile the Sikh scriptures. Other gurus followed similar paths.

With the ascension of the fifth guru, Arjan Dev (1563–1606), both the office and the religion underwent significant changes. Arjan is remembered for beginning the compilation of the official scriptures of Sikhism, the *Granth*. The Granth has become increasingly important in Sikhism since the days of the gurus. Basically it is a collection of hymns, a large portion of which came from Nanak. The remainder of the hymns that make up the Granth came from Kabir and other gurus. The Granth contains 3,384 hymns and is roughly three times the size of the Rig-Veda.

In addition to his contribution as the compiler of the Granth, Arjan is remembered for giving Sikhism its militant aspect, in direct contrast to the pacifism of Nanak and the earlier gurus. Between the time of Nanak and that of Arjan, the Sikh movement had grown and was beginning to be recognized as a threat by the Muslim authorities. The Muslim emperor ordered Arjan to remove from the Granth any doctrine that was contrary to the teachings of the Quran. When Arjan refused, he was put into jail and tortured to death. However, before his death he instructed his son Har Gobind, who was to become the sixth guru (1595–1645), to arm and surround himself with bodyguards. The advice of Arjan was accepted, and henceforth the Sikhs were more militant and aggressive in their attitude toward their enemies.

The last of the Sikh gurus was Gobind Singh (1666–1708). He was given the leadership of the Sikhs when he was only a boy because his father, the ninth guru, had been imprisoned and executed by the Muslims. It was Gobind Singh, more than any other guru, who or-

Parade for the ninth Sikh guru.

ganized and prepared the Sikhs for self-defense and war. He introduced into Sikhism the worship of the terrible Hindu goddess of death, Durga. He also established the Granth as the final word for Sikhs. Since Sikhs were to be governed by the Granth there were no more gurus after Gobind Singh's death. Because of his love of weapons he is said to have introduced, as a religious ritual, the baptism of the sword. In order to strengthen his people further and prepare them for war he developed an elite class of Sikhs who made unusually fine warriors. This corps was known as Singhs ("Lions"). They were distinguished in the following ways: They wore the *kes* or long hair on their heads and faces; they adorned their hair with the *kangha* (comb); they wore *kachk* (short trousers); they wore a *kara* (steel bracelet); and they were equipped with a *khanda* (steel dagger). The members of this corps were not allowed the use of wine, tobacco, or any other form of stimulant. They were encouraged to eat meat. The order of the Singhs was open to men of all castes. These factors, combined with the theology of reincarnation, made the Singhs incredible warriors.

Gobind Singh, the last of the gurus, was assassinated in 1708. From that time until the present the Sikhs have been governed by their scripture, the Granth, and their history has been full of strife. At certain times the Sikhs have been the victims of violence, and at other times they have been the aggressors. By the early nineteenth century they controlled most of the Punjab region. When the British sought to enter that area the Sikhs fought bloody wars against them but were finally subdued. Because of their valor as warriors the British came to admire and utilize the Sikhs as soldiers and policemen throughout India. However, with the departure of the British in 1940s and with the

Golden Temple of Amritsar. Devout Sikhs try to visit this temple at least once during their lives.

partition of India into Hindu and Muslim states by the United Nations, the Sikhs have lost their privileged status and once more find themselves in areas of conflict between Hinduism and Islam.

SIKHISM TODAY

Modern Sikhs are found mainly in India, although there are Sikh communities in many other parts of the world. Within the main body of modern Sikhism there are three divisions. Each of these divisions accepts the central teachings of Nanak, each accepts the Granth as sacred scripture, and each accepts the ten gurus as inspired leaders of the faith.

The first sect is called the Udasis and is basically an order of holy men. These Sikhs follow many of the same principles and rules that govern the ascetics of Hinduism, Buddhism, and Jainism. They are celibate, and they wear coarse yellow garments like the Buddhist monks or go naked like Jain monks. Their only possession is a begging bowl. Unlike other Sikhs, the Udasis frequently shave their heads and beards. Often they are active missionaries, seeking to convince nonbelievers of the merit of their religion.

The second sect of Sikhs are the Sahajdharis ("conservative" or "slow-going"). Their development as Sikhs seems to have stopped at some point before Gobind Singh. They reject the militant stance that has become characteristic of much of Sikhism and prefer to be clean shaven.

The third sect is the Singhs, who already have been described.

The religious life of the modern Sikh tends to be simple, probably because of the distrust of elaborate ceremonies that moved the early founders of this religion. One joins the Sikhs not by being born into a Sikh family but by undergoing a ritual of baptism when one is mature enough to accept it. In this ritual a bowl of sweetened water is stirred by a dagger, and the water is sprinkled upon the initiate as the initiate is instructed in the truths and prohibitions of the faith. Just as the initiatory ceremony of Sikhism is simple, so are the ceremonies surrounding marriage and death.

Daily rituals for a Sikh include an early morning bath which is followed by the reading of certain hymns and the recitation of prayers. At night there is another ritual involving hymns and prayers. When Sikhs gather for congregational worship they meet in temples called *gurdwaras*. In these temples the central object of worship is a copy of the sacred Granth. Congregational worship involves prayers to the Granth, various hymns, a sermon, and a communional meal. There are no Sikh priests and the group services may be led by any member of the community. Also there are no caste or sexual differentiations in worship. Men and women of all castes worship side by side.

An object of special attention to Sikhs all over the world is the *Takht* ("throne") of Sikhism at Amritsar. Although there are three other such thrones throughout the Sikh world, the one at Amritsar with its golden temple is central. It is here that the authorities of the Sikh world make decisions regarding the worship and practice of their people. Although Nanak specifically prohibited pilgrimages as worthless for true religion, most Sikhs like to go to Amritsar and plan to visit there at least once in their lives.

SUGGESTED READING

Archer, John Clark. *The Sikhs*. Princeton: Princeton University Press, 1946.

Frost, S. E., ed. *The Sacred Writings of the World's Great Religions*. New York: McGraw-Hill, 1972.

Singh, Harbans. *The Heritage of the Sikhs*. New York: Asia Publishing House, 1964.

Until fairly recent times the religions of China and Japan were relatively unknown to the Western world. However, the missionary movement and modern travel and communication technology have brought us the texts and traditions of Taoism, Confucianism, and Shinto. Within them are found a deep and very modern love for the beauty of nature and the family. Because of this, the Tao Tê Ching of Taoism has become one of the most read and quoted religious texts among college students in the late twentieth century. Today these religions seem to be in decline in the lands of their origin, and yet they have much to teach us.

RELIGIONS ORIGINATING IN
CHINA ᴬᴺᴰ JAPAN

CHINESE RELIGIONS

Portrait of Confucius.

The Wise Man chooses to be last
And so becomes the first of all.

LAO-TZU

It has been said that the Chinese people have no native religions; having been influenced by missionaries from Buddhism, Islam, and Christianity, many Chinese have adopted these religions, giving them Chinese characteristics, but they have never developed a religion of their own. According to this argument Taoism and Confucianism, which are native to China, are not truly religions but philosophies of life or systems of ethics. Indeed Taoism and Confucianism lack many of the elements common to other religions of the world. In their purest forms they are more philosophy than religion. However, religious factors were added to them in later years, and therefore both Taoism and Confucianism deserve discussion in any text that describes the religions of the world.

Another aspect of Chinese religions the Western student may find puzzling is their syncretistic nature. The European or American finds it impossible to be an advocate of more than one religion at a time. The Christian may be tolerant of the views of a Jewish neighbor but could never say, "I am a Christian and I am a Jew," or "I am a Christian and I am a Muslim." The very nature of these religions makes it impossible to adhere to more than one of them at a time. This is not the case with Chinese religions. It is perfectly acceptable for the traditional Chinese to say that he or she is a Buddhist, a Taoist, and a Confucian. This is illustrated in the story of the emperor who asked a Buddhist scholar if he were a Buddhist. The scholar pointed to his Taoist cap. "Are you then a Taoist?" the emperor asked, and the scholar pointed to his Confucian shoes. "Are you then a Confucian?" he asked, and the scholar pointed to his Buddhist scarf. It is not at all unusual for a Buddhist priest to tend a Taoist temple and memorize the teachings of Confucius. This willingness on the part of the Chinese to harmonize the teachings of widely diverse religions must have been maddening to Muslim and Christian missionaries.

Another element that makes the study of Chinese religions difficult for the modern student is that for the past twenty-five years the government of China has been at best neutral and sometimes hostile to any form of religion. All missionaries have been excluded, and the teachings of Lao-tzu and Confucius have been suppressed as hostile to modern China. Therefore we are dealing with religions with which we have had no direct contact for more than twenty-five years, and our sources are at least that old.

The history of religion in China falls into several broad categories. From earliest recorded history until the end of the Shang Dynasty in the eleventh century B.C., the Chinese people apparently followed a basically polytheistic religion intermingled with ancestor worship. From the development of the Chou Dynasty in the eleventh century B.C. until the beginning of the Christian era, the Chinese became aware of one supreme god above all other gods and spirits. The second period was also characterized by an emphasis upon morality, particularly the morality of the rulers. And this was the era that produced Lao-tzu, the legendary founder of Taoism, and Confucius. From the beginning of the Christian era until the eleventh century A.D. Buddhism and religious Taoism developed in China, and for the first time fully developed religious cults are to be found. The fourth general period of religious development extends from the eleventh century to the present. In this period we find an eclectic movement bringing about a synthesis among Buddhism, Taoism, and Confucianism for most of the Chinese people.

BASIC CHINESE RELIGIOUS CONCEPTS

From earliest times the Chinese have held certain religious concepts and practices that later played a part in the development of the philosophies of Taoism and Confucianism. Although the ancient records are sketchy in their description of these concepts, we must examine them first in order to better understand Chinese religions.

The Recognition of Multiple Gods and Spirits

As already stated, the earliest religion of the Chinese people seems to have been based upon the recognition of many gods and spirits which controlled the universe. As it was in the case of many other basic religious groups, the ancient Chinese were apparently polytheistic and animistic in their understanding of the cosmos. The gods of the heavens and the earth received particular attention and sacrifice. In the spring and fall the emperors of ancient China performed elaborate and expensive sacrifices to the gods of the heavens and the earth. Many of these rituals were intended to incur the fertility of the soil and bountiful harvests. Lesser rulers and the common people also performed sacrifices to these spirits.

In addition to the major deities of heaven and earth, the Chinese also recognized several kinds of local deities and spirits. In general the beneficial spirits were known as *Shen*. They were to be found in the bright and lighted places of the earth and were associated with the sun and the spring. The evil spirits were known as *Kwei* and were associated with dark and gloomy places. Generally the common people performed sacrifices and rituals that would put them on good terms with the Shen and keep them safe from the Kwei. Usually animals or grain were sacrificed, but there were occasional records of human sacrifice as the supreme offering to the deities. Archaeological investigations have revealed tombs of wealthy men that have contained the bodies of hundreds of servants and wives who were presumedly buried alive with their master. One record speaks of an emperor who was buried along with all of his wives who had failed to bear him children. One wonders if this was a matter of religious sacrifice or simple revenge. By the end of the Chou Dynasty in the pre-Christian era this practice had ceased. Apparently the practice of burying straw figures or paper likenesses of the victims was instituted as a substitute.

The Yin and the Yang

In searching for a principle to explain the true nature of the universe, the ancient Chinese philosophers developed the concept of the *yin* and the *yang*. What made the universe operate the way it did was understood to be a balance between these two forces. The yin was the negative force in nature. It was seen in darkness, coolness, femaleness, dampness, the earth itself, the moon, and the shadows. The yang was the positive force in nature. It was seen in lightness, brightness, warmth, maleness, dryness, and the sun. Traditionally the yin and the yang were represented by this symbol:

No value judgment was placed upon the yin and the yang. No one said that yin was better than yang or vice versa. No philosopher said that yang was good and yin was evil. The interaction between yin and yang was simply the way the universe operated. Except for a few objects such as the sun or the earth, which were clearly yin or yang, all the rest of nature, humankind, and even events were a combination of both forces. When these two forces were at work in harmony, life was what it should be.

Filial Piety and Ancestor Worship

A characteristic of the Chinese people throughout history has been their respect for and even veneration of aged members of the family. Perhaps the most difficult aspect of Chinese life for modern Western students to understand is this veneration of old age. The legendary founder of Taoism was named Li-poh-yang, but his disciples called him Lao-tzu, which means "Old Master" or "Old Boy." To the Chinese the term *old* or *aged* is not the sign of disrespect that it often is in many Western countries; rather it is the ultimate term of respect. To the Chinese, life may truly be said to begin at sixty when a person reaches the age when he or she is respected. Historically it is the aged father, mother, grandfather, or grandmother who dominates the Chinese home. It is the obligation of the children to support the elderly, to obey them, and to give them proper burial after their death. Even after the parents' death the child is obligated to maintain their grave site, to remember them and their deeds, and to offer sacrifices to them. Western students of Chinese life have often referred to this attitude as "ancestor worship." Indeed there is a religious aspect to these practices. Individuals revere their parents while they are alive and after they are dead. While they are alive the aged represent the wisdom of the family, and after their deaths they may be in a position to help the family further because of their contact with the spirit world. Therefore support of the dead ancestors with remembrance and sacrifices is essential. The Chinese who forget their ancestors are disgraces and will one day become homeless ghosts. Historically the Chinese home is apt to have a small shrine or altar at which the names and deeds of many previous generations of the family are remembered and where small sacrifices of rice and wine may be offered.

Divination

Like many other basic religious groups, the early Chinese believed that the unity of the universe allowed future events to be predicted by some means. Whereas certain ancient religions sought out the future in the patterns of the flight of birds or in the entrails of sacrificed animals or in the ravings of various oracles, the ancient Chinese sought the future in the patterns of the shell of the tortoise or in the stalks of grain. The shell of the tortoise was thought to be especially in touch with the rhythms of the universe because of the long life of its inhabitant. Frequently the shell was heated, and the future was divined by the cracks that appeared in it. Divination among the ancient Chinese probably reached its peak in the development of a book called the I Ching (The Book of Changes), which was edited by Confucius and is still in use today. With the casting of coins or stalks of a plant certain patterns emerge. By identifying these patterns among some sixty-four presented in the I Ching, a statement or prediction is evoked.

Development of Belief in the Shang Ti

Prior to the eleventh century B.C. the religious nature of the Chinese people was basically polytheistic as previously described. In the eleventh century, however, certain political events affected the theology of the Chinese, perhaps for all time. In that century the Chou clans rebelled against the ruling Shang Dynasty. By the end of the century the Chou warriors had effectively completed the rebellion and began a new dynasty that was to rule China for several centuries. The Chou rulers, realizing that they did not have the strength to maintain their empire as the Shang rulers had, began to assert that true rulership had to be based upon morality and religion. They further asserted that there was one supreme god who controlled the destinies of men and rulers. This god was Shang Ti, who had previously been regarded as the patron ancestor of the Shang Dynasty. The Chou rulers showed their genius by asserting that Shang Ti was more than an ancestor; he was the supreme god, and he had been responsible for the fall of the Shang Dynasty because of their immorality. Shang Ti was seen as the rewarder of good morality and the punisher of immorality, particularly among rulers. Therefore government had to be founded upon virtue. While Shang Ti might delight in elaborate sacrifice and ritual, he still loved morality more, and all the sacrifices in the world could not cover up evil. We read of his concern for morality in the ancient *Book of Documents (Shu Ching)*.

> The capital of Shang was full of crime. [The king] was not distressed that the kingdom of Yin was ruined. Nor did he care that the fragrance of virtue should rise up from the sacrifices to plead with *T'ien (Shang Ti)*. Instead the complaints of the people and the rank odour of drunken orgies were felt on high. Therefore *T'ien* determined to destroy Yin. It loved Yin no more, because of Yin's excesses. It is not *T'ien* that is cruel. It is people who bring evil on themselves.[1]
>
> His [King Wen] fame reached up to *Shang Ti* who blessed him. *T'ien* therefore bestowed its great command on King Wen to extirpate the dynasty of Yin, to receive the mandate, and take over its territories and people, that they might be well governed.[2]

Some scholars have suggested that the Chinese at this period were very close to developing an ethical monotheism similar to that enunciated by the Hebrew prophets in the eighth century B.C. However, the emphasis upon morality as a means of satisfying the high god remained in the hands of the rulers, and prophets never arose in this period of Chinese history. Nevertheless, the emperors of China held their thrones with one eye upon the heavens and a concern for personal morality and good government.

The Decline of the Feudal System

During the Chou Dynasty China had been organized and governed by a feudal system similar to that which existed in medieval Europe. The empire was divided into vassal states whose princes were subject to the emperor. The states in turn were subdivided into districts ruled by governors who were vassals to the princes. Each substate supported its lord financially while the lord in turn provided protection for the state. Society was then stratified into ranks. Members of the society knew their ranks and duties. They also knew who was above and below them.

---

[1]Chiu Kao, 11.
[2]K'ang Kao, 4.

In the five centuries between the eighth and third centuries B.C. the feudal system in China began to break down. Lords were no longer able to protect their vassals from invading armies. This led to the development of warlords who could provide protection and command respect. Serfs sometimes became landowners in these upsetting times. Merchant classes began to appear in the cities, and their economic power began to be felt. Old aristocratic families began to find themselves without either wealth or power. In general the feudal world turned upside down. Into this era came the great Chinese schools, each with its own distinctive answer to the problems facing the nation. The Confucians dreamed of a restored idealized form of feudalism as the best government; the legalists wanted nothing to do with feudalism but wished for a strong centralized government; the Taoists wanted no government at all or at least as little government as possible. It was out of this confused milieu that the great Chinese philosophy-religions were born.

TAOISM

Taoism is extremely difficult to define. It can be described in terms of its history and its effects upon the Chinese people, but it cannot be clearly delineated as a religion with a certain body of doctrines and rituals in the same way Islam or Christianity can be described. Its origins are lost in the mists of Chinese antiquity. Little is known of its founder, and indeed there are those who even deny his existence. Its sacred book is more a brief poetical statement of philosophy than a scripture. The name *Taoism* is taken from the title of this book, *Tao Tê Ching*, and is probably best translated as "the way" or "the way of nature." In spite of this seemingly religious title the earliest teachers of Taoism were only vaguely theistic in their beliefs. By the early Christian centuries, however, Taoism had been converted into a religion complete with gods, priests, temples, and sacrifices. In modern China Taoism is mainly associated with ignorance, superstition, and magical attempts to prolong life. A philosophy of nature, a religion, a system of magical practices—Taoism is all of these.

The Life of Lao-tzu

Traditionally the founder of Taoism is thought to be Lao-tzu, who lived in the sixth century B.C., although the basic philosophy of Taoism is probably much older. Little is known about Lao-tzu, and some scholars doubt that he was an historical figure. Legends about him state that he was born approximately fifty years before Confucius, and according to Confucian materials there was a meeting between the two. His original name was Li-poh-yang but he was given the title Lao-tzu ("Old Master" or "Old Boy") by his disciples as a title of respect. It is said that he was the keeper of royal archives in the court of the Chou Dynasty during the tumultuous period when order was breaking down. He tired of the artificial life in court and retired from his post. Journeying to the west, he reached a pass in the mountains at the northwest boundaries of China where he sought to leave the country. The guard of the pass recognized the wise man and refused to allow him to leave until he had committed to writing the sum of his wisdom. Thereupon Lao-tzu sat down and wrote the Tao Tê Ching. When this was completed he was allowed to leave the country and was never seen again. The truth of this story has never been verified. Certainly we know less about the founder of Taoism than we know of any of the other founders of world religions.

The Tao Tê Ching

The book that Lao-tzu was supposed to have written in the sixth century B.C., the Tao Tê Ching, has become the most influential book in Chinese literature except for the Analects of Confucius. The title literally means "The Classic of the Way and Its Power or Virtue." It is a small book made up of slightly more than five thousand words contained in eighty-one chapters and usually translated in poetical form. It has been the object of at least a thousand commentaries and has been translated into English more than forty times. In fact, it has been translated more times than any other book in the world except the Bible and thus is probably the best known of all Chinese books.[3]

That the Tao Tê Ching was written by Lao-tzu in the sixth century B.C. as he waited to be allowed to leave China has been the subject of much scholarly doubt for some time. It is generally agreed that the book was developed over many centuries and evolved into its present form sometime around the fourth century B.C. Arthur Waley suggests that the book was written in the third century B.C. as a polemic against the Confucians and Legalists who wished for either an idealized form of feudalism or some strong central government.[4] The theme of the

---

[3] An exception to this in the last twenty-five years would be the writings of Chairman Mao.

[4] Arthur Waley, *The Way and Its Power* (London: George Allen & Unwin, 1956), p. 86.

Tao Tê Ching is that all of peoples' achievements are folly, especially elaborate government.

The Teachings of the Early Taoist Philosophers

The beliefs of the early Taoists are difficult to ascertain. Our two major sources for the Taoism of the pre-Christian era are of course the Tao Tê Ching and the writing of a fourth century B.C. disciple of Lao-tzu, Chuang-tzu. Chuang-tzu covered the field of Taoism as it was practiced by the early devotees. He collected this material into a book and used it to try to convince the Chinese to accept Lao-tzu instead of Confucius as their main teacher. The teachings of early Taoism as found in these books center around the following themes:

1. *The basic unity behind the universe is a mysterious and undefinable force called the Tao.* Usually the word *Tao* is defined as "the way," and it may best be understood in terms of "the way of the universe" or perhaps "nature's way." Yet the true Tao is impossible to define. The Tao Tê Ching begins with the following admonition:

> The Way (Tao) that can be told of is not an Unvarying Way
> (Tao);
> The names that can be named are not unvarying names.[5]

Nameless and undefinable though it may be, the Tao is the source of the universe.

> It was from the Nameless that Heaven and Earth sprang;
> The named is but the mother that rears the ten thousand
> creatures, each after its kind.[6]

Even the gods, along with all the rest of the universe, seem to have evolved from the flow of the Tao.

Though the Tao is defined as "the way," it is most often compared to a stream or a moving body of water as it progresses endlessly and inexorably. As water wears away the hardest stone or metal and carries off buildings in its path, it is useless to struggle against the Tao. Therefore the ancient Taoist philosophers believed that all humankinds' accomplishments and monuments will sooner or later be destroyed by the Tao. Peoples' greatest buildings will fall into decay, their hard-won

---

[5] Ibid., p. 141.
[6] Ibid.

knowledge will be superseded, their wealth will fail, and even the sharpest sword will become dull. For this reason it behooved people not to struggle against the Tao but to seek to blend with it and be guided by it. True Taoists live quiet and simple lives. They avoid any achievement except that of seeking to understand the Tao.

2. *Life is the greatest of all possessions.* Because of their belief in the Tao as the source of all life and their belief in the folly of achievement, the early Taoist philosophers taught that life itself was the greatest of possessions; all others were doomed to decay. Fame, wealth, power, and education were mere flitting, transient illusions, literally here today and gone tomorrow. If people are not interested in the acquisition of goods, power, or education, then they can give their full attention to the enrichment of their own lives. This led the Taoists to search whereby life might be lengthened, and eventually they employed various magical practices in an attempt to prolong and enrich life.

3. *Life is to be lived simply.* Believing that all life originated from the Tao which would ultimately destroy peoples' achievements, the early Taoists turned their backs upon civilization with all its ills and benefits and sought to live as simply as possible. Some of them were literally hermits. Possibly they were motivated by the same emotions that drove some Hindus into the ascetic life or some early Christians into the deserts to live on pillars or in caves. Possibly Thoreau was motivated by these same feelings when he turned his back upon early American life and chose to live simply at Walden Pond. In every generation there are those who see the folly in civilization and seek to avoid it. The Taoist philosophers may have carried this dream to its greatest extreme. They considered that education, wealth, power, family ties were all worthless and in fact impediments to living.

> Banish wisdom, discard knowledge,
> And the people will be benefited a hundredfold.
> Banish human kindness, discard morality,
> And the people will be dutiful and compassionate.
> Banish skill, discard profit,
> And thieves and robbers will disappear.
> If when these three things are done they find life too plain and
>   unadorned,
> Then let them have accessories;
> Give them Simplicity to look at, the Uncarved Block to hold,
> Give them selflessness and fewness of desires.[7]

---

[7] Ibid., p. 166.

Ideally, individuals should turn their backs upon the advancements of civilization and live as simply and as quietly as possible. The word *innocence* characterizes the ideal state. Like the plants and the creatures of the earth, innocent human beings are content with what the Tao has ordained for them. According to early Taoist philosophers, there should be little government in the ideal state. In fact it was an axiom of the Taoists that the least government is the best government. Lao-tzu is remembered for saying, "Govern a great nation as you would cook a small fish"—do not overdo it.[8] The small village is the ideal unit of society. The best ruler is the one who rules least and is virtually anonymous. If all this were the case, all strivings, quarrels, and wars would cease. Taoism is pacific, not out of any moral commitment to pacifism, but because warring is useless and wasteful. If a larger, stronger state wished the territory of the quiet Taoist village, the village should simply submit to the larger state. In the long run there will be no grief because of this decision, and the village ultimately will conquer the large state with its humility.

The early Taoists looked upon the innocence of the child as an ideal towards which all human beings should strive. The infant knows no craft; and has no ambitions but to live; yet the child is cared for, fed, and clothed. The weakness and softness of the infant are the ideals of Taoism.

4. *Pomp and glory are to be despised.* Because the Taoists were concerned with living according to the path of nature as simply as possible, they despised the fame, pomp, and glory that most people seek. They saw such things as the cause of strife and discord in society. If each person were only content to live as the Tao intended, without seeking to rise above other people, then life would be as it was intended. This attitude also contained a condemnation of pride. It was a Chinese teaching, perhaps older than Taoism, that pride invited destruction, that the tree which stood taller than its neighbors would be the first felled by the woodsman. Therefore it is better to be humble, small, or imperfect than to stand out from all the rest.

> To remain whole, be twisted!
> To become straight, let yourself be bent.
> To become full, be hollow.
> Be tattered, that you may be renewed.
> Those that have little, may get more,

---

[8]Herbert A. Giles, *Religions of Ancient China* (Freeport, N.Y.: Books for Libraries Press, 1969), p. 47.

Those that have much, are but perplexed.
Therefore the Sage
Clasps the Primal Unity,
Testing by it everything under heaven.
He does not show himself; therefore he is seen everywhere.
He does not define himself, therefore he is distinct.
He does not boast of what he will do, therefore he succeeds.
He is not proud of his work, and therefore it endures.
He does not contend,
And for that very reason no one under heaven can contend
with him.

So then we see that the ancient saying "To remain whole, be twisted!" was no idle word; for true wholeness can only be achieved by return.[9]

Perhaps the best example of the Taoists' contempt for pomp, glory, rank, and wealth is the story of Chuang-tzu, the fourth century B.C. Taoist philosopher. Chuang-tzu was widely regarded for his wisdom and was offered the position of prime minister by Prince Wei of Ch'u. When the messengers of the prince brought this offer, Chuang is said to have replied in the following manner:

You offer me great wealth and a proud position indeed; but have you never seen the sacrificial ox? When after being fattened up for several years, it is decked with embroidered trappings and led to the altar, would it not willingly then change places with some uncaring pigling? . . . Begone! defile me not! I would rather disport myself to my own enjoyment in the mire than be a slave to a ruler of a state. I will never take office. Thus I shall remain free to follow my own inclinations.[10]

History does not record the response of the prince whose offer was spurned with such contempt.

There is little in this early form of Taoism that can be called religion. The Tao itself is a vague and impersonal force behind the universe and is more of a First Cause than a god, in any traditional sense of the word. In one translation of the Tao Tê Ching the word *god* is

---

[9]Waley, *The Way and Its Power*, p. 177.
[10]D. Howard Smith, *Chinese Religions* (New York: Holt, Rinehart & Winston, 1968), p. 71.

此是老君爺手托八卦面放金

爐鐵行人供之

Watercolor of Lao-Chün. The inscription reads, "This is Lao-Chün, worshiped by ironsmiths."

used only once[11] and in many translations it does not appear at all. Only rarely does the term *heaven* appear. The Tao is not conceived of as a force to whom one can pray or sacrifice, and the early Taoists seem to have had no rituals for worship. In fact, they may have been rejecting religion and all its accoutrements as a part of their rejection of the Confucians who placed a very high value upon rituals.

---

[11]"How pure and still the Tao is. I do not know whose song it is. It might appear to have been before God." *The Sacred Books of the East* (Second Impression. New York, 1927), Vol. XXXIX. Tao-Tê-Ching, 1:4, 2b, 3.

173

The early Taoists also seem to have had no concern for life after death. One of the most frequently remembered tales of Chuang-tzu concerns an occasion following his wife's death. His disciples sought to comfort him in his time of mourning but found him singing and beating time on a wooden bowl.

> "To live with your wife," exclaimed Hui-tzu, "and see your eldest son grow up to be a man, and then not to shed a tear over her corpse—this would be bad enough. But to drum on a bowl and sing; surely this is going too far!" "Not at all," replied Chuang-tzu. "When she died I could not help being affected by her death. Soon, however, I remembered that she had already existed in a previous state before her birth, without form or even substance; that while in that unconditioned condition, substance was added to spirit; that this substance then assumed form; and that the next state was birth. And now, by virtue of a further change, she is dead, passing from one phase to another like the sequence of spring, summer, autumn and winter. And while she is thus lying asleep in eternity, for me to go about weeping and wailing would be to proclaim myself ignorant of these natural laws. Therefore I refrain."[12]

If there was any concern for life after death among the ancient Taoists, it does not appear in any of the extant writings. In general the Taoists were concerned about the quality of life as it is lived on a day-to-day basis without much interest in the heavens, the gods, rituals, or life after death.

Schools that Rivaled the Early Taoists

The fourth and third centuries B.C. were eras of chaos in China. The old governmental structure of feudalism was breaking down; invaders regularly made inroads into the country; the social order was in a state of flux; and the ancient systems of values were seriously being questioned. The Taoist philosophers and their challenge to existing values and structures were, of course, a part of that era. Other philosophers, politicians, and teachers held other views of life and government and toured the nation. According to Arthur Waley,

---

[12] Ibid., p. 73.

Every Court in China was infested by "journeying philosophers" each in turn pressing upon a bewildered ruler the claims of Activism, of Quietism, of morality, of non-morality, of force, of non-resistance, of individualism, of State supremacy. In one thing only were they united; each claimed to possess the secret "art of ruling" whereby the Ancestors had grown mighty in the past.[13]

In addition to the Taoists there were three major schools of thought that were dominant in those days. These were the Confucians, the Legalists, and the Mohists.

The Confucians. More will be said about the school of Confucius in the following section. However, it must be noted here that its members were rivals to the Taoists in the fourth and third centuries B.C. in advising the rulers of China on government. Whereas the Taoists believed that the least government was the best government, the disciples of Confucius believed that an idealized feudal system was the best form of government. Whereas the Taoists had little use for formal religion, the Confucians at least believed that the rites and rituals of religion served the function of uniting the people. Whereas the Taoists believed that the best society was one with little structure, the Confucians taught that society needed an elaborate structure reinforced by etiquette to be effective.

The Legalists. A second group that vied for the attention of the rulers of China during this period was a large one that followed no specific teacher; its members were known as "Legalists" or "Realists." These people believed that human nature and the condition of China at the time demanded strong, tough leadership. To them human nature tended to be wicked and lazy. People followed the line of least resistance. If left to their own devices people would make decisions that would be bad for society as a whole. Therefore government should be run under what Westerners might call Machiavellian principles. Government should not be affected by morality or pity. People do not need love or pity . . . they need food and houses. Thus leaders of government should determine what is best for the majority of society and take the hard steps necessary to achieve these ends. If this means hardship

---

[13]Waley, *The Way and Its Power*, p. 70.

for the minority it should not affect the decisions. In their scheme of things the Legalists had no room for religion. Money and time spent on sacrifices to the gods could be better spent on good government. Naturally these teachers had little in common with the passive Taoist sages.

The Mohists. The third group that sought to influence government during the fourth and third centuries were the Mohists. These teachers were disciples of Mo-tzŭ, who lived in the fifth century B.C. (ca. 468–390). Mo-tzŭ began his career as a Confucian but later broke away to form his own distinctive philosophy. He and his disciples believed that the best government operates under the direction of the traditional Chinese religions. Under these religions people are taught to love one another; thus, the government would operate from a position of love. The Mohists were pacifists who despised warfare, yet they recognized the necessity of self-defense and allowed the possibility of building fortifications.

Though there were probably many representatives of each of these distinct philosophies, it is doubtful that any of them had serious influence on the governors of China except perhaps the Legalists. Nevertheless the teachings of the Taoists, the Confucians, and the Mohists have been held up as ideals for the Chinese people in a strange eclecticism for thousands of years.

The Later Development of Taoism

Basically Taoism as it is seen in the Tao Tê Ching and in the essays of Chuang-tzu was concerned with living life in harmony with the basic force behind nature, the Tao. As a pure philosophy this appealed to a small group of persons who were malcontent with the intricacies of society and government, but it probably never had wide appeal to the populace.

However, after the period of the early philosophers, Taoism did develop wide appeal for the masses and is frequently listed among the major religions of the world. This development from a philosophy for the few to a religion for the many is a fascinating story.

Following the period of the early Taoist philosophers two kinds of Taoists seem to have developed. One group followed the philosophical writings of Lao-tzu and Chuang-tzu. The second group were searching for immortality, not in the sense of life after death as taught by many other religions, but in an endless extension of the present life through various devices. The philosophers had taught that life was the greatest of all possessions and that the person whose life was properly attuned to the Tao might have long life. This appealed to the Chinese people, who look forward to old age and the relative ease and honor that it has traditionally brought in Chinese culture. Taking up this aspect of Taoism, scholars, priests, and magicians began to seek the means whereby life could be extended indefinitely. They sought every possible means, including special dietary regulations. Some came to believe that all foods, particularly solid foods, were poisonous and tried to train their bodies to live on only a very little liquid food. Some claimed that eventually they were able to live on only saliva and air. Others practiced fasting and breath control in a manner similar to that of the Indian Yogin.

Still another popular means of extending life was the use of alchemy. Some believed that since dead meat could be preserved from decay by salt, living flesh might be preserved by some other mineral such as gold. One can only guess at the outcomes of some of these experiments in longevity. Nevertheless the hope that immortality might be achieved did not die among the Chinese. Regarding one of the leaders of these movements it was said by a contemporary:

> He abstained from cereals, escaped old age, knew the method to avoid dying, and transmuted cinnabar. When he died, it was said that he had been transformed and, on opening his tomb several years later, they found no corpse there but only his cap and clothing.[14]

The Taoist alchemist seeking to work his magic soon became concerned with gods that might be involved in the process. Since the alchemists worked at the stove they began to offer sacrifices to the god of the stove, Tsao Chun. Thus it is said that Tsao Chun by third century A.D. became the first god of Taoism. The process of apotheosis continued until there were many, many Taoist gods. And so a philosophy that began by essentially denying personal gods developed its own gods.

By the second century A.D. the Tao Tê Ching had been officially recognized as a Chinese classic and soon was on its way to becoming the Taoist scripture. Those who were seeking immortality came to believe that the only way they could achieve this was through the

---

[14]Smith, *Chinese Religions*, p. 100.

practice of morality and virtuous deeds toward their fellow human beings. Thus the elements found in most religions gradually began to creep into Taoism.   •

Also in the second century the Han Dynasty, which had ruled China for several centuries, began to break down. During this time of chaos there arose certain charismatic Taoist leaders. Several of these people not only led in the search for immortality but also gathered together great armies of followers and participated in wars in a most un-Taoist fashion. With the organization that these people brought, with the concern for faith healing, the search for immortality, and the other religious accoutrements of gods, morality, temples, priests, rituals, and so on, Taoism became one of the religions, if not *the* religion, of the masses of the Chinese people by the beginning of the third century A.D.

Since there were contacts between India and China from very early times and since Buddhism under the influence of Asoka had become a missionary religion, doubtless there were Buddhist missionaries and traders in China as early as the third century B.C. However, the early contacts the Chinese had with Buddhism were with its Theravada branch. It is likely that this version of Buddhism with its emphasis on individual salvation through a monastic life was far too Indian for the Chinese, and therefore it made little headway in China. In later years there came the development of Mahayana Buddhism with its rich rituals, its many gods, its heavens and hells, and its promise of salvation through more traditional religious means. There also came extraordinary missionaries like the legendary Bodhidharma who brought the *dhyana* version of Mahayana Buddhism from India to China in the fifth century A.D. In China as in most Asian nations, this version of the teachings of the Buddha appealed tremendously to the masses.

By the fourth century A.D. Mahayana Buddhism was a force to be reckoned with by the Taoists. At first there seems to have been no rivalry between the two religions. The Taoists helped the Buddhists translate their texts into Chinese, and the Buddhists used Taoist terms to explain Buddhist concepts. However, as Buddhism became more popular among the Chinese people the Taoists began to recognize it as a threat. Fierce struggles arose between the two groups to determine who would have influence with the various rulers and thus control the provinces. In a most uncharacteristic fashion each religion became hostile to the other, and even persecution developed. In the ninth century the emperor Wu Tsung, who was greatly influenced by Taoist priests, ran a vast persecution of the Buddhists, destroying numerous temples. At other times Buddhists influenced the rulers to discriminate against the Taoists.

The struggle between the Buddhists and the Taoists was settled more by syncretism than by persecution. Each religion borrowed from the other until they both became associated, along with the teachings of Confucius, as the common religion of the Chinese people. Taoism borrowed widely from the Mahayana teachings of an afterlife with heavens and hells and judgment. The Buddhists followed their traditional pattern of accepting the native gods and heroes of the land as Buddhist bodhisattvas and the Taoists sought to turn the tables by asserting that Lao-tzu and others were created before the foundations of the earth and were thus superior to the Buddha. All in all the Taoists seem to have copied the most. By the sixth century A.D. the Taoists had taken the Buddhist pattern of monasticism. Their priests could now live in monasteries and in some cases were commanded to be celibate. Nunneries were established fo the Taoist women who wished the celibate life. By the tenth century the shape of Taoism was established, and it changed little during the next ten centuries.

Taoism, with its religious side fully developed and with its traditional emphasis upon magical means of extending life, continued to have its hold upon the common people of China into the twentieth century. The upper classes and the intellectuals of China continued to read the Tao Tê Ching and other classics of philosophical Taoism, but they tended to regard the religion itself as fit only for the ignorant masses. The twentieth century with its various revolutions in China brought about the end of any official support for Taoism, however. The current Chinese government looks upon it as superstition and tends to discourage it as it discourages all forms of religion.

CONFUCIANISM

Since Confuciansim is generally considered to be one of the major religions of the world, it might be appropriate to discuss it in a separate chapter rather than include it as a part of a general chapter on the religions of China. However, in its origins and development, Confucianism, like Taoism, is inextricably interwoven into the total philosophy of the Chinese people. Therefore, to lift Confucianism out and set it into a chapter apart from Taoism and Chinese religious thinking would be to present it in an unreal situation.

As in the case of Taoism, we begin the discussion of Confucianism by asking if it is truly a religion. There are those who contend that the teachings of Confucius and his disciples were never intended to be a religion, that Confucius was probably an atheist who discouraged prayer to the gods as worthless, and whose main concern was the nature of human society. If Confucianism is a religion it is a very different kind of religion. It has no priesthood, its sacred writings have never been considered a revelation from the gods like the Vedas or the Quran, it has frowned upon asceticism and monasticism, and it has no doctrine of an afterlife. In spite of all of these nonreligious aspects there have been some cultic developments in the history of Confucianism, and its philosophy has deeply affected the Chinese character. Therefore Confucianism deserves at least to be inspected as a possible world religion.

The Life of Confucius

The man whom the West knows as Confucius was really named Kung. When he became a famous teacher his disciples referred to him as Kung, the master (Kung Fu-tse). As his teachings became known to Western missionaries and scholars the name was Latinized to "Confucius."

Although Confucius was born in the sixth century B.C., because of the influence that he and his disciples had upon the Chinese people, the biographical material about him is extensive and fairly reliable. This is in marked contrast to the life of Lao-tzu, who also lived in the sixth century but about whom we know almost nothing. The earliest and most authentic material about Confucius is the Analects of Confucius, a collection of his teachings that was compiled about seventy years after his death. In addition to the biographical material in Confucian literature, Confucius is mentioned in the writings of the contemporary Taoists and Mohists. No one seriously doubts the historicity of Confucius.

Confucius was born in 551 B.C. in the state of Lu (now in modern Shantung). He was the child of an aristocratic family which had lost its wealth and position in the decline of the feudal states of China during that chaotic period. His father was said to have been a famous warrior of gigantic size and strength who was seventy years old when Confucius was conceived. The father died shortly before the birth of the child, and Confucius was reared in poverty by his widowed mother. Although his mother had to struggle for survival she was determined to provide her son with an education. Therefore Confucius was allowed to study with the village tutor. The biographies say that he studied subjects that were the traditional fare of Chinese students of his time: poetry, the history of China, music, hunting, fishing, and archery. He seems to have been extremely interested in the interworkings of society even as a youth; particularly in what constituted good government. This was to be his main theme for the rest of his life.

In his late teens he accepted a minor position in government, where he was to closely observe the ruling process. He married and fathered one son but the marriage ended in divorce. We know little about the wife or family of Confucius beyond these scanty facts. However, there are still Chinese today who claim to be the physical descendants of Confucius. While in his mid-twenties his mother died, and, being the devoted son that he was, Confucius mourned for her for three years.

Sometime during his twenties Confucius began his true career, that of a teacher. His reputation as a man of learning allowed him to establish himself as a teacher of young people. In the following years his reputation spread widely and he attracted many students. They lived in his home and followed him in his journeys. He taught them history, the principles of good government, and divination.[15]

Legend has it that at the age of fifty Confucius was finally able to put some of his principles of good government into practice when he was asked to join the government of the Duke of Lu as its prime minister. According to these pious Confucian legends Confucius's government was ideal. During the period of his leadership the state was so well governed that the crime rate dropped to almost nothing. People stopped locking their doors and a wallet dropped on the street was left untouched for days. However, the enemies of Confucius became jealous of his success and conspired against him. Consequently he was forced to retire from government at the age of fifty-five.

During the next twelve years of his life Confucius was a man without a position. He wandered from place to place with a few of his faithful disciples. Sometimes he was accepted by the populace and treated hospitably. At other times he and his friends were jeered at and even placed in jail. Finally, when he was sixty-seven years of age, a position was found for him as an advisor to the Duke of Ai. While this was not as important as the position he had formerly held, it at least gave Confucius a home for himself and his disciples. During the next

---

[15]The principal form of divination taught by Confucius was probably the Chinese classic, the *I Ching*. Current versions of the *I Ching* are believed to have been edited by Confucius.

Confucius' birthday ceremony at Taipei, Taiwan.

years he spent his time teaching and compiling some of the classical Chinese texts. The master died in the year 479 B.C. and was widely mourned by his disciples. According to one tradition his most faithful disciple built a hut beside the grave and stayed to mourn Confucius for three years.

The Teachings of Confucius

Confucius's attitude toward religion has been a point of great debate; on the one hand some regard him as the founder of one of the world's great religions, and on the other there are those who believe that he was an agnostic if not an atheist. The truth about Confucius's teachings on religion probably lies somewhere between the two extremes. Relative to his contemporaries he was somewhere in the middle of the spectrum with Lao-tzu on the left, denying the validity of religions, and Mo-tzŭ on the right, advocating a return to the ancient religions of China.

Confucius seems to have believed that, while the gods existed and worship and rituals were of value in bringing people together, these things were of secondary importance when compared to an equitable social order. When praying to the spirits interfered with a person's proper social duties, prayer should be secondary. His attitude seems to have been that ideally one should respect the spirits but keep them at a distance.[16] Even though Confucius was not an atheist or antireligious, there is no evidence to suggest that he was interested in starting a religion. In the strictest sense of the word, Confucianism cannot be called a religion. Rather it is a system of ethics, a theory of government, a set of personal and social goals that have deeply influenced the Chinese for almost twenty-five centuries

The teachings of Confucius were based around certain central themes. One of these themes is represented by the word *li*. *Li* has been variously translated into English as "propriety," "rites," "ceremonies," and "courtesy." Originally it may have meant the grain found in wood or the pattern in jade. Basically the word seems to mean "the course of life as it is intended to go," and of course it has religious and social connotations. When society lives by *li* it moves smoothly. Men and women respect their elders and superiors. The proper rituals and ceremonies are preformed. Everything and everyone is in its proper place. Naturally the principle of *li* was most closely followed when an idealized form of feudalistic government existed. In such a state all people know their superiors and inferiors and are able to act in the genteel manner that Confucius believed was necessary for a smooth society. Furthermore Confucius believed that China in his day was in a state of chaos because the people were no longer living according to the principles of *li*.

One of the Confucian classics, the Li Chi, whose primary subject is *li*, records the following conversation:

> Duke Ai asked Confucius, "What is the great *li*? Why is it that you talk about *li* as though it were such an important thing?"
> Confucius replied, "Your humble servant is really not worthy to understand *li*."

---

[16]Analects 6:20.

"But you do constantly speak about it," said Duke Ai.

Confucius: "What I have learned is this, that of all the things that people live by, *li* is the greatest. Without *li*, we do not know how to conduct a proper worship of the spirits of the universe; or how to establish the proper status of the king and the ministers, the ruler and the ruled, and the elders and the juniors; or how to establish the moral relationships between the sexes; between parents and children, and between brothers; or how to distinguish the different degrees of relationships in the family. That is why a gentleman holds *li* in such high regard.[17]

According to Confucius, there were five basic relationships in life. If *li* were present in these relationships throughout society, then the social order would be ideal. These five relationships are:

1. Father to son. There should be kindness in the father and filial piety in the son.

2. Elder brother to younger brother. There should be gentility in the elder brother and humility in the younger.

3. Husband to wife. There should be righteous behavior in the husband and obedience in the wife.

4. Elder to junior. There should be consideration among the elders and deference among the juniors.

5. Ruler to subject. There should be benevolence among the rulers and loyalty among the subjects.

In Confucian ideals the principle of *li* was the outward expression of the superior man toward others in his society. The inward expression of Confucian ideals was called *jen*. *Jen* is frequently translated into English with words such as "love," "goodness," and "humaneness." According to Confucius, only the great sages of antiquity truly possessed *jen*, but it was a quality that all men should seek to develop. The pursuit of this quality is mentioned many times in the Analects of Confucius.

Jen is of more importance to people than fire and water. I have seen men die through walking through water or fire, but I have never seen a man die through walking in *jen*.[18]

---

[17]Li Chi, XXVII.
[18]Analects 15:34.

> *Jen* is self-denial and a return to propriety *(li)*. For by self-
> denial and a return to propriety the whole world would return
> to *jen*.[19]

Thus Confucius taught that people should love one another and
practice respect and courtesy toward each other in their daily lives. He
did not go so far as Jesus did and command that people should ex-
change good for evil nor did he command, "So whatever you wish that
men would do to you do so to them. . . . "[20] Rather Confucius taught
that society was best served when people acted toward each other with
reciprocity.

> Tzu Kung asked: "Is there any one word that can serve as a
> principle for the conduct of life?"
> Confucius said: "Perhaps the word, 'reciprocity': Do not do
> to others what you would not want others to do to you."[21]

(Confucians know the law of reciprocity as *shu*.)

If the principles of *li* and *jen* were present and operative in a person
the end product is the Confucian goal, the superior human being.
Apparently Confucius believed in the natural goodness or at least in
the natural perfectibility of humankind, although it is not so clear in
his teachings as it is in the work of his disciple Mencius. This teaching
places the Confucians in direct contrast to those philosophies such as
Christianity that believe people's natural state is evil and needs divine
intervention for salvation. Confucius apparently believed that under
the proper circumstances it was possible for individuals to achieve
goodness and to eventually achieve the status of the superior human
being.

One of the circumstances necessary for persons to achieve goodness
was a good government. Confucius believed that poor government
with bad laws caused people to do evil, and that a generation of good
rulership can cure most of the moral ills of a people. A good example
set by the ruling classes will bring out the true morality of the people.
Because of the natural morality of humanity Confucius believed that it
was not necessary to offer people rewards or punishments in order to
induce them to good conduct. Good conduct is its own reward. Therefore, whatever Confucius might have believed about the gods, he

---

[19]Ibid.,12:1.
[20]Matthew 7:12.
[21]Analects 15:23.

never spoke of an afterlife in heaven or hell to reward good deeds or punish evil. Under the proper conditions people simply grow and develop into what Confucius called the "Superior Man."

The Development of Confucianism

When Confucius died in 479 B.C. his teachings were remembered and followed by only a small group of disciples. He had not had the success as a ruler he had hoped for, and his teachings had not received widespread support. Nor did the rulers of China open their doors to his immediate disciples. However, in the next five hundred years the disciples of Confucius began to take a major part in training and advising the rulers of China to such an extent that his teachings became an integral part of Chinese culture.

After the death of Confucius approximately seventy of his disciples scattered out across the empire. Some sought positions as advisior to rulers while others tried to begin schools of their own. They were not spectacularly successful in either of these attempts for at least two reasons. First, there was the opposition of the rival schools, the Taoists, the Legalists, and later the Mohists, who all claimed to have the key to good government for the official who would listen. Second, the disciples of Confucius taught that the best form of government was an idealized feudalism, and they were teaching this in a time when the feudal society was breaking down all over China. They were out of step with their time. Nevertheless the disciples did manage to reach a few attentive ears with both their teaching and their advising, and Confucius's teaching was perpetuated. In the fourth and third centuries B.C. there arose two of the most outstanding Confucians of all times, Mencius and Hsün Tzǔ, who did much to popularize and spread the teachings of Confucius.

In Chinese thought the sage of China second only to Confucius is Confucius' latter-day disciple, the man who is known to us as Mencius.[22] Mencius was born approximately one hundred years after the death of Confucius and lived from 372–289 B.C. We are not certain about a great many details in his life, but like many of the ancients there is an abundance of legend about him. Much of the legendary material about Mencius apparently is intended to draw parallels between him and Confucius. We are told that like Confucius, Mencius

---

[22]His real name was Meng and his private name was K'o, but his Chinese name has been Latinized by Western scholars to Mencius.

was the only child of a poor widow who struggled to support her son and to provide him with education. Like Confucius, Mencius became a teacher and sought a position as a political advisor. Also like his master his advice was not wanted, and he too wandered about teaching his disciples. More substantial tradition says that Mencius studied under the disciples of Tzu Ssu, the grandson of Confucius, and was in fact an ineffective advisor to some of the Chinese rulers of his day.

The teachings of Mencius have been maintained in the Book of Mencius. From this text and others his contribution as a Confucian scholar can be learned. Like Confucius, Mencius was not terribly interested in religion. Little is said about the gods in his writings, and no attempt is made to influence people to return to the worship of the traditional Chinese gods. Mencius's major ethical position was a reinforcement of Confucius's teaching of the natural goodness of human beings. Whereas this teaching had not been terribly clear in Confucius, it become crystal clear in Mencius. The latter strongly asserted that human nature was basically good. He observed that all people did not act in a virtuous manner, but this is because of their environment. Given the proper environment it is possible for all people to be virtuous. Naturally for a Confucian scholar the best environment is that which occurred in a government based upon paternalistic feudalism which was operated for the benefit of the people. Thus he distinguished between the feudal tyrant and the sage-king.

He who uses force and makes a pretence of virtue is a *pa* (tyrant). He who using virtue practises human-heartedness is a king. . . . When one subdues men by force, they do not submit in their hearts and only submit because their strength is insufficient. When one subdues men by virtue, in their heart of hearts they are pleased and sincerely submit.[23]

Since war destroyed the possibility for the kind of just and honorable conditions under which human goodness could develop, Mencius was opposed to war. On the other hand, since people were the most important element in any state, if the government were oppressive Mencius believed that persons had the right to revolt against it. In many ways Mencius sharpened the focus of Confucius's teachings, and in other ways he added his own distinctive ideas to the Confucian canon.

---

[23]The Book of Mencius, 2a.4.

The second most famous Confucian interpreter was Hsün Tzǔ, who lived in the generation after Mencius (298–238 B.C.). Whereas Mencius has come to be regarded as the orthodox interpreter of Confucius, Hsün Tzǔ is regarded as the heterodox interpreter; yet Hsün Tzǔ had a greater impact upon his times. Some authorities even give him credit for the development of Confucianism during the Han Dynasty (206 B.C.–220 A.D.).[24] He was a native of Chao and a widely respected and revered scholar. In his later years he served as a magistrate of the city of Lan-Ling. Beyond these bare facts we know little about the man.

Hsün Tzǔ is remembered for two major contributions to Confucian thought. First, he, even more than Confucius himself, believed in the worth of rites (li) as devices that would bring people together and educate them.

> What is the origin of rites? I say: Man is born with desires. If he does not get what he desires, he can but seek for it. If there are no degrees or limits to his seeking, he can but contend with others. Contention leads to disorder and disorder leads to exhaustion. As ancient kings hated such disorder, they established rites and moral principles to bring about the proper shares in order to nourish men's desires and meet their demands. They made it possible that men's desires did not exhaust the material supplies and the material supplies did not suppress the desires. Both desires and material supplies support each other and thus grew. This is how rites originated. . . . [25]

The second contribution of Hsün Tzǔ, and the one for which he is more famous, is his denial of the basic goodness of humankind. In direct contradiction to the teachings of Mencius, Hsün Tzǔ contended that people were basically evil in nature. He believed that goodness can only come through proper training. Therefore training, laws, and restraint are necessary in order that society might survive. This made rites all the more important, because it is through rites that people are trained in proper living. Added to this teaching was Hsün Tzǔ's belief that the spirits of the heavens were basically impersonal forces. For

---

[24]D. Howard Smith, *Chinese Religions*, p. 54.
[25]Hsün Tzǔ, Chapter 19.

this reason Hsün Tzŭ appears as the most nonreligious of all the early Confucian scholars.

The rise of the Han Dynasty marked a new era in Chinese history. The period preceding it had been one of chaos and political upheaval. When the Han rulers came to power they needed great numbers of new administrators and advisors. This new market for political theorists attracted many scholars who had been trained by the disciples of Confucius. The Confucians' position was further strengthened when in 136 B.C. they were placed in charge of the education of Chinese youth, particularly those youth who would eventually govern. From that date until 1905 A.D. Chinese education included a study of the teachings of Confucius. Master Kung himself could not have devised a system in which his philosophy would have had more influence over the future of China.

In addition to the development of Confucianism as the leading educational theory of China, in the years of the Han Dynasty there developed a cult of Confucius himself. The ruler of the state of Lu is said to have mourned for Confucius after his death and built a shrine to him. However, with the coming of the Han rulers and the ascendancy of the Confucian scholars the reverence for him increased dramatically. In 195 B.C. the first of the Han emperors visited the grave of Confucius and offered a pig, a sheep, and an ox as sacrifices. Fifty years later a temple was built to Confucius in his native town. By 8 B.C. titles and land were given to his descendants. The practice of awarding posthumous titles to Confucius himself began, and he was given the title of Duke. Gradually the temples and the ceremonies increased in number all over China. By the sixth century A.D. every prefecture in China had a temple to Confucius, and some people came to look upon his as a god. However, there never developed a popular religion about Confucius. He was generally regarded as the patron saint or ancestor of the Chinese scholar, and he was remembered and revered as one would remember any ancestor.

The growth of the Confucian cult was set back in 1503 when the images of Confucius were ordered removed from the temples and replaced with wooden tablets upon which were inscribed his teachings. In addition all the titles that had been given were removed, and he was known simply as "Master Kung, the perfect teacher of antiquity." In 1906 there was an attempt to restore the Confucian cult to some of its original glory, but with the birth of the People's Republic of China the sacrifices to Confucius, along with the other "great sacrifices," were abandoned.

SUGGESTED READING

Giles, Herbert A. *Religions of Ancient China*. Freeport, N.Y.: Books for Libraries Press, 1969.

Smith, D. Howard. *Chinese Religions*. New York: Holt, Rinehart & Winston, 1968.

Thompson, Laurence G. *The Chinese Way in Religion*. Encino, Calif.: Dickenson Publishing Company, 1973.

Waley, Arthur. *The Way and its Power*. London: George Allen & Unwin, 1956.

Yang, Y. C. *China's Religious Heritage*. New York: Abingdon-Cokesbury Press, 1943.

SHINTO

Mount Fuji, Japan.

Think not God is something distant, but seek for him in your heart, for the heart is the abode of God. That which in Heaven begets all things is, in man, that which makes him love his neighbor, so doubt not that Heaven loves goodness of heart and hates its opposite. Reverence for Heaven and one's ancestors is the foundation of the Way of the sages.

MURO-KIUSO

Shinto, a loosely organized native religion of the Japanese people, embraces a wide variety of beliefs and practices. Indeed this variety is so wide that it is as difficult to define Shinto as Hinduism. Therefore we can only list some of the areas that it covers. In its most basic sense Shinto is a fervent religious form of Japanese patriotism. Its mythology describes the formation of Japan as a land superior to all lands; its shrines commemorate the great heroes and events in the history of Japan. Historically it has taught the Japanese people that their emperors were literally the descendants of the sun goddess. Commentators have frequently compared Japanese Shinto to Americans visiting Gettysburg, the Washington Monument, or the Alamo. Probably the closest comparison would be that which takes place in some American towns and villages on Memorial Day when graves of the war dead are visited by the community, the blessings of God are invoked upon the nation, and great events in the national history are remembered in the beauty of a late spring day.[1]

Shinto further involves the Japanese in a worshipful attitude toward the beauties of their land, particularly its mountains. As practiced by the common people it may also include various aspects of animism and

[1] For a discussion of Memorial Day as American Shinto see W. Lloyd Warner, *American Life, Dream, and Reality* (Chicago: The University of Chicago Press, 1953), pp. 1–12.

ancestor worship. In addition it embraces the religious activity that takes place in the numerous shrines throughout Japan—which prior to 1945 received the financial support of the government—the simple rituals that are carried out in shrines in Japanese homes, and the highly organized and active religious sects that have developed from basic Shinto. Thus the term *Shinto* may refer to a multitude of varying Japanese religious and national practices.

The word itself was not officially coined until the sixth century A.D. It was developed then to distinguish native Japanese religion from the newer religions being imported from China and Korea during the period, Buddhism, Taoism, and Confucianism. The word *Shinto* actually comes from the Chinese words *shen* and *tao*, which may be roughly translated in this context as "the way of the gods." The preferred Japanese term which describes this native religion is *Kami-no-michi*, which also may be defined as "the way of the gods."

JAPANESE MYTHOLOGY

In order for us to understand Japanese religion prior to the sixth century, it is necessary to take a quick look at some of the traditional myths surrounding the origin of the nation of Japan, its native gods, and the early history of the country. In the beginning there were the *kami*. The term *kami* is usually defined as "gods" but that is inexact. Some scholars have chosen to define kami as *mana*.

> Kami in its original meaning is practically identical with *mana*, the name adopted by science from the language of the Melanesians to indicate the occult force which preliterate man found emanating from objects and experiences that aroused in him emotions of wonder and awe.[2]

Others have identified the kami with the Greek term *daimon*. However, this too is inadequate. Even the great Japanese Shinto scholar Motoori Norinaga in the eighteenth century confessed: "I do not yet understand the meaning of the term *kami*."[3] Kami certainly refers to the deities of heaven and earth worshiped by the Japanese people, but

---

[2]Daniel Clarence Holtom, "Shinto" in *Religion in the Twentieth Century*, ed. Vergilius Ferm (New York: The Philosophical Library, 1948), p. 147.
[3]William T. deBary, ed., *Sources of the Japanese Tradition* (New York: Columbia University Press, 1958), p. 23.

it can also refer to the spirit that is in human beings, animals, trees, plants, seas, and mountains. Any thing, any person, any force that possessed superior power or was awesome in any way was described by the ancient Japanese as kami. While kami may be defined in these broad terms, in ancient mythology it generally refers to gods or humans with godlike powers.

The major source for our knowledge of Japanese mythology is the Kojiki, "Chronicles of Ancient Events." These chronicles were collected in the seventh and eighth centuries A.D. as a response to the entrance of Chinese culture and religions. In these centuries the Japanese, while willing to accept the advanced culture of the Chinese, looked about for their own heritage. The results of this search yielded the chronicles, which contain a section called "The Age of the Gods." In this material one finds the mythological background of Japanese culture.

In Japanese mythology there is no creation story. Gods and goddesses simply appear and begin to develop that which became Japan.[4]

> At the beginning of heaven and earth, there came into existence in the Plain of High Heaven the Heavenly Center Lord Kami, next, the Kami of High Generative Force, and then the Kami of Divine Generative Force.
>
> Next, when the earth was young, not yet solid, there developed something like reed-shoots from which the Male Kami of Excellent Reed Shoots and then Heavenly Eternal Standing Kami emerged.[5]
>
> Then, there came into existence Earth Eternal Standing Kami, Kami of Abundant Clouds Field, male and female Kami of Clay, male and female Kami of Post, male and female Kami of Great Door, Kami of Complete Surface and his spouse, Kami of Awesomeness, Izanagi (kami-who-invites) and his spouse, Izanami (kami-who-is-invited).[6]

After this the first kami are no longer mentioned, and attention is focused entirely upon Izanagi and Izanami.

---

[4]The selections from the Japanese myths are taken from Basil Hall Chamberlain's translation in "Kojiki," *Records of Ancient Matters, Transactions of the Asiatic Society of Japan* 10 (1882), Supplement.
[5]Kojiki, Chapter 1.
[6]Ibid., Chapter 2.

The heavenly kami at this time gave the heavenly jeweled spear to Izanagi and Izanami and instructed them to complete and solidify the land. Thus, the two kami, standing on the floating bridge in Heaven, lowered the spear and stirred around, and as they lifted up the spear, the brine dripping from the tip of the spear piled up and formed an island. This was the island of Onogoro.[7]

Descending from heaven to this island, Izanagi asked his spouse Izanami as to how her body was formed. She replied, "My body is formed in such a way that one spot is not filled." Then Izanagi said, "My body is formed in such a way that there is one spot which is filled in excess. How would it be if I insert the portion of my body which is formed to excess into that portion of your body which is not filled and give birth to the land?" Izanami replied, "That would be excellent." Then Izanagi said, "Let us then walk around the heavenly pillar and meet and have conjugal intercourse."[8]

After giving birth to the land, they proceeded to bear kami (such as the kami of the wind, of the tree, of the mountain, and of the plains). But Izanami died after giving birth to the kami of fire.[9]

Because of his love for his wife, Izanagi journeyed to hades to seek her out. The existence of a land of the dead, which we translate as hades seems to have been taken for granted in the myth, but it is seldom mentioned again as a part of the Shinto world view. When Izanagi reached hades and found his wife he wished to look upon her face and persuade her to return to the land of the living, and thus he lit a torch. Upon seeing her ruined and decayed body crawling with maggots, he turned and fled to the land of the living.[10]

Izanagi, seeing this, was afraid and ran away, saying, "Since I have been to an extremely horrible and unclean land, I must purify myself." Thus, arriving at (a river), he purified and

---

[7] Ibid., Chapter 3.
[8] Ibid., Chapter 4.
[9] Ibid., Chapter 7.
[10] The theme of a hero figure searching the underworld for his lost love is fairly common in many mythologies and has been the object of much speculation regarding its universal meaning.

exorcised himself. When he washed his left eye, there came into existence the Sun Goddess, or Heavenly Illuminating Great Kami (Amaterasu), and when he washed his right eye, there emerged the Moon Kami (Tsukiyomi). Finally, as he washed his nose there came into existence Valiant Male Kami (Susanoo).[11]

From this point Izanagi is no longer mentioned in the myths and major attention is focused upon Amaterasu and her sibling kamis. Her brother the storm god, Susanoo, played a prank upon Amaterasu and she went away into a cave to pout. The other kami could not conceive a world without the presence of the sun goddess, and they made a concerted attempt to bring her out of the cave. They hung beautiful beads and a mirror before the entrance of her cave and made a great deal of noise.

The Sun Goddess, intrigued by all this, opened the rock-cave door slightly, wondering why it was that the 800 myriads of kami were laughing. Then Kami of Heavenly Headgear said, "There is a kami nobler than you, and that is why we are happy and dancing." While she was speaking thus, Kami of the Little Roof and Kami of Grand Bead showed the mirror to the Sun Goddess. Thereupon, the Sun Goddess, thinking this ever more strange, gradually came out of the cave, and the hidden Kami of Grand Bead took her hand and pulled her out. Then as the Sun Goddess reappeared, the Plain of High Heaven was naturally illuminated.[12]

The next event of importance in the Kojiki myth occurred when Amaterasu sent two messenger kamis to pacify the land of Japan. When this was accomplished she sent her grandson, Ninigi, to become the first emperor of Japan, with the following instructions:

This Land of the Plentiful Reed Plains and of the Fresh Rice-ears has been entrusted to you as the land to be governed by you. Therefore, you must descend from heaven in accordance with the divine command.

---

[11]Kojiki, Chapters 11, 12.
[12]Ibid., Chapter 17. It is always a dangerous thing to try to interpret the myths of the past, particularly those of another culture, but this one seems clearly to be the retelling of the events surrounding the eclipse of the sun.

Kinkakuji Temple, Golden Pavilion, Kyoto, Japan.

Thus, Ninigi, now leaving the heavenly rock seat, pushed through the myriad layers of heavenly clouds and descended on the peak of Mount Takachiho[13]

Thus deeply rooted in the mythological past is the legend that the emperors of Japan were descended from the sun goddess, the founder of the land.

THE HISTORY OF SHINTO

Shinto Prior to 300 A.D.

According to the mythological tradition the first Japanese emperor was enthroned in the seventh century B.C., but most modern scholars

---

[13]Ibid., Chapters 38, 39.

197

agree that the actual history of Japan does not begin until the third century A.D. At this point the Japanese people became known to other nations and began to keep historical records. Therefore the culture of Japan is one of the youngest of all the Asian nations. It is difficult to say what the exact worship of the Japanese was prior to this period. The coming of Buddhism in the sixth century A.D. caused the Japanese to collect their various myths and rituals under the title of *Kami-no-michi* to distinguish native religion from those brought in by the Chinese and Koreans. Prior to this, Japanese worship probably consisted of a loosely organized and widely varying collection of practices. The myths allowed for a limitless number of gods, goddesses, spirits, ancestor worship, and various forms of animism. Shrines were established all over the Japanese islands for the worship of the various kami, and shrines were built in individual homes for ancestor and kami worship. Amaterasu and Susanoo were probably the most popular gods and received more than their share of attention at the shrines built for them and in private homes. Beyond these very general statements it is difficult to say anything more about Japanese worship in its prehistoric period.

Chinese Influence upon Shinto

Early in its history Japan became an object of interest to Chinese and Korean merchants and missionaries. These persons brought with them much of the older culture of China including its arts, its language and alphabet, and of course its various religions and ethical systems. After the fourth century A.D. the Japanese came under the influence of Buddhism, Taoism, and Confucianism. All of these had a lasting effect on Japanese civilization. The Kojiki records the entrance of Chinese culture into Japan.

> [During the reign of the fifteenth emperor, Ojin, son of Empress Jingu] some immigrants crossed over from Silla. Also, the king of Paekche presented as tribute one stallion and one mare which were sent together with Master Achiki (who became the ancestor of the clan of scribes). He also presented as tribute a sword and a large mirror. Then, the emperor commanded the land of Paekche to send a wise man as tribute, whereupon a man called Master Waniki was presented together with the Confucian *Analects* in ten volumes and the *Thousand-Character Classic* in one volume, totaling eleven

volumes. Paekche also presented two artisans, a Korean smith and a Chinese weaver. Then there came over the ancestor of the chieftains of the Hata clan, the ancestor of the chieftains of the Aya clan, a man who knew the art of distilling liquor, whose name was Niho, also known as Susukori, and others. This man Susukori, distilled some liquor and offered it to the emperor, who greatly enjoyed it.[14]

In the years that followed, intercourse between China and Japan greatly increased. Prior to this period the Japanese had no written language. They subsequently adopted the Chinese script and many other elements of Chinese culture. Japan was organized and governed by a feudal system during this era and Confucian ethics were therefore welcomed. Ancestor worship had always been practiced in Japan and thus the Confucian and Taoist elements that emphasized filial piety were readily accepted by the Japanese. The Chinese arts, particularly those connected to Buddhist ritual, were also adopted. Altogether the period between the fourth and the eighth centuries was one of dramatic change for Japan.

The entrance of Buddhism from China and Korea was extremely important in the development of the religious traditions of Japan. According to the Japanese chronicles it was in the year 522 A.D. that Mahayana Buddhism was first introduced from China. In that year the emperor of Japan was presented with an image of Buddha and several volumes of Buddhist scripture. Though the emperor was delighted his advisors warned him that the introduction of a foreign god might arouse the anger of the native kamis. In light of the extremely polytheistic nature of Shinto it would seem that their warning was based more upon fear and distrust of foreign culture than upon any theological grounds. Shortly after the introduction of the Buddha a pestilence broke out in Japan. Fearing that it was the work of the vengeful kamis, the emperor had the statue thrown into a canal, and the temple that had been built for the Buddha was burned, whereupon the pestilence ceased.

Buddhism could not so easily be turned away from Japan, however. In succeeding generations other statues of the Buddha were introduced along with prayers, rituals, and Buddhist magic. By the end of the sixth century Mahayana Buddhism had taken a firm foothold on Japan.

---

[14]Ibid., Chapter 104.

Japanese reaction to Buddhism was fourfold. First, there was the introduction of the name *Shinto* or *Kami-no-michi* to distinguish the native Japanese religion from the new foreign religion. As we have suggested before, this may have been the first point at which the Japanese actually began to think of their native worship as a distinct religion.

The second reaction was for the Japanese advocates of Shinto to recognize the many Buddhas and bodhisattvas of Buddhism but to think of them as the revelation of the kamis to the Indian and Chinese people. Naturally the Buddhists tended to reverse this line of thinking and identify the kamis as Japanese revelations of the Buddhas and bodhisattvas.

The third reaction was a syncretism between Shinto and Buddhism which developed in Japan between the sixth and the ninth centuries and was called *Ryobu*, i.e., "Two Aspect," Shinto. There gradually developed an identification between the various Shinto kami and the Buddhist deities. Little by little the boundaries between the two religions were obliterated. The Shinto sanctuaries also came to serve Buddhist priests. The rituals performed in these sanctuaries made little distinction between the two religions. Buddhist architectural elements were added to Shinto temples. Generally Japanese life began to be divided into two spheres. The concerns of day-to-day life became the domain of the Shinto side of the religion while the concerns for the afterlife were served by the Buddhists. Thus a traditional citizen of Japan might be said to have been born a Shintoist but to die a Buddhist. For ten centuries Shinto and Buddhism lived side by side in Japan, each serving a special need of the people.

The fourth reaction of the Japanese to Buddhism was the development of some distinctively Japanese forms of Buddhism. Mahayana Buddhism is an extremely elastic religion allowing for many variations. This is true to such a degree that it may be considered a family of religions rather than a single branch of the religion of Buddhism. Within a few centuries of the time that Buddhism came to Japan new variations on the Buddhist theme began to develop. Buddhism had emphasized meditation (dhyana) as a means of insight into religious truth. The Chinese Buddhists had picked this up through the missionary work of Bodhidharma and called it *Ch'an*, but it remained for the Japanese to develop meditative Buddhism to its fullest form under the name of *Zen*. Likewise the Japanese originated or developed other forms of Buddhism such as Pure Land and Nichiren. (For a further discussion of these forms see chapter 6.) These and other forms of

Buddhism became so popular in Japan that even though Shinto was intermingled with them, it was almost forgotten as a viable religion for the Japanese people.

The Revival of Shinto

From the eighth century onward Shinto and Buddhism were submerged into a syncretistic form of religion to the point that Shinto was almost obliterated. Nevertheless there often arose reformers who wished to revise and revitalize the native religion of Japan. As early as the fourteenth century various scholars tried to point out the strengths of Shinto and to restore it to its place of prominence with the people. However, it was not until the seventeenth century and the rise of the Tokugawa regime (1600–1867) that Shinto got the boost it needed. This was an era in which the Japanese people were unified by tough-minded military leaders who sought to isolate the nation from outside influences. Since religions such as Buddhism and Christianity were foreign-born they were pushed aside; since Shinto was native to Japan it was given new strength and support by the national government. A Japanese version of Confucianism was the only foreign system that was allowed support during this period because Confucian ethics were supportive of the militaristic regime of the Tokugawa rulers.

One of the most colorful aspects of Japanese life during the Tokugawa era was the feudal knights called the *samurai*. Throughout the history of Japan individual warriors hired themselves as bodyguards or mercenary soldiers to lords, but it was in the Tokugawa era that the samurai was idealized and a code of conduct was established for him. In the seventeenth century the government set up the Shushi School of Confucianism as the orthodox model for the conduct of the upper classes. One of the leaders of this school was Yamaga Soko (1622–1685), who led in a combining of Shinto and Confucianism to develop the warrior code called *Bushido*, "the way of the fighting knight." The standard of conduct established for the Japanese feudal knight was similar in many respects to that of the idealized Christian knight of medieval Europe except for the absence of any form of romantic love. Generally Bushido may be summarized under the following categories:

1. The samurai is bound to be loyal to his master in the hierarchy of the feudal system. The extremes to which this loyalty was carried is best illustrated by one of the most famous stories in Japanese literature, the tale of the forty-seven ronin. Told very briefly, in 1702 a certain lord was insulted by a government official. He drew his sword

Samurai parade. This procession of armor-clad paraders seen passing through the torii is held twice a year, in the spring and the autumn.

and wounded the official. For his act the lord was required to commit suicide and his property was confiscated by the government. He had in his employ forty-seven samurai who, since their lord was dead, were officially known as *ronin* (men without a master). These knights took a vow of vengeance for the injustice brought against their master. In order to avoid suspicion they disbanded and acted publicly as if they had no concern for their master. When their enemies ceased to be watchful they gathered together, attacked the castle of the one who had humiliated their master, and killed him. Then they quietly waited for the government to order them to commit suicide. Thus the forty-seven ronin became the ideal example of the loyalty that samurai are to have toward their masters.

2. The samurai must have great courage in life, in battle, and in his willingness to lay down his life for his master.

3. Above all, the samurai is to be a man of honor. He prefers death to dishonor and is expected to take his own life rather than face a situation in which he is dishonored.

4. Like a true Confucian the samurai is expected to be polite to his master and to people in a position of authority above him. However, this politeness and gentility did not extend to everyone in society. There are stories of samurai who felt quite justified in trying out the edge of their swords on peasants if there were no battle at hand. The age-old story of the man who struck out at a peasant with his sword seven times and had no apparent effect until the peasant fell into eight pieces probably originated in samurai lore.

5. In spite of his attitude toward peasants the samurai is expected to be a gentleman in every sense of the word. He is supposed to be a man of benevolence, to right wrongs, and to bring justice to the victims of injustice. A popular Japanese movie, The Seven Samurai, is probably a good example of this sense of justice.

The willingness of the proper samurai to commit suicide before dishonor and the attitude of the Japanese people toward suicide as a whole have long amazed Westerners. Many European religious traditions teach directly against the practice of suicide, but in Japan suicide has often been encouraged as a means of avoiding dishonor, as a means of escaping a bad situation in life, as a means of protest, and in World War II as a very effective means of destroying enemy warships. Perhaps no culture in the history of the world has had this attitude toward suicide.

In Bushido the warrior is expected to kill himself in a very slow, painful manner called seppuku. (Westerners prefer the term hara-kiri,[15] which means "belly slitting.") This is a form of suicide by disembowelment. At the proper time the warrior is expected to slit open his abdomen in such a way that his intestines fall out. Thus he dies in a very slow and painful manner. In more recent times it became common for a friend to stand by and chop off the head once the necessary

---

[15]One frequently hears this term further corrupted to something that sounds like "harry karry."

slitting had taken place. This form of death was reserved for warriors
and nobility. Women and peasants were forbidden to commit *seppuku*
and were expected to kill themselves in a quicker manner by stabbing
themselves in the throat. A. B. Mitford, a secretary to the British
Consulate in Japan in the nineteenth century, was allowed to witness a
ritual suicide, and he recorded the incident in the following manner:

> The condemned man was Taki Zenzaburo, an officer of the
> Prince of Bizen, who gave the order to fire upon the foreign
> settlement at Hiogo in the month of February, 1868.
>
> The ceremony, which was ordered by the Mikado himself,
> took place at 10:30 at night in the temple of Seifukukji, the
> headquarters of the Satsuma troops at Hiogo. A witness was
> sent from each of the foreign legations. We were seven for-
> eigners in all.
>
> After an interval of a few minutes of anxious suspense, Taki
> Zenzaburo, a stalwart man, thirty-two years of age, with a
> noble air, walked into the hall attired in his dress of ceremony,
> with the peculiar hempen-cloth wings which are worn on great
> occasions. He was accompanied by a *kaishaku* and three offi-
> cers, who wore the *jimbaori* or war surcoat with gold-tissue
> facings. The word *kaishaku*, it should be observed, is one to
> which our word "executioner" is no equivalent term. The of-
> fice is that of a gentleman: in many cases it is performed by a
> kinsman or friend of the condemned, and the relation between
> them is rather that of principal and second than that of victim
> and executioner. In this instance the *kaishaku* was a pupil of
> Taki Zenzaburo, and was selected by the friends of the latter
> from among their number for his skill in swordsmanship.
>
> With the *kaishaku* on his left hand, Taki Zenzaburo ad-
> vanced slowly towards the Japanese witnesses, and the two
> bowed before them, then drawing near to the foreigners they
> saluted us in the same way, perhaps even with more deference:
> in each case the salutation was ceremoniously returned.
> Slowly, and with great dignity, the condemned man mounted
> to the raised floor, prostrated himself before the high altar
> twice, and seated himself on the felt carpet with his back to the
> high alter, the *kaishaku* crouching on his left-hand side. One
> of the three attendant officers then came forward, bearing a
> stand of the kind used in temples for offerings, on which,
> wrapped in paper, lay the *wakizashi*, the short sword or dirk of

the Japanese, nine inches and a half in length, with a point and an edge as sharp as a razor's. This he handed, prostrating himself, to the condemned man, who received it reverently, raising it to his head with both hands, and placed it in front of himself.

After another profound obeisance, Taki Zenzaburo, in a voice which betrayed so much emotion and hesitation as might be expected from a man who is making a painful confession, but with no sign of either in his face or manner, spoke as follows: "I, and I alone, unwarrantably gave the order to fire on the foreigners at Kobe, and again as they tried to escape. For this crime I disembowel myself, and I beg you who are present to do me the honor of witnessing the act."

Bowing once more, the speaker allowed his upper garments to slip down to his girdle, and remained naked to the waist. Carefully, according to custom, he tucked his sleeves under his knees to prevent himself from falling forwards. Deliberately, with a steady hand, he took the dirk that lay before him; he looked at it wistfully, almost affectionately; for a moment seemed to collect his thoughts for the last time, and then, stabbing himself deeply below the waist on the left-hand side, he drew the dirk slowly across to the right side, and, turning it in the wound, gave a slight cut upwards. During this sickeningly painful operation, he never moved a muscle of his face. When he drew out the dirk, he leaned forward and stretched out his neck; an expression of pain for the first time crossed his face, but he uttered no sound. At that moment the *kaishaku*, who, still crouching by his side, had been keenly watching his every movement, sprang to his feet, poised his sword for a second in the air; there was a flash, a heavy, ugly thud, a crashing fall; with one blow the head had been severed from the body.

A dead silence followed, broken only by the hideous noise of the blood throbbing out of the inert heap before us, which but a moment before had been a brave and chivalrous man. It was horrible.[16]

The willingness of warriors to die in such a horrible manner for personal honor or for the good of the Japanese nation may seem out of place to the Westerner who has been trained in the sacredness of life

[16]A. B. Mitford, *Tales of Old Japan*, Vol. I (London: Macmillan, 1871), pp. 231–236.

and the evils of suicide, but in the coming together of the Shintoist's love of and worship for his nation and its heroic figures and the Confucianist's high sense of honor, *seppuku* is considered to be very religious.

The Modern Era

During the Tokugawa era Japan did its best to avoid foreign influence in any form. It closed itself off from foreign trade, from tourism, and from any kind of foreign religion. During this period it attempted to draw only from its native resources. In the meantime the rest of the world, particularly the Western world, moved toward industrialization. In 1853 Japan was brought to a sudden confrontation with the modern world when Commodore Perry of the United States Navy appeared in Tokyo Bay and asked that the Japanese ports be opened and trade relations begun between the United States and Japan. In 1854 Perry appeared again with more ships, troops, and cannon, and the Japanese rulers were forced to open their nation to foreigners. Since that date Japan has been racing to catch up with and get ahead of the rest of the world in industrialization. This race toward modernity has of course had its effect upon the religions of Japan.

After a period of some confusion over what role religion was to play in the new Japan, it was decided in the Constitution of 1889 that the nation would follow the pattern of many Western nations in that there would be a state-supported religion but all other religions would be allowed the freedom to exist and propagate. There would be state-supported Shinto that would essentially consist of patriotic rituals at certain shrines. In addition, those who wished could develop Shinto sects, which would be supported by their adherents. Further, Shinto could be carried on in every home around simple domestic shrines. Beyond these forms of Shinto any other religion, Buddhism, Christianity, and so on, was free to exist in Japan. However, only the patriotic rituals at the state shrines would receive financial support from the government of Japan.

THREE FORMS OF SHINTO

State Shinto

Following the Constitution of 1889 the state took over the support of some 110,000 Shinto shrines and approximately 16,000 priests who tended these shrines throughout the nation. This version of Shinto became known as *Jinja* (shrine) to distinguish it from the more religious *Skuha* (sectarian) versions.

Each shrine supported by the state was dedicated to some local deity, hero, or event; the grand imperial shrine at Ise was dedicated to the mother goddess of Japan, Amaterasu. The visitor approaches the shrine by way of a distinctive Japanese archway called a *torii*, which was so inseparably connected to Shinto that it became known world wide as its symbol.

The typical major shrine consists of two buildings, an inner and an outer shrine. Both are built of unpainted wood and must be torn down and rebuilt once every twenty years. Anyone may visit the outer shrine, but the inner one is reserved for priests and government officials. The inner shrine contains objects of importance to the deity or event it commemorates. For example, at the grand imperial shrine the sacred objects are a mirror, a sword, and a string of beads, all of which are important to the myth of Amaterasu. On certain occasions or holidays these relics are publicly displayed.

The visitor who enters the outer shrine meditates on the importance of the deity or the event celebrated there, offers a modest offering, and perhaps a brief prayer. No one is obligated to visit the shrine, but it is an unwritten assumption that every loyal Japanese will try to visit the shrine at Ise at least once during his lifetime.

State Shinto was established for the purpose of engendering patriotism and loyalty toward the nation of Japan; it was to have no religious functions. After the 1889 Constitution, the Japanese government forbade the priests who tended the state shrines and were supported by the state from performing any religious act such as conducting funerals. The Constitution of 1889 began with these words: "The Empire of Japan shall be reigned over and governed by a line of Emperors unbroken for ages eternal. . . . The Emperor is sacred and inviolable."[17] This constitution also made the military leaders responsible to the emperor rather than to the parliament. State Shinto therefore became an instrument of support for the military leaders in the wars that Japan participated in during the last part of the nineteenth century and the first part of the twentieth. It was particularly supportive of the Japanese war effort during World War II. Shinto had become such an inseparable part of Japanese militarism that the American occupation forces felt it necessary to direct the abolition of state support for Shinto in

---

[17]Floyd Ross, *Shinto: The Way of Japan* (Boston: Beacon Press, 1965), pp. 138, 139.

December of 1945. In January of 1946 the occupation forces directed the emperor to issue a statement declaring that he was not divine.

Since 1945 the shrines once supported by the Japanese government have continued to exist, but they are now sustained with the financial support of private citizens. Immediately following World War II, attendance at these shrines dropped off and many fell into disuse. However, in the ensuing years interest in them revived.

Sectarian Shinto

With the developments of the Meiji era (1868–1912), specifically when the government said that Shinto was not a religion but rather an institution which fostered patriotism, the religious side of Shinto was forced to identify itself separately and find its own support as did all other religions in Japan. (The adherents to these religions are presently thought to number over eighteen million; however, statistics regarding any religion are always suspect, and this is especially true in Japan, where a person may in good conscience be a Buddhist, a Confucian, and a member of a Shinto sect all at the same time.)

The thirteen major sects of Shinto may be divided into three categories. First there are the sects whose primary emphasis is on mountain worship. The beautiful and graceful mountains of Japan have always been objects of reverence to its people. Somewhere it became popular for people to climb the mountains during seasonal pilgrimages in a combination of nature worship and asceticism. Some made exhausting climbs from the valleys to the peaks while others took up temporary dwellings in the mountains for ascetic purposes. Mountains Ontake and Fuji were the special favorites for these purposes. During the Meiji era three groups dedicated to nature worship and asceticism became established Shinto sects.

A second category developed from the basic practices of shamanism and divination of the Japanese peasants. The basic appeal of these sects in modern Japan is their promise of faith healing. Representative of such sects is *Tenri-kyo* ("Teaching of Heavenly Reason"). *Tenri-kyo* was founded in the nineteenth century by a peasant named Nakayama Miki (1798–1887). When she was forty-one years old this woman felt that she was possessed by the kami of Divine Reason. She believed that she had been miraculously healed from a serious illness and began to teach others as a result of this experience. Her religion emphasized various elements that had always been a part of the basic religion of the Japanese peasant such as shamanism, ecstatic dance, and faith heal-

Torii at Mijajima, Hiroshima, Japan. The typical Shinto Torii is a refinement of the primitive symbolic design of vertical and horizontal tree trunks.

ing. Today this sect emphasizes volunteer labor for public charity and, of course, faith healing. Because of its teachings on healing and because it was established by a woman, *Tenri-kyo* is often referred to as "the Christian Science of Japan," but outside of these two common features the two religions are scarcely alike.

A third type of sectarian Shinto includes those sects that are classified as more or less pure Shinto. When the rulers of Japan took over the shrines of Shinto in the Meiji era and declared that it was not a religion, this left behind a basic residue of the religious tradition of Shinto, its mythology, and its rituals. Three major sects developed to emphasize these religious elements. These sects revived the myths of the origin of Japan from the ancient chronicles. They believed that there was a religious and ethical dimension as well as a political aspect to Shinto. They emphasized purification of the body through fasting, breath control, bathing in cold water, chanting, and many other devices similar to the Yoga cults of Hinduism. Today these sects seem to be losing ground among the people of Japan while groups like *Tenri-kyo* are growing.

Domestic Shinto

Beyond the organized forms of state and sectarian Shinto there is another and more basic form. This is the very simple and common form of Shinto that takes place in many Japanese homes. The basic

209

unit or symbol of domestic Shinto is the *kami-dana* (god shelf), which is found in many Japanese homes, particularly in rural areas. The *kami-dana*, whether it is elaborate or simple, contains the symbols of whatever may be of religious significance to the family. It usually contains the names of the ancestors of the family since a part of the religion of the household is filial peity. The *kami-dana* might contain statues of the gods which have been beneficial to the family or are highly regarded. In the homes and shops of many Japanese artisans the images of the various patron deities are present, and the literature of Japan contains many stories of skilled workers creating masterpieces under the direction of an unseen patron god. The traditional *kami-dana* contains objects that have been bought at the great shrines such as the one at Ise. Any object the family considers to be sacred is fit for veneration at the god shelf. There is a story that the *kami-dana* in one household contained the cast-off shoes of a man who had been a benefactor of the household when it was in trouble. The shoes were believed to be symbolic of the friend's goodness or to contain the mana or kami that prompted the good deeds. At any rate they became objects of veneration.[18]

Worship at the *kami-dana* in the Japanese home is a very simple affair. Offerings of flowers, lanterns, incense, food, and drink may be placed before this altar daily. A simple daily service in which the worshiper washes his hands, makes an offering, claps his hands as a symbol of communication with the spirits, and offers a brief prayer may also be held here. On special occasions such as holidays, weddings, or anniversaries, more elaborate ceremonies may be held at the *kami-dana*. However, if the occasion is decidedly religious—a funeral, for example—it is not to the Shinto deities or priest that the Japanese family turns but to the Buddhist priest. In the special religious syncretism of Japan, Shinto is for this life, but Buddhism is for the life beyond. Therefore in addition to their *kami-dana* many Japanese homes will have a *butsu-dan*, a Buddhist household altar, where worship to the Buddhist deities is also carried on.

As we have seen, Shinto, the native religion of Japan, is many things to many people. To some Japanese it is a set of myths and rituals that remind them of the special origin of their nation. They are occasionally reminded of these myths and rituals on national holidays or on

[18]It has been suggested that the closest parallel to the Japanese *kami-dana* in American life is the dashboard of the automobile, where in many cases objects that promise good fortune or bring back good memories are displayed.

visits to a national shrine. Religion in terms of more regular worship and a concern for the future life is likely to be Buddhism. To those who are members of specific Shinto religious sects, Shinto may be related to faith healing, ascetic practices, or purification of the body. To many rural families of Japan, Shinto includes the daily worship that is carried on in the home at the *kami-dana* and contains elements of ancestor worship and animism.

SUGGESTED READING

Anesaki, Masaharu. *Religious Life of the Japanese People*. Tokyo: The Society for International Cultural Relations, 1961.

de Barry, William T., ed. *Sources of Japanese Tradition*. New York: Columbia University Press, 1958.

Earhart, H. Byron. *Japanese Religion: Unity and Diversity*. Encino, Calif.: Dickenson Publishing Company, 1969.

Kitagawa, Joseph M. *Religion in Japanese History*. New York: Columbia University Press, 1966.

Ross, Floyd Hiatt. *Shinto, the Way of Japan*. Boston: Beacon Press, 1965.

In the twentieth century Christianity and Islam have more adherents than any other religions in the world, sharing perhaps more than one half of the world's population between them. Their influence upon the values and aspirations of humanity is therefore enormous, and a basic knowledge of them is essential. These two giant missionary religions arose from the milieu of the ancient Middle East which first produced Zoroastrianism and Judaism. It was from these two religions that Christianity and Islam drew much of their world view, ethics, and especially their view of world history beginning with a creation and ending with a divine judgment. Therefore a study of these four religions is essential for the student who would truly be aware of the past and the future of many of the people of planet Earth.

RELIGIONS
ORIGINATING IN THE
MIDDLE EAST

CHAPTER TEN
ZOROASTRIANISM

PAUL POPPER, LTD.

Parsee girl being invested with the kusti, *the sacred string worn around the waist, which is one of the symbols of Zoroastrian faith.*

Make thy own self pure, O righteous man! Any one in the world here below can win purity for his own self, namely, when he cleanses his own self with good thoughts, words, and deeds.

VENDIDAD, 10,19.

One of the world's oldest living religions is Zoroastrianism; depending upon the date accepted, it may be as much as three thousand years old. Unlike its kindred religions, Christianity and Islam, Zoroastrianism is today a minor religion, with adherents numbering less than 150,000. Nevertheless, this religion cannot be overlooked in any study of the religions of the world because of its great contributions to Judaism, Christianity, and Islam. It should also be studied by the student of world history because it was the religion of the mighty Persian Empire that once controlled the entire Middle East and attempted to conquer the Greek city-states in the fifth century B.C. Students of philosophy may be interested in the founder of this religion, Zarathustra,[1] who was chosen as the key figure in Friedrich Nietzsche's *Also Sprach Zarathustra*.

PRE-ZOROASTRIAN PERSIAN RELIGION

The origins of Zoroastrian religion are shrouded in great mystery. Existing literary sources are contradictory as to dates and events. Naturally our knowledge of the pre-Zoroastrian Persians and their religion

---

[1] The true name of the founder of this religion is probably "Zarathustra." The name has been latinized into the more familiar form "Zoroaster" by Western writers.

is also confused. The major literary sources that deal with this period are the Gathas or hymns of early Zoroastrianism. The Gathas are to the people of this religion what the Torah is to the Jews. These hymns are looked upon as the very words of the prophet Zoroaster, and all remaining scriptural books are based upon them. Naturally these books present the preceding religious practices of the Persian people in a negative light, and for this reason the real truth is difficult to ascertain.

The ancient inhabitants of the land that later became the Persian Empire were a group of people who are generally known as Aryans ("noble ones").[2] A portion of the Aryan population migrated into the Indus valley and laid the foundations for the Indian peoples and their religion. Other Aryans continued to live in the region east of Mesopotamia and became the basis of the Medo-Persian Empire. Originally the Aryans who migrated to India and those who remained probably both worshiped the same deities.

The Gathas indicate that the Aryans were nature worshipers who venerated a series of deities. Many of these gods are also mentioned in the Indian Vedic literature. They were generically known as *daevas*, and were associated with the sun, moon, earth, fire, and water. Above this series of daevas there were higher gods such as Intar, the god of war; Asha, the god of truth and justice; and Uruwana, a sky god. The most popular and most important of all of these gods was Mithra, who was known as the giver and benefactor of cattle, a god of light, and the representative of loyalty and obedience. Although Zoroaster attempted to discount all gods but one, Mithra could not be displaced in the minds of the Aryan people. He reappears as a judge in the Zoroastrian judgment day; he is seen as Mitra in the Indian Vedic literature; and in the times of the Roman Empire, a religion based on the myth of Mithra became popular among Roman soldiers and merchants and rivaled Christianity in some parts of the Empire.

Above and beyond the local nature gods, there was one supreme lord who was recognized as the one reality and was called Ahura Mazda, "The Wise Lord." As is the case in many other basic religions, there was the recognition of one supreme deity, but the actual day-to-day worship seemed to revolve around the less important localized gods.

Since the predecessors of Zoroaster were nomadic people, it is likely

---

[2] It is suggested by some that the name of the modern nation, Iran, is actually a shortened version of a name which meant "the land of the Aryans."

that they worshiped the nature gods on crude altars with blood sacrifices. They also favored the sacramental use of the juice of the sacred haoma plant. The actual reason for this is not clear, but some suggest that the juice may have been drunk by the worshiper for its psychedelic qualities. Fire worship also seems to have been a part of the religion of the ancient Aryans.

The pre-Zoroastrian Aryans further believed that whenever religious practices strayed from the truth, prophets or reformers, called Saoshyants ("those who benefit the community"), would come and restore the purity of the religion. They believed that prior to Zoroaster there had been a series of Saoshyants who had restored pure religion, and some saw Zoroaster himself as one of the last and greatest of these reformers.

THE LIFE OF ZOROASTER

Several diverse sources provide information on the life of the prophet Zoroaster. There are, of course, the Gathas, which reveal many of the events of his life. In addition there are the writings of many ancient Greek and Roman authorities who showed a great interest in Zoroaster's life. Writers such as Plato, Pliny, and Plutarch made many references to Zoroaster. It is said that Pythagoras visited him, and that later Plato attempted to go to Persia to study with the magi, the Zoroastrian priests, but was forbidden because of the outbreak of war between Greece and Persia. Some of the material in these sources is obviously legendary, but some bears the mark of authenticity.

Zoroaster's birth date is uncertain. Many of the ancient Greek writers placed it at various points between 1000 and 600 B.C. Others place it approximately three hundred years before the time of Alexander the Great. While there are no clear records on this, the later date of the seventh century B.C. seems most likely in light of the historical development of the religion.

Since biographical data are scanty and much of them are heavily laced with legendary material, it is difficult to know more about Zoroaster than the broad outline of his life. His name, Zarathustra Spitama, indicates that he was born into a warrior clan that was connected to the royal family of ancient Persia. The name Zarathustra may mean "possessor of camels" and is taken by some to indicate that he came from a nomadic family. Regarding his early life we know little. Legendary material states that demons attempted to kill the infant

Zoroaster several times because they recognized him as a potential enemy.

> They rush away shouting, the wicked, evil-doing Daevas; they run away shouting, the wicked, evil-doing Daevas; "Let us gather together at the head of Aresura! For he is just born, the holy Zoroaster, in the house of Porushaspa. How can we procure his death? He is the weapon that fells the fiends; he is a Druj to the Druj!" Vanished are the Daeva-worshipers, the Nasu made by the Daevas, the false speaking lie.[3]

Each attempt on the infant's life was thwarted by the powers that looked over him. Regarding his childhood we have no information beyond the fact that at age fifteen he put on the *kusti*, the sacred string belt symbolic of his passage into manhood as a member of his religion. The literature on his life informs us that Zoroaster had three wives and was the father of six children. Regarding his occupation, his training, or the influences upon his life, we know nothing.

At the age of thirty Zoroaster received a revelation from Ahura Mazda. At this most critical time in his life he was wandering about seeking answers to the religious questions that troubled him. By the banks of a river he had a vision of the angel Vohu Mana, who appeared nine times the size of a man. In this meeting the angel told Zoroaster that there was only one true God, Ahura Mazda, and that he was to become the prophet of Ahura Mazda. During the next ten years Zoroaster had other visions in which each of the archangels of Ahura Mazda appeared and revealed further truth to him. He began to preach his new revelation at once but with absolutely no success. For ten years no one converted to the message of this new prophet. He was condemned by his people as a heretic and a sorcerer and tempted by evil spirits to cease his preaching. Finally he was able to convert his cousin Maidhyomah.

The turning point in the career of Zoroaster came when he and his cousin journeyed to Bactria to the court of a monarch named Vishtaspa. Zoroaster sought an audience with Vishtaspa in an attempt to convert him, but neither the audience nor the conversion was easy to attain. Although the stories of these events are mixed, it seems clear that Zoroaster stayed at the court of Vishtaspa for several years. During that time rival priests conspired against him and had him thrown into prison. Finally, however, he converted the prince to his new

---

[3]From the Zend-Avesta, Vendidad, Fargard XIX c. VI, 45, 46.

religion. Some of the legends say that the conversion was achieved when Zoroaster healed the favorite horse of Vishtaspa. At any rate, Vishtaspa and his entire court and kingdom became followers of the prophet. In the ensuing years Zoroastrianism spread rapidly in the lands of the Aryan people. Sometimes the conversion rates were speeded up by means of the holy wars. During a war with the Turanians, the city in which Zoroaster lived was invaded. An enemy soldier found the seventy-seven-year-old prophet tending the sacred flame in the fire temple and killed him.

THE TEACHINGS OF ZOROASTER

The Nature of God

As it was with the life of Zoroaster, so it is with his original teachings; the sources are distant and confused. The problem is compounded by the fact that over the years other teachings and legends have been added to the original message of the prophet. However, the central teaching of Zoroaster seems clear: There is only one true God in all the world and his name is Ahura Mazda. It is he who created the world.

> This I ask Thee, tell it to me truly, Lord! Who set firmly earth below and kept the sky Sure from falling? Who the streams and trees did make? Who their swiftness to the winds and clouds hath yoked? Who, O Mazda, was the Founder of Good Thought?
> This I ask Thee, tell it to me truly, Lord! Who, benignant, made the darkness and the light? Who, benignant, sleep and waking did create? Who the morning, noon and evening did decree As reminder, to the wise, of duty's call.[4]

It was with this point that Zoroaster began. All the many gods of nature (the daevas) that his people worshiped and the gods to whom they offered sacrificial animals were declared to be false gods. For its time Zoroaster's monotheism must have been revolutionary. Prior to him there were few who believed that there was one and only one god. There was the monotheism of Aten supported by Amenophis IV (Akhenaten), the Pharaoh of Egypt in the fourteenth century B.C., but apparently this religion survived less than twenty years, and then the

---

[4]Yasna 44.

Egyptians went back to their polytheism. Moses, living in the thirteenth century B.C., is said to have taught the Israelites that they were to have no other gods before Yahweh, but he never denied the existence of other gods. It is no wonder that Zoroaster's assertion that there was only one god was so controversial in the seventh and sixth centuries B.C.

The one true god in Zoroaster's religion, Ahura Mazda, was the same god who had been worshiped by the Aryan people for centuries as the distant high god. Zoroaster simply declared that he was the only god. The name *Ahura* means "lord" and indicates one who created and governs the universe. The name *Mazda* means "all wisdom." Thus Ahura Mazda is usually translated as "Wise Lord." Zoroastrian scripture attributes another twenty names to this god, such as He of Whom Questions Are Asked, Giver of Herds, Strong One, Perfect Holiness, Understanding, Blessing, the Unconquerable, Healing, the Creator, etc.[5] Ahura Mazda is understood to be the invisible and intangible creator and ruler of the universe.

In Zoroaster's understanding of his god, Ahura Mazda revealed himself to humankind through the agency of six modes. These are the *Amesha-Spenta* (usually translated as "Holy Immortals"). Western scholars have tended to equate these six modes with the archangels found in Christian theology or with some form of secondary deity. The analogy is not exact, however. The six figures are really six outstanding attributes of Ahura Mazda. Since people cannot properly comprehend the nature of god, Ahura Mazda comes to them as one of these aspects of his total nature. Three of the immortals bear masculine names and carry masculine qualities, while the other three bear feminine names and represent feminine qualities. Thus the total nature of Ahura Mazda is an equal balance of the male and female. The three masculine or father types of these immortals are *Asha* ("knowledge of the law of God and the law itself"), *Vohu-Mana* ("love"), and *Kshathra* ("loving service"). The three feminine immortals are *Armaiti* ("piety"), *Haurvatat* ("wholeness" or "perfection"), and *Ameretat* ("immortality"). Faithful Zoroastrians pray that these six immortals may come into their homes and bless them.

In addition to these expressions of the total nature of Ahura Mazda, there are other beings who serve him and who may be helpful to human beings. If the six immortals were the archangels of Zoroastrianism the multiple *Yazata* ("Adorable Ones") would be the hosts of

---

[5]Ormazd Yast, 5, 7.

angels surrounding the throne of God. They are limitless in number, but only about forty are mentioned in the Zoroastrian texts and only three receive any regular mention. These angels are *Sraosha*, the guardian of humanity who shows obedience to the law of God; his sister and feminine counterpart, *Ashi Vanguhi*, who is the rewarder of good deeds; and the ever-popular *Mithra*, the strongest of these beings and the ideal of soldiers.

The God of Evil

Perhaps Zoroaster's greatest contribution to the religions of the world was in the area of the problem of evil. The world is full of both good and evil. It is easy enough to ascribe the good in the world to the good God who has created the world, but who is responsible for the evil? If the creator God is responsible for the evil of the world, then where is his goodness and justice? Many religions have their powers of darkness, their demons, but it remained for Zoroaster to systematize and delineate the forces behind the world's evil.

Zoroastrianism is often referred to as dualistic, that is, as a religion that sees two supreme forces contending with each other for control of the universe. The usual interpretation of Zoroastrianism is that it recognizes a good god and his angels who are in charge of the good that happens in the world, and it recognizes an evil god and his demons who are responsible for all of the world's evil. But if this were Zoroaster's understanding of the universe, then he would not be teaching a monotheism but a dualism. In the same vein one might say that since Christianity recognizes a Satan figure, it too is not monotheistic. This is not the case in the teachings of Zoroaster. According to him there are two spirits emanating from Ahura Mazda; one is Spenta Mainyu, the Beneficent Spirit; the other is Angra Mainyu, the Evil Spirit. These two have coexisted since the beginning of time.

> Now the two primal Spirits, who revealed themselves in vision as Twins, are the Better and the Bad in thought and word and action. And between these two the wise once chose aright, and the foolish not so.
>
> And when these twain spirits came together in the beginning, they established Life and Not-Life, and that at the last the Worst Existence shall be to the followers of the Lie, but the Best Thought to him that follows Right. . . .[6]

---

[6]Yasna 30:3, 4.

These two spirits do not exist independently but relate to one another and meet in unity of Ahura Mazda. In this sense they are much like the yin and yang of Taoism. Neither is free from the influence of the other and each is bound by the other. In the truest sense Zoroastrianism remains a monotheism with the forces of both good and evil under the control of Ahura Mazda.

Angra Mainyu is also known by other names. He is sometimes known as Ahriman and at other times, as Shaitin or Satan. He is surrounded and abetted by a host of demons who do his bidding in tempting and tormenting human beings. Zoroastrianism may have been the first religion to develop a full scheme of demonology. All of the daevas of pre-Zoroastrian Aryan religion came to be identified as demons in the corps of Angra Mainyu. One of the most frequently mentioned of these demons is Aeshma, the demon of wrath.[7] Aeshma is second in command to Angra Mainyu and stalks the earth, polluting it and spreading disease and death.

The Nature of Humankind

Zoroaster saw the forces of good struggling with the forces of evil in the world, and he taught that human beings played a part in this struggle by cooperating with either of the forces. To Zoroaster men and women were born in a pure, sinless state and could choose to serve either good or evil. Their lives and ultimate destiny depended on the exercise of their free will. If they wished individuals could serve the forces of evil—they could cooperate in lies, hate, corruption, and every sort of evil—but they could also choose to be a part of good acts that would improve the world. The choice of conduct was entirely up to the individual. In this respect Zoroastrianism is markedly different from other religions. Christianity speaks of original sin that causes humankind to do evil unless redeemed by God. Islam sees human lives as determined by Allah, with people having little choice about their conduct. Other forms of determinism see the events in people's lives as determined by social or economic forces. Unlike these philosophies of human nature, Zoroastrianism taught that men and women were genuinely free to decide if they would do good or evil and thus were to be held accountable for those choices.

---

[7]Some scholars have suggested that Aeshma is the demon Asmodeus, who tormented Sarah and killed her seven bridegrooms in the Apocryphal book of Tobit.

Hear with your ears the Highest Truths I preach,
And with illumined minds weigh them with care,
Before you choose which of Two Paths to tread,—
Deciding man by man, each one for each;—
Before the great New Age is ushered in
Wake up, alert to spread Ahura's Word.[8]

By exercising the reason with which they were endowed, it is possible for human beings to choose the path of righteousness and in fact achieve perfection in this life. Therefore a scheme of multiple lives such as that of Hinduism is not necessary for Zoroastrianism.

Within the span of this one life of Earth
Perfection can be reached by fervent souls,
Ardent in zeal, sincere in their toil.[9]

Thus we see that in Zoroastrianism, perhaps more than in any other religion, ethical conduct is urged. Ethical conduct is possible since people have a free choice, and ethical conduct is important since it will determine people's ultimate destiny.

The Destiny of Humankind

Because people have freedom of choice they must stand responsible for their choices. Each deed, either good or evil, will bear its own fruits. Therefore Zoroastrianism sees a law of retribution at work in this life. That which is called karma in Hinduism and that which is stated by St. Paul as "whatsoever a man soweth, that shall he also reap"[10] is also taught in Zoroastrianism: "Evil to Evil, Good to Good."[11]

Falsehood brings on age-long punishment,
And Truth leads on to fuller, higher life.[12]

In this case Zoroastrianism may be unique among all religions. Zoroastrians so firmly believe in the freedom of people to choose good

[8] Yasna 30:2.
[9] Yasna 51:12.
[10] Galatians 6:7.
[11] Yasna 43:5.
[12] Yasna 30:11.

Sassanian period relief, Kermanshaw Province, Iran, 226
A.D. *Zoroastrianism was proclaimed the official religion of*
Persia during this period.

or evil and in the inevitability of retribution for those choices that there
is no means of atonement for evil deeds. There is no one to intercede
for the sinner, there are no prayers that can change the results of the
deed, and there are no offerings that can cover the sin. Human beings
choose how they will live, and they are wholly responsible for that
choice.

Another of Zoroaster's gifts to the world of Western religions was his
organized scheme of eschatology (belief concerning the end of the
world). In religions prior to Zoroastrianism there were sometimes
elaborate preparations for the life beyond the grave as it was with the
ancient Egyptians. However, in most religions it was simply assumed
that with death, life essentially came to an end. The ancient Hebrews,

for example, believed that the dead lived in a realm called Sheol for a time and then gradually faded into nothingness. Perhaps the Aryan kinsmen of Zoroaster living in India had begun to think in terms of reincarnation by this time, but that is not clear. Zoroaster and his followers developed a complete eschatology that was the consistent outworking of his theology of free choice and complete responsibility.

According to Zoroastrianism upon the death of an individual the soul stays with the body for three days and meditates upon the deeds that were done in life. On the fourth day the soul journeys to the place of judgment. There Mithra judges the soul based on the deeds performed during life. These deeds are balanced on a scale. If the preponderance of a person's life has been given over to evil, that person's soul will be sentenced to hell, but if the scale tips even slightly toward good, that person's soul will go to paradise. The soul on its way to paradise crosses the Chinvat bridge, which is a wide, easy path. The soul is greeted by beautiful maidens who escort it into heaven. Zoroastrian paradise is a place of beauty, light, pleasant scents, and noble souls who have lived life according to Zoroastrian ethics.

For the person whose balance is weighted down by evil deeds and thoughts, the Chinvat bridge becomes an entirely different experience. Once condemned, the soul is forced out upon this bridge which turns up on its edge and becomes as hard to walk on as the edge of a sword. Moreover, the soul is tormented by an old hag and eventually falls off the bridge and into hell. Zoroastrian hell is one of the most terrible hells of all. It is vividly described in a work called the *Vision of Arda Viraf*, which was written sometime between 226–641 A.D. In this work the hero is allowed to travel to both heaven and hell, and there to see the miseries and delights of its inhabitants.

> I saw the greedy jaws of hell: the most frightful pit, descending, in a very narrow, fearful crevice and in darkness so murky that I was forced to feel my way, amid such a stench that all whose nose inhaled that air, struggled, staggered, and fell, and in such confinement that existence seemed impossible. Each one thought, "I am alone"; and when a mere three days had elapsed supposed that the end of the nine thousand years of time had come, when time would cease and the resurrection of the body occur. "The nine thousand years are run," he would think, "yet, I am not released." In that place even the lesser noxious creatures are as high as mountains, and these so tear, seize, and worry the souls of the wicked as would be

unworthy of a dog. But I passed easily thereby in the guidance of Obedience and Thought.

I saw the soul of a man through whose fundament a snake went in, like a beam, and came forth out of the mouth; and many other snakes ever seized his limbs. "What sin," I inquired, "was committed by this body whose soul suffers so severe a punishment?" "This," I was told, "is the soul of a man who, in the world, committed sodomy."

A woman's soul I saw, to whom they gave to drink one cupful after another of the impurity and filth of men. I asked, "What sin was committed by the body whose soul thus suffers?" "Having failed to abstain," they replied, "this wicked woman approached water and fire during menstruation." I saw also, the soul of a man, the skin of whose head was being flayed . . . who, in the world, had slain a pious man. I saw the soul of a man into whose mouth they poured continually the menstrual discharge of women, while he cooked and ate his own child . . . "While in the world," I was told, "that wicked man had intercourse with a menstruating woman."[13]

The scene continues with all sorts of horrors. It seems the Zoroastrian hell is filled with men and women who have broken the laws of clean and unclean and who are being punished accordingly. Also there is a large category of men and women who have violated the sexual taboos of Zoroastrianism and who are being punished in a particularly horrible manner.

In the Zoroastrian scheme the souls of the dead abide in their heaven and hell until that point when time ends. The cycle of time will run out as a specified point in the future, and the world will come to its final consummation as established by Ahura Mazda when he created the world. He will wipe out every trace of the evil work of Angra Mainyu. The souls from hell will be brought up and purified and will join the resurrected souls of the righteous. Then the world will enter a new cycle without the evil and misery of the past. The Saoshyant will restore the world, and in this restored world no one will ever grow old or decay. Angra Mainyu and his demons will be destroyed forever, and the will of Ahura Mazda will reign supreme.

---

[13] Joseph Campbell, *The Masks of God: Occidental Mythology* (New York: The Viking Press, 1964), pp. 198, 199.

Zoroastrian Ethics

Since the essence of Zoroastrian theology is that people are free to choose between good and evil in this life and will be held responsible for their choices in an afterlife, one would expect Zoroastrians to have a lengthy and involved code of ethics. This is in fact the case, and Zoroastrians as a people have long been noted in both the ancient world and the modern for their high ethical standards.[14]

The basis for much of Zoroastrian ethics and worship is the understanding of the sacredness of the elements of the earth, fire, water, and air. Whatever violates or pollutes these sacred elements is wicked. Thus in the Zoroastrian hell those who have polluted the earth or the water with their excrement are subject to unusually harsh punishments. The concern for the elements is seen again and again in Zoroastrian life.

Zoroastrianism also teaches a concern for *Humata, Hukhta,* and *Hvarshta,* good thought, good word, and good deed. A prayer is "Henceforth let me stand firm for good thoughts, good words, and good deeds, which must be well thought, must be well spoken, and must be well done."[15] Based upon these rather general concerns are the specific demands of Zoroastrianism for righteousness as expressed in truthfulness, chastity, justice, compassion, care of the soil and cattle, charity, education, and service. The ancient Persians were known to the Greek historians for these virtues, particularly for the virtue of truthfulness. In modern India, where most contemporary Zoroastrians live, they are known for their purity of life, for their honesty as businesspeople, and for their concern over the education of their children.

Zoroastrian Worship

Pre-Zoroastrian Aryan worship depended heavily upon blood sacrifices to the various deities, but Zoroaster drastically changed these patterns. Zoroastrian worship consists mainly of prayers offered to Ahura Mazda requesting assistance in living a righteous life and in avoiding temptations. The only form of sacrifice that currently exists is the offering of sandalwood to sacred flames which burn eternally in

---

[14]The Hebrew Bible pays tribute to the ethics of the Persian when it refers to "the law of the Medes and Persians which altereth not." Esther 1:19.

[15]Sir Rustom Masani, *Zoroastrianism: The Religion of the Good Life* (New York: Macmillan, 1968), p. 78.

Zoroastrian fire temples. These fires are tended by priests who have been especially trained for their tasks and who wear surgical masks over their faces lest their breath contaminate the sacred flames. On special occasions during the year Zoroastrians visit the fire temple, offer bundles of sandalwood, and receive the ashes of the sacred flames.

In addition to these forms of worship there are Zoroastrian rituals for each of the points in life that are normally associated with rites of passage. There are ceremonies that attend the birth of a child. Zoroastrian scripture lays out very careful regulations regarding the state of purification of the household and the mother at the time of the birth of a child.

At a certain age (seven years in India and ten years in Iran) young Zoroastrians are received into this religion with the investiture of a sacred shirt *(sadre)* and sacred thread *(kusti)*. Except when bathing they must wear these two items for the rest of their lives. The *kusti* is to be tied and untied on at least five occasions during each day as a form of prayer. This sacred belt is made up of seventy-two threads which represent the seventy-two chapters of the Zoroastrian scripture, the Yasna. Other threads and constructions of threads represent other aspects to the faithful Zoroastrian.

There are, of course, Zoroastrian ceremonies at other important points in life such as marriage, periods of purification, and initiation into the priesthood for those who choose it. The most distinctive ritual of all, however, is that which occurs at death. If one believes that earth, fire, water, and air are the most sacred elements in life and if one believes that the corpse is the most contaminating element of all, then how is one to dispose of the dead? The body cannot be buried lest it contaminate the soil; it cannot be cremated lest it contaminate the sacred fire; and it cannot be buried at sea lest water be polluted. The Zoroastrian solution to this problem is one which has attracted widespread attention.

When a Zoroastrian dies, the corpse is washed, a clean suit of clothes is placed upon it, and the *kusti* of the deceased is wrapped around the body. After certain purification ceremonies the body is carried out of the house by corpse bearers. The corpse bearers, along with the mourners, take the body to an enclosure called a *Dakhma*, or "tower of silence." This enclosure looks something like a small version of an American football stadium. It is a round structure, open to the sky. Inside the *Dakhma* there are open compartments and, in the center, a dry well. The body is placed in one of the compartments and its clothing is either removed or torn open. The mourners leave the site and within a few moments vultures descend upon the body and begin to strip it of its flesh. In an area where there are fairly frequent deaths, a large number of vultures usually stay near the *Dakhmas* and within thirty minutes they are able to strip the body cleanly. After a time, when the bones are dried out by the sun, they are washed down into the central well of the *Dakhma*. Thus the body of the Zoroastrian is disposed of without risking contamination of the soil, fire, or water.

The principle of exposing the dead to birds and beasts of prey seems to have been a part of Zoroastrian life from earliest times. The Zend-Avesta commands the following procedure:

> And two men, strong and agile, having changed their gar-
> ments, shall lift the body from the clay or the stones, or out of
> the plastered house, and they shall lay it down at a place where
> they know that there are always corpse-eating dogs and corpse-
> eating birds.[16]

Zoroastrian disposal of the dead occasionally runs into problems when the community is small and deaths are so infrequent that there are not large numbers of vultures about the *Dakhmas*. On some occasions there is protest against this procedure by non-Zoroastrian majorities. In such situations it is permissible to bury the body in a stone casket that has been lined with lead to prevent contamination of the soil. Modern Zoroastrians living in Western cities where the practice of exposing the dead may be frowned upon have begun thinking in terms of cremation by means of an electrical oven, since the body might be burned in this fashion without exposing it to a flame.

THE HISTORICAL DEVELOPMENT OF ZOROASTRIANISM

If it were certain that Zoroaster was born in the seventh century B.C. and if he lived to be seventy-seven years old, then he would have died early in the sixth century B.C. One could then assume that his religion had begun to take hold of the Aryan people and that it was the religion of the first emperor of the Medo-Persian Empire, Cyrus, who reigned from 558–530 B.C. and who is mentioned in the Jewish Bible as the one

---

[16]Vendidad Fargard VIII, c. II, 10.

who liberated the Jews from Babylonian captivity about 538 B.C. However, none of the sources is that clear about these events. As we have said before, the events in the life of Zoroaster are not clearly supported even as to the century in which he lived. We have no proof that Cyrus was a Zoroastrian. The only sources of early Persian Empire religion are the inscriptions of Darius (522–486 B.C.), which indicate that his people worshiped Ahura Mazda. The inscriptions, however, do not mention Zoroaster.

> A great god is Ahuramazda, who created this excellent work which is seen, who created happiness for man, who bestowed wisdom and activity upon Darius the king.
>
> Says Darius the king: By the favor of Ahuramazda I am of such a sort that I am a friend to the right, I am not a friend to wrong; it is not my desire that the weak man should have wrong done to him by the mighty; nor is that my desire, that the mighty man should have wrong done him by the weak.
>
> What is right, that is my desire. I am not a friend to the man who is a Lie-follower. I am not hot-tempered. What things develop in my anger, I hold firmly under control by my willpower. I am firmly ruling over my own [impulses].[17]

It was not until the era of the Sassanid rulers of Persia (226–642 A.D.) that Zoroastrianism officially became the religion of the empire. Zoroastrianism may have had a great influence upon the Persians prior to the Sassanids, but we have little proof of it.

Zoroastrian influence upon peoples and religions other than the Persians is also a matter of some speculation. Many of the ancient Greek and Roman writers were apparently enamored with Zoroaster and his thoughts, and he is featured in many of their writings. However, the Persian emperors of the fifth century B.C. failed in several attempts to conquer Greece. Consequently Persian influence was never strong there. Persia did conquer and hold the Middle East for two centuries, and its influence was very strong upon the peoples of that world. The Jews came under Persian control in 538 B.C. when Cyrus conquered Babylon, where many Jews lived in captivity. According to the Bible, Cyrus allowed the captive Jews to return to Jerusalem. Apparently a minority of the Jews returned, but most

---

[17]Jack Finegan. *The Archaeology of World Religions* (Princeton: Princeton University Press, 1952), p. 95.

*The birth of Mithras. Mithras was believed to have been
born from a rock. He holds his short sword and the torch,
symbols of his obedience to the god Sol Invictus (the
unconquered sun). Other symbols of events in his life
surround his birth scene.*

stayed in Mesopotamia and became a part of the culture there. If the
book of Esther is correct, a Jewess even became the wife of the king of
Persia.

How much influence did Zoroastrianism have upon Judaism during
this period? We cannot be certain. However, there are certain changes
in the theology of Judaism between the preexilic days of 586 B.C. and
the postexilic period beginning in 538 B.C. Biblical books which reflect
the period prior to 586 B.C. have no Satan figure. However, the literature that was written after the exile speaks of a Satan figure four
times.[18] In the Intertestamental literature Satan and his demons are
mentioned frequently, and in the New Testament literature they are

---

[18]I Chronicles 21:1, Job, Zechariah 3, and Psalm 109.

accepted as a regular part of life. Jesus is confronted by Satan as he begins his public ministry, and a large part of that ministry is devoted to exorcising demons. Preexilic biblical books have no mention of the resurrection of the body, little concern for life after death in either a heaven or a hell, no mention of God's plan for bringing the earth to an end, only an occasional mention of angels, and no word about a day of judgment. Each of these themes, which were a part of the teachings of Zoroastrianism, developed in Judaism after the exile and had become vital parts of the religion by the time of Jesus.

The early Christians incorporated these items into their religion. In later years it was the eschatology of Judaism and Christianity that most deeply influenced the prophet Muhammad, and judgment day, resurrection, heaven, hell, Satan, demons, and angels all became a vital part of Islam. It may be that all of these major religions drew their eschatology from Zoroastrianism.

The Persian Empire was conquered by Alexander the Great in the fourth century B.C. In the years that followed, Zoroastrianism suffered a decline. The entire Persian culture was invaded by the pervasive Hellenistic culture. During the era of the Roman Empire Zoroastrianism was quiescent also. All that seems to have been active in this period was the cult of Mithra. The Roman Empire became acquainted with Mithra in the first century A.D. Mithra, the god of light and obedience, appealed especially to the Roman soldier, and soon Mithraic cults were established over the entire Mediterranean world. The worship of Mithra became so popular that some suggest it was a major rival to early Christianity. However, when Christianity was declared to be the official religion of the Roman Empire, Mithraism was suppressed.

A revival of Zoroastrianism occurred in the third century A.D. under the Sassanid rulers of Persia. These rulers established official support for Zoroastrianism and had the ancient scriptures translated into contemporary language. The religion continued to flourish until the seventh century. At this time Islam was arising out of the desert regions to the south of Persia. By 642 the Muslim warriors had, with three major battles, caused the collapse of the Sassanian empire. At first the Muslims were tolerant of the Zoroastrians. The latter were, after all, a people with a book (scripture) and they worshiped only one god. However, by the ninth century Muslim persecution of the Zoroastrians had grown to such a point that most Zoroastrians were forced to either convert to Islam or flee the country. Those who chose to flee followed the path of their ancient Aryan relatives and went to

India. There they found tolerance by the Hindu majority and were known as the Parsees (that is, those who came from Persia). They remained an insignificant minority in India until the nineteenth century when the British arrived. Because the Parsee were not encumbered with the caste system or intricate food taboos and because they valued education, they quickly became favorites of the British. As a result of this favored position in British India, the modern Parsee community leads in fields such as education, business, and finance in a far greater way than its minority status would indicate.

Today the religion of Zoroaster is kept by an insignificant minority (approximately 11,000) in Iran known as *Gabars* ("infidels"), by a larger minority (approximately 100,000) in India, and in other small communities around the world.

SUGGESTED READING

Duchesne-Guillemin, Jacques. *Symbols and Values in Zoroastrianism*. New York: Harper & Row, 1966.

Herzfeld, Ernst. *Zoroaster and His World*. 2 vols. Princeton: Princeton University Press, 1946.

Masani, Rustom. *Zoroastrianism: The Religion of the Good Life*. New York: Macmillan, 1968.

Vermaseren, M. J. *Mithras, The Secret God*. Translated by Therese and Vincent Megaw, New York: Barnes & Noble Books, 1963.

Zaehner, R. C. *The Dawn and Twilight of Zoroastrianism*. New York: Putnam, 1961.

CHAPTER ELEVEN
JUDAISM

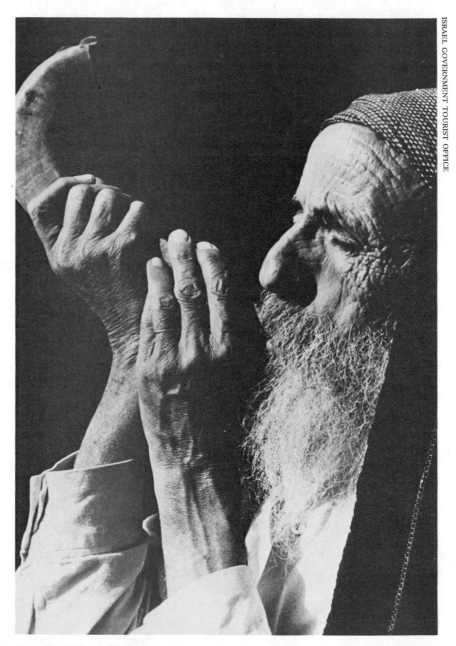

Raising the ancient ram's horn.

Hear, O Israel: The Lord our God is one; and you shall love
the Lord your God with all your heart, and with all your
soul, and with all your might.

DEUTERONOMY 6:4, 5

One of the most perplexing problems that arises in any discussion of Judaism is its definition. If we were to define Judaism as we define any other religion, we might say that a Jew is anyone who adheres to a certain set of Jewish religious beliefs or practices. Indeed in many cases this may be a very effective definition. Unfortunately the issue has been clouded so that it is not always so simple. Alan W. Miller in his introduction to *The God of Daniel S.: In Search of the American Jew* lists eight different types of persons who are called Jews in American society. These range all the way from the extremely orthodox Hasidic Jew to the person whose parents or grandparents happened to be born Jewish.

Judaism cannot be defined primarily in terms of religious beliefs because there are some people who are called Jews but consider themselves atheists. Adolph Hitler found it expedient to define Judaism in terms of race, but in modern Israel Jews display the physical characteristics of nearly every race. There are European Jews, African Jews, and Oriental Jews. The problem of identifying the Jew is so complex that someone has suggested that "a Jew is anyone, anyone else chooses to call a Jew." Indeed the history of Judaism, especially its last fifty years, would seem to give some truth to that statement.

If we cannot define Judaism in terms of all people who might be called Jews, we can speak of those people who identify themselves with the religion of Judaism. Though religious practices among Jews differ widely, generally the unifying feature among all Jews is a belief in the oneness of a God who works in and through historical events and who has in some manner chosen the Jewish people as agents. Around this basic principle Judaism is built.

THE BIBLICAL PATRIARCHS

Since Judaism is concerned with God's activity in history, it is necessary to describe Jewish beliefs and practices historically. According to the Bible, God found it necessary to call out one man and his family from all the people on earth. This calling of Abraham is recorded in Genesis 12. It came after a series of disastrous dealings with all humankind (Adam and Eve, Cain and Abel, the flood, the tower of Babel, etc.). Because of these disasters God chose to communicate with only one nation, the descendants of Abraham. Abraham was called to enter a covenant with God in which Abraham was promised that he would become the father of a great nation, would possess a land, and would become a blessing to all people if he would be faithful to his part of the covenant. Abraham is succeeded in this covenant by his son Isaac, his grandson Jacob (or Israel), and Jacob's twelve sons. These figures are called the patriarchs of the Jewish people because they are the physical forebears of the nation, and their stories are found in Genesis 12–50. These tales were probably written by authors generations after the times of the patriarchs. Though some scholars doubt the historicity of these figures, their names and their ways of life fit into history of the Fertile Crescent at the beginning of the second millennium B.C.

If there were people like Abraham and Isaac who were the forebears of the Jews, what was the nature of their lives and their religion? The biblical narratives present the patriarchs as nomads following their flocks from place to place. Abraham is described as a citizen of the city of Ur of the Chaldees (Genesis 11:31) who left his home to follow the voice of God to the land of Canaan on the western side of the Fertile Crescent. Historically he could have been one of the waves of Amorites who flooded the Fertile Crescent between 2000–1750 B.C. The Mari letters from Mesopotamia in this era reveal the use of such names as Benjamin and Jacob, indicating the historical plausibility of the biblical narrative.

Though the Bible does not give the reader a systematic presentation of the religious beliefs and practices of the patriarchs, the narratives reveal a great deal about their theology. They worshiped one God who was guiding their destinies. The generic name for God among the

Semites is *El*. This name is frequently used in various combinations in the patriarchal literature to refer to their God. He is called *El Shaddai* ("God of the mountains" or "God Almighty"); *El Elyon* ("God Most High"); *El Olam* ("God Everlasting") and most frequently, *Elohim* ("Gods").[1]

This God was worshiped by burning animal sacrifices on crude altars built in the open. The Israelites apparently did not worship their God in a building or a temple until the time of Solomon (961–922 B.C.). In the story of Abraham's attempt to offer his son Isaac upon the command of God (Genesis 22) there is a hint that the patriarchs may have practiced human sacrifices in previous times.

There are also indications of basic animistic practices in the worship of the patriarchs. Abraham made a covenant with Abimelech in Beersheba and called upon the name of God. To seal the covenant Abraham planted a grove in Beersheba (Genesis 21:32, 33). God appeared to Isaac and reaffirmed the covenant while Isaac was digging wells near Beersheba (Genesis 26:17–25). Jacob slept upon certain stones and in his dreams God spoke to him and renewed the covenant (Genesis 28:11–16). The connection between the appearance of God, the reaffirmation of the covenant, and the typical animistic symbols of trees, wells, and stones may be significant.

From very early in the worship of the patriarchs, circumcision of the male was practiced. Genesis traces the ritual back to a commandment of God to Abraham (Genesis 17:10, 11). However, circumcision is a very ancient and widespread religious custom which probably did not originate with Abraham. In addition, the practice of keeping a Sabbath may have been a part of the worship of the patriarchs. Genesis attaches the custom to the days of creation, when God rested on the seventh day after laboring for six days (Genesis 2:2). It is not clear in the patriarchal stories what the practices of these figures were on the Sabbath.

THE EXODUS

Whatever their religious practices may have been and whatever gods they may have worshiped, the stories of the patriarchs are in Genesis to give the reader a reason for the most important event in Judaism, the

---

[1]The use of the plural here is a mystery. While it might be tempting to assume that at one point the patriarchs may have been polytheists, there is nothing in the narratives to indicate worship to any but the one God, and the term is used only in a singular sense.

Exodus. God promised Abraham that a great nation would spring from his seed, that this nation would have a homeland (Canaan), and that the entire world would be blessed by this nation. The book of Genesis closes with a great nation springing up from the descendants of Abraham, but they were not in Canaan. They were in Egypt, where they were bound in slavery. Therefore, the Exodus from Egypt and their slavery, the journey back to Canaan, and the conquest of the land had to be accomplished before God's promise to Abraham could be fulfilled. The events and characters of the Exodus—in which God acted to save his chosen people, the Israelites; in which he miraculously delivered them from slavery at the hands of the most powerful nation in the world at that time; in which he revealed his name and his laws to its leaders and finally brought the former slaves as a conquering army into Canaan—became the heart and soul of the Jewish religion. These events are remembered annually in the various major holidays of Judaism. The legal material which is attributed to the Sinai experience became the most important material in the Jewish Bible.

The book of Exodus opens with the descendants of Abraham, the Israelites, crying out for deliverance from their enslavement by the Egyptians. The key figure in this drama of salvation is Moses. Like many great figures in religion, Moses was endangered as an infant by the forces of evil and was miraculously delivered. He was rescued and reared by the daughter of the Pharaoh of Egypt. Since the name *Moses* is an Egyptian name, there may be a factual basis for the story. Recognizing his Israelite heritage and killing an Egyptian in defense of a slave, Moses was exiled to the Sinai desert, where he lived for forty years as a shepherd. In the desert the God of Abraham revealed himself to Moses, speaking through a bush which burned but was not consumed. The God revealed that his name was YHWH[2] and commanded Moses to lead the Israelites from their slavery. Moses returned to Egypt and, after a series of ten miraculous plagues upon the Egyptians, was able to gain the release of the Israelites. The final plague was death to the firstborn of every house in Egypt. Israelites who ate a sacred meal of roasted lamb, bitter herbs, and unleavened bread and who smeared lamb's blood upon their doorposts were passed over by the angel of death.

When the Israelites fled Egypt, they were pursued by the Pharaoh, who had changed his mind about their release. The waters of the Sea

[2]The vowels of this name have been lost because Jews preferred not to pronounce the divine name lest they take it in vain. Many modern scholars vocalize it as Yahweh.

of Reeds[3] were parted by YHWH, and the Israelites crossed through on dry land. When the Egyptians attempted to follow them, the waters receded, and the Egyptians were trapped and drowned. This event, along with the Passover, became a part of Jewish history as an act in which God intervened to deliver his chosen people.

The next event of significance was the giving of the law on Mt. Sinai. After crossing the Sea of Reeds, the Israelites came to Mt. Sinai on their journey to Canaan. From this mountain, YHWH communicated his law to the Israelites through Moses. Ten absolute laws that are basic to Jewish life are found in Exodus 20:1–17. They may be summarized as follows:

1. I am the Lord your God, who has brought you out of the land of Egypt, out of the house of bondage. You shall have no other gods before me.

2. You shall not make any graven image.

3. You shall not take the name of the Lord your God in vain. . . .

4. Remember the sabbath day, to keep it holy.

5. Honor your father and your mother.

6. You shall not kill.

7. You shall not commit adultery.

8. You shall not steal.

9. You shall not bear false witness against your neighbor.

10. You shall not covet your neighbor's property.

Basically, these commandments stress obedience and loyalty to YHWH and decent behavior towards members of the community. In the books of Exodus, Leviticus, and portions of Numbers and Deuteronomy which follow, elaborate codes of law regulating every area of life are laid out. These laws purport to have been given by God through Moses during the wilderness experience, but many of them reflect a community which has been established in agricultural life for centuries.

Whenever they may have been codified, the legal material in the Pentateuch (the first five books of the Bible) became the single most important part of the Bible for Judaism. It is to this material that Jews have turned for centuries, looking for inspiration and guidance. It is

---

[3]The usual reading of this as "Red Sea" is based upon an ancient mistranslation.

this material which became the basis for the later Mishnah and Talmud, which in turn became central for Judaism. It is at this point that Judaism is defined as a religion of the law and Jews as a people primarily concerned with obedience to the laws of God.

In addition to the laws of God, the years in the Sinai wilderness gave the Israelites two other religious institutions. These were the Ark of the Covenant and the Tent of Meeting. The Ark of the Covenant was a coffinlike box which contained the sacred relics of the Exodus and which may have been the portable throne of YHWH. This box was the most treasured sacred possession of the Israelites and was eventually placed in Solomon's temple in the tenth century B.C. It presumably remained there until the temple was destroyed by the Babylonians in 586 B.C. The Tent of Meeting was not so popular or long lived as the Ark. It was literally a tent which could be moved from place to place with the nomadic Israelites. It provided a place for the worship of YHWH and sacrifice to him. After the Israelites entered Canaan, it is mentioned only once in connection with the cult at Shiloh.

After a period of wandering in the wilderness, the Bible records that the Israelites conquered the territories on the east bank of the Jordan River. Then, under the leadership of Joshua, Moses' successor, they crossed the Jordan and conquered the cities of Canaan. Two conflicting accounts are given. According to the book of Joshua, the Israelites swept across the country and destroyed every major city held by the Canaanites. The book of Judges tells another story, however. Here we have a picture of the worshipers of YHWH living side by side with the native dwellers of Canaan and sometimes even being subjected to them. Later events seem to support the second story.

When the Israelites settled in Canaan, they renewed their covenant with YHWH. The cult of YHWH, its ark, its priests, and its sacrifices was centered in Shiloh. Worship at this time seems to have been a rather informal matter. The cultic priests attended to those who came to the center for special needs and on special days. They were in turn supported by the gifts of those who came to worship and perhaps the donations of the various tribal groups who surrounded the cult center.

THE RELIGION OF THE HEBREW MONARCHY

The religion of Israel took a more formal turn when David became the first truly effective king of the Israelites. David, who was from the southern portion of the country, needed a central capital and a cult to

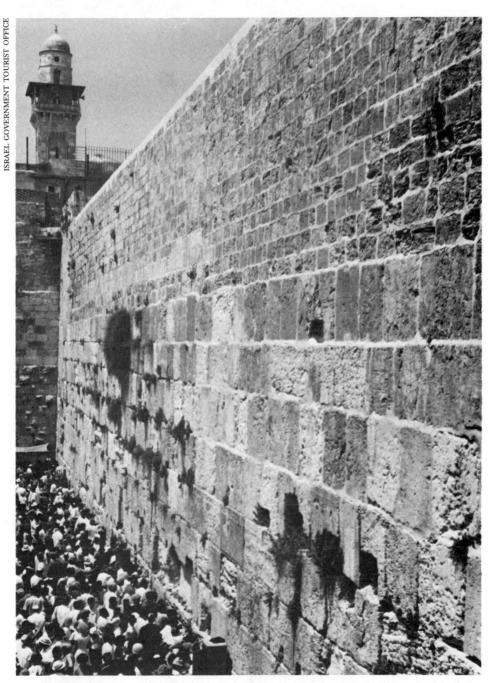

All that remains of the outer wall that once enclosed the temple area of Jerusalem is a portion of the western side known as the Wailing Wall, one of the most sacred sites of Judaism. Pilgrims come here to pray and recite from the Torah.

unify his nation. He captured Jerusalem in the central hill country and made it his capital. Jerusalem had little to recommend it except its location, its easily defended hills, and perhaps a history as a sacred site. David and later historical events parlayed these features into making Jerusalem one of the most important, most disputed cities in the world. David's abilities as a military leader and administrator helped Israel to develop into a fairly powerful and wealthy small nation of the ancient Middle East. The Bible tells us that David wished to build a magnificent temple for YHWH in Jerusalem but was forbidden.

The Temple

It remained for Solomon, David's son and successor, to build the temple. With all the wealth that his father had amassed, Solomon built a palace for himself and a temple for his God. Strangely enough, the temple was designed by Tyrian builders who were worshipers of the Baalim, the gods of the Canaanites and Phoenicians, condemned in the Bible. The temple naturally took the form of other Canaanite temples for the Baalim. The Ark of the Covenant was placed in the temple, and a class of priests were attached to the temple. Worship of YHWH thus took on a more formal status. The main form of worship remained the animal sacrifice with its flesh burned in the courtyard. In the temple prayers were offered to YHWH, and, if the example of David is typical, there may also have been sacred dancing before the Ark (II Samuel 6:14).

The Prophetic Movement

With the development of the temple cult another aspect was introduced into the worship of Israel. Other ancient religions, including that of the worship of the Baalim, had developed bodies of religious leaders called prophets. In their earlier forms, the prophetic figures were persons involved in the ecstatic aspects of worship. Unlike the priests, whose duties involved the proper offerings of sacrifices, the prophets of ancient religions danced, sang, breathed incense, and worked themselves into an ecstatic state in order to hear the voices of their gods. The prophets of Israel may have begun in this fashion.[4] Occasionally they performed the function of the witch doctors of other

---

[4]See I Samuel 19:24.

religions. They healed the sick, cursed, blessed, produced food for their followers, and worked other miracles.[5]

Eventually a portion of the Israelite prophetic movement became attached to the royal household. The first of these prophets to be involved with the palace was Nathan, who was part of the court of David. It was Nathan who accused David after David had murdered Uriah and taken Uriah's wife, but it was also Nathan who was instrumental in placing Solomon on the throne at the death of David. Others who were more or less attached to the royal houses or at least had the ear of the kings were Elijah, Isaiah, and Jeremiah. Still other prophets were common men who preached fiery denunciations against wickedness among peasants and royalty. Outstanding in this group were men like Amos and Micah. These prophets must have been but a few of many who preached in troubled times. Their messages were remembered and preserved by their disciples and eventually written into the Bible.

In contemporary English, the word *prophet* has the connotation of prediction, but to label all the works of the prophets of Israel as predictions is to do them injustice. In the social and political upheavals of the eighth century B.C., the prophetic movement produced four classic figures—Amos, Hosea, Isaiah, and Micah—who are remembered not so much for their predictions as for the boldness with which they denounced the social injustices of their times and the beautiful, poetic language with which they bade the Israelites to return to their God.

> Thus says the Lord:
> "For three transgressions of Israel,
>   and for four, I will not revoke the punishment;
> because they sell the righteous for silver,
>   and the needy for a pair of shoes—
> they that trample the head of the poor into the dust of
>   the earth,
> and turn aside the way of the afflicted."[6]
>
> Seek good, and not evil,
>   that you may live;

---

[5]The prophet about whom there is the most information in the Bible that fits this pattern is Elisha. See II Kings 2:1-13, 13:21.

[6]Amos 2:6, 7a. This quotation and those which follow will be taken from the *Revised Standard Version of the Bible.*

and so the Lord, the God of hosts, will be with you,
   as you have said.
Hate evil, and love good,
   and establish justice in the gate;
it may be that the Lord, the God of hosts,
   will be gracious to the remnant of Joseph.[7]

"With what shall I come before the Lord,
   and bow myself before God on high?
Shall I come before him with burnt offerings,
   with calves a year old?
Will the Lord be pleased with thousands of rams,
   with ten thousands of rivers of oil?
Shall I give my first-born for my transgression,
   the fruit of my body for the sin of my soul?"
He has showed you, O man, what is good;
   and what does the Lord require of you
but to do justice, and love kindness,
   and to walk humbly with your God?[8]

These are not the words of starry-eyed seers who were predicting the future but of men who were busy speaking the word of God to their people. The prophetic movement of ancient Israel stands out as one of the major moral and literary contributions of any religion to the world.

THE EXILE AND THE RETURN

In 922 B.C. the nation of Israel was split into two nations. The northern nation was called Israel and was the larger and more productive of the two. It was destroyed by the Assyrians in 721 B.C., and ten of the twelve tribes of Israel disappeared from history. The people who made up this nation were either killed or deported and enslaved. Whatever their fate, they were never to be a distinctive people of Israel again and are known as the ten lost tribes.

The southern nation was called Judah and was made up of the remaining two tribes. Judah survived the Assyrian years but was eventually destroyed by the neo-Babylonian empire in 586 B.C. With the Babylonian conquest the city of Jerusalem was destroyed, Solomon's

---

[7]Amos 5:14, 15.
[8]Micah 6:6–8.

temple torn down, and the citizens of Judah either killed or carried into captivity. Whereas the northern nation had simply ceased to exist after its destruction, the nation of Judah clung to its identity, customs, and religion while in captivity. It was led by a man who was both a prophet and a priest, Ezekiel. Ezekiel and others so forged the identity of the Jews in captivity that when the Persians captured Babylon in 538 B.C., many Jews were freed and returned to Jerusalem to reestablish their lives and their temple there.

During the Babylonian captivity certain theological changes were forced upon the Jews. Previously they had thought of YHWH as their local diety, perhaps residing in the temple at Jerusalem. Now the temple was destroyed and the people were scattered in a strange land. An unknown poet of that period wrote of their sadness.

> By the waters of Babylon,
>   there we sat down and wept,
>   when we remembered Zion.
> On the willows there
>   we hung our lyres.
> For there our captors required of us songs,
>   and our tormentors, mirth, saying,
>   "Sing us one of the songs of Zion!"
> How shall we sing the Lord's song
>   in a foreign land?[9]

Ezekiel answered that YHWH was mobile and was available to his people in Babylon as easily as he was in Jerusalem.[10] Another prophet, Isaiah,[11] stated that YHWH was no longer just the God of the Israelites but was in fact the one true God for all the people of all the world. Even the Zoroastrian Cyrus, king of Persia, is but an instrument of YHWH.

> Who says of Cyrus, "He is my shepherd,
>   and he shall fulfill all my purpose;"
> saying of Jerusalem, "She shall be built,"
>   and of the temple, "Your foundation shall be laid."[12]

---

[9]Psalm 137:1–4.
[10]See Ezekiel 1.
[11]Isaiah chapters 40–66 are usually attributed to a sixth century B.C. prophet.
[12]Isaiah 44:28.

Indeed the mission of the Jews as YHWH's chosen people is to present his message to all the nations of the world.

> I will give you as a light to the nations,
> that my salvation may reach to the end of
> the earth.[13]

Among the most influential of Jews to return from Babylon to Jerusalem was Ezra (ca. 428 B.C.). Ezra was a priest who brought with him a copy of scripture that he read to the citizens of the rebuilt Jerusalem. The nature and exact content of this book are not known, but whatever they were, it had a profound effect upon the people. They reformed their lives according to the laws in this book. For all times Jews became identified, not only as a people of God's laws, but as a people dominated by a book. Ezra was probably the person who began the process of canonizing books as the word of God. From this time onward it was believed that God no longer spoke through the prophets but through his book. It remained only for the followers of YHWH to read his book and interpret it for their lives.

In addition to the growth of a scriptural canon, the religion of the period of the second temple (520 B.C.–70 A.D.) included sacrifices at the rebuilt temple with a cult of priests, singers, and attendants. At first the temple as it was rebuilt in the sixth century B.C. was a rather simple structure. In the time of Herod the Great (37–4 B.C.) and later, it was restored and decorated to a magnificent state far beyond the glory of Solomon's temple. Just a few years after the second temple was finally finished, it was destroyed for all time by the Romans in 70 A.D.

RELIGIOUS INSTITUTIONS OF THE DIASPORA

The years following the Babylonian captivity saw the beginning of the Diaspora. The Diaspora was the scattering of the Jewish people all over the world. Sometimes it was forced upon them as it was in 586 B.C. by the Babylonians. In other cases Jews moved by choice to other nations or stayed by choice in nations such as Babylon and Persia. By the year 250 B.C. there was such a large Jewish community in Alexandria, Egypt, that it was necessary to translate the Bible from Hebrew to Greek.[14] Jews in Babylon lived well under Persian rule. The book of

[13]Isaiah 49:6b.
[14]The Septuagint.

Esther says that a Jewess became Queen of Persia in the fourth century B.C. In later years Jews were found in all the cities of the Roman Empire.

The Synagogue

Judaism away from the land of Israel was forced to accept a new concept of God and new institutions of worship. The notion of YHWH as the only God of all the peoples of the world, as enunciated by Second Isaiah, was accepted, and various books were accepted as his word. Because they could not get to the temple to worship except on rare occasions and because blood sacrifices were no longer appropriate for Jews living in such cosmopolitan centers as Rome, Athens, and Alexandria, the Jews of the Diaspora developed the institution of the synagogue. The English word *synagogue* is derived from the Greek word *synagoge*, which means "assembly." The synagogue is literally an assembly. Synagogue can occur wherever there is a copy of the scripture (Torah) and ten adult (over thirteen years of age) Jewish males. Ten adult males constitute a quorum, or a *minyan*. Whenever this combination exists, there can be prayer and instruction. Synagogue may be held under a tree or in an elaborate building set aside for the purpose. No one knows exactly when the institution of the synagogue was developed, but whatever the specific date, it arose during the Diaspora when Jews could no longer worship at the temple in Jerusalem, and it serves Judaism to this day.

Along with the synagogue there arose the figure of the rabbi. The rabbi is not a priest or a minister in the traditional sense. The word *rabbi* literally means "my teacher." With the establishment of the Torah as the voice of God, there also arose the need for someone to spend time studying the scripture and teaching the community. Those persons who had the time, the interest, and the intelligence to study gradually began to be singled out and sought after by inquiring members of the Jewish community. They eventually became known as rabbis.

As rabbis sought to interpret scripture to Jews living lives very different from those of Abraham, Moses, or David, many problems arose. How does one apply laws intended for nomadic or agricultural peoples of the Iron Age to persons living in imperial Rome in the time of Augustus Caesar? Rabbis struggled with these problems, sought hermeneutical (interpretive) principles, and interpreted God's laws to their people. Outstanding rabbis arose; their fame as wise men and

Lifting the Torah after the reading.

interpreters spread; students came to study with them; great rabbis disagreed with one another and entered into debate with each other. Gradually an accepted corpus of rabbinic opinion developed.

In addition to the synagogue and the rabbis, the Diaspora Jewish communities maintained other distinctive features that set them apart from the gentiles who surrounded them and maintained their separateness as Jews. Jews separated themselves from gentiles by refusing to work on the Sabbath. In the worlds of the Greeks and the Romans, where only religious holidays were days of rest from labor, the Jews were regarded as lazy loafers because of their refusal to work one day out of seven. In addition, Jews refused to eat certain foods which gentiles ate. Kosher food laws in the early Diaspora were not as broad

248

or as complex as they later became, but Jews of the Diaspora doubtless had to refuse many foods that their neighbors ate. The story of Daniel, a Jewish captive in Babylon, •refusing to eat the king's food must be representative of the plight of many. Jews also practiced circumcision. This ritual was looked upon with disgust at least by the Greeks, who believed in the beauty of the unmarred human body. Undoubtedly circumcision was the object of humor and disgust among other gentile nations also.

In 66 A.D. the cup of bitterness between Jews and Romans in Judea overflowed into violent revolution. At first the Jews were successful, but by 68 A.D. the tide had turned. The Romans, under Titus, gradually subdued the land and finally besieged Jerusalem. By the summer of 70 A.D. the city was defeated. Jewish revolutionaries were slaughtered or enslaved by the thousands. Worst of all, the magnificent temple was looted and burned, never to be rebuilt. This was surely the most severe blow of all to the Jews.

From the ashes of destruction there arose a new Judaism. The phoenix was modest indeed. A rabbi living in Jerusalem during the siege, Yohanan Ben Zakkai, escaped in a coffin borne by his disciples to the tent of Titus. The rabbi asked permission to establish an academy to discuss the future of Judaism on the Mediterranean seacoast at the town of Yabneh. Titus granted permission, and Ben Zakkai gathered about him the rabbis of Israel to discuss and debate the future of Judaism. The debate lasted for years. Among the issues that were decided was the exact list of books that belonged in the sacred Torah. The books of the law (Genesis-Deuteronomy) were widely accepted, as were most of the books of the prophets.[15] The books that were the object of the debate were called "the writings," These were books such as the Psalms, Job, Esther, Ruth, Tobit, Judith, I and II Macabees. After much debate the canon that we know today was established.

The Mishnah

After the years at Yabneh, the leadership of post 70 A.D. Judaism moved to the region of Galilee. Here the debates over the meaning of the law continued for years. The greatest leader of Jews during the second century A.D. was a man named Judah ha-Nasi (Judah the Prince). Judah's great contribution to Judaism was to bring together all

---

[15] In the time of Jesus the Bible was defined as "the law and the prophets."

the commentary about the law that had been collected since the days of Ezra. The commentary along with the disputes was collected into a series of tractates arranged into six divisions. This collection by Judah was called the *Mishnah* (learning or repetition) and became one of the great literary milestones in Jewish history.

Within the pages of the Mishnah the reader finds the attempt of second-century Jew to live by the law of God. At this time there was no more Jewish nation, and after 135 A.D. there was no hope of rebuilding the temple or reestablishing a priesthood. All that was left was the law, and it had to be obeyed. How does one keep the law? By building a structure of additional, complementary laws as an adjunct to the primary law so that in keeping the second law, the first will not be violated. For example the Ten Commandments say, "Remember the sabbath day and keep it holy." People must not work on the Sabbath, but what does that mean? The only form of work specifically forbidden in the Bible is lighting a fire. Some literalists would have had the observant Jew simply sitting in cold and darkened rooms all the Sabbath. The rabbis who produced the Mishnah tried to interpret what the Torah really meant by keeping the Sabbath. They tried to develop interpretations and secondary laws which would make the Sabbath a day of worship and joy. The Mishnah has one entire section set aside for opinions relating to the Sabbath. The rabbis taught that extra lamps should be lit on the eve of Sabbath to make the house more cheerful. Gentiles could be employed to light or extinguish cooking fires on the seventh day.

> If a gentile lighted a lamp an Israelite may make use of the light, but if he lighted it for the sake of the Israelite it is forbidden. If he filled (a trough) with water to give his cattle to drink, an Israelite may give his own cattle to drink after him, but if the gentile did it for the Israelite, it is forbidden. If he made a gangway by which to come down (from a ship) an Israelite may come down after him, but if he did it for the Israelite, it is forbidden. Rabban Gamaliel and the elders were once travelling in a ship, and a gentile made a gangway by which to come down, and Rabban Gamaliel and the elders came down by it.[16]

According to the Mishnah the Sabbath was to be a happy day. The best food the family could afford was to be served on Sabbath; the best

---

[16]Mishnah, Shabbath 16:8.

clothes were to be worn on that day; and even emergency situations that might arise on the Sabbath were to be taken care of by the rabbis. Every step was taken to preserve the sanctity of the law on the one hand and to make life under the law as comfortable and agreeable as possible on the other.

The Talmud

Following the compilation of the Mishnah, the center of Jewish life and learning gradually moved from Galilee to Babylon, where Jews had lived since 586 B.C. While there was occasional persecution of the Jews by the Zoroastrians of that area, life for the Jews in Babylon was easier and more profitable than it had become in Galilee. In 323 A.D. Constantine became sole emperor of what was left of the Roman Empire. Because of his wife and mother, Constantine was favorably inclined toward Christianity and took steps toward making it the official religion of the empire; this was finally accomplished near the end of the fourth century. The rise of Christianity brought about pressure and hostility against the Jews in Galilee and throughout the rest of the empire.

Christianity had begun as a sect of Judaism with Jesus and all his immediate disciples as practicing Jews. Chirstianity drew its scripture, its forms of worship, and its eschatology directly from Judaism. In fact the early church first met in synagogues across the Roman Empire.

The New Testament records the first splits between Judaism and Christianity in the middle of the first century, when first Peter and then Paul invite non-Jews into Christianity. In the missionary ministry of Paul not only are non-Jews brought in, but they come without benefit of circumcision or kosher food laws; they did not have to convert to Judaism or keep its laws. Whether it was Judaism drawing away from Christianity or the reverse is not clear, but the schism occurred and was intensified after 70 A.D. Jesus' messiahship was doubtless one of the issues of separation, but it was not the only issue. Jews were willing enough to accept potential messiahs such as Simon Bar Cochba in the second century and Sabbatai Zevi in the seventeenth century. The greatest issue must have been the Christian acceptance of gentiles who were not required to keep the laws of Judaism. Christian hostility toward Judaism centered around Jewish refusal to accept Jesus as Messiah and the supposed guilt of all Jews for the death of Jesus. Jewish minorities living in Christian-dominated lands began to feel the hostility from the majority. Byzantine Christianity soon made life for Jews in

Palestine less pleasant than it had been under pagan Roman domination, and life in Zoroastrian Babylon became more acceptable.

In the Jewish community of Babylon the discussion over the laws of God continued. Additional interpretative, illustrative, and sermonic material was brought together under the title of Gemara ("study"). Gemara was more than additional commentary on the Mishnah and Torah; it was a body of literature which dealt with every area of Jewish life. Gemara grew up in both the Palestinian and the Babylonian communities. When Gemara was added to the Mishnah the resultant product was called Talmud.

The Palestinian Talmud was completed about 425 A.D. The body of this Talmud is about one-third the size of its Babylonian counterpart. Both Talmuds are written mainly in Aramaic with some Hebrew mixed in, while the Mishnah texts are entirely in Hebrew. The Babylonian Talmud is the larger (it runs to 2.5 million words) and more influential of the two; it was completed about 500 A.D. Both Talmuds are made up of two kinds of material: legal material, discussions, and decisions that are called Halachah ("the proper way") and sections that deal with history, folklore, and sermons that are called Haggadah ("tale," "narrative"). About 30 percent of the Babylonian Talmud is Haggadah. The following tale is an example of Haggadic material found in the Talmud.

> Another time the Emperor said to R. Joshua b. Hananiah, "I wish to see your God." He replied, "You cannot see him." "Indeed," said the Emperor, "I will see him." He went and placed the Emperor facing the sun during the summer solstice and said to him, "Look up at it." He replied, "I cannot." Said R. Joshua, "If at the sun which is but one of the ministers that attend the Holy One, blessed be He, you cannot look, how then can you presume to look upon the divine presence!"[17]

As the repository of the oral law, the Talmuds became the most important nonbiblical material in Judaism. Since the time of their completion they have been the object of many commentaries and endless study by all generations of Jews. Indeed, Judaism may be more talmudically oriented than biblically oriented.

With the completion of the Talmuds in Babylon at the beginning of the sixth century A.D., a portion of the life of Judaism came to an end.

---

[17]B. Talmud, Hullin 60a.

Those scholars who had compiled the Talmud were followed by scholars who founded and ran academies for the study of the Talmud. The presidents of these academies were called *Gaon* (excellency), and the period between 600–1000 A.D. was known as the Gaonic period. These Geonim lived mainly in Babylon and were the leading religious authorities in Judaism during that period. The last of the great Geonim was Saadia ben Joseph (882-942), who became Gaon of the academy at Sura. Saadia was best known as the leading spokesperson of talmudic Judaism against the Karaites, a group within Judaism that denied the authority of the Talmuds and desired to live exclusively by the legal material within the Hebrew Bible. With the passing of Saadia the great Jewish academies of Babylon faded.

MEDIEVAL JUDAISM

Judaism and Islam

In the seventh century A.D. a new religion and a new culture sprang from the Arabian desert; the religion was Islam. Muhammad (570-632 A.D.), the founder of Islam, had contact with Judaism early in his life through the Jewish tribes in the Arabian desert. He had picked up from them a garbled version of the Jewish Bible. When these tribes refused to recognize him as the true prophet of God, Muhammad turned against them.

In the years following the death of Muhammad, the religion of Islam exploded out of the desert into the Fertile Crescent and conquered most of this territory. By the end of the seventh and the early years of the eighth century, Jews living in Babylon, Palestine, Egypt, Turkey, North Africa, and Spain fell under the control of Muslim conquerors. Theoretically Muslims should have treated the Jews better than other infidels. The Jews were not polytheists, and they were people with a scripture. Therefore they, like Christians and Zoroastrians, should have been treated tolerantly. However, it did not always work this way. The Umayyad caliphs, who were the first Muslim dynasty (640–750), sporadically persecuted then tolerated the Jews.

The Abbasid dynasty which followed the Umayyads was more tolerant. They built their capital at Baghdad, which soon became the center of science, philosophy, and medicine of the Middle Eastern world. Jews became a part of this golden society. Arabic became the language of the Jews, and Saadia translated the Bible into Arabic. Jewish and Muslim scholars worked side by side to translate Greek and

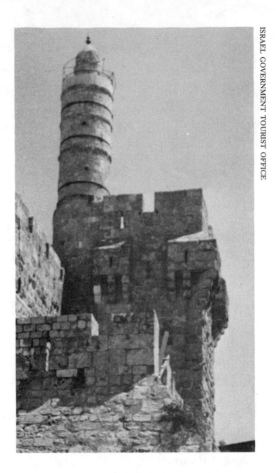

The Tower of David,
Jerusalem. According to the
Bible, David erected the walls
of Jerusalem. Tradition has it
that this tower may also have
been built by David, or
possibly by Solomon.

Latin philosophers into Arabic and thus preserved them from destruction until the European world rediscovered them during the Renaissance. It was in this tolerant world that the Jewish academies flourished, and Baghdad became the center of Jewish religious authority during the period.

The golden age did not last long, however. Renewed persecution of the Jews began again in 847. Heavier taxes were levied against non-Muslims, and Jewish synagogues were converted into mosques. Harassed from the outside, the Jewish world was also torn internally. One group of Jewish leaders, the exilarchs, struggled against the academic heads, the Geonim. The Karaite heresy challenged talmudic authority and drained the energies of the community. With the exception of Saadia, no outstanding minds arose to lead the academies. Gradually the academies declined and closed down. The leadership of Jewish life and thinking passed across the Mediterranean to Spain, although Jews continued to live in Babylon for many more centuries.

Judaism in Spain

Jews were in Spain as early as the first century A.D., and St. Paul mentions his hopes of visiting the Jewish community there (Romans 15:24, 28). They were treated fairly well by the Visigoths of that era, but when the empire converted to Christianity in the fourth century, Jews were given the choice of conversion or expulsion. Apparently, however, this was not evenly enforced, and Jews continued to survive in Spain as Jews. Judaism probably welcomed the conquest of Spain by the Muslims in 711 A.D., because in Spain as in Babylon a golden age of tolerance and freedom for Jewish people followed the Muslim conquest. Jews freely entered the fields of government, science, medicine, philosophy, and literature. With the decline of the Babylonian community, Spanish Jews became the leaders of worldwide Judaism.

There were many outstanding Jews in Spain in the early Middle Ages. Samuel Ibn Nagdela was the grand vizier of Granada and wrote an introduction to the Talmud. Judah ha-Levi was a physician and a Hebrew poet. Moses Ibn Gikatella was a biblical scholar who advanced theories of biblical criticism that were not espoused by Christian scholars for almost one thousand years. Moses ben Nachman (Nachmanides, 1195–1270) was a talmudic authority who was challenged to debate Judaism against Christian monks before the king of Aragon in 1263. He debated so rationally and refuted the Christian claims so clearly that he was rewarded by the king. Even so, he was banished in 1267 and spent his last years in Jerusalem.

By far the greatest figure from Spanish Judaism spent most of his life out of Spain. He was Moses ben Maimon (Maimonides, 1135–1204). Like others of his time, Maimonides was expert in several fields. He was an outstanding philosopher, a talmudist, and a physician. He and his family fled from religious persecution in Spain when he was thirteen. After traveling in many lands, they eventually settled in Egypt, where Moses became the personal physician of Saladin, the Sultan of Egypt. Maimonides' two most famous works are his *Mishneh Torah* and *Guide to the Perplexed*. The *Mishneh Torah* contains fourteen volumes and is a summary of the laws of the Talmud. *Guide to the Perplexed*, completed in 1190, is an attempt to harmonize Judaism with the philosophy of Aristotle. This book caused a storm of controversy among the Jews of the time.

The Arab rule of Spain began to decline at the beginning of the thirteenth century with a consequent rise of Christian rulership, which meant hardship for the Jewish people. Persecutions and forced conversions increased. In 1391 a massacre of thousands of Jews occurred. Many Jews accepted conversion rather than endure persecution, while others converted openly but secretly continued to practice Judaism. The persons were called *Marranos* ("the damned") in Spanish. The pressure continued until 1492, when Ferdinand and Isabella not only sent Columbus on his historic mission but also expelled the Jews and the Moors from Spain. Thousands of Jews fled to Portugal, Italy, Morocco, and Turkey from yet another area which once had been their home.

The Cabala

Jewish mysticism is as old as Judaism. Elements of the occult in Judaism have been found in the Bible, in the Talmud, and in the writings of many of its leading figures. The concern for angels, demons, magical incantations, charms, witches, ghouls, interpretation of dreams, the date of the coming of the Messiah, numerology, and the name of God have been lumped together under the heading of *Cabala* (tradition). The codification of these elements in Judaism probably began in Babylon between approximately 500 and 900 A.D. when books containing speculations in these areas began to appear. The outstanding book from this period was the *Sefer Yetzirch* ("the book of creation"), which came from the Babylonian Jewish community. After this period the cabalistic movement shifted to Spain, Italy, Germany, and Poland.

By far the most outstanding compilation of cabalistic material was the *Sefer Hazohar* ("the book of splendor"), which is more simply known as the Zohar. The book is attributed to Tanna Simeon Ben Yohai, a Jewish leader of the second century A.D. Internal evidence has caused modern scholars to assign the Zohar to Moses de Leon, a thirteenth-century Spanish mystic from Cordova. De Leon probably attempted to attribute the book to a figure one thousand years earlier in order to give it more authority. Whoever its author may have been, the Zohar soon became the most widely read book in Judaism, replacing for a time even the Talmud.

The cabalistic literature became popular with Jews during a very difficult time for them. With their expulsion from Spain in 1492 and from other European countries, and with the collapse of the Babylonian community, world Judaism entered a period of persecution, exile, poverty, and depression. The Talmud is a book for reasonable people who live under rather normal circumstances. The cabalistic literature is for the oppressed and despised who have little hope. Jews fleeing from Spain and from ghetto to ghetto in Europe needed a messiah to deliver them more than ever. Therefore they searched the Zohar for magical clues that would lead them to the Messiah and to salvation.

The Zohar is concerned with such themes as the nature of God, the theory of the emanations from God, cosmogony, the creation of humankind and of angels, the existence of evil, and the work of angels in the world. Like some of the Gnostics, the cabalists asked how an essentially good and spiritual God could have created this sensual world. The answer to this question that most satisfied them was that the nature of God is truly incomprehensible to humanity. Therefore God reveals himself to the world through ten emanations. These emanations are named for the various attributes of God, such as "wisdom," "strength," and "beauty." It was by the work of these ten forces that the sensual world was created. Humans are the highest of all creation and are endowed with three souls. These souls are preexistent and immortal. The cabalists also taught that evil is nonexistent. That which is called evil is but the negative side of good. By such teachings the cabalists differed markedly from orthodox Judaism.

In order to achieve its unorthodox teachings the followers of Cabala utilized unique and far-fetched systems of interpretation. For example, in reading the story of Abraham and the angels who visited him at Mamre (Genesis 18:2a), the cabalists found the following phrase: "Behold, three men stood in front of him." Nowhere in the text are the angels named, but the cabalists ascertained that they must have been Michael, Gabriel, and Raphael. They acheived this knowledge by totaling the numbers of the letters in the phrase. Hebrew, like Latin and Greek, utilizes the letters of its alphabet for numerals. Therefore, by adding the numerical values of the letters used in the Hebrew phrase, "Behold, three men stood in front of him," the interpreter totals 701. The numerical value of the names Michael, Gabriel, and Raphael is also 701. Therefore, the cabalists reason, these three must have been the angels who visited Abraham.

One of the outstanding cabalistic groups was founded in upper Galilee in the village of Safed by Jews fleeing from Spain in the sixteenth century. They were led by Isaac Luria (1534–1572). Luria and his friends established a whole system of amulets, words, and numbers that would overcome evil. Luria himself is said to have believed that he was Elijah, the forerunner of the Messiah. Wherever Jews were found during these troubled times, they studied the cabalistic literature and dreamed of the Messiah.

Jews in Europe

Jews had lived in Europe since the time of the Roman Empire, although the European nations were not widely favored as settlements for large Jewish communities while Babylon and Spain flourished. However, with the decline of favor and the increase of persecution in these areas, Jews began to move to Europe in larger numbers until by the tenth century Europe became the major ground for Jewish life. Jews settled down to live alongside Christians in France, Germany, England, and Italy. Frequently they were invited into communities by Christian leaders. Because of the usury laws of the medieval Christian church, Christians were forbidden to lend money at interest. Jews were not bound by church laws and frequently became the money-lenders to the Christian nobility. Naturally this role did not endear Jews to the common people.

Jewish people living in European communities were often subjected to outrages against their persons and property by the Christian majority. The major reasons for this persecution seem to be as follows:

1. Jews were held responsible for the death of Jesus.[18]

2. Jews were frequently accused of ritual murder of some member of the Christian community and of using this person's blood to bake the unleavened bread for Passover. Jews so accused were usually lynched by mobs and their property taken by local authorities.

3. Jews were accused of desecration of the Sacred Host. The consecrated wafer which became the body of Christ in the Christian mass was said to be stolen by Jews so that they could pierce it with pins, pour boiling oil over it, or pound it so as to further torment Christ.

4. Jews were accused of encouraging lepers to poison Christian wells during the period of the plagues.

These and other charges raised sporadically intensified Christian hostility toward the Jews in isolated areas. During this period synagogues sometimes were built like fortresses to offer some protection to the beleaguered Jews.

---

[18]The biblical basis for this charge was usually taken from the Gospel of Matthew 27:25 and from the passion narrative in the Gospel of John in which the enemies of Jesus are simply referred to as "the Jews."

The Christian Crusades set off widespread attacks on Jews in Europe. The Crusades were instituted by Pope Innocent II in 1096 when he urged Christian Europe to attack the infidel Muslims and win back the holy places in Palestine. Christian princes and their knights took up the challenge for a variety of reasons. However, it seemed easier to attack the infidel Jew who lived in Europe on the way to Palestine. Jewish communities all over Europe, particularly those in the Rhineland, were ravaged by the Crusaders. Many were killed, others were forced to convert to Christianity and still others committed suicide. A few were hidden by sympathetic Christian bishops. The wave of persecution set off by the Crusades was so severe by 1286 that many Jews fled to Poland or to the Islamic countries where authorities were more tolerant.

JUDAISM AND THE MODERN WORLD

By the end of the fifteenth century Jews had been officially expelled or made to feel unwelcome in nearly every European nation. Most devastating, of course, was the expulsion of the Jews from Spain in 1492. Other nations had officially taken this step earlier. Edward I of England expelled them in 1290; Philip the Fair of France moved to drive all Jews from his country in 1306; they were also driven from Germany in the fourteenth century. Portugal followed Spain's example, and after 1498 there were no open Jews in that country. Many fled the persecution of Christian governments and found homes in the Muslim states of the Ottoman Empire. The Jewish refugees from Spain and Portugal in the Ottoman world became known as Sephardim and developed their own *lingua franca*, which was mainly Spanish with some Hebrew loan words. The Sephardim also developed their own liturgy and a distinctive pronunciation of Hebrew.

Other refugees turned to Eastern Europe. Poland particularly attracted persecuted Jews because authorities allowed Jews to enter many vocations that were closed to them in other nations. Many became landlords and tax collectors for the absentee Polish nobility. By the end of the sixteenth century it is estimated that there were more than one-half million Jews in Poland, the largest concentration of Jews in the world. Jews in Eastern Europe became known as Ashkenazim. Their language was Yiddish, which is a combination of Middle High German and Hebrew and is written in the Hebrew alphabet.

Jews and the Reformation

In the sixteenth century Christianity was seized by a revolution that became known as the Protestant Reformation. The leader of this movement in Germany was Martin Luther. Luther was a biblical scholar who knew Hebrew and emphasized the study of both the Old and New Testaments as a true basis for faith. In his early writings he denounced the Catholic Church for its treatment of the Jews. However, when it became apparent that Jews were no more interested in converting to his brand of Christianity than they had been in converting to the Catholic faith, Luther turned against them and made fierce anti-Jewish statements in his later writings.

The Counter-Reformation of the Catholic Church against the Protestant movement in the sixteenth century reinstituted the Inquisition, and the Jews again became its victims. Another feature of the Counter-Reformation in Rome was the formation of the *Ghetto*. Jews of that city were forced to move into a special section, known as the Ghetto where they were confined. Later ghettos were found wherever Jews lived throughout Europe. At first they probably entered these ghettos voluntarily for their own protection and as a place where their culture could be maintained, but later they had no choice. The ghettos became crowded, filthy, sunless places in the very worst parts of the cities. They were walled, and their gates were locked after a certain hour each day, enforcing a curfew upon the inhabitants. To be certain that Jews could be distinguished from gentiles, the fourth Lateran Council in 1215 decreed that Jews should wear a yellow badge. In addition, many European communities demanded that Jews wear distinctive hats or caps.

In the seventeenth century Jews living in Poland saw the end of their sheltered existence. In 1648 the Cossacks and the Ukrainian peasants rose in revolt against the Polish nobility. The Jews who had served the nobility were caught and became the objects of cruel abuse, robbery, rape, and slaughter known as pogroms. Between 1648 and 1656 it is estimated that from 300,000 to 500,000 Jews were slaughtered. Many of those who survived fled into western Europe.

Jewish Response to the Modern World

Because of the misery of the Jews in the ghettos and during the pogroms, there arose in the sixteenth century a strong messianic hope. The object of this hope in the seventeenth century was a charismatic

Bar Mitzvah ceremony. Usually at age thirteen young Jewish boys go through the ceremony of Bar Mitzvah (Son of the Commandment). This rite of passage marks the boys' entrance into the responsibilities of manhood.

figure named Sabbatai Zevi. Sabbatai Zevi was born in Smyrna in 1626. As a young man he studied the mysticism of the Cabala and eventually gathered about him a band of disciples. Sabbatai Zevi and his followers wandered from place to place in the Middle East. In Egypt he married a girl named Sarah, who claimed that she was destined to be the bride of the Messiah, and Sabbatai Zevi was eventually declared the Messiah by his disciples. These claims raised Jewish hopes all over the world. Jews danced for joy in the streets of many European cities; bets were taken in Lloyd's of London as to the exact day when Sabbatai Zevi would enter Jerusalem. In 1665 the Messiah and his party entered Constantinople with the purpose of dethroning the Sultan of Turkey. The Turkish rulers imprisoned him and gave him the choice of conversion to Islam or death. Sabbatai Zevi converted and thus bitterly crushed the hopes of Jews everywhere.

Where Sabbatai Zevi had failed, another figure arose in Germany whose life and influence would do much to deliver the Jews from their misery. In 1743 a frail, hunchbacked boy appeared at the only gate through which a Jew could enter Berlin. When asked his purpose in the city, he replied that he had come to learn. This was Moses the son of Mendel of Dessau. He had been born in 1729, and indeed his passion was learning. The long hours spent in studying under poor conditions had ruined his health and stooped his shoulders. After his arrival in Berlin he spent his time learning and soon began to write essays in German that caused him to be widely accepted by the poets and philosophers of eighteenth-century Germany and the court of Frederick the Great. Moses Germanized his name to Mendelssohn. That a Jew could write in German prose and be accepted by the learned of that nation was phenomenal. Mendelssohn became the friend of German critic and dramatist Gotthold Ephraim Lessing and is believed to be the hero of his play, *Nathan the Wise*. He encouraged the Jews to come out of the ghettos and enter the modern world, to write and speak German rather than Yiddish.

At the same time another movement that would influence modern Judaism was developing in Poland. About 1750, in Podolia, a simple, uneducated man named Israel ben Eliezer (1699–1760) began to preach to his Jewish brethren that God was not to be found in scholarly research in the Bible or the Talmud but in simple, heartfelt faith. Israel became known to his followers as Baal Shem Tov ("master of the good name"), and his followers became known as the *Hasidim* ("pious ones"). The following is an example of the teaching of the Baal Shem Tov.

> Frequently we observe a Zaddik lamenting unto the Lord because of his poverty, yet failing to gain any improvement of his position. This should not be construed to mean that the Lord does not concern himself for the Zaddik. Nay, it is rather a sign of God's great love for him. A parable will illustrate this: A prince of tender age built himself a little house of toy boards. A careless servant inadvertently struck it with his foot, and the fragile structure fell to pieces. The weeping child complained to the king and besought him to punish the servant. The king, however, had secretly intended to surprise his beloved son by building for him a miniature palace of solid and beautiful materials. Therefore, knowing of the rare gift in store for the prince, he did not act upon the lad's complaint.

It is the same with the Zaddik, God's cherished son. The Lord has made ready for him a splendid abode in Paradise. He, therefore, gives slight attention to the Zaddik's complaints of temporary discomforts in this insignificant world below.[19]

The Hasidic movement was widely accepted by the Jews of Eastern Europe, although many of them were excommunicated by the orthodox rabbis. One could not find more distant opposites than the two stellar figures of Judaism in the eighteenth century, Moses Mendelssohn and Baal Shem Tov.

The end of the eighteenth century brought new winds of thought to Europe and North America, and these were to have an effect upon Judaism. In North America there was a revolution and a subsequent constitution which stated that all people are to be treated equally under the law. For the first time in modern history a gentile nation declared that the Jews were to be treated as people with equal rights. In France the revolution of 1789 was followed by a declaration of the rights of men, including the Jews. Wherever the armies of France went in the following years, ghettos were torn down and Jews were given civil rights. In that same year Jews were first admitted to the European universities. On the one hand Mendelssohn encouraged the Jews of Western Europe to come out of the ghettoes and join the Christian societies in the adventure of modernity. On the other hand the Baal Shem Tov and his followers in the Hasidic movement encouraged the Jews of Eastern Europe to search within their own traditions and find the resources to maintain Judaism as an independent entity in the midst of Christian societies.

Reform Judaism

With Jews following the lead of Mendelssohn and entering European society on all levels, the demand for reforms in Judaism became apparent. If Jews were to be a part of Western civilization, many felt, some of the historical practices of Judaism were out of place. In 1843 a group of German Jewish leaders met and made the following declarations:

1.   There is a continuation in the development of Judaism.

2.   The Talmud has no authority for the modern Jew.

---

[19]Louis I. Newman, trans., *The Hasidic Anthology* (New York: Scribner, 1934), p. 3.

3. We seek no Messiah, and we know no homeland but the land of our birth.

This declaration became the basis for Reform Judaism. Reform Jews began to use more vernacular and less Hebrew in their worship; their synagogues were called temples; kosher food laws were not stressed; choirs and organs were introduced. Indeed, Reform worship in the nineteenth century was in many respects like Christian worship. Many of the Jewish immigrants to the United States in the early nineteenth century were Reform.

While Jews were enjoying new freedoms and rights in Western Europe in the nineteenth century, the lot of their kinspeople in Eastern Europe had scarcely changed in two hundred years. Czarist Russia allowed fierce pogroms against the Jewish population. Harassment and second-class citizenship were their lot. In Russia they were squeezed into certain areas called the Pale of Settlement and forbidden even to travel into other parts of the nation. In 1881, after the assassination of Alexander II, the worst series of pogroms against the Jews broke out. As a result a great exodus from Eastern Europe took place. Thousands of Jews fled to any country that would have them; the greatest number took refuge in the United States.

Zionism

In Western Europe the Jewish population may have believed that it had been accepted into the modern world as an equal. Indeed civil rights had been granted to Jews, and Jews were making great contributions in every profession. But the anti-Jewish feeling of Christian Europe still lay beneath the surface. These feelings were brought into the open by the Dreyfus case. In 1894 Captain Alfred Dreyfus was accused of betraying French military secrets during the Franco-Prussian War. On the basis of flimsy evidence Dreyfus was convicted and condemned to life imprisonment on Devil's Island. During the trial the hostility of the French toward the Jewish Dreyfus and all Jewish people erupted. Captain Dreyfus was granted amnesty in 1899 and his court-martial declared "erroneous" seven years later.

The Dreyfus case was to have long-range effects upon modern Judaism because of a young Austrian journalist named Theodore Herzl who covered the trial for his newspaper. Herzl and others came to realize that regardless of the liberal façade of European countries, Jewish people would never be treated fairly until they had a land of their own. In a movement known as Zionism, Herzl and others pleaded the cause of a Jewish state. Attempts were made to find land anywhere in the world where Jews might develop a state, but all locations took second place in Jewish hearts to the land which they had left hundreds of years before, the land now called Palestine.

In the early 1900s Jews began buying land and developing settlements in Palestine. Herzl worked himself into an early grave on behalf of Zionism, but the seeds had been sown for what would eventually become the nation of Israel. In 1909 the Jewish city of Tel Aviv was founded, and by 1920 approximately 50,000 Jews had immigrated to Palestine.

With the end of World War I, the defeat of the Turks, and the breakup of the Ottoman Empire, Palestine became governed by mandate by the British. In 1917 Chaim Weizmann, a Zionist who had rendered service to the British as a chemist, persuaded the British Foreign Secretary, Lord Balfour, to issue a declaration which said: "His majesty's government views with favour the establishment in Palestine of a national home for the Jewish people. . . ." With the issuance of this document by a sympathetic government that ruled Palestine, it would seem that it should have been clear sailing for Zionists. Their objective, however, was not to be easily achieved.

In many cases the native populations of Palestine reacted strongly against great numbers of Jewish immigrants and put pressure upon the British to restrict the immigration. By 1928 there were 100,000 Jews in Palestine; by 1931, 175,000; by 1933, 220,000. The Arabs reacted with riots and strikes. In 1939, fearing to further offend the Arab nations, the British government issued a white paper in which a quota was set, limiting Jewish immigration to 15,000 per year for the following five years. This quota came at a time when the Jews of Europe were desperately seeking refuge from the Nazi holocaust.

The Nazi Holocaust

In 1933 Adolph Hitler became chancellor of Germany. Very quickly thereafter that nation was changed into an anti-Semitic, Nazi dictatorship. Little by little the rights of the Jews in Germany were taken away. The Nuremburg Laws of 1935 reduced Jews to second-class citizens who could not vote, hold office, work in most professions, or marry non-Jews. Jews who could see the handwriting on the wall fled to whatever refuge they could find. Immigration laws in the United States prevented large numbers of them from entering this country. Palestine was virtually closed as a result of the white paper of 1939.

Menorah in front of the Knesset, Israel's parliament. The seven-branched candelabrum is one of the oldest symbols of Judaism.

When Hitler began to move into Eastern Europe in 1939, millions of Jews in Poland, Hungary, and Czechoslovakia fell into his hands. In most cases the non-Jewish citizens of these countries were only too happy to cooperate with the Nazis on the Jewish question. (The yellow badges and ghettos of the Middle Ages were restored for the Jews.) How was the extermination of European Jews to be accomplished? There were millions of Jews trapped in Europe, and their numbers made a solution to the Jewish problem difficult. The first solution was deportation of all Jews in occupied countries to concentration work camps in the east. Hundreds of thousands were jammed into cattle cars and sent to Eastern Europe, where they were forced to work until they died.

By 1941 a final solution was reached by the Nazis: The Jews were to be biologically annihilated. Many extermination methods were attempted, but the one which was eventually accepted as cheapest and most efficient was death by Zyklon B gas. Methodically, Jews from the concentration camps were driven into gas chambers and asphyxiated. Their bodies were shorn of all valuables, including hair and gold teeth. Skin, bones, and even body fat were put to use by the thorough Nazis. Bodies that were of no more use were then burned in special ovens.

There are various estimates of the number of Jews killed during the Nazi years. The usual number given is six million. In Poland alone, prior to World War II the Jewish population was 3,350,000. In 1945 there remained only 50,000.

One might ask how such a thing could happen in the twentieth century. How could it happen in one of the most civilized nations in the history of the world? Germany had given the world great musicians, philosophers, theologians, scientists, and leaders in nearly every profession, art and craft. How could such a nation produce such evil? A number of explanations for the Nazi holocaust have been suggested.

1. *German racism.* Adolph Hitler appealed to a very basic emotion in his people when he asserted that the Aryans were the supreme race and that other races, expecially the Semites, were inferior.

2. *German troubles following World War I.* Germany had been defeated in World War I and humiliated in the peace treaty that followed. German pride demanded that some reason be found for the defeat. The most common excuse was that Germany had been "stabbed in the back," and the most common traitor was the Jew. Germany also suffered from severe economic conditions following the war, and this too was blamed on the Jews. The fraudulent *Protocols of the Elders of Zion* was believed to be the plan for an international Jewish conspiracy to destroy the economies of Christian nations. At the same time many Germans also believed that the Jews were behind the international Communist conspiracy. Therefore Jews were accused of being the international bankers and financiers who would wreak havoc in world economy at the same time that they were considered to be the Marxist enemy of capitalist economies!

3. *Nazi madness.* It would seem that in some cases the destruction of the Jews was more important to the Nazis than anything else. There were occasions when trains that were needed to take German troops and supplies to the front were diverted to take Jews to concentration camps.

4. *Modern efficiency.* The very number of Jews murdered could not have been achieved at any other time in history. Neither the Romans nor the Cossacks could have killed so many persons in such a short period of time. Only modern, efficient technology made it possible.

5. *The silence of the rest of the world*. At a time when Jews most needed a refuge, doors were shut to them all over the world. Christian nations and Christian leaders did very little to rescue the victims, and little protest was raised. No attempt was made by Allied bombers to wreck the machinery of the holocaust. It was as though the rest of the world were willing to allow Hitler to have his way with the unfortunate Jews in his trap.

The holocaust reduced the world population of Jews by as much as one-third. When the enormity of the crime was made public in the Nuremburg trials of the late 1940s and the Eichmann trial of 1960, it had a profound effect upon Jewish thinking. It was one of the primary causes for the development of the nation of Israel in the years after World War II. The holocaust may have had a lasting effect upon Jewish theology also. At least one Jewish thinker, Richard Rubenstein, has said in his book *After Auschwitz* that for Judaism, God died in the holocaust. Before the Nazi years, whenever there was a serious threat to the Jews, no matter how severe it was, God somehow answered the cries of his people. At Auschwitz and in other concentration camps, there seemed to be no answer to their prayers as they were led to the ovens. The full story of the holocaust and its effects upon Judaism is not yet told.

The State of Israel

The development of the state of Israel came quickly after World War II. By 1947 it was obvious that Britain could no longer control Palestine and its two warring factions. Zionists were determined to build a home for the thousands of displaced Jews, and the Palestinian Arabs were just as determined that it would not be established in Palestine. In 1947 the United Nations voted to partition Palestine into a Jewish and an Arab state. The British left Palestine in May of 1948, and immediately Israel proclaimed statehood. Ironically the United States and Russia vied to see who would be the first to recognize the new nation. Immediately Israel was attacked by five neighboring Arab states. She survived these attacks and others and has answered, at least in part, the Zionists' dreams of a homeland for the Jews.

Unfortunately, with the development of the state of Israel, thousands of Palestinian Arabs fled their homes in what became the new nation. Since 1948 many of them have eked out miserable existences in various refugee camps. During the war of 1967 other large portions of territory formerly held by the Arab nations fell to the Israelis, including the city of Old Jerusalem and one of the most sacred shrines of all to the Jews, the Wailing Wall, that one portion of the temple area remaining after the war of 70 A.D. The governance of the city of Jerusalem and the west bank of the Jordan and an equitable solution to the difficulties of the Palestinian refugees remain serious problems.

Current Varieties in Judaism

Recent statistics estimate that there are 14,435,900 Jews in the world. Three million are in Israel; 2,620,000 are in Russia; and 5,870,000 are in the United States. The largest concentration of Jews anywhere in the world is in New York City, with 1,836,000. As already stated, the term *Jew* covers a multitude of religious practices and beliefs. The Jews of the world are widely divided in terms of their belief and practices.

Those called Orthodox are the largest group within Judaism. The Orthodox attempt to stay as close as possible to the nature of biblical and talmudic Judaism. Kosher food laws are stressed, along with strict observance of the Sabbath. In worship, men and women are separated in the synagogue and both must cover their heads. Hebrew is the language of Orthodox worship.

Reform Judaism is popular mainly in the United States and Europe. It attempts to be as modern as possible in Judaistic beliefs and practices. Its worship is usually on Friday evenings, and its synagogues are called temples. Men and women sit together with uncovered heads. The vernacular is used through most of the service, with Hebrew interspersed only occasionally. Organ music and choirs are common. Few members of Reform temples attempt to keep all of the kosher food laws or the talmudic restrictions on the Sabbath.

In between the Orthodox and the Reform is the Conservative movement. It arose in the nineteenth century, led by Sabata Morais, as a reaction against the extremes of the Reform movement. Shocked at the excesses of the Reform leaders at the Pittsburgh Conference of American Rabbis in 1885, Sabata Morais and others organized the Jewish Theological Seminary of America in New York City. This seminary has been the voice of Conservative Judaism in America ever since. Conservative Judaism is distinguished from the Orthodox by its greater concern with the scientific study of the Bible and rabbinical material. In its worship the vernacular is used more than Hebrew. Unlike Reform Jews, Conservatives tend to worship on Saturday morning. Men are required to cover their heads with the traditional skull cap (*yarmulke*) during worship. There is an attempt by many Conservatives to abide by the biblical and talmudic laws regulating food and Sabbath observance.

Growing out of the Conservative movement is Reconstructionist Judaism. Mordecai M. Kaplan, a professor of homiletics at the Jewish Theological Seminary in the 1930s, is regarded as the founder of Reconstructionism. He understood Judaism not only as a religion but as a culture, with its own history, laws, and arts. Therefore, it is not enough to practice Judaism as a religion only; the entire Jewish culture must be studied and experienced. The numerous Jewish community centers in American cities today are an organizational attempt to deal with Kaplan's ideals. Naturally the Reconstructionists give complete support to the state of Israel as the home of Jewish culture.

In addition to these groups there are numerous smaller sects of Judaism throughout the world that, because of geographical isolation or differing religious practice, are out of the mainstream. There are the Falashas of Ethiopia, a group of black Ethiopians numbering between 15,000 and 25,000 who practice a form of Judaism which retains Jewish beliefs and practices from the first century A.D. Other small, variant Jewish groups also exist in India and China.

JEWISH HOLIDAYS

Judaism has always been defined and understood by its adherents in terms of the actions of God on behalf of his people. Therefore, commemorations of these acts of God tend to be extremely important. The holidays on which these great events are remembered are a unifying factor, bringing together Jews of all degrees of belief and practice. Judaism also depends upon community for its very existence. Therefore, although many portions of its annual festivals may be carried out in the Jewish home, most depend heavily upon the community meeting in the synagogue. Because of this reliance upon the group, the events of *Bar Mitzvah*, when the young are officially recognized as adult members of the Jewish community, also are a significant festival.

Sabbath (*Shabbat*)

The most important and distinctive of all Jewish holidays is the Sabbath. Judaism gave the world the six-day workweek, with the seventh day reserved for worship and rest. The Sabbath begins on Friday at sundown and continues until sundown on Saturday. On Friday night the Sabbath is ushered in with the *Kiddush*, the benediction over wine or bread, and the lighting and blessing of Sabbath candles by the woman of the house. Traditionally, the best food of the week is served at the Friday evening meal. Conservative and Orthodox Jews attend synagogue on Saturday morning and also read the week's section of the Torah. Orthodox observance of the Sabbath forbids lighting or extinguishing fires or lights, riding in automobiles, smoking, carrying money, or performing any type of labor.

Passover *(Pesach)*

Another important festival in Judaism is the celebration of the Passover. This holiday begins on the fifteenth of the Hebrew month of Nisan[20] (March–April) and lasts for eight days. It commemorates the deliverance of the Israelites from slavery in Egypt. On the first two nights of Passover the Jewish family gathers for a ritual meal called *Seder*. The foods associated with the Exodus (lamb, unleavened bread, bitter herbs, etc.) are eaten as the family engages in rituals that recall the Exodus.

The Feast of Weeks *(Shavuot)*

Fifty days after *Pesach*, on the sixth and seventh days of Sivan (May–June), the celebration of Weeks, or *Shavuot*, occurs. This holiday is called Pentacost in the New Testament. *Shavuot* was originally a festival celebrating the first grain harvest, but it later was related to the Exodus event as the time when Moses received the Ten Commandments on Mt. Sinai. Jewish homes and synagogues are decorated with plants and flowers during the celebration of this holiday.

New Year *(Rosh Hashanah)*

The Jewish new year is celebrated on the first and second days of the month of Tishre (September–October). Tradition says that the days of *Rosh Hashanah* were also the first days of creation. The season begins a

---

[20]For its religious festivals Judaism relies upon an ancient lunar calendar which is synchronized with the solar calendar by adding an extra month each leap year. This calendar is dated from the supposed date of creation, which would make the year beginning in the fall of 1979 A.D. the Jewish year 5740.

period of penitence that culminates in the next holiday, the Day of Atonement *(Yom Kippur)*. The new year is celebrated by special prayers and by eating sweets in the hope of a good year to come.

The Day of Atonement *(Yom Kippur)*

The holiest of all Jewish holidays is the Day of Atonement. It is celebrated on the tenth of Tishre and at the end of the period of penitence begun at *Rosh Hashanah*. The day is traditionally celebrated by an abstinence from work, food, and drink. The day is to be spent in the synagogue, where prayers are offered for forgiveness of sins and reconciliation. It is also an occasion for charity.

The Feast of Tabernacles *(Sukkot)*

Five days after *Yom Kipper*, on the fifteenth of Tishre, the feast of tabernacles is celebrated. Originally this was a celebration of the autumn harvest. Like many of the other holidays, *Sukkot* became attached to the Exodus experience and is now kept as a remembrance of the times when the Israelites wandered in the Sinai wilderness and lived in makeshift tabernacles *(sukkot)*. For either reason the festival is a joyous one. Some speculate that the American Thanksgiving festival was modeled after the biblical *sukkot*.

The Feast of Dedication *(Chanukkah)*

On the twenty-fifth of the month of Kislev (November–December) Jews celebrate one of the few holidays not associated with the Exodus. In 165 B.C. Judas Maccabeus retook the Temple from the Syrian Greeks and rededicated it. A cruse of oil used in the rededication which should have burned but one day miraculously provided light for eight days. In remembrance of that event, Jews light candles each day for eight days. It is thus a festival of lights as well as a festival of dedication. *Chanukkah* has been a minor holiday in Judaism until fairly recent times.

The Feast of Lots *(Purim)*

Another festival not associated with the Exodus is *Purim*, celebrated on the fourteenth of Adar (February–March) as a remembrance of Jewish victory over gentile foes. The book of Esther says that Esther, the Jewess who had become the Queen of Persia, was made aware of a plot to destroy her people. By boldly approaching the king and revealing this plot to him, Esther was able to save her people from a massacre and see her enemies hanged upon the gibbet they had prepared for the Jews. Since lots were cast to determine the day when the Jews were to be destroyed, the festival is known as *Purim* (lots). On this day the scroll of Esther is read, gifts are exchanged, and a special meal is eaten. Generally it is a day of great joy and merrymaking.

The Son of the Commandment *(Bar Mitzvah)*

Though the *Bar Mitzvah* is not an annual festival in the Jewish calendar, it is an important occasion in the life of the community. According to Judaism, when a boy has reached his thirteenth birthday, he is technically a man. He can be a member of the ten adults necessary for a *minyan*. Usually the boy is prepared for the occasion by several years of instruction in his religion and in Hebrew. On the Sabbath after his thirteenth birthday he reads from the scripture at synagogue and may deliver a speech. This is a festive occasion for the boy and his parents, and the young man may receive many presents from his friends. The *Bar Mitzvah* may have been introduced as late as the fourteenth century as a counter to Christian confirmation, although the age of thirteen has always been the age of majority in Judaism. A modern innovation is the *Bat Mitzvah* ("daughter of commandment"), a similar ceremony for girls. The *Bat Mitzvah* is practiced mainly among Reform congregations.

SUGGESTED READING

Baron, Salo W. A *Social and Religious History of the Jews.* 3 Vols. New York: Columbia University Press, 1952.

Buber, Martin. *Tales of the Hasidim.* 2 Vols. New York: Schocken Books, 1948.

Cohen, A., ed. *Everybody's Talmud.* New York: Dutton, 1932.

Hertzberg, Arthur, ed., *Judaism.* New York: George Braziller, 1961.

Neusner, Jacob. *Between Time and Eternity, the Essentials of Judaism.* Encino, Calif.: Dickenson, 1975.

Trepp, Leo. *Judaism: Development and Life.* Encino, Calif.: Dickenson, 1966.

CHAPTER TWELVE

CHRISTIANITY

Altar, United Methodish Church.

Jesus said to him, "I am the way, and the truth, and the life;
no one comes to the Father, but by me."

JOHN 14:6

In terms of the number of its adherents, Christianity is by far the largest religion in the world. In 1972 the estimated number of Roman Catholics, Eastern Orthodox, and Protestant groups was 985,363,400.[1] This means that approximately one of every three persons on earth is identified in some way with Christianity. Naturally a religion that encompasses so many people contains a great variety of beliefs and practices. In general Christians share a common belief in the uniqueness of Jesus of Nazareth, that he in some way provided for the redemption of humankind by his death and was himself resurrected from the dead. Christians generally also believe in baptism as initiation into the religion and in the communion meal. They hold to the idea that the believer has one life in which to determine his or her destiny for life after death. This destiny is usually thought to be either an eternity of bliss in heaven or an eternity of torment in hell. Around these basic themes are thousands of variations within the body of Christendom.

THE WORLD OF THE FIRST CENTURY A.D.

Christianity arose as a sect of Judaism in the first century A.D. when the Roman Empire was at its peak. According to Christian scripture,

---

[1]Statistics on the number of adherents of any religion are vague at best. The number of Christians is often determined simply by giving the populations of nations known to be "Christian nations."

Jesus was born when Augustus Caesar ruled the world, and Christianity became known in the Roman capital in the last third of the first century. Some knowledge of the condition of both Judaism and the Roman Empire of those days will help us understand the forces that created Christianity.

If there were ever a time in the history of the world when there was "one world" in the sense that the peoples of the earth were ruled by one government, with a basic common language and a basic common culture, it was the world of the first century A.D. Under the rule of Augustus Caesar and his successors, the mighty Roman legions had conquered almost everything that could be conquered. Wherever they went they took with them Roman civilization, efficient administrators, and thorough engineers. They built cities and roads. They swept the Mediterranean of the pirates and made sea travel safe. Communication and travel across the vast empire had never been safer and surer. When Christian missionaries like St. Paul began to spread the gospel of Christianity, the Roman Empire provided the path.

In addition to material benefits the Roman Empire gave the world one language. Of course each captive nation continued to speak its own native tongue, but wherever one went in the Roman world the leaders of government and business would in addition be able to speak koine Greek. Though the language of the common people of Rome was Latin, many of the leaders had been educated by Greek slaves and tutors, and they found Greek to be the more beautiful and expressive language. Furthermore, Alexander the Great had conquered much of the same world that became the Roman Empire, and he had sowed the seeds of Hellenistic culture and its Greek language wherever his armies had gone. Because ancient Greece had been the home of philosophy, the beautiful and accurate language of Greece is considered by many to be one of the best vehicles for expressing philosophical and theological thoughts. A Christian missionary like Paul could go anywhere in the Roman Empire and be sure that he could converse with the populace in koine Greek. He could also write letters or epistles to Christian communities in Greek and know that they would be read and understood.

The world of the first century A.D. was also a world of governmental stability. The Romans governed with great cruelty, but they produced a world of relative peace. Augustus and his successors imposed their *Pax Romana* ("the peace of Rome"), and though it was harsh, it was peace nonetheless. To be sure, there were local revolts against Roman government such as the Jewish revolt of 66–70 A.D., but there were no major international wars during this period. Christianity developed in a time of stable government and international calm.

The Roman world of the first century had no major religious commitment. The Greeks and the Romans had their pantheons, but belief in them had largely ceased. Sacrifices to the Roman gods were still carried on officially, but there was little popular support for them. The nations within the empire had their own national religions, and many of these were alive and well. In Judaism the rabbis were developing material that would eventually become the Mishnah and Talmud. Indeed Judaism was finding many converts from other religions. However, the empire itself had no vital religion during this era, and many people were seeking a new religion to take the place of the dead religions. Many sought out astrology as a solution to the problems of life. Others turned to new religious cults that developed from various Eastern religions. Mithraism, which was a development from Persian thought, entered Roman life during the reign of Nero and quickly became a very popular cult among Roman soldiers. The cult of Osiris spread from Egyptian religions into the empire. In Greece the worship of Dionysus was popular. These and other so-called mystery religions gained large followings from among the citizens of the Roman Empire. Each offered the believer life after death in one form or another. Many had secret rituals to which only the initiated were invited. Many had sacred communion meals and baptisms that aided the participant in the search for eternal life. Most of the mystery religions accepted people into their groups without regard to race or social status. In the homogenized life of the Roman Empire, where a large portion of the population was made up of slaves, this was an important feature indeed.

Another aspect of the first century world that is becoming increasingly clear today is that, in Judaism at least and possibly in other religions, there was an anticipation among some that the world was nearing its end or at least a climactic moment. Among the political groups of Palestine there was the hope that a messiah would rise up and lead the people in the overthrow of the Roman monster. This was therefore a time in which many would identify themselves, or at least allow themselves to be identified, as Messiah. Among the people who lived by the Dead Sea and produced those documents popularly called the *Dead Sea Scrolls*, there was an anticipation of a swiftly approaching end of time. These people were so certain that the end was at hand that they had left their normal lives and come to this lonely, godforsaken wilderness to await the coming of the Lord in the wilderness. Into this forlorn and hopeful world came Jesus of Nazareth.

THE LIFE AND TEACHINGS OF JESUS

Jesus of Nazareth was not mentioned in non-Christian literature until the end of the first century A.D. Even then the references to him were vague and not very helpful in constructing the events in his life. Non-Christians sometimes assert that Jesus was not a historical figure since up until the end of the first century there were only Christian stories about his life. Whether or not this is true cannot be proved, but the limited first-century, non-Christian material on his life is a fact. The only truly objective facts we have about the life of Jesus are that a group of people who were called Christians began to be recognized in the Roman Empire around 60–65 A.D., and they aroused hostility and persecution in an empire that was normally tolerant of religious variations. Christianity became the object of many official and unofficial persecutions but continued to grow until finally in the fourth century it became the official religion of what remained of the Roman Empire. While modern students of Christianity may not know exactly what the early church taught, the existence of this group cannot be questioned.

Central to the existence of early Christians was the idea that Jesus of Nazareth had been crucified in Jerusalem during the reign of Pontius Pilate and had been resurrected from the dead. About forty years after his death members of this group began to write biographical statements about Jesus centering on his death and resurrection. Modern scholarship usually agrees that the earliest Gospel, Mark, was written about 70 A.D. It is the briefest of the four Gospels that have been retained by the church. The Gospel of Mark was followed by those of Matthew and Luke, both written about 85 A.D., and then by that of John, written between 90 and 100 A.D. These Gospels are not biographies in the true sense of the word but give most of their attention to the last few months in the life of Jesus. Only rarely is Jesus' childhood or early adult years mentioned, and none of the Gospels contains a physical description of Jesus. Even the exact details of Jesus' last few months are in dispute among the four Gospels. If the earliest Gospel was written forty years after the death of Jesus and if all of the Gospels were written by confessed Christians who had a biased point of view, then admittedly they are not the most reliable sources of objective material. However, with all of their imperfections the Gospels still provide the best information we have about the life of Jesus.

Two Gospels, Mark and John, begin with the ministry of a mature Jesus. Only Matthew and Luke speak of his birth, and only Luke contains material relating to his childhood. The reader must assume that for the early church, the years before Jesus' actual ministry were not terribly important. In those Gospels that do tell of his birth there are problems in harmonizing details. However, they do agree that Jesus was born in the ancestral home of David, Bethlehem. Matthew places the time of Jesus' birth in the years prior to the death of Herod the Great (4 B.C.).[2] Both Matthew and Luke assert that Jesus' birth was unique in that he was born from Mary, who was a virgin. They tie this event to the words of the eighth century B.C. Hebrew prophet, Isaiah:

> Behold, a young woman [virgin][3] shall conceive and bear a son, and shall call his name Immanuel.[4]

All Gospels agree that Jesus was a native of the village of Nazareth in the province of Galilee. Of his childhood and young maturity we are told only of the event recorded in Luke in which the twelve-year-old Jesus went to Jerusalem for a festival with his parents and became so involved in discussion with the teachers of the law that he failed to find his way into the party returning to Nazareth. Except for this lone incident, the life of Jesus prior to his thirtieth year is not mentioned. Naturally this blank has led to all sorts of speculation by Christians and non-Christians.

The Gospel of Luke tells its readers that Jesus was about thirty years of age when he began his ministry, and all the Gospels agree that his first public act was his baptism by John the Baptist in the Jordan River. The figure of John also is not clear in the Gospel accounts. Luke says that he was Jesus' second cousin. Whatever his relationship may have

---

[2] If Matthew is correct in this, Jesus would have been born between 6 and 4 B.C. This is possible since those who established the Christian calendar, marking time into B.C. (before Christ) and A.D. (*Anno Domini*, in the year of our Lord), lived several hundred years after the time of Jesus and simply miscalculated the date by a few years.

[3] The translation of the Hebrew word *almah* has been a source of contention between Christians and Jews for years. In other contexts, the word nearly always means "young woman." Matthew translates it with the Greek word *parthenos*, which always means "virgin."

[4] Isaiah 7:14. This quotation and those that follow are taken from *The Holy Bible: Revised Standard Version* (New York: Thomas Nelson & Sons, 1952).

been, John was a powerful, charismatic figure in Judea. When he preached his message of repentance, large crowds came down to Jericho to hear him. A body of disciples followed him. Years later, the apostle Paul encountered Jews in Corinth who had heard of John but not of Jesus.

Following his baptism Jesus went into the nearby Judean wilderness where he fasted for forty days and pondered the nature of his ministry. According to the Gospels Jesus was tempted by Satan to accept all sorts of easy paths to glory during this time. After the period of temptations Jesus returned to Galilee, where he began to preach. From the Galilean villages he chose a band of followers who would be his disciples for the next few years. Some of them had originally been disciples of John the Baptist. The Gospels list twelve disciples, but this number must have been flexible. There were times in Jesus' ministry when only three or four of this group were close to him. At other times he seems to have been followed by thousands of disciples.

The exact length of Jesus' public ministry is not known. The events of this ministry that are given in the synoptic Gospels (Matthew, Mark, and Luke) could fit into one year, beginning and ending at Passover. However, the Gospel of John presents Jesus' ministry over several seasons that seem to fit into a three-year period. Traditionally Christians accept John's outline and talk of a three-year ministry. The location of Jesus' ministry is also a matter of some dispute. The synoptic Gospels present Jesus working mainly in Galilee and appearing in Jerusalem only for special occasions. John's account has Jesus spending more time in the province of Judea around Jerusalem.

All the Gospels agree that during his public ministry Jesus spent his time teaching and healing. Whether it was to a small group of disciples or to a large crowd in a public place, he was a teacher. In the truest sense of the word he was called *rabbi* ("my teacher") by his disciples. Both the form and the content of Jesus' teachings are recognized and respected as outstanding among those of the great religious innovators of the world. Occasionally Jesus conveyed his message in direct, simple statements such as the Beatitudes of the Sermon on the Mount:

> Blessed are the poor in spirit, for theirs is the kingdom of heaven.
> Blessed are those who mourn, for they shall be comforted.
> Blessed are the meek, for they shall inherit the earth.
> Blessed are those who hunger and thirst for righteousness, for they shall be satisfied.

Blessed are the merciful, for they shall obtain mercy.
Blessed are the pure in heart, for they shall see God.
Blessed are the peacemakers, for they shall be called sons of
  God.
Blessed are those who are persecuted for righteousness' sake,
  for theirs is the kingdom of heaven.
Blessed are you when men revile you and persecute you and
  utter all kinds of evil against you falsely on my account.
Rejoice and be glad, for your reward is great in heaven, for so
  men persecuted the prophets who were before you.[5]

Jesus is most often remembered, however, for his use of a teaching device called the parable. The parable is a short, easily recognized story about very human characters and events. Because of the brevity and beauty of these stories, the parables of Jesus are among the best remembered and most quoted teachings of all the religions of the world. The Gospel of Luke is particularly well stocked with Jesus' parables. Here the reader finds the stories of the prodigal son, the lost sheep, and, perhaps the best known of all, the parable of the Good Samaritan.

A man was going down from Jerusalem to Jericho, and he fell among robbers, who stripped him and beat him, and departed, leaving him half dead. Now by chance a priest was going down that road; and when he saw him he passed by on the other side. So likewise a Levite, when he came to the place and saw him, passed by on the other side. But a Samaritan, as he journeyed, came to where he was; and when he saw him, he had compassion, and went to him and bound up his wounds, pouring on oil and wine; then he set him on his own beast and brought him to an inn, and took care of him. And the next day he took out two denarii and gave them to the innkeeper, saying, "Take care of him; and whatever more you spend, I will repay you when I come back."[6]

It is difficult to find one central theme in all of the teachings of Jesus. Different groups within Christianity tend to isolate those statements that seem to support their position and claim that this was indeed the main message of Christ.

---

[5]Matthew 5:3–12.
[6]Luke 10:30–35.

Many of Jesus' teachings seem to be pacifistic. For example:

> You have heard that it was said, "An eye for an eye and a tooth for a tooth." But I say to you, Do not resist one who is evil. But if any one strikes you on the right cheek, turn to him the other also; and if any one would sue you and take your coat, let him have your cloak as well; and if any one forces you to go one mile, go with him two miles.[7]

Yet it would be a mistake to say that his total answer to the problems of his times was pacificism. At one point he urges his disciples to be armed (Luke 22:36), and at another he states that he has not come to bring peace, but a sword (Matthew 10:34).

Other groups within Christianity contend that the central message of Jesus was people's superiority over the Jewish law. Indeed many of Jesus' actions and teachings seem to suggest an attitude of indifference toward the laws of Judaism. He healed on the Sabbath, and he allowed his disciples to pluck grain on the Sabbath while they walked through the fields. He also stated that

> Not what goes into the mouth defiles a man, but what comes out of the mouth, this defiles a man.[8]

This statement seems to put Jesus in conflict with the kosher food laws. However, at times Jesus has a very reverent attitude toward the laws of Judaism:

> Think not that I have come to abolish the law and the prophets; I have come not to abolish them but to fulfill them. For truly I say to you, till heaven and earth pass away, not an iota, not a dot, will pass from the law until all is accomplished. Whoever then relaxes one of the least of these commandments and teaches men so, shall be called least in the kingdom of heaven; but he who does them and teaches them shall be called great in the kingdom of heaven.[9]

Indeed many of the teachings of Jesus are similar or parallel to those of the great rabbis of that era whose words are remembered in the Mishnah.

---

[7] Matthew 5:38–41.
[8] Matthew 15:11.
[9] Matthew 5:17–19.

Still others have chosen to see the central message of Jesus in terms of an overwhelming concern on his part for the coming end of the age. Albert Schweitzer, in his classic *The Quest for the Historical Jesus*, has pointed out the heavy emphasis on eschatology found in the words of Jesus. Those who agree with Schweitzer see Jesus as a leader who believed that the world was very near the end of an old age and the beginning of a new one.

In truth there are many aspects to the teachings of Jesus as found in the Gospels. Like all great teachers he was concerned with human values, warning people about the perils of riches and preaching compassion among humans. Yet he was also a man of his times, aware of the hateful oppression of his people by the Romans but similarly aware of the disastrous possibilities of revolution against the Romans. He was a man who had been schooled in the laws of his religion and saw in them the great potential for human good if properly applied, as well as the potential for oppressiveness if improperly applied. Jesus was also a man of his times in that he, like the Essenes of Qumran and others, was acutely aware that the age was drawing to a climax. Thus Jesus cannot easily be forced into one dogmatic mold.

All of the Gospels record that Jesus was a worker of miracles. Regardless of the attitude that modern readers may have toward the nature of miracles, and regardless of the embarrassment that the miracles may cause modern Christians as they try to find a rational explanation for them, the Gospels and the sermons of the early Christians are quite clear: Jesus worked miracles. He healed the sick, the blind, and the lame; he fed the hungry; he raised the dead; he cast out demons; he walked upon the waters and stilled the storms. Miracles were a very real part of the world of Jesus, and he performed them regularly without great fanfare.

After a time of public ministry the opposition against Jesus began to grow. It became necessary for him to go away from the crowds of both friends and enemies and rest periodically. On one such occasion he went to the north to Caesarea Philippi to be alone with his closest disciples. Here he asked his disciples:

> "Who do men say that I am?" And they told him, "John the Baptist; and others say, Elijah; and others one of the prophets." And he asked them, "But who do you say that I am?" Peter answered him, "You are the Christ."[10]

---

[10]Mark 8:27–29.

Crucifixion *by Matthias Grunewald (center panel of the exterior of the* Isenheim Altarpiece); *completed in 1515.*

This is the clearest statement of Jesus' identification as a messianic figure by his disciples and by himself. He followed this statement with the warning that he would soon go to Jerusalem and be put to death.

After these events Jesus and his followers began their journey southward to Jerusalem. They arrived at the time of celebration of the Passover. The city was crowded with pilgrims from the Diaspora communities all over the world. It was a season of high theological expectation since it commemorated YHWH's greatest intervention in history on behalf of his people. On the Sunday before his death Jesus entered the city and was widely accepted and acclaimed by the citizens. On this day and those that followed Jesus spent time in the temple teaching and engaging in debates with his opponents. Each afternoon he left the city and went a few miles to the village of Bethany, where he stayed at the home of Mary, Martha, and Lazarus.

On Thursday evening Jesus entered Jerusalem and partook of a final meal with his disciples. It is not clear in all of the Gospels whether this was the Passover Seder or simply a common meal. He shared bread and wine with his disciples and indicated that they were symbolic of his broken body and shed blood. Following the meal Jesus and his party went out of the city to the Garden of Gethsemane, where he prayed for a few hours. Here he was betrayed by Judas, one of his closest disciples, and arrested by the temple guards. He was tried by the Jewish high court, the Sanhedrin, early the next morning. This trial was followed by a series of trials, interviews, and beatings by Pontius Pilate, the Roman Procurator of Judea, and by Herod, the ruler of Galilee. Finally, at about nine o'clock in the morning he was sent out of the city and crucified with two felons. The Gospels record that a series of cataclysmic events occurred as Jesus was dying. By three o'clock in the afternoon he was dead. He was taken from the cross and buried in a nearby borrowed tomb.

The Gospels state that the opposition to Jesus and the responsibility for his death came mainly from within the body of Jewish leadership, especially from the party of the Pharisees. The Pharisees were a group within Judaism made up mostly of the common people. They were fairly liberal and progressive in their theological outlook. They believed in resurrection of the dead and accepted as canon books in the Bible beyond the first five books of Moses. The New Testament lists several of Jesus' disciples as Pharisees, including Paul, the great missionary of the early church. In truth there were more similarities between Jesus and the Pharisees than there were differences. Indeed some have suggested that Jesus himself was a Pharisee.

Other opposition came to Jesus from the Sadducees, an aristocratic group who controlled the temple in Jerusalem. Theologically they were very conservative, accepting only the first five books of the Bible as the word of God. The Gospels present the Sadducean leaders as the ones who tried Jesus in Jerusalem and were ultimately responsible for his death.

Undoubtedly Jesus was opposed by another party within Judaism, the Zealots. The Zealots, who had arisen in Galilee soon after the birth of Jesus, were fanatical anti-Roman patriots who stirred up revolution at every opportunity. Even though one of Jesus' closest disciples is listed as a Zealot, this party could not have been pleased with Jesus because he refused to be the leader of a political revolution against Rome.

Although the Gospels fix the major share of the opposition to Jesus upon these groups within Judaism, the ultimate and fatal opposition must surely have come from the Roman government. Because of the Zealots and other dissident groups, Roman rule of Judea was never easy. From the time of Pompey's entry into Jerusalem in 63 B.C. through the reign of Herod the Great in the first century A.D. and into the era of 130–135 A.D., Judea was not quiet for the Romans. The Gospels say that Jesus began the last week of his life by entering the city of Jerusalem during Passover week, riding upon a donkey, and being received by the crowds as though he were a conquering hero. Because Jesus was from Galilee, the home of the Zealots, and because some of his close followers were known to be armed, it was only natural for the Roman authorities to assume that this was a potentially danger-ous man. The Gospel accounts place the responsibility for Jesus' death upon the Jewish leaders and the crowds in Jerusalem who were there for the Passover, and thus lay the foundation for much of the anti-Jewish feeling and persecution that has followed in the past two thousand years.[11] But Jesus surely would not have been executed had it not been the wish of the Roman authorities. He was crucified Roman fashion, by a group of Roman soldiers, by the order of the Roman procurator of Judea, Pontius Pilate.

Jesus was crucified on Friday and was in the tomb by Friday eve-ning. The following Sunday morning when women came to tend to his body they found the tomb empty. A reading of the four Gospels about the events that followed is confusing. Mark records that the women found the tomb empty and conversed with a young man there who told them that Jesus had risen and gone into Galilee. The other Gospels present more elaborate statements. In them Jesus appeared to different groups of disciples in Jerusalem and Galilee at various times over the next forty days. Eventually he gathered his friends together at the Mount of Olives outside of Jerusalem and ascended into heaven. All of the Gospels agree, however, that the tomb was empty and that Jesus had conquered death. Most agree that he was seen after his resurrec-tion by a number of reputable witnesses. The resurrection event be-came central to the early Christian church.

[11]The Second Vatican Council (1962–1965), after much debate, issued a statement which said that although Jewish authorities were the ones who pressed for the death of Jesus, his execution cannot be charged against all Jews.

EARLY CHRISTIANITY

The Jerusalem Church

After Jesus' resurrection and ascension, his followers met in Jerusalem. They probably banded together out of fear that they might share Jesus' fate. However, at the festival of Shavuot[12] fifty days after Passover, the Christians were feeling more courageous because of the coming of the Holy Spirit and went out into the streets of Jerusalem to preach about their faith. Miraculously they were able to preach in languages that they had not known before, and as a result persuaded many people to join with them.

It is important to note that this original group of Christians in Jerusalem and those groups that later sprang up throughout the world were considered by others and by themselves to be another sect of Judaism. The members of this group were Jewish by background; their Bible was the Jewish Bible; and they continued to worship at the Temple in Jerusalem. The only thing that distinguished them from other Jews was their belief that Jesus of Nazareth was somehow unique. The exact faith of these early Christians is difficult to define precisely. The systemization of Christian theology was not to come for several centuries and after long years of debate.

Our knowledge of the Jerusalem church is drawn from the accounts of the New Testament book, Acts of the Apostles. The leadership of the group seems to have resided in two men. The first was Simon Peter, who had been among the inner circle of Jesus' disciples. Though the organization was loose in the early days, Peter was certainly a major spokesperson for the church. Other of Jesus' disciples are mentioned in Acts, but none seems to have had the authority of Peter. A second man who came to have more and more influence in Jerusalem was James, the half-brother of Jesus. Tradition says that James was not a follower of Jesus during his ministry but came to believe in him after the resurrection. James assumed leadership of the Jerusalem church when Peter moved out to other communities. Beyond these two, there seems to have been no official leadership.

The Acts record that seven men were chosen to serve the Christians in the distribution of charity. One of these was Stephen, who not only acted as a servant of the church but also preached in the streets. His preaching so enraged the authorities in Jerusalem that he was officially denounced and stoned to death. Thus Stephen became the first martyr

---

[12]Christians refer to this festival by its Greek name, *Pentecost*.

of the Christian faith. His death was but one event in a series of persecutions against the Christians in Jerusalem as hostility against them increased. These persecutions caused many of the Christians to leave Jerusalem and carry their faith elsewhere in Judea and into other centers of the Roman Empire.

The Life of Paul

Because almost one-half of the book of Acts is given over to the missionary activities of Paul and because he is traditionally considered to be the author of fourteen books in the New Testament, Paul is the best-known early Christian. Undoubtedly there were other missionary figures in the early church who went as far and did as much as Paul, but they escaped the attention of the New Testament. Not only was Paul important as a missionary of the early faith, but he also made a great contribution as a theologian. He was among the first to attempt to state systematically the beliefs of Christianity. Indeed, Paul is sometimes called the "Second Founder of Christianity."

According to the biographical material presented in Acts and that which may be gathered from his epistles, Paul was reared in the Diaspora Jewish community of Tarsus in Asia Minor. He undoubtedly received an education in both Judaism and in Hellenistic culture. He studied with the great Rabbi Gamaliel and was a member of the Pharisee party. Paul was originally part of the anti-Christian group, and when opposition to the Christian sect in Jerusalem became active persecution, Paul became a leader and observed the stoning of Stephen. On a mission to persecute the Christians in Damascus, he was struck down by a light from heaven and became converted from an enemy of the Christians to a spokesperson for them. After a time of study he began to preach on behalf of Christianity. With various companions he traveled across the Roman Empire, preaching first in the Jewish synagogues and then to gentile audiences. It was Paul, perhaps more than anyone else, who led the movement to allow gentiles to become Christians without first becoming Jews and following the laws of Judaism. This became both the strength and the weakness of Christianity. Its strength lay in the fact that converts could come very easily into the church from almost any background without a lengthy and arduous preparation for Judaism. Its weakness was that it set the wedge between the church and the synagogue, a wedge that has never been removed.

Paul and his companions carried out three missionary journeys which are discussed in Acts. These journeys took them to many of the great cities of Asia Minor and Greece. Upon completion of his travels, Paul returned to Jerusalem, where he was arrested by the Roman authorities. He was imprisoned in Caesarea for several years and eventually sent to Rome, where he was to be tried by Caesar. Acts concludes with Paul entering Rome somewhere around 60 A.D., and there is no biblical material on the remainder of his life. Tradition says that he was imprisoned in Rome during the period of the Neronic persecution of the church (64 A.D.) and executed. Tradition also states that Peter, who had become bishop of the church at Rome, was executed there at approximately the same time. The *Annals* of Tacitus, a Roman historian who wrote approximately fifty years after the Neronic persecution (54–68 A.D.), claims that Nero set out to persecute the Christians in order to shift the blame from himself for having set a great fire in Rome. This was the first of the official persecutions of the Christians by the Roman government.

The Worship of the Early Church

Clearly the church modeled its worship after the forms used in the Jewish synagogue. The Jerusalem church, which continued to exist and exert authority until its destruction along with the city in 70 A.D., still used the Temple as a place of worship. It may even have continued to practice the animal sacrifice that was a part of Temple worship at that time. Wherever Paul went he first sought out and preached at the local Jewish synagogue. Undoubtedly the prayers, the scripture reading, the hymns, and the simple sermons so much a part of synagogue worship were also a part of early Christian worship.

In addition to these modes of worship Christians added others. Baptism was apparently a part of Christian worship from earliest times. Baptism as an initiation into a new faith was practiced by the Pharisees when they took converts into Judaism. John the Baptist baptized people in the Jordan River as a symbol of repentance. Jesus' disciples baptized converts even during his ministry, and Paul baptized converts wherever he went.

Both the mode and the meaning of Christian baptism have been objects of debate throughout the history of the church. The word *baptize* comes from the Greek word *baptidzo*, which means "to immerse." Presumably John immersed his converts in the Jordan. As Christians grew in number, the inconvenience of finding a body of water large enough to immerse the candidate perhaps argued for a more moderate form of baptism. Pouring or sprinkling water upon the head became accepted as the proper mode of baptism.

It is not clear why Jesus' disciples baptized, nor does the New Testament tell the reader clearly why the early church continued the practice. It appears to have originally been an outward sign of the change in status from the pagan life to the Christian life. In later years it took on deeper meanings. Eventually baptism was understood to be the washing away of original sin. The converts who were baptized in the New Testament accounts were adults, but baptism became more and more important to salvation, and eventually infants were baptized in order to wash away the stain of original sin as quickly as possible. Whatever the manner and meaning of baptism may have been, before very long it was administered by a sprinkling of water on the infant children of Christian parents and became a sacrament of the church.

The second addition of the early Christians was the eucharist, or communion meal. This was probably modeled on the Seder meal of Judaism in which the community recalls divine history as they partake of sacred foods. Specifically it was adopted by Christians from the model of Jesus' last supper with his disciples on the evening before his death. In the early years of the church it became customary for Christians to gather together and eat a meal recalling the death of Jesus. Perhaps it was simply a meal of bread and wine, or it may have included other foods. Again, both the manner and meaning of the communion meal have been debated within the church. Eventually the eucharist became a sacred meal in which the bread and wine actually became the flesh and blood of Jesus; individuals who received these elements were actually eating and drinking the body of Jesus and thus their souls were somehow sanctified and aided in their journey toward eventual salvation.

Leadership in the Early Church

Apparently the early church was not a highly organized structure. It was small and not quite sure of itself. Both the Acts and the epistles of Paul indicate that many Christians were expecting Jesus to return to earth at almost any time, and therefore the church had no need of a highly organized structure. As the years passed and it became apparent that Jesus was not returning immediately, as the number of Christians grew, and as the various interpretations of Christianity increased, it became necessary for the church to organize more fully.

There had always been outstanding leaders such as Peter, Paul, and

One of the most common and widely accepted rituals in Christianity is baptism. This is usually considered the initiatory rite that brings individuals into the Christian community.

James, but apparently they held no titles and drew whatever authority they had from their relationship to Jesus and the force of their personalities. The claim of the Roman Catholic Church is that Peter was intended by Jesus to be the cornerstone of the church. This claim is based upon the following biblical passage:

> Simon Peter replied, "You are the Christ, the Son of the living God." And Jesus answered him, "Blessed are you, Simon Bar-Jona! For flesh and blood has not revealed this to you, but my Father who is in heaven. And I tell you, you are Peter [Greek *Petros*], and on this rock [Greek *petra*] I will build my church, and the powers of death shall not prevail against it. I will give you the keys of the kingdom of heaven, and whatever you bind on earth shall be bound in heaven, and whatever you loose on earth shall be loosed in heaven."[13]

---

[13] Matthew 16:16–19.

Although it is not mentioned in the New Testament, a strong tradition says that Peter went to Rome and became the leader of the church in that city. The bishops who were his successors became the popes of the Roman church.

The New Testament mentions several kinds of leaders in the early church, but their roles are never very clearly delineated. One such leader was the bishop. The Greek word for bishop is *Episcopos*, which literally means "shepherd." Qualifications for this office were laid out by Paul in both the epistles to Timothy and to Titus, and the bishop seems to have managed the church in a certain geographical area. Another officer was the deacon. The first seven servants chosen by the church of Jerusalem are frequently referred to as deacons, although the New Testament never calls them this. The office of deacon was as the word *diakonis* ("servant") implies, one of service. The qualifications for deacon were as stringent as those for the bishop. Elders (*presbeuteroi*) are also mentioned as leaders of the church. Acts makes a clear connection between the elders of Judaism and those of the church. Apparently the latter were older persons who had been given authority to make decisions on religious matters by virtue of their age and wisdom. Paul's letters indicate that the elders also had the function of teaching and preaching. In addition to these offices the New Testament mentions evangelists, prophets, apostles, pastors, and teachers. Never, however, is the reader given a complete list of the functions of these leaders.

The Christian church of the New Testament period (ca. 30–150 A.D.) seems to have been amorphous both in belief and structure. There was no strong organization to impose a creed upon the Christian groups, and therefore they varied greatly in what they believed and practiced. Paul was constantly having to correct what he considered false doctrine among Christians in various parts of the Roman world. He was in disagreement with many of the Jerusalem leaders over the issue of the admittance of gentiles into the church. The churches of the various cities within the Roman Empire seem to have been loosely organized, meeting in the synagogues when they were welcome and in private homes when no other arrangements could be made. They soon changed their day of worship from the Jewish Sabbath of Saturday to Sunday, the day when Jesus rose from the dead. Their clergy apparently had little official status and usually were not paid for their preaching. Occasionally offerings were taken for Christian preachers, but for the most part they lived by whatever trade or skills they had.

The Production of the New Testament

The Bible of the early church was the Jewish Bible. Christians read the prophets Isaiah, Micah, and Zechariah and saw in them predictions of the life of Jesus. As the years passed, specifically Christian literature began to be developed. Probably the earliest Christian writings were the letters or epistles that Saint Paul wrote to the congregations of Christians he had established. These letters began in the 50s and 60s of the first century. Fourteen of the current twenty-seven books of the New Testament are letters attributed to Paul, although modern scholarship denies that all of the fourteen came from his pen. These letters are an anthology of Pauline thought. They contain advice to the early church on doctrine, leadership, and worship. Additionally they contain some biographical material about Paul and other early church leaders that is not found elsewhere. In his letters to the Romans and Galatians particularly, Paul sets forth the first systematic understanding of the importance of the life, death, and resurrection of Jesus.

In the years following Jesus' death Christians undoubtedly wrote their remembrances of the events of his life as well as his sayings. We may speculate that collections of his teachings were compiled for use in the instruction of converts. However, Christians may not have made a careful attempt to write the story of Jesus because they were expecting his imminent return. As the years went by and as the people who personally knew of Jesus began to die, either from old age or from persecution, fewer and fewer Christians were able to recount the events in Jesus' life with any certainty. In 70 A.D. the Roman armies closed in on Jerusalem to finish off the Jewish revolution that had begun four years earlier. By the end of the summer Jerusalem and its temple were destroyed, along with the Jerusalem church and many witnesses to the life of Jesus. It may have been this event that caused a Christian to collect a brief statement of the events in the last few months of Jesus' life and to publish it as the Gospel of Mark. In the next decade two more elaborate Gospels, Matthew and Luke, used Mark as a base. The Gospel that differs most from the others in terms of content, chronology, and message is the Gospel of John. This supposedly was written between 90 and 100 A.D., although its date is by no means certain. The account of the early church in Jerusalem, Acts of the Apostles, was probably written by the author of Luke as a sequel to that Gospel.

Other epistles by anonymous authors were probably written between 90 and 150 A.D. and make up eight books in the current New Testament. In addition to these books there must have been many other epistles, gospels, and histories that were written in these early centuries, circulated and read by Christians, but were not popular or authoritative enough to have been maintained. The twenty-seven books that make up the New Testament were probably well established as canon in Christendom by the end of the second century.

Early Heresies

As we have noted, because early Christianity was not a highly organized body with an established creed and because it encompassed a wide variety of members, many different beliefs were held by the early Christians. In subsequent years the church did establish creedal statements and supported an orthodox theology. Later Christians, looking back on the early believers who did not conform to the content of these creeds, referred to such predecessors as heretics. Therefore some of the best early Christian thinkers are today called heretics.

The most famous heresy within the early church centered around the widespread and diverse group called Gnostics.[14] The term *Gnostic* has come to encompass so many beliefs and practices among early Christians that it is difficult to define accurately. However most authorities seem to agree that the Gnostics had in common belief in a divine spark within all humans. This spark is immortal and came from an unknown god. Gnostics also believed that the universe as we know it is controlled by evil forces. Therefore it was necessary for a redeemer figure to come to earth from the unknown god and provide knowledge whereby the divine spark in humanity might be able to rejoin its maker. Some Gnostics seem to have believed that spirit was good and flesh was evil. Therefore the supreme God, who was pure spirit, could not have created this fleshly world; it must have been created by some secondary deity. The major thrust of Gnosticism against orthodox Christianity was that it denied that the Godly Christ could have been fully identified with the human Jesus. Many of the Gnostics said that Jesus only appeared to be human but was actually pure spirit, and therefore his life, teachings, death, and resurrection were of little con-

---

[14]The name is derived from the Greek word *gnosko*, which means "to know." Those called Gnostics claimed to know certain secrets that mere mortals could not know.

sequence.[15] Gnosticism was also a syncretistic movement, taking its doctrines from late Judaism, Christianity, Greek, Persian, and Egyptian religions, Greek philosophy, and the mystery religions. Though the Gnostics were branded as heretics and their teachings condemned by the early church councils, their belief that flesh was evil and spirit was divine had its long-range effects upon Christianity. The church has historically placed more emphasis on the divinity of Jesus than upon his humanity, and Christians have been encouraged to deny the flesh in order to glorify the spirit.

Another version of Gnosticism that developed in the second century A.D. was Marcionism. It was named after Marcion, the son of the Bishop of Pontus, who came to Rome in 140 A.D. seeking an office in the church. Although his theology attracted many followers, he was excommunicated from the church in 144. He basically taught that the God of the Old Testament was not the true picture of the God of love that Christians found in Christ. Therefore Christians should not waste time reading the Old Testament. Even the Gospels were suspect because they were written by Jewish Christians. Marcion died in 160, but his teachings continued to be popular in some circles. To this day one still hears Christians saying that the God of the Old Testament is a God of wrath and judgment, while the God of the New Testament is a God of love.

Another heresy which sprang up in early Christianity was Montanism. In the middle of the second century Montanus taught that the Holy Spirit, the third member of the Trinity (Father, Son, and Holy Spirit), was not to be stifled by dogma but was to be free to move among Christians, causing them to speak in tongues and prophesy. He also taught that the end of the world was coming soon along with the return of Christ. Although Montanus had a zealous band of disciples and was very influential in shaping early Christian theology, his movement had almost died out by the fourth century. Still there have been occasional charismatic movements similar to Montanism throughout the history of the Christian church.

To counter these and other heretical groups it became necessary for orthodox Christians to develop a statement of faith. The statement had to be simple enough to be memorized and used regularly; at the same time it had to be thorough enough to combat effectively the heresies. The result was the so-called Apostles' Creed. The critical mind cannot

---

[15]This particular aspect of Gnosticism is called Docetism.

believe that this creed was developed by Peter, James, and John, although it does have the ring of early authority. The following statement of this creed comes from about 340 A.D.

> I believe in God almighty.
> And in Christ Jesus, his only son, our Lord
> Who was born of the Holy Spirit and the Virgin Mary
> Who was crucified under Pontius Pilate and was buried
> And the third day rose from the dead
> Who ascended into heaven
> And sitteth on the right hand of the Father
> Whence he cometh to judge the living and the dead.
> And in the Holy Ghost
> The holy church
> The remission of sins
> The resurrection of the flesh
> The life everlasting.[16]

Growth of the Church of Rome

In the early years of Christianity Jerusalem exercised leadership over the church. After 70 A.D. other cities, such as Alexandria and Antioch, took over this leadership. These cities produced many of the outstanding thinkers who are known as the church fathers and whose writings influenced Christianity for all time. Each of the great cities of the Roman Empire had a bishop; the larger and more influential the city, the greater the authority of its bishop. The bishops of Alexandria, Antioch, Caesarea, and Rome all were considered to be leaders in the early church. Eventually the bishop of the Church of Rome came to be recognized as the most important bishop of all and finally was designated pope. There were several reasons for this ascendancy.

First, Peter, whom Jesus had singled out as the rock upon which he would build his church, had become the first bishop of the Roman church and had passed on his authority to the bishops who succeeded him. Thus the Roman church had a very strong tradition.

Second, Constantine, the first Roman emperor to support Christianity, moved his political capital from Rome to Constantinople in 330. This left the city of Rome without a strong political leader. A series of

---

[16]Martin E. Marty, A Short History of Christianity (Cleveland and New York: World Publishing Company, 1958), p. 75.

strong bishops of the Roman church filled this void and were looked upon by Western rulers as extremely important people.

Third, the churches of the East were split apart by various doctrinal controversies, and no one bishop could speak for all Eastern Christians. The West, however, was relatively free from these controversies, and the bishop of Rome was the spokesperson for a widely accepted orthodoxy.

Fourth, in the seventh century the Muslims conquered most of the great cities of the Christian Byzantine Empire, and the dominant religion of cities such as Alexandria and Antioch became Islam. This left Rome as the single leading Christian city in what was left of the Roman Empire.

Thus, through a series of fortuitous events and able leadership, the Church of Rome came to be the dominant church in Christendom, and its bishops became the Christian popes.

The Emergence of Christianity as the Religion of the Roman Empire

During the period between 64 and 330 A.D. Christianity went through several periods of persecution and acceptance by the Roman Empire. Officially the empire was tolerant of all religions. However, the Christians occasionally found themselves in trouble because of their refusal to accept the official Roman gods and to worship them on state occasions. Jews also were in difficulty over this issue. In addition the Christian sect was accused by the Romans of a variety of evils. Since the Christians were often from the slave classes and often met in secret they were accused of evil secret rituals that included eating flesh and drinking blood. They were also accused of sexual immorality. As their numbers grew, as they refused to give first allegiance to the emperor, and as they occasionally refused to be members of the Roman army, the opposition to them grew. Frequently persecution was the result. Nero's persecution of the Christians was local and brief. The Emperor Domitian (81–96 A.D.) insisted that citizens of the empire worship his person, and he instituted the first widespread persecution of Christians who refused to worship him. This persecution may have formed the background from which the Revelation of John was written.

In the second century there were again quiet periods followed by severe persecutions. The legal status of Christians in the empire was never secure, and at any time local officials could begin to pressure them. Widespread persecution broke out under the Emperor Hadrian (117–138) and Marcus Aurelius (161–180). In this era the old Roman Empire was falling apart from internal and external forces, and the emperors frequently looked upon the Christians as a threat to the unity and the strength of the old Roman ways. Therefore they persecuted Christians in hopes of renewing Rome to what it had been in the days before Christianity.

The on-again, off-again persecution of Christians reached its peak in 303 under the Emperor Diocletian in an empire-wide movement that lasted for more than ten years. This period was followed by the reign of Constantine. Constantine was not Christian but was strongly influenced by his wife and mother, who were. Although he did not make Christianity the religion of the Roman Empire, he treated it with the same toleration extended to other religions and brought a halt to persecution. In 325 Constantine called the Church Council of Nicea to stop the warring within Christian factions over the nature of Christ. Two years later, when he was dying, Constantine finally accepted baptism and officially became a Christian.

Several of the emperors who followed Constantine tried to reverse the tide and return to the old Roman religions. But with the reign of Theodosius (379–395) Christianity officially became the religion of the Roman Empire, and all other religions were suppressed.

Augustine

Perhaps no other Christian after Paul so deeply influenced the life and the direction of Christianity as did Augustine (354–430). Like many of the other leaders of the early church, he was born in North Africa. His mother was a devout Christian, but his father was pagan. Although he received Christian instruction as a child, he did not accept the faith until later in life. As a young man he took a concubine and had a child by her. For a time he was interested in Manichaeism, a religion that was a syncretism of Christian and Zoroastrian ideas. After a few years with Manichaeism, Augustine followed the teachings of Neoplatonism, but he was not completely satisfied with this either. In Milan he came under the influence of the Christian bishop, Ambrose. In a very dramatic conversion experience Augustine became a Christian. He returned to North Africa, where he became a writer and eventually the bishop of Hippo. Two of his writings have become classics in Christian literature: his autobiographical *Confessions* and his *City of God*, an interpretation of history written in response to those who blamed the Christians for the fall of the city of Rome to the Goths.

Augustine is also widely known for his formulations of the doctrine of original sin, the fall of man, and predestination. Taking his support from Paul's letter to the Romans, he believed that the original man and woman had willfully chosen to sin against God and thus had passed to all future generations a sinful nature. For this reason all humankind was incurably sinful and fallen. To Augustine, God in his infinite mercy had sent his son to die for the sins of a handful of sinners who had been predestined for salvation. All the rest of humankind was doomed to eternal damnation. Augustine was challenged in these views by the monk Pelagius, who believed that humankind was free to act as it would. Therefore salvation to Pelagius and his followers was something initiated and mainly carried through by human will. Only a little help from God was needed. Although the Pelagians were denounced by orthodox Christianity, the teachings of Augustine never really became orthodox either. It was not until the time of John Calvin in the Protestant Reformation of the sixteenth century that Augustine's doctrines received wider attention.

The Monastic Movement

Introduced by the early medieval church, the monastic movement became a major part of Christianity. Of all the major religions of the Western world, Christianity is the only one to encourage monastic orders. Neither Judaism nor Islam has encouraged its members to move apart from the evils of normal life and live alone, although there have been minor movements in both religions.

The monastic movement in Christianity did not really begin to develop until the third century. To be sure, there were statements in the New Testament from both Jesus and Paul that supported some forms of celibacy, fasting, and sharing possessions with the needy. Nevertheless, the first two and a half centuries of Christianity saw no widespread application of these teachings in the form of monasticism. The tradition of celibacy for the bishops, priests, and deacons was established in the Western churches by the end of the fourth century. The Eastern churches commanded celibacy for the bishops, but priests and deacons were allowed to marry before they were ordained.

The movement toward asceticism and monastic community life apparently began in Egypt in the middle of the third century. Christians in Egypt may have been influenced by the asceticism of Hinduism or

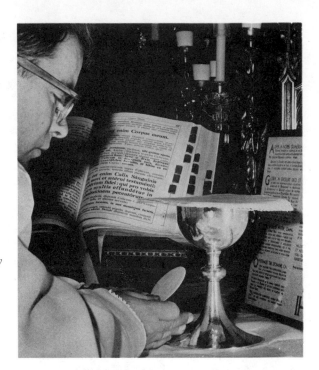

Roman Catholic priest consecrating the host or sacred bread during a mass. The bread is believed by many Christians to represent the body of Christ.

native Egyptian religions, or they may have been influenced by the basic distrust of the flesh taught by the Manichaeans, the Gnostics, and the Neoplatonists. Egypt itself, with its deserts and wild places, offered the ideal setting for men and women who wanted to leave the problems of normal life behind them and seek solitude in the wilderness. Some began to sell their possessions and go out into the desert regions to live simple lives dedicated to God. A number of them were widely known for their feats of asceticism. Simeon Stylites (d. 459), for example, is said to have lived atop a pillar in the desert for thirty-six years. Others fasted for long periods, went without sleep, ate only the simplest of food, gave up bathing, and wore irritating garments. Still others gathered together and formed monastic communities.

The first Christian monastery is attributed to Pachomius, who was born in Egypt in the last decade of the third century. For a variety of reasons the monastic movement soon became popular throughout Christendom.

Basically the monasteries were secluded places where men and women were dedicated to a simple life of hard manual labor, prayer, fasting, and sometimes study. What little learning and scholarship that existed in the medieval period was kept alive in the monasteries. Historically some of the best minds of the church were produced by these communities. St. Jerome (b. 342), who translated the Hebrew and

Greek biblical material into the Latin Vulgate, the standard Bible for the Roman Catholic Church for over 1500 years, was a product of the monastic movement. Some have suggested that the vitality and strength of the monasteries at any given time was an accurate gauge of the vitality of the entire church.

MEDIEVAL CHRISTIANITY

That period between the fall of the Roman Empire and the rise of the modern European nations is usually called the "medieval" period. During this period the Christian Church was a major force in the total culture of both Eastern and Western Europe.

The Division between Eastern and Western Christianity

From the time of the establishment of the city of Constantinople and the new capital of the Roman Empire (330) there developed a gradually widening division between the Christians of the East and those of Western Europe. This basic division was political and geographical as well as theological. When Constantine set up his capital in the East he took an active role in the development and direction of the church and called the Council of Nicea to settle theological differences. His successors followed his example and usually took an active part in directing religion. In the West, Rome had been left without effective political leadership. Into this vacuum stepped the able bishops of the Roman church, who even took some of the titles of the ancient Caesars. When the barbarians massed at the walls of Rome, it was the popes who negotiated with them for the city.

The theological differences between East and West were basic ones. Most of the great thinkers and leaders of the early church were from North Africa and Asia Minor. Most of the early councils that established Christian doctrine were held in the East. Eastern Christians tended to be more interested in theological formulations and became bitterly divided over certain issues. Western Christians tended to be more practical and were concerned with survival in a hostile and decaying world. Eastern theologians tended to emphasize the divine nature of Christ, while those of the West emphasized his humanity.

The largest issue dividing Eastern and Western Christians was the papacy. The great cities of the East each had outstanding bishops who became known as patriarchs. Although Constantinople was the capital, its patriarch could never gain authority over the patriarchs of the other major cities. In the West there was only Rome, and the bishop of that city clearly led the Western church. Gradually the bishop of Rome claimed to be the leader of all Christendom, but the Eastern patriarchs refused to accept his authority.

Numerous minor differences also developed between these churches that came to be known as Eastern Orthodox and Roman Catholic. The Eastern church used icons, two-dimensional pictures of Jesus, Mary, and the disciples, in their worship, while the Western church allowed statues. The East baptized infants by immersion, while the West allowed sprinkling. The East gave the people both bread and wine in the communion meal, while the West gave them only bread. The East allowed its clergy the possibility of marriage before ordination, while the West came to insist upon celibacy. The East used Greek as its language of worship, while the West used Latin until the mid-twentieth century.

The rift between the two branches of Christendom continued to grow during its first thousand years. Western Christians were busy repelling various barbarian invasions and building what has become Western Europe, while the East saw almost all of its empire fall into the hands of the Muslim invaders in the seventh and eighth centuries. Antagonism reached a climax in 1054, when Pope Leo IX sent delegates to Constantinople to excommunicate the Patriarch Cerularius. Even this breach might have been healed, but Christian Crusaders from European nations stopped at Constantinople in 1204 on their way to the Holy Land and sacked the city. Even today the modern ecumenical movement within Christendom is still seeking a reunion between these two branches of the church.

The Medieval Papacy

Because of its great missionary activities and basic attractiveness, by the medieval period Christianity virtually became the only religion of Western Europe. The thrust of the Muslim movement into Europe was stopped by Charles Martel at the Battle of Tours in 732, and although there were Muslims in Spain for another seven centuries Europe was maintained as a Christian realm. The implications of this for the papacy were immense. For Europeans there was only one Holy Catholic Church and outside it there was no salvation. This church had one head, Christ, who ruled through his vicar, Peter, and his successors on the throne of the church in Rome. The line of succession from Peter to the various popes was said to be an unbroken line of authority. This power and its potential were the occasion for both excellence and abuse by the medieval popes.

In the chaos that followed the decline of the Roman Empire, the papacy was often the only secure leadership in Europe, and the popes of the Christian church exercised much of the same power as did temporal rulers. Indeed they were the makers of many temporal rulers, as it was the custom of those who would be emperors of the "Holy Roman Empire" to be crowned by the popes. Naturally this power led to abuses. The papacy gathered lands, wealth, and art treasures and went to war in a manner similar to that of any other feudal fiefdom. Frequently ecclesiastical offices were given to relatives (nepotism) or sold to the highest bidder (simony) because they carried so much potential power and wealth.

The strength of the papacy over European politics was never more clearly illustrated than in the conflict between Pope Gregory VII (1073–1085) and Emperor Henry IV (d. 1106). The issue between them was who was to appoint German bishops, the pope or the emperor. The emperor wished to appoint his own bishops, for obvious reasons, but when he did so, the pope excommunicated him. In order to gain a reversal of this decision, the emperor crossed the Alps in the dead of winter, January 1077, and stood for three days as a barefoot penitent before the palace of the pope. Finally Gregory absolved him. Such was the power of the church over the secular rulers of that time.

In terms of its moral leadership the papacy reached its weakest point between 1309 and 1377, a period called the "Babylonian Captivity of the Church." During this period the headquarters of the papacy moved from Rome to Avignon, near the French border. The popes and most of the cardinals of this era were all French, and at times the papacy was virtually captive to the king of France. This weakened its power and prestige with nations that were not friendly to France. This was also a period of papal wealth, luxury, moral laxity, and abuse. The result was the Great Schism.

In 1378 the Avignon cardinals elected a new pope, Urban VI, who then refused to return to Avignon with them and restored the papacy to Rome. The cardinals declared Urban's election to be void and elected another pope who would rule from Avignon. Urban selected another college of cardinals. The European nations were divided in their support of the two men who claimed to be the successor to Saint Peter. The Council of Pisa was called in 1409 to settle the issue but instead selected a third pope, who also claimed to be Christ's vicar on earth. The Great Schism was finally healed by the Council of Constance, which met from 1414 to 1418, and the papacy was returned to one pope with his capital in Rome.

Thomas Aquinas

No discussion of medieval Christianity, or Christianity in general, would be complete without some mention of one of the greatest—if not *the* greatest—thinkers the church ever produced, Thomas Aquinas (d. 1274).

The tenth through the fourteenth centuries in Western Europe were a time of intense intellectual activity. During this period many of the great universities were founded, and their main intellectual pursuit was theology. The writings of Plato, Aristotle, and others were preserved from destruction by the Arab philosophers, and by the late medieval period there was enough peaceful contact between Muslim and Christian scholars to allow Christians access to these writings so that they could translate them into Latin. These translations gave impetus to the intellectual movement.

The issue that most concerned Christian thinkers was the relationship between faith and reason. Were Christian beliefs, which had been communicated through scripture and the church, consistent with what people perceived to be the truth by means of their ability to reason?

The most outstanding Christian scholar to address this issue was Thomas Aquinas, a Dominican monk whose entire life was given over to scholarship. He was a student of Albertus Magnus at the University of Paris and at Cologne. Although Aquinas was a prolific writer of hymns, commentaries, and theological studies, he is best remembered for two works. The first was *Summa Contra Gentiles*, a series of arguments defending the Christian faith against infidels. The second and best known of his works was *Summa Theologiae*, a massive systematization of the Christian faith that became the standard theological formulation for the Roman Catholic Church. Aquinas, more than any other, attempted to Christianize Aristotle. He utilized Aristotle's arguments for the existence of God based upon reason to prove a part of the Christian scheme. However, Aquinas believed that reason could only take the Christian so far; beyond this point, there had to be divine revelation to complete the message. Therefore both reason and revelation were necessary for Christian belief.

THE PROTESTANT REFORMATION

In the sixteenth century the Western church was torn asunder by a violent revolution from which it has never fully recovered. This revolution has been called the Reformation, but it went far beyond reforming Christianity; it upset it, destroyed its unified hold on Europe, challenged its authority, and disrupted it for centuries. The causes for this revolution are many, varied, and intricate. However, the major ones may be listed broadly as the rise of European nationalism, the new learning of the Renaissance, and the decline of the papacy.

Early Reform Movements

The date of the beginning of the Protestant Reformation is usually established at 1517, when Martin Luther posted his ninety-five theses on the door of the church in Wittenberg, but there were reformers and reform movements more than a century before Luther. One of the earliest reformers was John Wyclif of England (1320?–1384). Wyclif was an Oxford scholar who eventually held most of the ideas that were later representative of the Protestant movement. His greatest contribution was the translation of the official Bible of the church, which was called the Vulgate, from Latin into English. To facilitate the reading of this Bible by the common people, Wyclif organized a band of wandering preachers known as Lollards who went about the country preaching and teaching. Wyclif died in 1384 but was condemned by the Council of Constance in 1415. His remains were unearthed and burned in 1428 as an expression of this condemnation. Even though the Lollard movement was intermittently persecuted by the kings of England, it survived long after Wyclif.

Early reformation in Bohemia was led by John Hus (1373–1415). Rector of the University of Prague, Hus was influenced by the writings of Wyclif. Hus denounced the evils of the current papacy and drew a large following from the citizens of Prague.

In order to raise money for various reasons, the medieval papacy had approved the sale of so-called indulgences. For a price, a Christian could buy an indulgence that, drawing upon the treasury of good that the saints had developed, would pay for a sin committed by the living or by the dead who were in purgatory. Hus was particularly bold in denouncing this practice that naturally led to all manner of corruption and became a target for the wrath of the reformers. Hus was condemned by the Council of Constance in 1415 and burned at the stake.

Early reformation was represented in Italy by the fervent preaching for personal moral reform from a Dominican monk, Girolamo Savonarola (1452–1498). Savonarola, who was a preacher to the city of Florence in the 1490s, was convinced that Florence was facing troubled times because of God's judgment on the moral laxity of the city. His preaching was so convincing that the Florentines changed their lives and publicly burned their pornography and objects of amusement. The stern Savonarola soon came into conflict with loose-living Pope Alexander VI, who excommunicated him. Eventually Savonarola and two of his disciples were hanged and their bodies burned.

Martin Luther

The most outstanding figure of the Reformation was Martin Luther of Saxony (1483–1546). Luther was born into the rapidly developing middle class of German society. Although he was reared in a very religious home he had no intention of pursuing a religious vocation. After completing his master of arts degree he began to study law and planned a career as a lawyer. However, in July 1505 Luther was struck down by a bolt of lightning, and in terror he vowed to become a monk. Against his father's wishes he entered an Augustinian monastery and began his search for the salvation of his soul. Two years later he was ordained a priest and celebrated his first mass. Still he sought salvation through fasting, vigils, confession, and self-mortification.

Luther's skills as a scholar were noted by his superiors, and he was sent as a teacher of theology to the University of Wittenberg. There he taught, preached, and took his doctorate of theology. While at Wittenberg he lectured on Paul's letters to the Romans and the Galatians. In both these books the phrase "the just shall live by faith" caught his eye and became a source of illumination to him.

Like many others, Luther began to call for moral reform within the church. He was particularly incensed by the sale of indulgences by a local man named Tetzel, who promised people that as soon as their money fell into the coffer, a soul rose from purgatory. On the basis of his opposition to this sale of indulgences, Luther chose ninety-five theses as grounds for debate and nailed them upon the door of the castle church of Wittenberg on October 31, 1517. These theses were widely read all across Germany and created an immediate sensation. In the publications and debates that followed, Luther was led into more and more controversy with the papacy. He came to declare that every Christian was a priest who could interpret scripture alone and that the popes and the church hierarchy were not superior to the believer. He also challenged the doctrine of transubstantiation, which taught that at the mass the bread and wine literally became the body and blood of Jesus. Luther's writings upon these and many other controversial issues were widely distributed through a new medium, the printing press.

Because of the controversy that Luther had caused, the emperor of the Holy Roman Empire, Charles V, called an imperial diet at the city of Worms in April 1521 to try Luther. When questioned Luther admitted that the writings under scrutiny were his, but he refused to recant or retract any of their contents. He is reported to have said, "Here I stand. I cannot do otherwise." As a result of his actions before the diet, he was placed under an imperial edict that banned the printing and sale of his books and forbade anyone to provide hospitality or shelter for him or his friends. It had been expected that Luther would suffer the same fate as Hus one hundred years before, but the emperor was too busy with other matters to properly pursue him. Instead Luther was kidnapped by his own friends and taken to the Wartburg Castle, where he lived in disguise for almost a year. During this time he wrote nearly a dozen books and translated the New Testament into German. Later he translated the Old Testament, and his translations of scripture became classics in the German language.

In 1522 Luther returned to Wittenberg, where he took charge of the rapidly developing Reformation. He repudiated the acts of radical reformers who wanted to destroy everything in the Christian church that was not specifically mentioned in scripture. His own style was to remove only those things that he felt were contrary to scripture. In the following years Luther was busy in many ways. He was, of course, organizing a reformed church in Germany. He was writing hymns such as the Protestant classic, "A Mighty Fortress Is Our God." He was encouraging former priests and nuns to marry, and he himself married a nun, Katherine von Bora, and became a father.

In the last years of his life Luther grew more conservative. His writings were sometimes bitterly anti-Jewish, because Jews were no more anxious to accept Lutheran Christianity than they had been to accept Catholic Christianity. He also turned against the peasants who were currently in rebellion and encouraged the nobility to slaughter them. Against all odds Martin Luther died peacefully in February 1546.

The Reformation sprang up in other nations during Luther's

A *simple wooden Protestant church*.

lifetime and immediately thereafter. In Germany the decision to be reformed or to remain Catholic lay with the prince of any particular region. If the ruler were reformed, the region became reformed; if the ruler chose to remain Catholic, the region remained Catholic. Thus the religious orientation of Germany became a kind of patchwork. The Scandinavian nations, Sweden, Denmark, and Norway, became Lutheran during the following decades.

Ulrich Zwingli

In Switzerland the reform movement was led by Ulrich Zwingli (1484–1531). Zwingli was a contemporary of Luther and was much influenced by his writings. At first the Reformed Church in Switzerland was very close to the Lutheran movement. However, Zwingli and Luther differed substantially over one central issue. Although Luther denied that the bread and wine of communion actually became the body and blood of Christ, he did believe that Christ was spiritually present in the elements. He believed that the words of Jesus at the Last Supper, "This is my body," were to be taken literally. Zwingli chose to emphasize the other words of Jesus at the Last Supper, "Do this in remembrance of me." Therefore, to the Swiss reformer, the communion meal was a memorial, a remembrance of Jesus' death. This issue prevented a union between the Swiss and the Lutherans.

John Calvin

Probably the greatest and most influential mind of the Reformation was John Calvin (1509–1564). Calvin was born in France and received a classical education at the University of Paris. By 1534 he had come under the influence of the Protestant movement and made his break with the Roman church. By the time he was twenty-six he had turned his fine mind to theological matters and written the massive book that became the classic of Protestant theology, *The Institutes of the Christian Religion*. This book, originally written in Latin and later translated into French, was revised four times in Calvin's lifetime. In it he set forth his understanding of the nature of the true Christian faith before it was corrupted by Rome. He repeated many of the teachings of Saint Augustine, stressing such ideas as the sovereignty of God, original sin, the total depravity of man, predestination, and election.

Eventually Calvin served as a minister in the Reformed Church of Geneva and then in Strassburg. He was invited back to Geneva a second time and remained there from 1541 until his death in 1564. Although he was never more than a minister in Geneva, Calvin's influence over the life of the entire city was enormous. Despite opposition from both theological and political foes, he was virtually the ruler of Geneva. He himself was given to hard work and simple living, and he impressed this upon the city. He discouraged frivolity of any kind. He encouraged commerce and industry along with the lending of money at reasonable rates of interest.[17] He encouraged education and founded the University of Geneva. Under Calvin's leadership Geneva became the home of oppressed Protestants from all over Europe.

---

[17]Indeed some scholars such as Max Weber have suggested that John Calvin was the father of modern capitalism.

The importance of John Calvin to the Reformed church cannot be stressed enough. His writings set the intellectual base for much of the later Protestant theology. His concern for the rightness of labor and thrift as expressions of religion is felt four hundred years later among those who have been reared in Calvinistic religion.

Other Reformation Leaders and Movements

Although the Reformation first centered around the writings and teachings of people like Luther and Calvin, and although it attracted large numbers of dissatisfied Christians throughout Europe, it soon became a fragmented movement. Within one hundred years of the death of Luther there were hundreds of denominations (and later, subdenominations) of the Reformed church. In the centuries that followed, the fragmentation continued. There were at least two major reasons for these divisions. First, Protestantism derived much of its force and early growth from nationalistic trends in sixteenth-century Western Europe. Whereas in medieval Europe one emperor, who was crowned by the pope, ruled the entire European society, postmedieval Europe began to demand monarchs over each nation, without outside interference from the emperor or Rome. Therefore, when the opportunity came for leaders of European nations to express their freedom from Rome through a new version of Christianity, many were willing to take it. The best example of this was the establishment of the Church of England. Although England had been the home of Wyclif and had theological differences with Rome, the major reason for the Reformation in that country was political. The strong king of England, Henry VIII, wanted a wife who would bear him a son. Since his wife Catherine could not bear him one, Henry asked the pope for an annulment so that he might remarry. When the pope refused, Henry married Anne Boleyn, established the Church of England, and appointed Thomas Cranmer archbishop of Canterbury in 1533. Although the ostensible cause of the breach between Rome and England was Henry's marital life, the drive toward political independence was perhaps the stronger force behind the establishment of the Church of England.

A second cause for the many divisions within Protestantism was the controversy about the "priesthood of the believer," which had been such a strong part of Luther's teachings. Many of the reformers thought that many priests, who heard confessions, administered the sacraments, and interpreted the Bible for the untrained parishioner—

indeed, the institution of the priesthood itself—was corrupt. Therefore these reformers taught that in the spirit of the New Testament each believer was a priest who was qualified to perform many of these tasks alone. The reformers were strongly in favor of the translation of the Bible into vernacular languages so it could be read by every Christian. Obviously if all Christians could read the Bible and were free to interpret it for themselves, differences of interpretation were bound to occur, and these ultimately caused divisions within Protestantism.

One of the most radical dissident groups was the Anabaptists. Whereas Luther and Calvin had rejected only those elements in the Catholic church that they felt were expressly forbidden in the Bible, the Anabaptists attempted to discard all those elements not expressly found in the New Testament. Luther and Calvin advocated infant baptism because it was not condemned by the New Testament, but the Anabaptists rejected it because they could not find such a practice in the New Testament. They therefore rebaptized adults who had formerly been baptized as infants—thus the nickname "Anabaptists" (rebaptizers). Because this movement was devisive in nature, there were many Anabaptist subgroups with a great variety of beliefs. Because they were different and their numbers were small, the Anabaptists were persecuted by both Catholics and other Protestants to the point that they were almost eliminated from the European continent. They survived in Britain and America as Baptists, Mennonites, and Amish.

Other Reformation groups existed in nearly every European nation. Many of these were suppressed by their governments and either fled their native lands or were crushed completely. One such group was the French Huguenots. The French were deeply impressed by the teachings of John Calvin, and his Reformation made many converts among the French middle class and even the aristocracy. Hostilities between the Catholic majority and the Protestant minority erupted into a series of wars between 1562 and 1594. Following these wars the Huguenots were guaranteed freedom of worship in certain specified locations by the Edict of Nantes. One hundred years later, in 1685, the edict was formally revoked, and hundreds of thousands of the Huguenots fled to other parts of Europe and America. Only a tiny minority of Protestants remained in France after the seventeenth century.

Italy, the home of both the papacy and Savonarola, never produced a Protestant Reformation of any magnitude, nor did Czechoslovakia, the home of Hus, nor did Spain. The Scottish Reformation was led by a Calvinist, John Knox, and became the basis for the modern Presbyterian Church.

MODERN CHRISTIANITY

Christianity, like all the other major religions of the world, has been forced to deal with the problems and challenges of the modern world. However, in entering the modern age, Christianity was first required to overcome the trauma of the Reformation.

The Catholic Counter-Reformation

Protestants were not the only ones who saw the problems within the sixteenth-century Catholic church. Others were aware of the same grievances that motivated Luther and Calvin, but they wished to purify the church without establishing another form of Christianity. They wanted a reformation without the attendant revolution. These individuals remained within the Roman Catholic Church and sought a Counter-Reformation as a response to the Protestant Reformation.

When it became apparent that large numbers of Christians were leaving the church and following the Reformers, the Catholic church responded immediately in 1545 by convening the Council of Trent. Some who came to the council wanted to achieve reforms that would bring reconciliation with the Protestants. Others wished to delineate the Catholic position so clearly that there would be no grounds for reconciliation. Generally the decisions of Trent favored those who preferred the second path. To counter the Protestant emphasis upon scripture as the sole word of God, the council declared that Catholic tradition was coequal with scripture as a source of truth for Christians. Therefore when Protestants pointed to a practice in the Catholic church that was contrary to scripture, the Catholics replied that the church had written scripture and therefore its traditions were at least equal if not superior.

As a response to Protestants such as Wyclif and Luther who insisted on translating scripture into the vernacular, the Council of Trent stated that the Latin Vulgate was to be the true sacred canon of the church. This was also a counter to Reformers who had chosen to exclude certain Old Testament books not found in the Jewish scripture. The council further declared that only the Roman Catholic Church had the right to interpret scripture. This too flew in the face of the Protestant doctrine of the "priesthood of the believer."

Whereas most Reformed churches had rejected all of the sacraments except baptism and communion, the Council of Trent reaffirmed the traditional seven sacraments:

1. *Baptism.* Baptism of infants was necessary to wash away the taint of original sin. Any infant who died without the benefit of baptism was technically destined for hell. However, it became popular later to say that the unbaptized infant was to spend eternity in a never-never land called *limbo.*

2. *Confirmation.* At some point before maturity, usually about age thirteen, children must be reconfirmed in the vows that were made for them when they were baptized as infants.

3. *Penance.* Christians must confess their sins regularly in private to priests and receive absolution. Absolution, or forgiveness, may be conditioned upon acts of penance ordered by the priest, depending on the seriousness of the sin confessed.

4. *Eucharist.* This sacrament is known throughout Christendom as the Lord's Supper, communion, or mass. In many Christian communities the bread and wine are given to the laity, but the Roman Catholic Church gives only the bread and reserves the wine for the priesthood. The Council of Trent not only reaffirmed this sacrament but also gave renewed support to the doctrine of transubstantiation. According to this doctrine, during the mass the bread and wine literally become the body and blood of Jesus. While the laity might be expected to take reasonable care of the body of Jesus, they could not be trusted with the blood.

5. *Extreme unction.* As a Christian nears death he or she is to be visited by a priest and anointed with healing oil. The priest then hears the last confession. In receiving these last rites, the Christian is properly prepared to die.

6. *Marriage.* By the fifteenth century the marriage of Christians had come to be regarded as a sacrament.

7. *Ordination.* For those Christians who chose the clergy as a career rather than marriage, taking the holy orders was considered a sacrament.

The Council of Trent also strongly supported relics, the veneration of saints, and sacred images, all contrary to most Protestant teaching. As a positive response to the challenge of Luther and others, the sale of indulgences was controlled and other abuses of the medieval church were corrected.

Another result of the Catholic Counter-Reformation was the development of the Society of Jesus (Jesuits). The founder of the society was Ignatius Loyola (1491–1556), a Spanish nobleman whose first career was the military. Loyola was wounded in a battle in 1521, and during his convalescence he read about the life of Christ and the various saints. He was so moved by this literature that upon his recovery he entered a monastery, took the vows of poverty, chastity, and obedience, hung up his armor in the chapel of the Virgin Mary, and dedicated himself to becoming a soldier of Christ. In the following years Loyola developed the *Spiritual Exercises* which were designed to serve as an agency for examining the conscience and as a guide for meditation. These exercises were usually given under the direction of a spiritual leader and required about four weeks.

Realizing his need for education, Loyola went back to school and eventually studied theology at the University of Paris. He gathered about him other scholars to whom he introduced the *Spiritual Exercises*. Among these early converts was Francis Xavier (1506–1552), who was to become a Christian missionary to India and Japan. Loyola and his friends went to Rome, and in 1540 the pope gave them official permission to found a new order, the Society of Jesus. This order was characterized by its military organization, its absolute obedience to the pope and the general of the order, its scholarship, and its missionary activities. Scholarship was stressed because Loyola and his early followers were university students. Before Loyola died in 1556 he saw his order grow from just a few friends to over a thousand members. Although it was an object of fear and suspicion by both Protestants and other Catholics, the Jesuit order continued to grow and attracted some of the ablest young men in Catholic Europe.

Catholic Dogmas Since the Counter-Reformation

The heart of the modern Catholic church was established by the end of the sixteenth century. Prior to the second Vatican Council called in 1959 there were no sweeping changes in Catholic theology. A series of dogmas were established by the church during this period, but many of them had been widely held for centuries. Their establishment as dogmas merely put the official seal of approval upon them. The following dogmas have been accepted as major doctrines since the Council of Trent.

1. *The Immaculate Conception of Mary*. It had long been held among Catholics that Mary, the mother of Jesus, not only had conceived as a virgin but that she had been born without the taint of original sin. In 1854 Pope Pius IX formally declared the Immaculate Conception to be a dogma that should be believed by all faithful Catholics.

2. *The dogma of papal infallibility*. After the Council of Trent

closed in 1563 the Roman Catholic Church called no general council until the Vatican Council of 1869. This council dealt with the sensitive issue of papal infallibility. After much debate and controversy the council declared as dogma that the pope was infallible when he spoke *ex cathedra*, that is, as the pastor of all Christians on the issues of dogma and morals. Naturally this dogma widened the gap between Catholics and Eastern Orthodox and Protestant groups.

3. *The dogma of the bodily assumption of Mary.* In 1950 Pope Pius XII declared as dogma the bodily assumption of Mary. This meant that Mary did not suffer decay in a tomb but was taken directly into heaven after her death.

Vatican II

Upon the death of Pius XII in 1958, John XXIII became the pope. John was determined to revitalize the church and bring it into line with the twentieth century. Therefore he called the second Vatican Council, which was to be the most revolutionary council since Trent. Invited to this council were representatives of Eastern Orthodox and Protestant Christian groups acting as observers to the proceedings. Meeting between 1962–1965, this council effected some of the most sweeping changes ever made in the Roman Catholic Church. Non-Catholics were recognized as true Christians, the vernacular was allowed in many parts of the mass, the Index of Prohibited Books was abolished, more congregational participation in worship was encouraged, and the church officially declared that Jews were no longer to be held responsible for the death of Jesus. In general the second Vatican Council attempted to bring the church up to date and took several steps toward reconciliation with Orthodox and Protestant groups.

Modern Movements

Modern Protestant movements. Because of the reasons already discussed, Protestantism has been, until the recent ecumenical movement, a denominational movement. Two Protestants might believe essentially the same doctrines but differ on baptism or on church government and belong to different denominations.

There are so many Protestant denominations that not even the most exhaustive text on the history of Christianity could hope to effectively deal with them all. Basically, however, there are four branches of Protestantism. There are the Lutherans, who are generally found in

•

the Germanic and Scandinavian nations and the immigrants from those nations. There are those Reformed and Presbyterian denominations that sprang from the teachings of John Calvin. A third branch is the group that sprang from the radical Reformers, the Anabaptists. This group includes the Baptists, the Mennonites, and the Amish. Although the lines of descent are not clear, Anabaptist influence also is apparent in several other Protestant groups such as the Quakers and the Disciples of Christ. The fourth branch includes the Church of England and the Methodists.

We have already considered all of these groups except the Methodists. Methodism began in the eighteenth century as a response to the emotional coolness of the Church of England and the plight of urban dwellers in the early industrial revolution. The founder of Methodism was John Wesley (1703–1791). Wesley, the fifteenth child in the family of an Anglican clergyman, attended Oxford and was ordained as an Anglican priest in 1728. While at Oxford he and his brother Charles organized a small group for the purpose of religious support. The group was first called the Holy Club but because of its disciplined ways was nicknamed the Methodists.

In 1735 John and Charles were sent to Georgia as missionaries, and on the voyage to America they encountered another Protestant group called Moravians, who spoke to them of religious conversion. The Wesley brothers experienced this conversion in 1738. They began to preach about their experience first in the churches and to religious societies and later in the fields and town squares. They were joined by an eloquent and fiery preacher, George Whitefield. Their emotional sermons mainly appealed to the lower and middle classes, and soon there was a large Methodist following. John organized the Methodists into societies that were formed into circuits and attended by preachers who traveled from society to society. Charles became the hymn writer and contributed hundreds of songs that are still treasured by many Protestants.

Although John Wesley had no desire to separate himself from the Church of England and form a new denomination, by the time he died, the break between the two groups was obvious. At the end of the eighteenth century there were over 70,000 Methodists in England, but the denomination's greatest growth came among the colonists in America. The Methodist meeting and its circuit rider were a familiar part of the American frontier, and Methodism became one of the largest Protestant denominations in the United States, second only to the various Baptist groups.

The Second Vatican Council meets in Rome's majestic St. Peter's Basilica, where 2,400 high church dignitaries gathered.

The squalor, poverty, despair, and alcoholism of the industrial society produced other Protestant movements. In the nineteenth century in England William Booth founded the Salvation Army in an attempt not only to save the souls of the ragged edges of humanity in the slums of industrialized cities but also to provide food, clothing, and warmth for their bodies. In 1844 a similar concern for the total person produced the Young Men's Christian Association in London. A concern for the ignorance of slum children caused Robert Raikes to organize the first Sunday school in Gloucester, England, in 1780. Raikes' first objective was to teach the children to read the Bible. Since then the Sunday school has become almost universally accepted by Protestant denominations as an agency of religious instruction.

The missionary movement.   If the central thesis of monotheistic religions is that there is only one God for all the earth, then anyone who does not accept this God must be in error. Therefore it becomes the duty of the monotheist to go to the person in error and convince that person to accept the one true God.

Christians, like other monotheists, have been missionaries from the earliest days. The great theologian of the early church, Paul, was a far-traveling, zealous missionary. There is a strong tradition that Thomas, the doubting disciple of Jesus, went to India to spread the Christian gospel. We have already spoken of Catholic missionaries such as Francis Xavier, who preached Christianity in Japan. Catholic missionaries accompanied the Spanish explorers in the sixteenth century. The Wesleys served as Anglican missionaries in America. Still,

317

Protestant groups, especially those that had been influenced by John Calvin, were slow to enter the mission fields. They were probably impeded by Calvin's doctrine of predestination, which taught that the sovereign God would save only those persons whom he chose to save, and it was therefore folly to send missionaries to the heathen. If God wished to save them, they would be saved without the help of missionaries; if God did not wish to save them, it was a waste of time and money. By the nineteenth century, however, this attitude had changed except among the sternest Calvinists, and most Protestant groups came to support some form of mission work. Occasionally this missionary activity was directed at the Roman Catholic population in areas such as Latin America, but generally it was carried on in non-Christian areas in Africa and Asia. The rising nationalism among many nations in these areas in the late twentieth century has brought an end to much missionary activity.

The ecumenical movement.   The most outstanding movement among Christians in the twentieth century has been the ecumenical movement. As we have noted, Christianity has long been divided into two main branches, Eastern and Western, and since the sixteenth century the Western church has been divided into Protestant and Catholic. However, in the twentieth century Christians have begun the long, hard journey to reunion. The Roman Catholic contribution to this journey was the second Vatican Council.

The most visible attempt at reunion was the organization of the World Council of Churches in Amsterdam in 1948. This organization has been supported by many Protestant denominations and some representatives of Eastern Orthodoxy. Although the World Council is organized to promote church unity, little actual unification has been produced. In fact there are few concrete examples of reunion within Christendom. One has been the uniting of a small number of Protestant denominations that had no great theological differences. Other, more dramatic, unions stemmed from the pressing needs of the mission fields in nations like India, where factions within Christianity had weakened its case for conversions. Still the reunification of Christianity is a long way off. Eastern Orthodoxy, whose largest branch, the Russian Orthodox Church, is beset by a hostile government, maintains an aloofness toward the Western church. The post–Vatican II Roman Catholic Church is more open to non-Catholic Christians than ever before, but the Protestant-Catholic dialogue, while progressing, still has many hurdles to clear. Protestants, as always, are vastly divided, and although some are quite anxious for church union and willing to pay almost any price for it, the majority apparently still prefer to go it alone.

SUGGESTED READING

Adam, Karl. *The Spirit of Catholicism*. New York: Macmillan, 1962.

Filson, Floyd V. *Opening the New Testament*. Philadelphia: Westminster Press, 1952.

Hordern, William. A *Layman's Guide to Protestant Theology*. New York: Macmillan, 1957.

Klausner, Joseph. *Jesus of Nazareth*. New York: Macmillan, 1934.

Marty, Martin E. A *Short History of Christianity*. Cleveland: World Publishing Company, 1959.

ISLAM

A page from the Quran written in Kufic script, one of the two main Arabic styles.

There is no God but Allah; Muhammad is the messenger of Allah.

THE SHAHADAH

The youngest of the world's major religions is Islam. It is also one of the largest, with one third of a billion adherents; one of the fastest growing, with its active missionary program in Africa; and the dominant religion of the so-called third-world nations of the Middle East and Africa. In addition it is one of the simplest and least complicated of the world's religions. These factors, coupled with a colorful founder and a rapid expansion period, make Islam one of the most interesting and important of all religions.

The basic belief of this religion is that there is only one God, who is called Allah, the same God worshiped by other religions under other names. He is the sole and sovereign ruler of the universe. Though Allah has made himself known through other prophets at other times, his best and final revelation was to the prophet Muhammad in the seventh century A.D. According to his teachings, the believer has only one life to live. How believers live this life will determine how they spend their eternal existence. During that one life believers must submit to the will of Allah. Thus the adherents of this religion are called *Muslims* ("submitters").

PRE-ISLAMIC ARAB RELIGION

Islam began with the Arabian desert peoples in the seventh century A.D. It did not spring out of a religious vacuum. The people of this area had developed religious forms of their own and had been exposed to various other religions for centuries. Although the influence was not strong, Byzantine Christianity had been a factor in the lives of these people. Judea, the home of Christianity, was not too distant from Arabia. Cities such as Damascus, Caesarea, Antioch, and Alexandria were neighbors to Mecca and Yathrib (Medina). Christian princes ruled from these cities, and many of the early Church fathers wrote and taught in them. Christian influence on the early Arab people was weakened by two factors. First, in the Byzantine world Christian theology was internally divided into many factions over the nature of Christ. Battles, both theological and physical, were fought over the precise relationship between God and Jesus. Perhaps these wars caused a yearning for a prophet who would say, "There is no God but Allah." Second, the Byzantine rulers on many occasions had treated the Arab Christians with hostility and cruelty. Undoubtedly this caused many to welcome the conquests of a new Arab religion in the seventh century.

The people of Arabia were also familiar with Judaism. Several of the desert tribes were Jewish. Although their origins are not clear, many historians believe that these tribes were the descendants of Jews who had been forced out of Judea when the Romans put down rebellion in the land in 70 A.D. and again in 135. When Muhammad, the prophet of Islam, entered Medina in 622 A.D. many of the citizens of that city were Jewish.

Another religion that may have had some influence upon the formulation of Islam was Zoroastrianism. While the effects upon Islam are not as strong as on Judaism and Christianity, it is possible that Muhammad and some of his disciples may have been in contact with the Persian Zoroastrians.

Perhaps the major religious force from which Islam grew and which it reacted against was the native religions of the Arab people. Actually we know very little about the basic religion of these people because the only material we have about them is the Muslim scripture, the Quran, which naturally is hostile. Apparently the pre-Islamic people worshiped a variety of gods. They recognized one supreme high god, who was separated and unapproachable by people, whom they called Allah (literally, "the God"). The deities that received most worship and attention were the local and tribal gods. Images of these gods were carved and cherished, and blood sacrifices were made to them. In addition to a great pantheon of the gods of heaven and earth, there were lesser divine creatures. There were angels and fairies who were kind and helpful spirits, and there were demonic creatures called *jinn* who usually sought to do harm to humans. There were also the universally evil spirits such as the ghouls who devoured the bodies of the dead.

Perhaps the most obvious characteristic of basic pre-Islamic religion is its animism. Gods and spirits were found in stones, trees, wells, and animals, and these spirits had to be placated and implored for aid. The city of Mecca became a holy place because of animistic associations. Mecca is located on the central western coast of Arabia and lay on the major north-south caravan route. Its claim to fame was rooted in a meteoric stone that had fallen there centuries before. The stone became an object of veneration to the animistic population, and by the time of Muhammad, pilgrims had built an enclosure around it called the Kaaba. The Kaaba gradually filled with images, relics, and paintings. One report claims that it even contained a painting of Jesus and Mary. Islamic legend says that the black stone fell from heaven during the time of Adam and Eve and that Abraham and his son Ishmael built the Kaaba. A period of several months each year was set aside as a time of truce so that pilgrims could travel safely to Mecca to worship at this shrine. Naturally the black stone was an object of both pride and profit to the Meccans, and there was a constant struggle between the various clans of Mecca over who would control the Kaaba.

THE LIFE OF MUHAMMAD

Because Islam is one of the youngest of the world's religions, the details of the life of its founder are more available than those of other founders. No one seriously questions the fact that Muhammad was a historical figure who lived in the seventh century A.D. From information on the life of the Prophet we assume that he was born about 570 A.D. into the clan of Hashim of the tribe of Quraysh, the group that controlled the Kaaba in Mecca. His father, Abd-al-Muttalib, died before Muhammad was born and his mother died before he was six years of age.[1] Thereafter Muhammad was reared by his uncle, abu-Talib, chief of the Quraysh tribe. Life for an orphan in those times must have been difficult. There was no chance for any kind of formal education, and Islam makes much of the fact that Muhammad was illiterate. Thus

---

[1] It is often observed that many of the founders of religions spent at least a portion of their formative years in homes without a father figure. This was the case in the lives of Moses, Muhammad, Confucius, Mencius, and others. Freud, in *Moses and Monotheism*, makes a great deal of this fact.

the revelation of the Quran to him was the more miraculous. The only occupation open to him was that of a caravan worker, and many of his formative years probably were spent in traveling across the Middle East as a camel driver. Of course, this in itself must have been quite an education. During these travels the young Muhammad had an opportunity to come into contact with representatives of the religions and the cultures of the world. Covering the Arabian peninsula, traveling to Byzantine cities such as Damascus he doubtless met Christians, Jews, and perhaps even Zoroastrians. Each of these religions had several things in common and must have had an influence upon Muhammad. They all believed in one God, though Byzantine Christians were in a constant state of dispute over the persons within the Trinity, and the Zoroastrians had developed a dualism of a god of light and a god of darkness. All of these religions had a scripture that was believed to be the word of God. All of them had an eschatology that taught that the world would one day end and that the righteous would be rewarded while the evil would be tormented in hell. Muhammad seems to have been especially affected by eschatology and began to be concerned about the future of his people who worshiped a multitude of gods and idols.

These years as a camel driver also afforded Muhammad the opportunity to meet the woman who would become his wife, the owner of the caravan, Khadija. Khadija was a wealthy widow who was about forty years old when she married the twenty-five-year-old Muhammad. Although it was permissible to have more than one wife, Muhammad was married only to Khadija as long as she lived. During their marriage of twenty-five years she bore him two sons and four daughters. The sons died in infancy and only one daughter, Fatima, survived her father. Khadija provided the wealth and love that the orphaned Muhammad had never had as a child. She became his strongest supporter and one of his first converts, and her wealth gave him the freedom to consider theological questions.

In the years following his marriage to Khadija, Muhammad began to go into the hills surrounding Mecca and ponder the fate of his people. He was especially concerned about their idolatry and the fate they would have on judgment day when the world ended. During these periods of meditation he received a visit from an angel whom he later identified as Gabriel, mentioned in both the Jewish and Christian bibles. Tradition says that during the month of Ramadan in a cave on Mt. Hira Gabriel brought the following command from God:

Read in the name of thy Lord who created, who created man
of blood coagulated. Read! Thy Lord is the most beneficent,
who taught by the pen, taught that which they knew not unto
men.[2]

At frequent intervals during the rest of his life, Muhammad received revelations from God in this fashion. Islamic tradition says that
the Prophet received many of these revelations through what must be
called ecstatic seizures. Inspiration came like the painful sounding of a
bell; his forehead became covered with sweat. At times visions came to
him in his sleep. These traditions have caused unfriendly critics to
suggest that Muhammad may have been an epileptic. Superficial interpreters of religious experience often seek to explain religious ecstasy
in terms of epilepsy, but this can seldom be proved. Muhammad
memorized the contents of these divine messages and eventually they
were committed to writing to become the scriptures of Islam, called
the Quran.

After a series of revelations, Muhammad became convinced that
there was only one God, whom his people had called Allah and whom
other religions called by other names. He also became convinced that
he was the last and the greatest in a series of prophets of this God,
which included Abraham, Moses, and Jesus, among others. These
former prophets had only an incomplete revelation of Allah, but
Muhammad had the complete and final revelation. Thus Islam at its
very inception did not deny the validity of other religions but rather
looked upon itself as the completion of what others had begun. It is
also worthy of note that Muhammad never considered himself any
more than a prophet. He was not divine; he died like any other person.
His mission was much like that of the classical Hebrew prophet: to
present the word of God to his people.

As the Prophet of Allah, Muhammad began to preach his new understanding of religion to the citizens of Mecca. He received little
encouragement from his neighbors; indeed, there was much discour-
agement and open hostility. He was preaching that there was only one
God who was not to be worshiped with idols, and this of course worked
against the livelihood of many Meccans who depended upon pilgrims
coming to Mecca to worship idols at the Kaaba. Muhammad's first

[2]Quran 96:1–5. This quotation and those that follow are taken from *The Quran*, translated by J. M. Rodwell, Everyman's Library, J. M. Dent & Sons,
London, 1909.

convert was his wife, Khadija. There is debate in the traditions as to who was his first male convert. It was either Ali, a cousin, or Zayd, a slave boy who had been freed by Muhammad. The third convert was a friend, abu-Bakr. In the following years a handful of other converts joined the Muslim movement. Mainly they came from the younger and poorer classes in Mecca. As opposition from the older, richer, and established clan leaders of the city grew stronger, Muhammad received protection from his uncle abu-Talib and other members of his clan, even those who were not Muslims. However, as the opposition and persecution became more severe, Muhammad finally had to urge some of his followers to leave the country. In the year 615 about fifteen Muslim families fled Mecca and took refuge in the Christian kingdom of Abyssinia. The Prophet and the remainder of the Muslims stayed behind in Mecca to continue to preach and face persecution. This persecution took the form of a boycott against Muhammad and his entire clan by the rest of the Meccans, but it proved ineffective.

In 619 Muhammad suffered the loss of his two greatest benefactors, his uncle abu-Talib and his beloved Khadija. After the death of his wife, the Prophet married the first of a number of wives whom he was to have during the remainder of his life. The death of abu-Talib left him without the protection of his clan, and life became very difficult for the Muslims. Muhammad tried to move out of Mecca to a nearby town but was rejected there and had to return.

One of the most significant events in the history of Islam occurred in the year 620, when a group of six men journeyed from the city of Yathrib (later renamed Medina in honor of the Prophet), located 250 miles to the north, to Mecca to confer with Muhammad. They were impressed with the power of his personality. Medina was a city torn by clan warfare and internal strife. It needed one who would come as an impartial judge and settle the disputes within the city, and the delegation believed that Muhammad might be the person. The following year twelve delegates came from Medina to meet the Prophet. Curiously enough ten of the twelve were from Jewish tribes who believed that Muhammad might possibly be the Messiah. An invitation was extended to him to come and be the judge over the city. It was 622 before Muhammad could leave Mecca because a group of assassins had pledged to kill him, and he had to avoid them with great care. His followers slipped out a few at a time, and finally the Prophet made his escape in September. On September 24, 622, Muhammad arrived to be the judge of the city of Medina. The journey from Mecca to Medina is called *Hijrah* ("migration"), and it is the time from which Muslims have since dated their calendars. Dates are listed as A.H. (*Anno Hegirae*).

In Medina the Muslims were established as a clan among other clans, and although Muhammad had been brought to the city as an arbitrator, his religion was by no means widely accepted. Many of the tribes in Medina were Jewish, and perhaps to gain their favor Muhammad commanded the Muslims to pray toward Jerusalem. With the passing of time, the divisions between Muslims and Jews increased, and the Prophet commanded his disciples to pray toward Mecca instead.

In 623 Muhammad married Aishah, the nine-year-old daughter of his friend abu-Bakr. This was also the year of the first conflict between the Medinans under the leadership of Muhammad and the Meccans. The natural rivalry between these two cities was of course intensified by Hijrah. At first the conflicts were merely scattered raids against the Meccan caravans, but later they developed into full military campaigns.

The process of raiding caravans was not a dishonorable matter among Arabs of this era, and it gave the Muslims a way not only to take vengeance against the Meccans but also to acquire money and goods. The most successful of these early encounters was the battle of Badr in 624, when the Muslims defeated the Meccans, killed up to seventy, and took many prisoners and much booty. Tradition says that this was accomplished because the Prophet was at the battle praying for his troops. A victory like this was a great stimulus for the Muslims. It reinforced their loyalty to the Prophet and his cause, and it attracted many others to Islam. The following year brought another battle with the Meccans. In this battle the Muslims lost more men than the Meccans, and Muhammad himself was wounded. Because the forces of Mecca had not altogether wiped out the Muslims, however, it was considered a victory for the Prophet.

Conflict between the Muslims and the Jewish tribes in the area also intensified during this period. The Jews apparently had rejected any notion that Muhammad was the Messiah and often ridiculed him publicly. At times they supported the Meccans against the Prophet. As a result the Jewish tribes were either expelled from Muslim territory or offered the choice of conversion or death. The final break occurred when a Jewess, Zainab, invited the Prophet and his friends to dinner and fed them poisoned lamb. Although Muhammad ate only a little of the meat, he suffered from the effects for the rest of his life.

In 627 a force of 10,000 Meccans attacked Medina, but no decisive

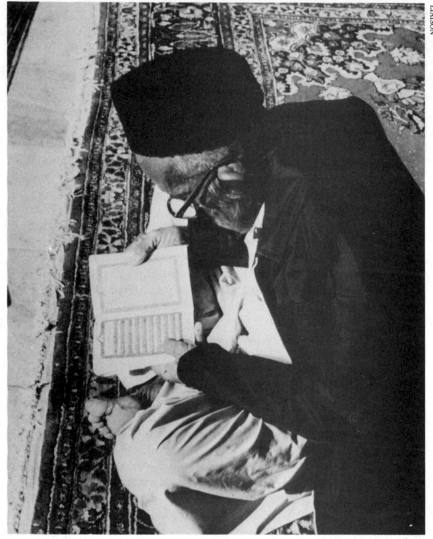

Old man reading the Quran.

battles were fought and the Meccans withdrew. The following year Muhammad attempted to go to Mecca for pilgrimage with his followers, but the Meccans barred the way. A peace treaty was arranged, and the Muslims were allowed to make the pilgrimage the following year. By 629 Islam had grown so strong that when the Muslims entered Mecca on their pilgrimage, no one dared to stop them. In 630 Muhammad, with a force of 10,000 men, entered Mecca as its complete conqueror. He went to the Kaaba and, although he respected the black stone and its enclosure, he destroyed the idols and images. With this symbolic act the Prophet became virtually the sole leader of the Arabian people.

During the next few years Islam grew stronger still. Muhammad sent out messages to surrounding nations inviting them to join the nation of Islam. His followers returned from Abyssinia to rejoin him. He married new wives, many of whom were the widows of Muslims who had died in battle. Other marriages strengthened political ties. Only one of his late marriages was open to criticism. This was his marriage to his cousin Zaynab, who was also the wife of Zayd, his adopted son. Because of her love for the Prophet, Zaynab is supposed to have made life unbearable for her husband until he divorced her. After a suitable period she and the Prophet were married. Muhammad was not criticized so much for taking another man's wife as for marrying his own cousin, which was considered incestuous by the Arab culture of the time.

In 632 Muhammad led the Muslims in another pilgrimage to Mecca. By this time he was sixty-two years of age and in poor health, having never fully recovered from the effects of the poison he had eaten a few years before. Upon his return to Medina he gave a farewell message to the Muslims and then died in the arms of his wife, Aishah. He had made no arrangements regarding his successor, and for a time there was confusion among the Muslims as to leadership. It was finally agreed that abu-Bakr should be the caliph, or successor. At Muhammad's funeral the following words, attributed to abu-Bakr, summed up the Muslim understanding of the Prophet:

O ye people, if anyone worships Muhammad, Muhammad is dead, but if anyone worships God, He is alive and dies not.[3]

THE QURAN

The scripture of Islam is called the Quran. The word *quran* literally means "reading" or "recitation." Thus the title indicates the basic belief that all Muslims hold about this book, that it is a copy of a recitation of an eternal scripture written in heaven and revealed chapter by chapter to Muhammad. The title may also reflect the first words of the

---

[3]W. Montgomery Watt, *Muhammad: Prophet and Statesman* (London: Oxford University Press, 1961), p. 228.

first *surah* or chapter, "Read, in the name of the Lord who created. . . . "

Perhaps no scripture has ever been so influential upon its people than the Quran. Surely no scripture is read so much or committed to memory so often. Whereas Christians and Jews take their bibles seriously, they have subjected them to textual and literary criticism for centuries. Therefore all but the most orthodox believe that the current texts of the Bible mean something less than the absolute word of God. Such is not the case in Islam; the Quran *is* the word of God: It is eternal, absolute, and irrevocable. It was literally revealed to Muhammad, who acted only as a stenographer for Allah, and it has been transmitted virtually unchanged since the days of the Prophet. Therefore it is recited and memorized by all Muslims. The first things Muslims hear when they are born are selections from the Quran. It is the source of their education and becomes a textbook for the study of Arabic. It is not unusual for a Muslim schoolchild to memorize the Quran in its entirety. Verses from it are inscribed upon the walls of the Muslim's home for decoration; its words may be the last a person hears before death.

The Quran is said to contain the exact words of Allah to the Prophet from the time of the first revelation to the end of Muhammad's life. Because Muhammad was illiterate the messages were memorized by him and passed on to Zayd, his secretary, who wrote them upon leaves, stones, bones, or parchments. After Muhammad's death these materials were collected. Tradition says that an early caliph, Uthman, worked with Zayd and others to develop an authorized version of the Quran which replaced several variations of the text.

The revelations that make up the Quran are organized into chapters called *surahs*. With the exception of a brief introductory statement the text is arranged according to the length of the *surah* in descending order. Therefore the non-Muslim reader is sometimes confused because there is no topical or chronological arrangement of the material. The revelations are a great deal like the materials one finds in the prophetic books of the Jewish Bible, an anthology of prophetic material without regard to arrangement. The longest *surah* contains 287 verses, the shortest only three.

The Nature of God

Because the Quran is the word of God, its messages become the authority for all Muslims on God, how God expects people to live, and the eternal destiny of humankind. Allah is revealed to be the one sovereign God over all the universe. The religion of Islam demands the strictest of monotheism, and its creed is this: "There is no God but Allah and Muhammad is his messenger." In contrast to the polytheists of Mecca and the Byzantine Christians who were in dispute over what part Jesus played in the Godhead, Muslims state that there is only the one God, complete, eternal, and undivided. Of all the world's religions only Judaism insists on such absolute monotheism.

> He unto Whom belongeth the sovereignty of the heavens and the earth, He hath chosen no son nor hath He any partner in the sovereignty.[4]

> Say: He is God, One,
> God, the Everlasting Refuge,
> Who has not begotten, and has not been begotten,
> and equal to Him is not any one.[5]

Allah is the omnipresent, omniscient, and omnipotent creator of the universe, and this role is heavily emphasized in the Quran.

> Lo! your Lord is Allah Who created the heavens and the earth in six Days, then mounted He the Throne. He covered the night with the day, which is in haste to follow it, and hath made the sun and the moon and the stars subservient by His command. His verily is all creation and commandment. Blessed be Allah, the Lord of the Worlds![6]

According to Muslim tradition Allah had ninety-nine names, such as the Holy One, the Keeper of Faith, the Guardian, and the Creator. Devout Muslims repeat these names in a manner similar to a Catholic Christian saying rosary.

While Allah possesses the characteristics of power, sovereignty, and majesty, he is also characterized by his justice and mercy. He will repay the evil with justice and the righteous with mercy.

> To God belongs every one dwelling in the heavens and the earth, that he may requite all those who have done evil and

---

[4]Quran 25:2.
[5]Quran 112.
[6]Quran 7:54.

requite all those who have done good with the fairest recompense, even them who avoid the great sins and abominations (save for the trifling faults). Truly your Lord is ample in forgiveness: very well He knew you, when He formed you of the earth and while you were yet hidden in your Mother's womb. Boast· not therefore of your own worth: very well He knows who is truly godly.[7]

Though Allah is alone as the God figure in Islam he is surrounded and aided by certain other heavenly figures. There are his angels who act as his messengers, as did Gabriel when he revealed the Quran to Muhammad, and as his warriors who fight at the side of believers against the infidels. There is another creation halfway between humans and angels who are called the *jinn*. The jinn are created of fire. Some are beneficial creatures who act as guardian angels for humankind while others are demons. The leader of the jinn is a fallen angel called Iblis.[8] Iblis acts very much like the Satan figure in the biblical book of Job. He is not so much a secondary god of evil as Angra Mainyu in Zoroastrianism, but he acts as tempter and prosecuting attorney against humankind. According to Muslim legend Iblis was responsible for the fall of Adam.

Predestination

In the Quran it is revealed that humans are the creation of Allah and must be obedient to him. Righteous persons who would win the favor of God must submit to his will. Because of the Muslim emphasis upon God's power and sovereignty, the words *fatalism* and *predestination* have been used to describe this religion. Carried to its ultimate extreme in Islam, Calvinism, and early Greek philosophy, the belief in an all-powerful force that rules the universe and knows all things leads one to believe that people have no choice in life. Whether one does good or evil, enjoys success or failure is all in the hands of the God who rules the world and has planned each event in advance. When carried to this extreme people do not possess freedom of choice and therefore are not responsible for their acts. God is all and people are but his puppets. Indeed there is a strong strain of fatalism in Islam. The most frequent statement among devout Muslims is *im shallah* (if God wills

---

[7]Quran 53:32, 33.
[8]It is believed that this word is the Arabic version of the Greek word for devil, *diabolos*.

it). Nevertheless it is not accurate to call Islam purely a fatalistic religion. All sects within it do not agree on this issue, although they do hold in common the idea that people are somehow responsible for the evil that they commit and will be judged for this. Allah in his wisdom and mercy allows human beings to make choices in the areas in which they will be judged. From this point of view people do have freedom.

Eschatology

The judgment of humanity at the conclusion of time by Allah is one of the basic beliefs of Islam. The eschatology of Jews, Christians, and Zoroastrians had a profound effect upon Muhammad, and his scheme of the end of time in the Quran reflects these influences. The Quran says that when a person dies the body returns to the earth and the soul goes into a state of sleep until resurrection day. On this day the angel of Allah will sound his trumpet, the earth will be split, and the bodies will rejoin their souls.[9] The resurrected are then judged by Allah. Those who have been faithful and virtuous will be rewarded, and those who have been evil will be punished. All people are judged on the basis of the record of deeds in a book kept for the purpose.

> And the Book is placed, and thou seest the guilty fearful of that which is therein, and they say: What kind of a book is this that leaveth not a small thing nor a great thing but hath counted it! And they find all that they did, confronting them, and thy Lord wrongeth no one.[10]

Both the hell and paradise of Islam are very real places that are graphically described.

> When the day that must come shall have come suddenly,
> None shall treat that sudden coming as a lie:
> Day that shall abase! Day that shall exalt!
> When the earth shall be shaken with a shock,
> And the mountains shall be crumbled with a crumbling,
> And shall become scattered dust,
> And into three bands shall ye be divided:
> Then the people of the right hand—Oh! how happy shall be
>   the people of the right hand!

---

[9]Quran 82.
[10]Quran 18:50.

And the people of the left hand—Oh! how wretched shall be
    the people of the left hand!
And they who were foremost on earth—the foremost still.
These are they who shall be brought nigh to God,
In gardens of delight;
A crowd of the former
And few of the latter generations;
On inwrought couches
Reclining on them face to face:
Aye-blooming youths go round about to them
With goblets and ewers and a cup of flowing wine;
Their brows ache not from it, nor fails the sense:
And with such fruits as shall please them best,
And with flesh of such birds, as they shall long for:
And theirs shall be the Houris, with large dark eyes, like pearls
    hidden in their shells,
In recompense of their labours past.
No vain discourse shall they hear therein, nor charge of sin,
But only the cry, "Peace! Peace!"
And the people of the right hand—Oh! how happy shall be the
    people of the right hand!
Amid thornless sidrahs
And tall trees clad with fruit,
And in extended shade,
And by flowing waters,
And with abundant fruits,
Unfailing, unforbidden,
And on lofty couches.
Of a rare creation have we created the Houris,
And we have made them ever virgins,
Dear to their spouses, of equal age with them,
For the people of the right hand,
A crowd of the former,
And a crowd of the latter generations.
But the people of the left hand—Oh! how wretched shall
    be the people of the left hand!
Amid pestilential winds and in scalding water,
And in the shadow of a black smoke,
Not cool, and horrid to behold.
For they truly, ere this, were blessed with worldly goods,
But persisted in heinous sin,

And were wont to say,
"What! after we have died, and become dust and bones shall
   we be raised?
And our fathers, the men of yore?"
Say: Aye, the former and the latter:
Gathered shall they all be for the time of a known day.
Then ye, O ye the erring, the gainsaying,
Shall surely eat of the tree Ez-zakkoum,
And fill your bellies with it,
And thereupon shall ye drink boiling water,
And ye shall drink as the thirsty camel drinketh.
This shall be their repast in the day of reckoning![11]

The student of world religions is immediately aware of the similarities among the Muslim eschatological scheme and those of Zoroastrianism, Judaism, and Christianity. The only differences in the Islamic heaven and hell are those that would be particularly appealing or distasteful to a desert dweller. Heaven is located in a beautiful garden with flowing water and shade. The righteous are fed wine— normally forbidden to Muslims—that does not disturb the senses and does not leave the drinker with a hangover. Hell is a horrid place filled with scalding winds, black smoke, and brackish water.

RELIGIOUS INSTITUTIONS

From the Quran and from the early years of Islamic life there developed certain religious institutions that are almost universally recognized by Muslims.

The Mosque

Islam is not a temple-oriented religion. Although certain places are venerated by Muslims it would not have suited the nomadic life of the Arab people to require that they worship in a temple of any sort. The nature of their lives demanded that they be free to worship Allah everyday wherever they might be. Generally Muslim worship is carried on in a variety of places. Muhammad decreed that Friday should be a special day of Muslim worship as Saturday was Sabbath for the Jews

---

[11]Quran 56:1–56.

and Sunday for the Christians. Unlike the Jewish and Christian Sabbath, however, Friday is not a day of rest; rather, it is the only day of the week when the Muslim is required to pray with his fellow Muslims at a mosque. There believers are led in prayer by an *imam*. The *imam* is not a priest in any sense of the word but rather a member of the community who has been chosen to lead the prayers because of his reputation as a pious man. The remainder of the religious duties of a Muslim can be performed away from the mosque and its leadership.

The Five Pillars

Those things which one must do to be a good Muslim are usually referred to as "the five pillars of Islam." These five pillars or obligations are repetition of the creed, daily prayer, almsgiving, the fast during the month of Ramadan, and the pilgrimage to Mecca.

1. *Repetition of the creed* (shahadah). The most common religious act of the Muslim is his frequent repetition of the creed of Islam: *La ilaha illa Allah; Muhammad rasul Allah.* ("There is no God but Allah; Muhammad is the messenger of Allah.") This statement is known as *Shahadah* (bearing witness). These are the first words that a Muslim child hears, and they are likely to be the last words uttered by the dying Muslim. The devout will utter this statement as often as possible everyday, and the mere utterance of it makes the reciter a Muslim.

2. *Daily prayer* (salah). In addition to the recitation of the creed, the Muslim is expected to pray daily. The Prophet commanded three prayers daily during his lifetime, but in later years this number was revised upward to five daily prayers. The five accepted times for prayer are dawn, midday, midafternoon, sunset, and nightfall. In Muslim communities strong-voiced men called *muezzins* climb to the tops of graceful towers known as minarets five times a day and cry out that it is time for prayer.[12] Wherever Muslims are they pause for a prescribed prayer. Before they pray, however, they must wash themselves and be cleansed of any impurities. Mosques are frequently built with facilities for washing the hands, feet, and face before prayer. If no water is available Muslims may cleanse themselves with sand. Properly cleansed, the worshipers prostrate themselves, facing toward Mecca, and offer their prayers. Prayer in the mosque is usually limited to men, as women are instructed to pray at home.

---

[12]Regrettably the muezzin is being replaced in many modern Muslim communities by tape recordings and loudspeakers.

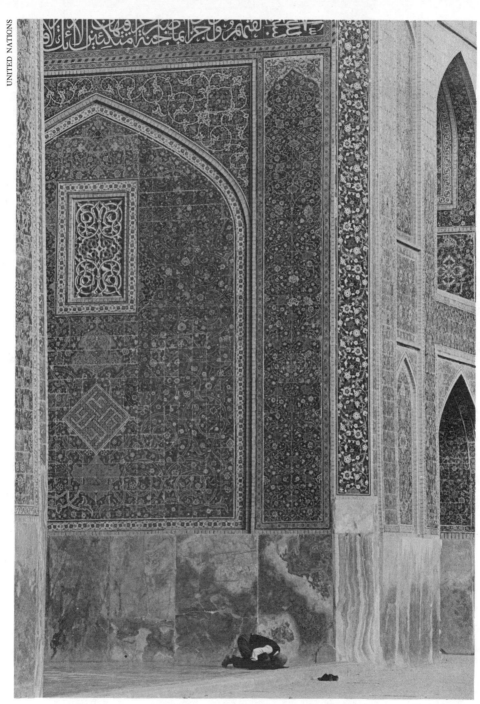

Muslim praying in front of the Shah Mosque. Muslims are required to pray five times each day.

3. *Almsgiving* (zakah). Proper Muslims are expected to share their possessions with the poor of the community.

> Establish worship and pay the poor-due and obey the messenger, that haply ye may find mercy.[13]
> Lo! those who give alms, both men and women and lend unto Allah a goodly loan, it will be doubled for them, and theirs will be a rich reward.[14]

Originally almsgiving was intended to be simply an act of charity toward the poor, widows, and orphans of the community, but in later Islamic life it became obligatory and was assessed as a tax amounting to between 2 and 3 percent of one's wealth. Because of its emphasis upon almsgiving, Islam has never looked upon begging as dishonorable.

4. *Fasting* (sawm). Many religions require fasting in one form or another during the year, but usually it is for a very brief period of time. Jews, for example, are to fast on the Day of Atonement. Other religions restrict certain foods at special times; for example, Roman Catholic Christians are expected to avoid meat during the season of Lent. Islam, however, requires the longest and most stringent fast of all. Each year during the entire month of Ramadan, Muslims are expected to abstain from all food, drink, smoking, and sexual relations during the daylight hours. The fast is kept in remembrance of the month when the Prophet first received his revelation, which became the Quran. Because of the Muslim lunar calendar the month of Ramadan varies from year to year. On some years it may fall in the summer months when abstinence from water during the long daylight hours is very difficult. By Muslim tradition all food and drink must cease when there is enough light in the morning to distinguish a black thread from a white thread. Nourishment may be taken again in the evening when light has passed so that the threads may not be distinguished. The only Muslims who are excused from this fast are those who are sick, those who are traveling, mothers nursing infants, and small children. When the month of Ramadan is concluded Muslims celebrate with a feast that lasts three days.

5. *Pilgrimage* (hajj). A pilgrimage to Mecca was part of pre-Islamic Arab worship for many years before the time of Muhammad. During a special season each year pilgrims came to Mecca, worshiped at the Kaaba, and paid respect to the sacred black stone. Although the Pro-

---

[13]Quran 24:56.
[14]Quran 57:18.

phet purged the Kaaba of its idols, he incorporated it and its black stone into his religion. It has become a requirement for every Muslim who can afford the trip to make the pilgrimage to Mecca and venerate the sacred shrines of Islam.

The pilgrimage takes place during a special month in the Muslim calendar called the dhul-Hijah. During this month pilgrims from all over the world arrive at Mecca. The poor sometimes use their life's savings to make this trip. Others who are elderly and sick begin the long journey with no real hope of completing it or of returning, but no devout Muslim could ask for a more blessed way to die than on the *hajj* to Mecca. Outside Mecca the pilgrims must leave whatever mode of transportation they used for the journey, and walk the rest of the way. They must be clad in simple pilgrim's garment with no head covering and only the briefest of sandals so that rich and poor cannot be distinguished by their apparel. During the month of the *hajj* the pilgrims must also fast in the same manner as during the month of Ramadan.

During the days of the pilgrimage visitors to Mecca visit the well of Zemzen established by Hagar and Ishmael. They make seven trips around the Kaaba and kiss the sacred black stone. They offer a sacrifice of a sheep or goat on the tenth day of the *hajj*. After these duties they may visit Medina and perhaps Jerusalem. When the pilgrims return home they may have the title *hajj* attached to their names so that all the world will know that they have fulfilled this religious obligation.

Calendar

Islam has its own distinctive calendar, which is made up of twelve lunar months of between twenty-nine and thirty days for a total of 354 days each year. To make up some of the difference between the lunar year and the solar year, one day is added to the last month of the year eleven times each thirty years. Even with this correction, however, 103 Muslim years are the equivalent of 100 solar years. Muslims date their calendars from the Hijrah, so the date of the Prophet's death is not known as 632 A.D. but as 10 A.H.

Islam and Women

The position of women in pre-Islamic Arabia was very low. Female infanticide was apparently common as a means of keeping down the female population. A woman was considered as chattel owned by her father, husband, or elder brother. If she displeased her husband he

could divorce her without any recourse on her part. Women like
Khadija, the first wife of the Prophet, who could control their own
wealth and destinies must have been extremely rare. While Muhammad did not raise the status of women to that of men, he did raise it
significantly.

The practice of murdering female babies was forbidden by Islam.
While Muhammad allowed polygamy[15] to continue and was married to
many women himself, he limited the number of wives a Muslim could
have to four, provided a man could afford them. In a society whose
males were frequently killed in tribal warfare and in which marriage
was the only acceptable state for a woman, the polygamy rules probably worked to the benefit of women. Many of the wives of the Prophet
were the widows of Muslims who had been killed in battle.

If a Muslim wished to divorce his wife it was an easy process compared to modern Western methods. When the husband said, "I divorce
you, I divorce you, I divorce you," the divorce was in effect. However,
the Muslim woman was not left totally destitute. She had as her possession the dowry that the husband paid the wife when the marriage
was initially arranged. If there was a divorce, the property of the dowry
remained the wife's.

In spite of the elevation of the position of women in Islam, they are
still regarded as inferior to men. Generally women are not encouraged
to pray at the mosque. Their status is mentioned in the Quran:

> Men are in charge of women, because Allah hath made the
> one of them to excel the other, and because they spend of
> their property [for the support of women]. So good women are
> obedient, guarding in secret that which Allah hath guarded.
> As for those from whom ye fear rebellion, admonish them and
> banish them to beds apart, and scourge them. Then if they
> obey you, seek not a way against them. Lo! Allah is ever High
> Exalted, Great.[16]

Muslim Taboos

The Quran and Muslim tradition have established a series of taboos
that in many ways are similar to those established in the Jewish Bible.
Pork is forbidden to the Muslim as the most unclean of all meats. In
Muhammad's day there must have been little temptation to eat pork by

[15]Technically "polygyny."
[16]Quran 4:34.

the desert dwelling nomads whose major meat supply was sheep and goats. Unlike Jews and Christians, Muslims are also forbidden to drink wine. Again this may have been an expression of the contempt that desert nomads felt for the settled farmer. Because Muslims are forbidden wine they gave the world coffee as a drink. Gambling is also forbidden to Muslims.

The Holy War (*Jihad*)

One of the more controversial requirements placed upon Muslims by their religion is that of the holy war. In the strictest sense a Muslim might feel a religious obligation to go to war and wipe out the infidel in the name of Allah. This requirement was invoked several times in the early days of Islam as its forces spread out across the Middle East and in later years when the movement was directed eastward. The Muslim warrior was offered two enticements to do battle with the infidel. One of course was the booty that he might win for himself, and the other was the promise that if he died in battle he would go straight to a reward in paradise. In modern times *jihad* has never been a clear issue. While the rewards are still there, modern Arab states have been less than anxious to enter wars unified as Muslims against non-Muslims. Even the modern wars against Israel have not enjoyed the complete support of all Muslim nations against a common enemy.

THE SPREAD OF ISLAM

Islam appeared and developed at exactly the right time in history for expansion. It came at a time when the Arab people were ready for a unifying force; when the Byzantine Empire was on the verge of collapse from internal corruption and misrule; and when the Persian Empire was also vulnerable. Within a century of the death of the Prophet the religion of Islam had become the unifying force for the Arab people; it had conquered Palestine, Persia, and Egypt and swept across North Africa into Spain. In the centuries that followed, Islam conquered all the Middle East and moved on into India, China, and eventually the islands of the Pacific. There were several reasons for this rapid and massive expansion.

1. Islam is a militant and intolerant religion that demands conquest of the infidel and rewards those who go into battle on its behalf.

2. Islam is a universal religion. Though it arose from the Arab world it recognizes no national barriers and knows no distinction between races. All are the children of Allah and all are accepted as Muslims.

3. Islam is a simple religion. Unlike other religions that require learning or meditation or great sacrifice, Islam is a simple and clear religion. A person who repeats the creed is a Muslim; a person who keeps the five pillars of Islam is a good Muslim.

4. The world that surrounded the early Muslims was a confused and corrupt one. Byzantine Christian rulers had mistreated and abused Arab Christians, and therefore the Muslim conquerors were frequently received not as an invading army but as deliverers.

Before the death of Muhammad, Islam had begun to conquer and unite the Arabian peninsula. With every conquest and every addition to Islam others were encouraged to join and share in the benefits. After the death of the Prophet the movement gathered momentum and moved outside Arabia. Damascus was taken in 634; Persia fell by 636; Jerusalem became Muslim in 638; Caesarea was conquered after stubborn resistance in 640; and Egypt was also taken in 640. In the following decades Islam consolidated its victories. Most of North Africa became Muslim by the end of the seventh century. In 711 the Muslims entered Spain, where they were dominant for the next seven centuries. In 732 they were turned back from further conquest in Europe by Charles Martel at the Battle of Tours. But for this battle the religious heritage of Europe may very well have been Muslim rather than Christian. On the eastern side of the Mediterranean the expansion also began to slow down. Constantinople, the capital of the Byzantine Empire, was able to resist the attacks of the Muslims until 1453. The island of Sicily fell in the ninth century and for a period was a base for raids against Italy. With the consolidation of the Islamic Empire of Spain, North Africa, and the Middle East, the Muslims moved eastward. In the eleventh century the caliphs of Baghdad extended their conquests into India and China. Today large portions of India are Muslim, and there are an estimated thirty million Muslims in China. In the fourteenth century Indonesia was virtually converted to Islam, and in the fifteenth and sixteenth centuries Islam made converts in the Pacific Islands. The Muslim world remained within these boundaries until the end of the nineteenth century, when missionary activity began to make renewed and rapid strides in Africa.

*From the time of Muhammad up to today, the life style of
the Middle Eastern nomad has changed little.*

THE CALIPHATE

Islam is not a highly structured religion in the sense that Roman
Catholic Christianity is. One of the reasons for this is the fact that
Islam is a religion that can be practiced privately. Most of the duties of
a good Muslim can be practiced at home without the presence of a
priest. Another reason for its lack of structure is that Muhammad
never clearly left a successor or a plan for the succession of his leadership. Only one of his children, Fatima, lived longer than the Prophet,
and he never clearly designated her as the leader who was to follow
him. The only hint of succession that the Prophet made was to appoint
his friend abu-Bakr to lead the community in prayers. Following the
death of Muhammad there was great confusion among the Muslims,
but after a time it was agreed that abu-Bakr should be the caliph (from
khalifa, "deputy" or "representative") who would rule the Muslims in
temporal matters. It was presumed that spiritual rule would be left to
the Quran.

The caliphate is the one central unifying office in the history of
Islam. At first the caliphs were friends of the Prophet and acted as
pious leaders of the faithful. They were chosen by election or common
consent. In later years the caliphate became hereditary and the office
was more like that of a king. The first four caliphs are often referred to
as the "orthodox caliphs" because they were selected from the circle of

343

friends of the Prophet and ruled from Arabia. These four were abu-Bakr, Umar, Uthman, and Ali, the husband of the Prophet's daughter, Fatima. Life was not easy for these caliphs: abu-Bakr had to suppress rebellion and also try to unify the nation which the Prophet had built; Umar and Uthman were murdered; and Ali had the caliphate wrested from his hands in 661 by those who formed the first dynasty of Islam, the Umayyads.

Between 661 and 750 Islam was ruled by the Umayyad caliphs, who made their headquarters in Damascus, Syria. The Umayyads were more interested in ruling as kings, in conquering territory, and in sharing booty than they were in being leaders of a religious community. They were succeeded by the Abbasid dynasty, which ruled from Baghdad in Persia between 750 and 1258. The Abbasids outdid the Umayyads and ruled with great pomp and splendor in the style which the reader may find in the *Arabian Nights*. It was during the years of the Abbasid caliphate that Islam reached the peak of its civilization. It was in Baghdad that Jews and Muslims worked together in studying and preserving the texts of the Greek philosophers and scientists. After the tenth century, however, the golden age of Muslim civilization began to decline, and the caliphate began to lose its power. The Abbasids were replaced by the Mamelukan Turks, who ruled the Muslim Empire from Egypt. The Mamelukes were replaced in the sixteenth century by the Ottoman Turks, who made the title *caliph* synonymous with that of *sultan* of Turkey. When the Ottoman Empire was broken up after World War I, the caliphate ceased to exist. However, by that time it was only a title that carried with it none of the glory and power it had once held in the days of the Abbasid caliphs.

VARIATIONS WITHIN ISLAM

Like most large religions Islam is not a monolithic body. Although most Muslims would agree on the basic principles of Islam, there are many variations in beliefs and practice.

The Sunnis

Eighty-five percent of all Muslims are classified as Sunnis (traditionalists) and are regarded as the orthodox of Islam. These representatives of normative Islam attempt to follow the path of their religion exactly as it was established by the Prophet and the first four orthodox caliphs. However, this is not always easy to do because

Muhammad was a man who lived in Arabia in the seventh century and there are difficulties in applying his teachings to persons living in other regions and in other centuries. It became necessary for Muslims to collect the sayings of Muhammad and his immediate disciples that are not found in the Quran and to interpret them as guides for problems not anticipated in the Quran. For example, the Quran orders very severe punishment for thieves.

> As for the thief, both male and female, cut off their hands. It is the reward of their own deeds, and exemplary punishment from Allah. Allah is Mighty, Wise.[17]

While this punishment may have been fair and effective for a few Muslims living in Medina in the seventh century, it could scarcely have worked in Damascus in the ninth century when Islam had grown into a world power. Therefore a tradition developed whereby thieves were punished by flogging. These traditions and interpretations relating to the laws of the Quran became known as *hadith*.

As Islam grew and took on the character of the many nations into which it spread, there arose schools of interpretation that varied in the amount of weight they gave to the Quran, the hadiths, and human reason in interpreting the life of Islam. There are four of these schools of thought, and every Sunni Muslim is a member of one of these schools. Generally the four schools represent different geographical regions. The first is the Hanifite group, which follow the teachings of abu-Hanifah (d. 767 A.D.). The Hanifites are found today in western Asia, India, and Lower Egypt. The second are the Malikites, who follow the teachings of Malik ibn-Anas (d. 795 A.D.) and are found in North and West Africa and Upper Egypt. The third is the Shafi'ite group, who follow the patterns established by al-Shafi'i (d. 820 A.D.) and are found in Lower Egypt, Syria, India, and Indonesia. The last group are the Hanbalites, who follow Ahmad ibn-Hanbal (d. 855 A.D.) and are today found in Saudi Arabia. Generally the Hanbalites are the most conservative of the four groups.

The Shi'ites

The Shi'ites constitute the second largest sect in Islam, making up about 14 percent of the total number of Muslims in the world. Today

---

[17]Quran 5:38.

they are found mainly in Iran and Iraq, those modern nations that share the borders of ancient Persia. The Shi'ites call themselves *Shiat Ali* ("Partisans of Ali"). The sect arose after the death of Ali, the son-in-law of the Prophet and the last of the first four orthodox caliphs. In 661 A.D. Ali was murdered and his son Hasan was forced to resign his claim to the caliphate by those who established the Umayyad dynasty. The Shi'ites believe that Ali and his descendants were the only true claimants to the caliphate. Furthermore they believe that in the centuries that followed there were twelve descendants of Ali who were the true leaders of Islam and were called *imams*. The twelfth *imam* disappeared in 878 without leaving a trace or an heir. This has led to the belief among Shi'ites that he will appear again to lead Islam into a golden age. This messianic figure is called the *Mahdi*, and the anticipation of his coming has been the cause of the rise of numerous pretenders.

The development of the Shi'ites as a splinter group in Islam opened the door for perhaps as many as seventy other minor groups. The Shi'ites themselves are divided into multiple sects. One of the most interesting of these was the Assassins. This sect arose in the eleventh century and became the scourge of the Christian crusaders who invaded Muslim lands. Its founder was Hasan ibn-al-Sabbah, who built an impregnable fortress for himself and was known by the crusaders as the "Old Man of the Mountains." He enticed his followers to join him by offering them large amounts of hashish and, when they were intoxicated with the drug, showing them the wonders of paradise that would be theirs if they died in his service. The followers then were sent out to murder selected victims. Because of their use of hashish they became known as the Assassins, and this word was eventually added to European languages. Fortunately, most of this group of terrorists were wiped out by the Mongols in the thirteenth century.

The Mystical Element

Islam, like Judaism, has always been a religion that emphasized obedience to the will of God in the here and now. Therefore it has never encouraged the ascetic life so characteristic of the Indian religions. In addition to its emphasis upon this world, Islam has been essentially an unemotional religion. Good Muslims need not enter a mystical experience with God; but must only obey the teachings of the Quran. Nevertheless in every religion there is a hunger for the mystical experience. Furthermore, Islam arose in a land dominated by Byzantine Christianity, which highly prized the ascetic life; and in later years it developed in India, where there is also a strong concern for communion with God through asceticism.

In Islam the concern for mystical union with God was expressed through a group called the Sufis. The word *sufi* means "woolen" and refers to the coarse wool garments worn by the members of this order as a symbol of their poverty and rejection of worldly niceties. The Sufis claim that they have always been a part of Islam and trace their origins back to the days of the Prophet and the first four orthodox caliphs. In Islam's earlier days Muslims were supposed to have been more pious and more concerned with true spiritual matters than they were later. With the expansion of Islam into a world empire it became more materialistic than it had been during the first fifty years of its history. With the development of the Abbasid dynasty and its grandeur in Baghdad, there came a cry among some for a simpler, more austere life. Therefore the ninth century probably was the era when the Sufi movement began.

One of the most outstanding Sufis of the early period was Mansur al-Hallaj. His quest for mystical oneness with God brought him to the point where he finally proclaimed, "I am the truth." For this offense and others, his fellow Muslims crucified him in 922 A.D. He went to his death asking forgiveness for his persecutors. The martyrdom of one of their number and similar persecutions in the following years forced the Sufi movement to go underground and teach its more unorthodox beliefs in secret. However, as the orthodox Muslim teachers emphasized more and more the formal and legalistic aspects of Islam, the Sufis emphasized the emotional and mystical aspects, and thus came to appeal to the common people. Islam finally accepted the major teachings of the Sufis in the twelfth century because of the life and teachings of Abu-Hamid al-Ghazali. Al-Ghazali, a professor of theology at the Nizamiyah school in Baghdad, found no personal satisfaction in orthodox Muslim doctrine. He abandoned his position and his family and, like the Christian Saint Francis, set out to find God in poverty and mystical experiences. He found his satisfaction among the Sufis. His books, *The Revivification of the Religious Sciences*, *The Folly of the Philosophers*, and the *Niche of the Lights*, had a great impact upon Islam and served to make orthodox doctrine more mystical.

Also in the twelfth century the Sufis began to organize themselves into monastical orders. These orders were usually centered around a Sufi saint. When a convert came to join the order he was known as a *fakir* or a *dervish*.[18] Traditionally novices stayed in the order and studied with the master until they became masters themselves. Sufi monastic practices vary but generally they emphasize discipline, poverty, abstinence, and in some cases celibacy. Sometimes there were the extremes of asceticism and emotionalism, which Westerners have come to associate with the titles *fakir* and *dervish*. There are recorded reports of Sufis swallowing live coals, walking on coals, swallowing snakes, and so on, and of course there are the various Turkish dervishes who seek oneness with God by whirling in one spot for hours. These are only the extremes of the Sufi movement, however, and are not representative of the totality in any sense. The real contribution of the Sufis to Islamic thought is their insistence of the possibility of union with God through a mystical experience.

ISLAM IN THE MODERN WORLD

In the years following the glories of the Caliphate of Baghdad, Islam settled down to a relatively routine existence. There were the battles with the Christian Crusaders over the holy sites in Palestine in the twelfth and thirteenth centuries that produced one of the most outstanding Muslim leaders of all time, Saladin; there was the eastward spread of Islam into India, China, and the Pacific Islands; and there was the development of the Ottoman Empire in the sixteenth century; but on the whole, Islam never achieved the golden era of wealth, power, and intellectual life that it had enjoyed during the reign of the Abbasid caliphs.

When the European nations were moving out of the medieval twilight into the industrial age, many Islamic nations continued to live in preindustrialized societies. Several reasons are suggested for this era of quiet in the Islamic world. One of the most obvious is the conservative nature of the religion itself. Most religions are essentially conservative, but Islam is especially so. The Prophet came as the last word from God to humankind, and the Quran is God's last great message. All that is necessary is to know the Quran and how to apply it to one's life. Therefore after the great era of the Baghdad caliphs there was little internal stimulus to encourage Muslims to seek new knowledge or to change their lives.

---

[18]The word *faqir* (fakir) literally means "a poor man," while the word *darwish* (dervish) connotes "one who comes to the door," i.e., a beggar. Thus both words indicate the monk's universal practices of poverty and begging.

Another reason for the lack of change among Muslims may have been their sense of self-satisfaction relative to European nations. The Muslims had decidedly defeated the Christian crusaders who had invaded their lands. Later they had taken the supposedly invincible city of Constantinople from its Christian defenders. The Islamic world therefore had a sense of military and cultural superiority toward the Christian nations. Some have suggested that it was not until the conquest of Egypt by Napoleon in the early nineteenth century that Islamic nations became aware that Europeans might be superior in any way.

A third reason for the slowness with which the Muslim nations moved into the modern era was the development of extremely conservative groups within Islam which took active leadership in a struggle against any change. The most outstanding force against change was the Wahhabi movement founded in 1744 by Muhammad ibn-Abd-al-Wahhab. The Wahhabis were traditionalists who opposed all forms of change. Naturally they opposed any acceptance of European ways, but they also opposed internal innovations such as those proposed by the Sufis. The Wahhabi movement came to be attached to the house of the Su'ud family, and when the Su'ud family came to control Arabia, this puritanical religious movement came with them. In the nineteenth century the Wahhabis suppressed the Sufis and others whom they considered to be compromising with change. Today the Wahhabi movement is not strong in the Islamic world, but its existence in the last century does speak to the latent desire among many Muslims to resist change.

The isolation of the Muslim world from the modern world came to an end in the early part of the twentieth century. By that time transportation and communication had advanced to the point that the Muslim world came within easy reach of the European world. World War I brought the Ottoman Empire into the struggle on the side of the Axis powers. With the defeat of the Axis forces the Ottoman Empire was broken up, and European powers took control of some parts of the Middle East. During the post–World War I years the various Muslim states that had constituted parts of the Ottoman Empire developed into independent nations. They eventually broke their ties with the European governments and achieved independent status. In addition many of the Middle Eastern Arab nations were found to have the world's largest supply of crude oil, thus raising the level of their wealth and political power almost overnight. These factors have caused a resurgence of interest in Islam both internally and externally. Whether

Modern-day pilgrimage to Mecca.

the world chooses to or not, the Muslim states of the Middle East can never again be overlooked; they are extremely important.

The internal resurgence of interest in Islam has manifested itself in several ways. First is the reform movements from within. Some Muslims have suggested and practiced textual criticism of the Quran in a manner similar to that practiced by Christians and Jews on their bibles. No one has yet suggested the higher criticism of the Quran. Other reformers have changed marriage and divorce laws in Muslim communities to help make them more compatible with those of the Western nations. Other reform movements in Islam have been syncretistic, picking up features from other world religions and changing the nature of Islam altogether.

The most obvious result of the resurgence of Islam in the twentieth century is its very active missionary movement in Africa. The move south of the Sahara by Muslim missionaries began in the late nineteenth century when the slave trade had ended and conversion of blacks was possible. Yet Islam has existed in portions of Africa since the seventh century. North Africa was among the first lands to be conquered and converted to Islam. Portions of the interior, particularly the cities, have also known Muslim influence for a long time. Muslim merchants and traders worked in many parts of the continent. However, the colonial forces of the European nations in the eighteenth and nineteenth centuries made Muslim missionary activity in the interior possible. The colonial powers opened Africa to both Christian and Muslim missions with maps, modern transportation, and communication. The abuses of the Africans by the colonial nations also opened doors for Islam in that when the African nations gained their independence, hostility toward the white Europeans and their religion could be expressed by conversion to Islam. Although Islam is a religion which knows no bias of color or ethnic origin, it can be thought of as the religion of the peoples of the third world who have been victimized by the Christian colonial powers. The Muslim missionaries have been so effective in Africa in the past fifty years that it was estimated in 1968 that perhaps as many as one-fourth of the inhabitants of Africa are Muslim. If the present rate of conversion continues, the entire continent may one day soon be regarded as part of the Muslim world.

Islam as a religion has gone through two major periods of growth, one at the beginning of its history and another in the twentieth century, with a rather long period of quiet between. With the emergence of the Arab states as major world powers and with Islam's rapid growth in Africa, Islam is now recognized as a major world religion that will continue to make its impression upon the philosophies, art, architecture, and politics of the world.

SUGGESTED READING

Andrae, Tor. *Mohammed, the Man and His Faith*. London: George Allen and Unwin, 1936.

Arberry, A. J. *The Holy Koran*. New York: Macmillan, 1953.

Cragg, Kenneth. *The House of Islam*. Encino, Calif.: Dickenson Publishing Company, 1975.

Guillaume, Alfred. *Islam*. Baltimore: Penguin, 1954.

Watt, W. Montgomery. *Muhammad, Prophet and Statesman*. London: Oxford University Press, 1964.

BAHA'I

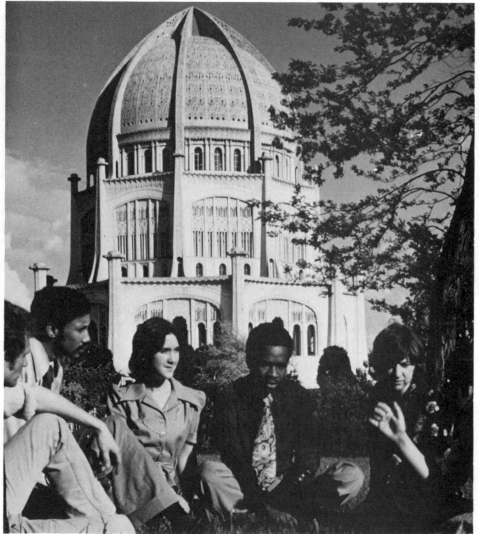

Young Baha'is in front of the Baha'i Temple, Wilmette, Illinois.

All the prophets of God proclaim the same faith.
BAHAULLAH

Baha'i began as a sect of Islam but has moved so far away from that religion as to be considered a separate religion altogether. Several themes are central to Baha'i. Baha'i assumes that all the religions of the world spring from one source, that there is a basic unity of all religious truth, and that all the prophets have had a partial message from the one God. Baha'i further maintains that religion must work in harmony with science and education to provide a peaceful world order and believes in the equality of opportunity among the races and between the sexes. By emphasizing these themes Baha'i has attracted followers in many of the nations of the world.

ORIGIN AND DEVELOPMENT OF BAHA'I

The Shi'ite sect of Islam, particularly in Persia, has always taught that there were twelve legitimate descendants of Ali, the son-in-law and legitimate successor to Muhammad. These twelve *imams* were often referred to as "gates" whereby the believers gained access to the true faith. The twelfth of these successors disappeared in the ninth century A.D., and the Shi'ites have always believed that one day he would reappear as a messiah.

In 1844 a Shi'ite Muslim named Mirza Ali Muhammad declared that he was the promised twelfth *imam* and called himself Bab-ub-Din ("the gate of faith"). Advocating sweeping religious and social reforms such as raising the status of women, the Bab gathered around him a group of disciples who called themselves Babis. The movement was short-lived as both the religious and political forces of Persia moved to crush it. The Bab was publicly executed in 1850, and many of his disciples were imprisoned or executed. Before he died, however, the Bab predicted that he had prepared the way for one yet to come who would found a universal religion. The body of the Bab was rescued by some of his followers and preserved for several years. Ultimately it was transported to the city of Haifa in Palestine where it was finally buried.

One of the Bab's imprisoned disciples was a man named Mirza Husayn Ali, the son of one of the most distinguished families in Persia. Because of his family Mirza was not executed with the Bab but was imprisoned in Tehran. In 1852 another of the Bab's followers attempted to assassinate the Shah of Iran, and this brought further persecution upon the group. Mirza Ali was exiled to Baghdad, and there he spent the next ten years of his life. During his imprisonment and exile it was revealed to Mirza that he was the one whom the Bab had foretold. In 1863 Mirza and the remaining Babis were exiled from Baghdad to Constantinople, and on the eve of their departure he revealed to the Babis that he was the one promised by the Bab. This revelation was made in Ridvan near Baghdad and today is commemorated annually by Baha'is with a feast. Mirza assumed the name Bahaullah ("the glory of God"), and those Babis who accepted him and followed his teachings became known as Baha'is.

In the following years Bahaullah and the Baha'is were forced from one capital city in the Middle East to another. From Constantinople they went to Adrianople. Finally they were banished to the Turkish prison city of Acca in Palestine. At first Bahaullah and about eighty of his followers were incarcerated for two years in an army barracks where they suffered from hunger and disease. After this period the group was transferred to other quarters that were somewhat more comfortable. Eventually more freedom was given to Bahaullah, but he spent the remainder of his life as a prisoner of the Turkish government in Acca. Although he was imprisoned during his years in Acca, Bahaullah was able to send out missionaries and receive guests and thus spread his teachings of unity and world peace. During this period he wrote many letters and books. One series of letters was sent to the pope and to the world heads of state announcing his mission and calling for their help in furthering world peace. He wrote books such as the *Kitab-i-Aqdas* ("The Most Holy Book"), the *Kitab-i-Iqan* ("The Book of

Abdul Baha, son of Bahaullah

Certitudes"), and *The Hidden Words*. He died in Acca in 1892 at the age of 75.

Leadership of the movement passed to the son of Bahaullah, Abbas Effendi, who became known as Abdul Baha (the servant of Baha). Abdul Baha carried on his father's program of writing, and in 1908 he was freed by the Turks. For the remaining years of his life he traveled widely in Europe and North America preaching the doctrines of Baha'i and establishing Baha'i assemblies in many nations. In 1920 the British conferred the knighthood of the British Empire upon Abdul Baha because of his work for world peace. Upon Abdul Baha's death in 1921 leadership of the movement was passed to his grandson, Shoghi Effendi, who continued the work of establishing local and national assemblies in many nations until his death in 1957. At this point Baha'i came to be governed, not by one of the descendants of Bahaullah, but by a body elected from Baha'is all over the world.

THE TEACHINGS OF BAHA'I

Although Baha'i originated within the Shi'ite sect of Islam it soon came to differ radically from it. Baha'i does not revere the Quran to the same

355

degree that Islam does. Much of the Quran is modified, explained allegorically, or treated symbolically. Belief in angels and evil spirits has been discarded by Baha'i, while heaven and hell are treated symbolically. The Quran takes its place along with the Christian and Jewish bibles and the sacred writings of other religions as a source for Baha'i worship. This attitude toward the Quran has made Baha'i most unpopular among Muslims, and it has even been outlawed in Iran, the land of its birth.

The basic belief of Baha'i is that all religions come from the same source. In nearly every era God has revealed his truth through prophets. Moses, Zoroaster, Jesus, Muhammad, Krishna, Buddah, and Bahaullah were the prophets of God, and all presented a portion of the truth of God in their times, but Bahaullah, as the last and the greatest of these prophets, revealed the final truth from God. Bahaullah's greatest message was the oneness of the human race. All of humankind, all races, both sexes, and all religious truths are the work of the one God. In the words of Bahaullah:

> Of the Tree of Knowledge the All-glorious fruit is this exalted word: Of one Tree are all ye the fruits and of one Bough the leaves. Let not man glory in this that he loves his country, but let him rather glory in this that he loves his kind.[1]

On the basis of these religious truths found in the writings of Bahaullah, Abdul Baha went out from Acca to preach the following Baha'i doctrines of the world:

1. The oneness of the entire human race is the pivotal principle and fundamental doctrine of the faith. This principle is essential to Baha'i. It is the basis for most of its teachings and practices.

2. There must be an independent search after truth, unfettered by superstition or tradition. Anyone who wishes to be a Baha'i must be willing to search out the truth of God without relying on the prophets and the traditions of the past. "The freedom of man from superstition and imitation, so that he may discern the Manifestations of God with the eye of Oneness, and consider all affairs with keen sight. . . ."[2] is one of the basic teachings of Baha'i.

3. There is a basic unity of all religions. Growing out of the belief that there is a oneness in the human race is the teaching that all

---

[1] J. E. Esslemont, *Bahaullah and the New Era* (Wilmette, Ill.: Baha'i Books, 1937), p. 59.
[2] Bahaullah, *Words of Wisdom.*

religions essentially teach the same message. This is not to say that differences do not exist among the religions of the world, but Baha'i doctrine states that the basic message of every religion is the same and that all minor differences should be forgotten. In a conversation with a visitor Bahaullah said:

> That all nations should become one in faith and all men as brothers; that the bonds of affection and unity between the sons of men should be strengthened; that diversity of religion should cease, and differences of race be annulled . . . these strifes and this bloodshed and discord must cease, and all men be as one kindred and one family. . . .[3]

4. All forms of prejudice, whether religious, racial, class, or national, are condemned. In one of his speeches in Paris Abdul Baha said:

> Religion should unite all hearts and cause wars and disputes to vanish from the face of the earth; it should give birth to spirituality, and bring light and life to every soul. If religion becomes a cause of dislike, hatred and division, it would be better to be without it. . . . Any religion which is not a cause of love and unity is no religion.[4]

5. Harmony must exist between religion and science. Baha'i arose in the nineteenth century when great battles were fought between the established religions and the newly emerging sciences. These two forces must be harmonized.

> Ali, the son-in-law of Muhammad, said: "That which is in conformity with science is also in conformity with religion." Whatever the intelligence of man cannot understand, religion ought not to accept. Religion and science walk hand in hand, and any religion contrary to science is not the truth.[5]

6. There is equality of men and women. Baha'i may be the only religion of the world which has asserted from the beginning that women are equal to men.

---

[3]Esslemont, *Bahaullah and the New Era*, p. 126.
[4]Ibid., p. 165.
[5]Abdul Baha, *Wisdom of Abdul Baha*.

Humanity is like a bird with its two wings—the one is male, the other female. Unless both wings are strong and impelled by some common force, the bird cannot fly heavenwards. According to the spirit of this age, women must advance and fulfill their mission in all departments of life, becoming equal to men.[6]

7. Compulsory education must prevail. Although neither Bahaullah nor Abdul Baha had the opportunity of formal education, both preached that universal education was a necessary condition for world peace and stability.

8. In addition to universal education, Baha'i teaches that there should be a universal language. Bahaullah said:

We commanded the Trustees of the House of Justice, either to choose one of the existing tongues, or to originate a new one, and in like manner to adopt a common script, teaching these to the children in all the schools of the world, that the world may become even as one land and one home.[7]

Abdul Baha was an advocate of the adoption of Esperanto as the universal language.

9. Extremes of wealth and poverty should be abolished. Coming from a family of high rank and then spending much of his life in prisons, Bahaullah was acutely aware of the extremes of wealth and poverty in the world. Believing that both extremes were unhealthy and abnormal, he urged their abolition. He did not offer an elaborate plan that would bring about this change. Rather, he suggested to the rich of the world that they should open their hearts and contribute to the poor. He also advocated that the governments of the world should pass laws to prevent the two extremes.

10. A world tribunal for the adjudication of disputes between nations should be instituted. Forty years before the establishment of the League of Nations, Bahaullah was urging such an organization from his prison cell in Acca. However, when the League of Nations was formed after World War I, Abdul Baha considered it too weak to be effective.

11. Work performed in the spirit of service should be exalted to the

---

[6]Abdul Baha as cited in Esslemont, *Bahaullah and the New Era*, p. 154.
[7]Bahaullah, *Tablet of Ishraqat*.

rank of worship. According to Baha'i a good society is one in which everyone works at some task. There are to be no loafers or idlers.

> It is enjoined on every one of you to engage in some occupation—some art, trade or the like. We have made this—your occupation—identical with the worship of God, the true One.[8]

Thus Bahaullah, like Calvin and the ancient Jewish Pharisees, believed in the religious efficacy of labor.

12. Justice should be glorified as the ruling principle in human society and religion, for the protection of all peoples and nations.

13. Finally, as a capstone to all of the teachings of Baha'i, the establishment of a permanent and universal peace should be the supreme goal of humankind.[9]

Unlike Islam and other Western religions, Baha'i believes that heaven and hell are not places but conditions of the soul. The soul, which is the reality of humankind, is eternal and in continuous progress. When the soul is near to God and God's purposes, that is heaven; when the soul is distant from God, that is hell. Thus the descriptions of heaven and hell that are found in other religions are regarded as symbolic rather than actual. When Baha'is speak of the unity of humankind, they mean not only the unity of humanity in this life but unity of the living and the dead as well. Thus it is possible that the living and the dead may commune with each other. Abdul Baha believed that this was the reason for the peculiar powers of the prophets and saints to see into the other world and commune with it.

According to the Baha'i belief in the total unity of God, there can be no such thing as positive evil. If God is one and all, there can be no Satan figure in the universe. Just as darkness is only the absence of light, so that which appears to be evil is only the absence of good. According to Abdul Baha:

> In creation there is no evil; all is good. Certain qualities and natures innate in some men and apparently blameworthy are not so in reality.[10]

---

[8] Bahaullah, *Glad Tidings*.

[9] These thirteen principles are taken from information supplied by the Public Information Department, National Baha'i Headquarters, 112 Linden Avenue, Wilmette, Illinois.

[10] Abdul Baha, *Some Answered Questions* (Wilmette, Ill.: Baha'i Publishing Trust, 1964), p. 250.

Baha'i Temple, Wilmette, Illinois. This building serves as the center for the Baha'i faith in North America. Like Baha'i temples the world over it is nine-sided, to Baha'is a symbol of unity.

BAHA'I PRACTICES

The daily life of Baha'is is governed by many regulations. The Baha'i is required to pray daily. In fact, the entire life of a Baha'i is supposed to be a prayer. One's work, one's thoughts, and one's deeds are all to be done in the spirit of a prayer. This is one of the most important aspects of Baha'i life. Bahaullah stressed this in the *Kitab-i-Aqdas*.

> Chant (or recite) the Words of God every morning and evening. The one who neglects this has not been faithful to the Covenant of God and His agreement, and he who turns away from it today is of those who have turned away from God.[11]

Although there are many formal prayers which a Baha'i may recite in daily devotions, Bahaullah established three obligatory prayers. Ba-

---

[11]Bahaullah, *Kitab-i-Aqdas*.

ha'is are free to choose any one of these three as a part of their meditations.

Baha'is are also encouraged to fast for one of the nineteen months in their calendar. During the month of *Ala* (loftiness), which begins near the first of March, Baha'is are expected to fast for nineteen days. A full fast, with a complete abstinence from food, is not required; Baha'is must not eat during the daylight hours only. Since the fast occurs during the early spring each year, no food or drink is taken between about 6 A.M. and 6 P.M. According to Abdul Baha:

> Fasting is a symbol. Fasting signifies abstinence from lust. Physical fasting is a symbol of that abstinence, and is a reminder; that is, just as a person abstains from physical appetites, he is to abstain from self-appetites and self-desires. But mere abstention from food has no effect on the spirit. It is only a symbol, a reminder. Otherwise it is of no importance.[12]

At other periods during the Baha'i year, followers engage in certain feasts which celebrate various events in the history of Baha'i. These include the feast of the new year, celebrated on March 21, and the feast of Ridvan, celebrated between April 21 and May 2, which commemorates Bahaullah's declaration that he was the promised one.

For Baha'is monogamy is the rule in marriage. Baha'is may marry only after they have the consent of both sets of parents. Bahaullah taught:

> Verily in the Book of Bayan (the Bab's Revelation) the matter is restricted to the consent of both (bride and bridegroom). As We desired to bring about love and friendship and the unity of the people, therefore We made it conditional upon the consent of the parents also, that enmity and ill-feeling might be avoided.[13]

Divorce is permitted for Baha'is but only in extreme cases of incompatibility. At such a point the couple must wait for one full year and seek to re-establish their relationship. If this does not happen then a divorce may be granted. If a Baha'i couple have children they are obligated to provide their children with the best possible education. Alcohol and narcotics are forbidden to Baha'is.

---

[12]Abdul Baha, cited by J. E. Esslemont, *Bahaullah and the New Era*, p. 189.
[13]Bahaullah, *Kitab-i-Aqdas*.

Baha'i differs from many other religions in its manner of worship. The basic unit of worship is the Local Spiritual Assembly. This group may meet in the homes of members or in other buildings, but there are no special houses of worship as in other religions. Neither is there a special clergy to conduct the worship. Worship for Baha'is tends to be very simple, with a minimum of form and no ritual. A respected member of the community reads from the writings of Bahaullah and from the scriptures of other world religions. The remainder of the service consists of private prayers and readings. Baha'i community worship is so simple in form that it rejects two elements that Christians and others often find essential, the sermon and the offering. While Baha'is are expected to contribute to the support of their religion, they refuse to take offerings from non-Baha'is.[14]

Baha'is are organized on three levels. The most basic is that of the Local Spiritual Assembly already mentioned. In every community where there are nine or more adult Baha'is a nine-member administrative body is elected each April 21 to govern the affairs of those Baha'is. As of 1968 there were 6,828 of these assemblies in the world. The second level of administration is the National Spiritual Assembly. This too is a nine-member body made up of people elected annually by delegates to the national conventions. In 1968 there were eighty-three National Assemblies. The top level of the Baha'i organization is the Universal House of Justice. This is a nine-member body elected by the members of the National Spiritual Assemblies throughout the world. These representatives serve a five-year term.

Although the Baha'is do not have local houses of worship they have constructed several magnificent temples around the world and plan eventually to construct one on every continent. Those already in existence are located in Frankfurt, Germany; Sydney, Australia; Kampala, Uganda; and Wilmette, Illinois, U.S.A. Each of these temples reflects a somewhat different style of architecture, but all must be nine-sided and covered with a dome. The number nine is symbolic for Baha'i because it is the largest unit number and thus represents the worldwide unity that Baha'i seeks to develop. In addition to these temples the world center of Baha'i is located on Mt. Carmel in Haifa, Israel, near Acca, where Bahaullah spent his last days. In the midst of splendid

---

[14]Israeli tour guides who take tourists to the Shrine of the Bab in Haifa tell the tourists that unlike the other holy places in Israel, the Baha'i shrine will neither attempt to sell souvenirs or relics nor accept any offering.

gardens stands the gold-domed shrine of the Bab and the archive building.

Like other religions Baha'i has established its own calendar and its own holy days. The calendar is a solar one made up of nineteen months, each containing nineteen days. To achieve 365 days, four days are added after the last month of the year (five days are added in leap years). The new year begins on March 21, at the birth of spring. As is the case with the Jewish calendar, the day begins at sunset.

Although exact statistics are not available it is estimated that there may be as many as five million Baha'is in the world today. While still relatively small in terms of members, this religion appears to be growing.

SUGGESTED READING

Bahaullah. *The Kitab-I-Iqan* (The Book of Certitudes). Translated by Shoghi Effendi. Wilmette, Ill.: Baha'i Publishing Trust, 1931.

Effendi, Shoghi. *God Passes By*. Wilmette, Ill.: Baha'i Publishing Trust, 1970.

Esslemont, J. E. *Bahaullah and the New Era*. Wilmette, Ill.: Baha'i Books, 1937.

INDEX